MW00758318

Ancient Greeks

CREATING THE CLASSICAL TRADITION

ΟΜΗΡΟ
ΑΝΔΡΩΝ ΗΡΩΩΝ
ΚΟΣΜΗΤΟΡΙ
ΛΙΑΣ
ΟΔΥΣΣΕ
ΕΙ ΘΕΟΣ ΕΣΤΙΝ ΟΜΗΡΟΣ, ΕΝ ΑΘΑΝΑΤΟΙΣΙ ΣΕΒΕΣΘΩ·
ΕΙ Δ ΑΥ ΜΗ ΘΕΟΣ ΕΣΤΙ ΝΟΜΙΖΕΣΘΩ ΘΕΟΣ ΕΙΝΑΙ

Ancient Greeks

CREATING THE CLASSICAL TRADITION

ROSALIE F. AND CHARLES F. BAKER III

OXFORD UNIVERSITY PRESS
NEW YORK • OXFORD

For our son, Chip

Oxford University Press
Oxford New York
Athens Auckland Bangkok Bogotá Bombay
Buenos Aires Calcutta Cape Town Dar es Salaam Delhi
Florence Hong Kong Istanbul Karachi
Kuala Lumpur Madras Madrid Melbourne
Mexico City Nairobi Paris Singapore
Taipei Tokyo Toronto Warsaw
and associated companies in
Berlin Ibadan

Published by Oxford University Press, Inc.
198 Madison Avenue, New York, New York 10016

Library of Congress Cataloging-in-Publication Data

Baker, Rosalie F.
Ancient Greeks / Rosalie F. Baker and Charles F. Baker.
p. cm. — (Oxford profiles)
Includes bibliographic references and index.
ISBN 0-19-509940-0
1. Greece—Civilization—To 146 B.C.—Juvenile literature.
2. Intellectuals—Greece—Biography—Juvenile literature.
I. Baker, Charles F., III. II. Title. III. Series.
DF77.B2531996
938—dc20 95-26637
CIP
AC

1 3 5 7 9 8 6 4 2
Printed in the United States of America
on acid-free paper

On the cover: (clockwise from top left) Solon, Pericles, and Sappho
Frontispiece: In a detail from the *Apotheosis of Homer* by the French painter Ingres, Pindar presents Homer a lyre to accompany his verses. In the background, the Greek letters on the temple spell "Homer."

Design: Sandy Kaufman
Layout: Loraine Machlin
Picture research: Patricia Burns
Consultant: Joseph Pucci, William A. Dyer, Jr., Assistant Professor of the Humanities; Assistant Professor of Classics and in the Program in Medieval Studies, Brown University

Contents

Part 5. A Lasting Influence (325–200 B.C.) 194

List of Maps

Preface

The influence of ancient Greek civilization has been felt throughout modern Western history. It began as soon as the Greeks moved beyond their borders and encountered other peoples, sometime in the 800s B.C., and has continued to the present day. Greek ideas can be found in our law codes, government policies, styles of architecture, literary works, and vocabulary. Because these ideas have become so much a part of our daily life, we tend to forget that they originated more than 2,500 years ago with people living in a relatively small area bordering the Mediterranean and Aegean seas. Reading about people whose accomplishments shaped ancient Greece also provides insight into our own thoughts and customs.

On the following pages you will meet Greeks from all walks of life, including a statesman who fostered the Golden Age of Athens, a playwright whose works continue to delight modern audiences, and a slave who became a well-respected banker. The names of some are familiar: the poet Sappho, one of the few ancient Greek women whose lives have been documented; the philosopher Plato; and the Macedonian ruler Alexander the Great. Others are not so well known. The long-distance runner Phidippides, for example, ran what became the basis of today's marathons. And Pytheas, who sailed into the Atlantic Ocean, seeking new lands, is considered the first scientific explorer.

Original sources documenting the lives of the ancient Greeks are rare. For each of the people whose stories are included in this book, however, we do have accurate and reliable information. They are included in this volume not only because their accomplishments significantly influenced Greek life but because these accomplishments continued to be important centuries later.

To be sure, there were many other Greeks whose work either influenced the people profiled here or who played other, less important roles in the development of Greek society. There are also people about whom reliable information does not exist. Further Reading, which begins on page 247, will help you locate information about these other Greek personalities and about Greek civilization in general. In addition, Further Reading selections appear at the end of each individual profile. Although there are relatively few books geared specifically to young adults, those listed are accessible to a general audience.

Rosalie F. and Charles F. Baker
New Bedford, Massachusetts

A note about spelling:

When the Romans conquered Greece in the 2nd century B.C., it was only natural for the Romans to Latinize Greek names. In the centuries that followed, the Latinized spellings became the accepted form and, in many cases, the only form used for Greek names. Only recently has there been a definite movement to transliterate Greek names from Greek into English. For example, when the name of the Greek philosopher Socrates is transliterated from Greek, it is spelled Sokrates. Because that spelling is still quite unfamiliar and not in many books or library catalogs, we have chosen to use the Latinized spelling of the ancient Greek names. Beginning on page 242, we have included a list of Greek names with the Latinized spelling and the transliterated Greek spelling.

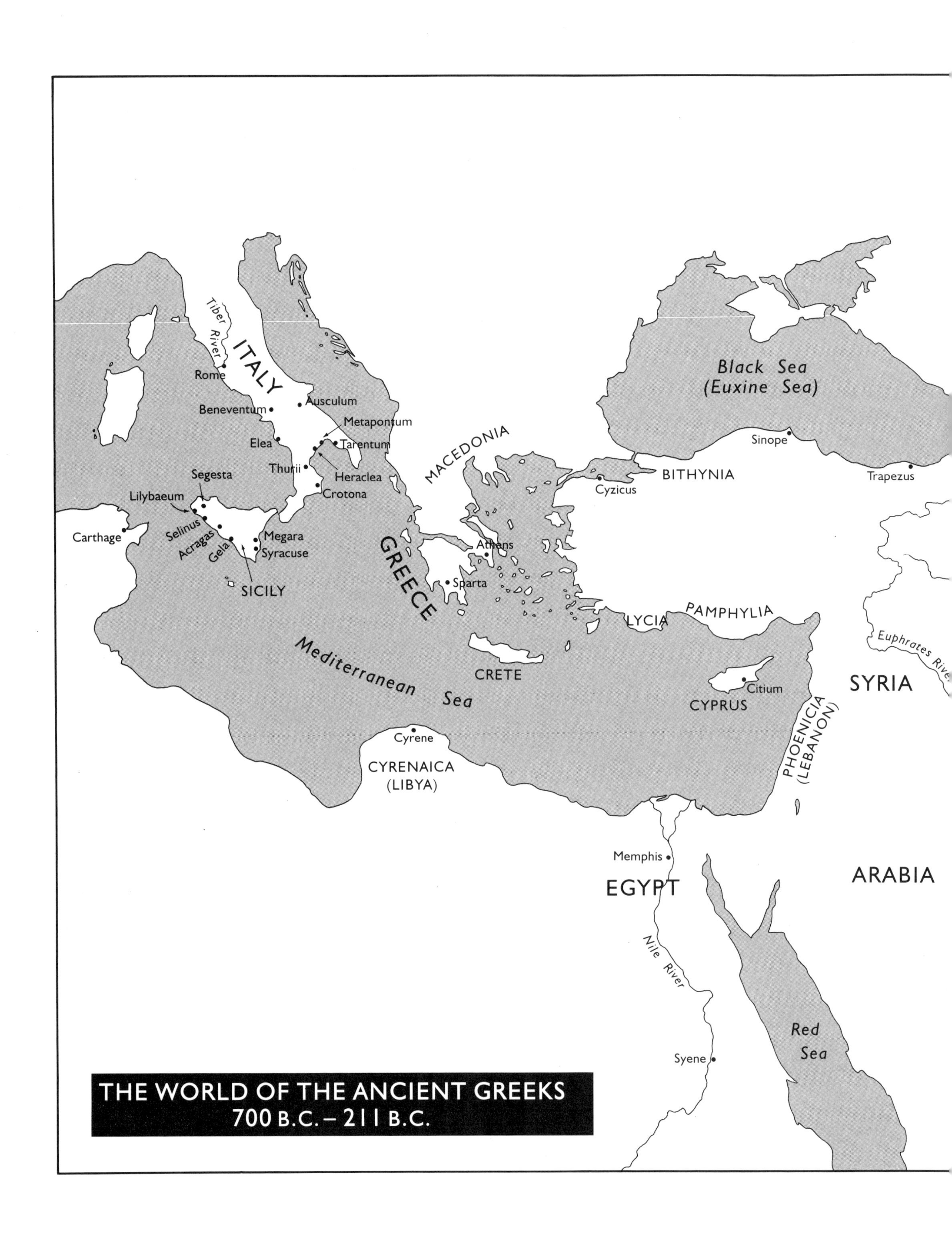

Tiber River
ITALY
Rome
Ausculum
Beneventum
Metapontum
Elea
Tarentum
Thurii
Heraclea
Crotona
Segesta
Lilybaeum
Carthage
Selinus
Acragas
Gela
Megara
Syracuse
SICILY
GREECE
MACEDONIA
Athens
Sparta
Black Sea
(Euxine Sea)
Sinope
Trapezus
BITHYNIA
Cyzicus
LYCIA
PAMPHYLIA
Euphrates River
SYRIA
Mediterranean Sea
CRETE
Citium
CYPRUS
PHOENICIA
(LEBANON)
Cyrene
CYRENAICA
(LIBYA)
Memphis
EGYPT
ARABIA
Nile River
Red Sea
Syene
THE WORLD OF THE ANCIENT GREEKS
700 B.C. – 211 B.C.

0 200 400 600 kilometers
0 200 400 600 miles
Aral Sea
Caspian Sea
ASIA
HINDU KUSH MOUNTAINS
BACTRIA
Tigris River
BABYLONIA
Indus River
PERSIA
INDIA
Persian Gulf
GEDROSIA DESERT
Arabian Sea

ANCIENT GREECE
700 B.C. – 211 B.C.
PAEONIA
MACEDONIA
ILLYRIA
EPIRUS
GREECE
THESSALY
CHALCIDICE PENINSULA
Amphipolis
Eion
Abdera
THASOS
Pella
Thessalonica
Methone
Vergina
Pydna
Stagira
Olynthus
Potidaea
Corcyra
Pherae
CYNOSCEPHALAE MTS.
Ambracia
Adriatic Sea
SCYROS
EUBOEA
PHOCIS
Elatea
Delphi
Chaeronea
Chalcis
Eretria
Aegean Sea
ITHACA
Leuctra
Thebes
Tanagra
BOEOTIA
Decelea
Eleusis
ATTICA
Athens
Elis
Sicyon
Corinth
ANDROS
Olympia
ARCADIA
Scillus
Mantinea
Argos
Bassae
Troezen
Cape Sunium
PELOPONNESUS
MESSENIA
Eurotas River
Sparta
DELOS
MELOS
Mediterranean Sea
CRETE

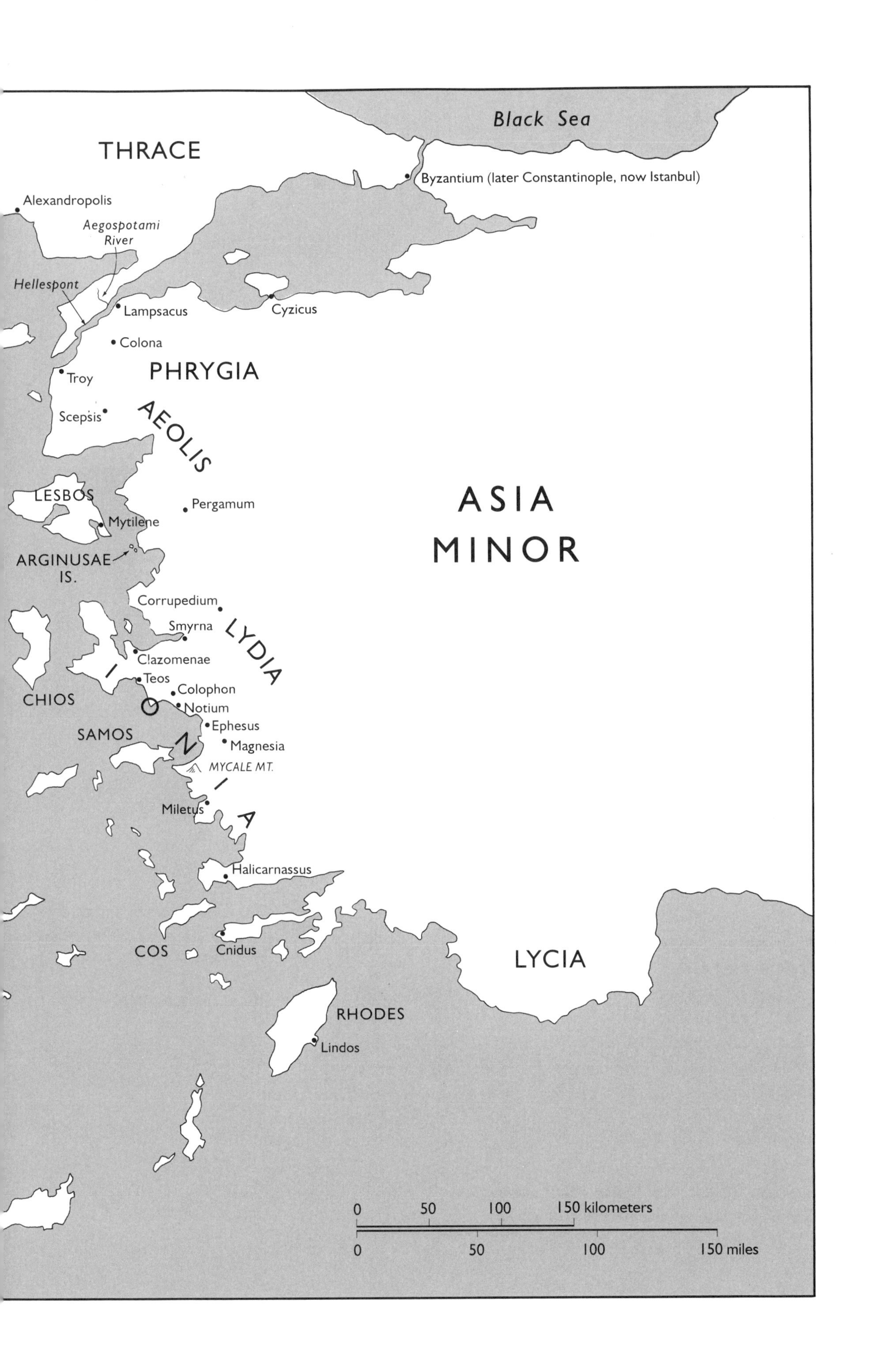

Black Sea
THRACE
Byzantium (later Constantinople, now Istanbul)
Alexandropolis
Aegospotami River
Hellespont
Lampsacus
Cyzicus
Colona
PHRYGIA
Troy
Scepsis
AEOLIS
LESBOS
Pergamum
Mytilene
ASIA MINOR
ARGINUSAE IS.
Corrupedium
Smyrna
LYDIA
Clazomenae
Teos
Colophon
CHIOS
Notium
IONIA
Ephesus
SAMOS
Magnesia
MYCALE MT.
Miletus
Halicarnassus
COS
Cnidus
LYCIA
RHODES
Lindos
0 50 100 150 kilometers
0 50 100 150 miles

1 Forging Greek Unity (700–500 B.C.)

The early history of Greece is so steeped in legend and myth that it is difficult to know what is fact and what is fiction. Because writing arose in Greece only in the 8th century B.C., no accurate records exist detailing Greece's beginning. And even the words *Greece* and *Greek* come from the Latin word *Graeci*, which is what the Romans, centuries later, called the Greeks. Bards were the official historians and orally retold the deeds and legends of their nation's heroes. Naturally, as the tales passed from generation to generation, incidents were omitted or edited, sometimes purposely, sometimes accidentally. Details were even added, because it was not the event or the person's birthdate that was important but what the event represented or what a hero had accomplished. As a result, historians today must often use approximate dates and questionable place names and sites when speaking of events that occurred prior to the 5th century B.C. Understanding this situation makes it easier for us to appreciate why archaeologists are always searching for clues that might allow scholars to fix time periods with greater accuracy.

IN THIS PART

HOMER

SOLON

LYCURGUS

SAPPHO

AESOP

PYTHAGORAS

ANACREON

What is certain about Greece's early history is that northern tribes invaded the land sometime between 2000 and 1000 B.C. Life remained relatively peaceful until the 11th century B.C., when a series of invasions by other northern tribes, known collectively as Dorians, caused much turmoil. Such invasions, which were common in early times, occurred when people tried to conquer new lands or escape war, famine, drought, and climate changes.

The Dorian invasion transformed Greece. Preferring military weapons to culture, the Dorians introduced iron making to Greece and established cities in southern and western areas of the peninsula. In time, Sparta became their most prominent city and was considered to be the home of Greece's best soldiers.

Not all Greeks, however, regarded warfare as supreme, and many chose to emigrate to the islands of the Aegean Sea and to the coast of Asia Minor (present-day Turkey). Those who settled the northern regions of Asia Minor were known as Aeolians, whereas those who settled the central regions were known as Ionians. Some Dorians also chose to leave the mainland, but the colonies that they established, including those on the islands of Crete, Rhodes, and Kos, were further south. Although the Dorians never extended their influence over Athens, many Athenians did choose to leave the mainland and set up new colonies. Even though Athens traditionally considered itself the protector and so-called mother of all Ionian colonists, the bonds between the people who stayed in Greece and those who emigrated always remained strong. In the years that followed, it was this bond that formed the basis of Greek unity.

For Greeks everywhere, the great Trojan War became the symbol of this unity. This was a legendary struggle that may have been based on a real war between the Greeks and the people of Troy over trade through the Dardanelles. From the *Iliad* and the *Odyssey*, two epic poems credited to Homer, Greece's master poet of the 8th century B.C., Greeks learned the story of this war. In the centuries after Homer, the events narrated in these poems influenced much of Greek life and culture. Because all Greeks shared a common language, worshiped the same gods, and observed the same cultural traditions, these poems served as a unifying element throughout the Greek world.

Still, each Greek was fiercely independent and loyal to his own city. Because the Greek terrain, with its mountains, valleys, rivers, and deep inlets, discouraged much interaction between regions, Greek cities were self-governing, independent states. In each polis, or city-state, the people and their leaders shaped the laws and customs that ruled and regulated life within that city-state. As a result, each one had its own characteristics and peculiarities. Athens and Sparta were the chief city-states, and their values were quite opposite. The Athenians stressed freedom of thought, culture, and democracy, whereas the Spartans believed in strict discipline, military preparedness, and a sparse lifestyle.

Part 1 of *Ancient Greeks* profiles some of those individuals responsible for crafting and laying the early foundations for what historians now call the Greek tradition.

Homer

MASTER OF EPIC POETRY

Homer has always been one of the world's best-known poets. The two works ascribed to him, the *Iliad,* a tragic poem about the Trojan War, and the *Odyssey,* a poem about the long return journey of Odysseus to Ithaca after the Trojan War, are among the most widely read and imitated epic poems ever written. Scholars consider both poems to be literary masterpieces of Greek and world literature. Judging from the vocabulary, the military tactics, and the information about daily life included in these two poems, scholars believe that Homer lived sometime in the 8th or 9th century B.C. But we know little else about the man called Homer.

The two areas with the strongest claim to Homer as a native son are the island of Chios off the coast of Asia Minor and the city of Smyrna on the west coast of Asia Minor. Both were part of the area known in ancient times as

In this scene from Homer's *Odyssey,* Odysseus (far right), disguised as a beggar to escape detection by his enemies, returns home from the Trojan War. Only after he secures the safety of his kingdom does he reveal himself to his faithful wife, Penelope (seated).

Ionia, and much of the vocabulary and sentence structure found in Homer's poems is Ionian. To honor Homer's memory, a group of Chians formed a society called the Homeridae (literally, Friends of Homer). The members met regularly to recite Homer's works and tell stories about his life, which undoubtedly contained a mixture of truth and legend. In time, truth became indistinguishable from legend.

Some scholars believe that Demodocus, the blind poet mentioned in the *Odyssey*, is Homer himself. By profession, Demodocus belonged to that class of people known as bards, national poets or storytellers who sing their verses to the accompaniment of a musical instrument called a lyre. Ancient kings and princes often employed bards to live at the palace and to compose verses praising their patrons and the greatness of the city. The fact that ancient bards were often represented as blind gave rise to the tradition that Homer was blind. Some scholars have suggested that the ancients felt a poet's lack of sight allowed him to concentrate more fully on composing and reciting his work. Greek sculptors usually represented Homer and other bards with closed eyes, probably to represent blindness.

Because there is so little known about Homer, many historians and scholars have disputed his authorship of the *Iliad* and the *Odyssey*. There are those who do not believe that he ever lived. The controversy over the composition of the poems, however, is not recent. Even some ancient Greeks questioned Homer's role as author of the works.

Over the centuries, those who have questioned Homer's authorship have argued that the poems were not written by one person, but by two individuals, or even by several people over a period of time. They believe that the two poems contain many inconsistencies and too much repetition. Yet we must remember that in 700 B.C. most people were illiterate. Writing is believed to have begun in Greece only around 750 B.C. Therefore, poetry was meant to be recited, not written. Because a poem as long as the *Iliad* (about 16,000 lines) or the *Odyssey* (about 12,000 lines) required a tremendous amount of memorization, it was possible that inconsistencies and repetitions could occur as each bard repeated the story. In addition, bards traditionally passed their tales orally from generation to generation. Many of the myths and tales included in the poems were known to most Greeks. It was how each bard, each storyteller, treated the tale that won him recognition and fame. In turn, a poet's treatment depended on how he adapted and

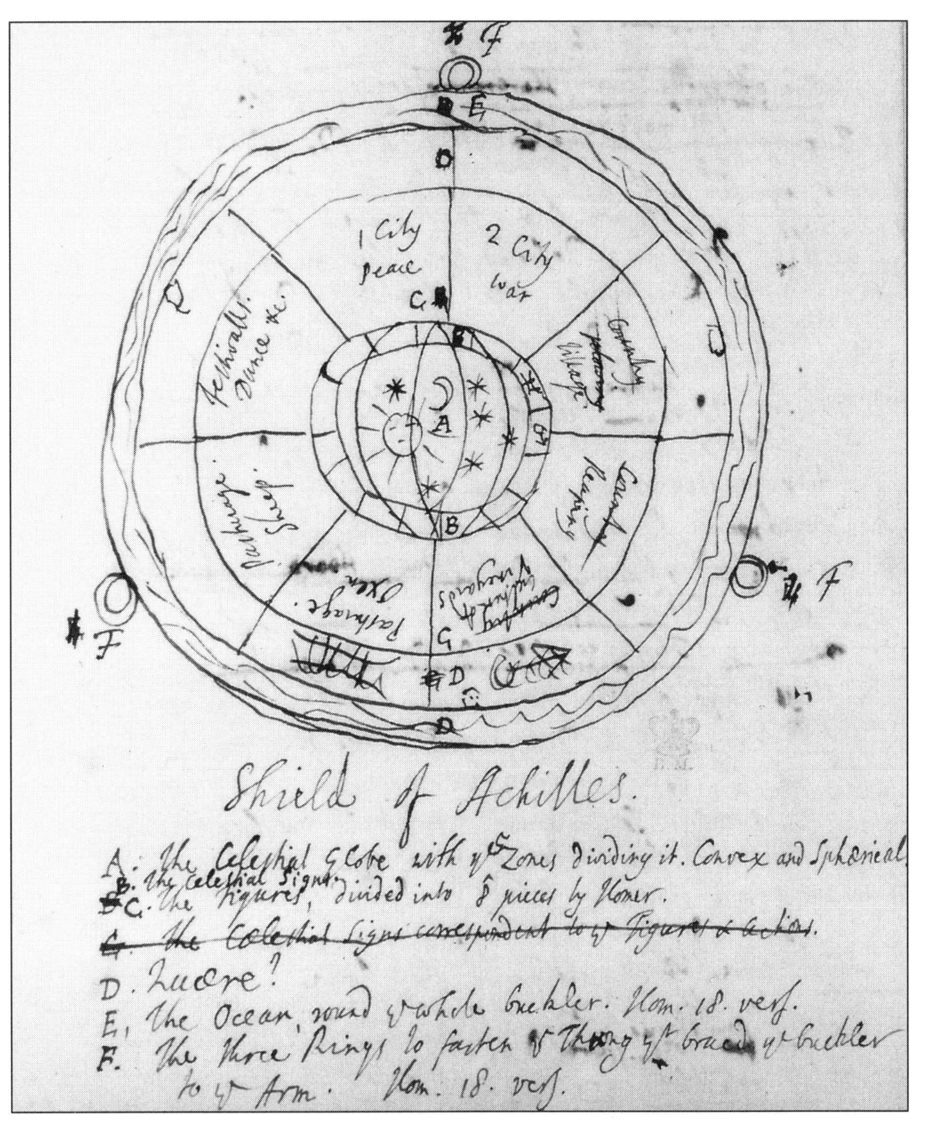

The 18th-century English poet Alexander Pope accompanied his translation of Homer's *Iliad* with a drawing of Achilles' shield, based on Homer's detailed description in Book 18.

He fell/thunderous/ly and/his armor/clattered u/pon him

spondee dactyl spondee dactyl dactyl spondee

Homer wrote this line about a soldier dying on a battlefield in the standard epic meter—the dactylic hexameter, which is a unit of verse containing six metrical feet, with the fifth foot a dactyl. In a dactylic foot, there is one stressed (or long) syllable and two unstressed (short) ones. In dactylic hexameter, the last foot is always a spondee, which is two stressed syllables.

added verses to the oral narrative poem to meet the needs of his audience.

Yet it is not the controversy surrounding the authorship of the poems that makes them great; it is the poems themselves. Each is a unified whole. Each poem revolves around a theme that praises the Greeks and stresses those qualities that made them heroes in the ancient world. Carefully and skillfully woven into each poem are many subplots and shorter tales.

Both the *Iliad* and the *Odyssey* belong to the class of poetry called epic, and the acknowledged master of the epic is Homer. His style and techniques have set the standards that all the epic poets since have followed. In fact, many later writers, including the Roman poet Virgil, borrowed directly from his works.

By definition, an epic is a poem that focuses on a national hero who performs superhuman deeds. An epic may be historical, legendary, or mythological—or it can include elements of all three. Because epics are always long and complicated, epic language is serious and includes certain literary styles and conventions, such as the constant use of specific, descriptive adjectives. For example, Odysseus, the hero of the *Odyssey*, is called "the crafty Odysseus," and dawn, the period of time between night and day, is referred to as "rosy-fingered." Known as epithets, these adjectives help listeners draw a clearer mental image of the people and incidents mentioned in the poem. In addition, the repetition of the same epithet gives continuity to the piece and to whomever or whatever is described.

Because the ancient epics were recited orally, poets needed to be very conscious of the sound and rhythm of their verses. By using harsh-sounding letters and single-syllable words, they could heighten the dramatic effect and convey a specific mood, such as approaching danger or violent storm squalls. By using some words that took time to say and others that were spoken quickly, poets were able to give a definite rhythm to each line. This arrangement of syllables in specific patterns is called meter. Both the *Iliad* and the *Odyssey* were written in dactylic hexameter, meaning that the syllables in the words of each line could be divided into six feet or measures, much like a line in music. *Dactyl* is Greek for "finger." A dactylic metrical foot, like a finger, has three parts—one long syllable and two short ones. In dactylic hexameter, the last foot is always a spondee, that is, two long syllables. Consequently, the final measure is always heavy. The fifth foot is almost always a dactyl with three syllables in the measure, the first long and the second and third short. A dactylic foot, then, gives a lightness to a line of verse. The first four feet in a dactylic hexameter line can be dactyls or spondees, depending on the sound quality the poet wishes to convey.

Another epic convention is the use of figures of speech, such as similes (a comparison using "like" or "as"), metaphors (a device that makes a comparison by substituting a word or phrase with another that literally means something else—as in, for example, "the ship plowed the seas"), personification (the representation of an idea or object in human form), oxymoron (the placing of opposites side by side, such as "bitter sweetness"), and assonance (the repetition of the same sound, such as "busy, buzzing bees"). Poets use figures of speech to vary the sound quality of the poem.

Besides the literary characteristics that define an epic, there are other prerequisites. Epic themes and heroes must be timeless and universal. Yet epic heroes are always mortals with human characteristics such as fear, courage, and love of family, attributes that introduce a human element into the poem and allow the audience to relate to the heroes on a personal level. Because religion played an important role in the everyday life of the ancient Greeks, the gods and goddesses also played active roles in epics and interacted with human heroes.

To heighten the excitement and drama of the story and involve the listener more quickly in the action, Homer used another convention in his epics: he started each tale in the middle of the story and then used a flashback to give the listener the details of events that had already taken place. For example, the *Odyssey* begins with Odysseus on the island of the nymph Calypso and then tells of his adventures during the past 10 years since he left Troy.

Because epics include so many conventions, they are extremely long works. The *Iliad* and the *Odyssey* are each divided into 24 books, with each book ranging in length from 424 lines

"More men who have a sense of honor survive than are slain, but those who flee difficult situations achieve neither glory nor receive help from others."

—from the *Iliad*

to 909 lines. Both poems are very complicated and contain simple and complex messages, as all epics do. The simplest level of meaning involves listening or reading for pure enjoyment; the next level has the audience analyzing the people and events in order to understand the time period during which the epic was written. At the highest level, the audience becomes involved in understanding the poem's spiritual and moral message and in applying it to everyday life.

The ancient Greeks recognized early the importance and value of Homer's works. By the 5th century B.C., Greek children were required to read and memorize lengthy passages from both poems. In addition, many professional poets recited Homer's works wherever people gathered, especially at festivals and games. Often these poets competed in public against one another, with each reciting a favorite section or a portion from one of Homer's epics. Never did the Greeks tire of hearing how their ancestors had defeated the Trojans, and they knew well the events that led to the Trojan War.

According to Greek mythology, Eris, the goddess of discord, was so angry at not being invited to the wedding of Peleus and Thetis (the future parents of Achilles, the hero of the *Iliad*) that she threw a golden apple into the reception area where the guests were talking. On the apple, Eris had carved the words "For the fairest." Hera (the queen of the gods), Athena (the goddess of wisdom), and Aphrodite (the goddess of beauty) all claimed the apple, but the decision was left to Paris, a son of Priam, king of Troy, which was a powerful city in Asia Minor. Determined to be the winner, Hera offered Paris control of Asia if he would pick her. Athena promised him victories on the battlefield if he chose her. But it was Aphrodite's prize that Paris could not resist, for Aphrodite offered him the most beautiful woman in the world, Helen, the queen of Sparta, a powerful city-state in southern Greece.

The *Iliad* tells how Helen's husband, the heartbroken and angry King Menelaus, marshalled Sparta's troops and then sent messengers asking the kings and heroes of Greece to join his fight against Troy. "The honor of Greece must be defended," he cried, and, for nine years, the Greeks laid siege to Troy. Defeats equaled victories, and the loss of thousands of lives disheartened those who survived. Yet it was the gods and goddesses who were mostly responsible for the endless war, because some deities favored the Trojans while others backed the Greeks. Neither side was about to acknowledge defeat.

Another reason for the stalemate was the Greek hero Achilles' refusal to fight until the Greek king Agamemnon returned to him a female prisoner of war named Briseïs. Only after Patroclus, Achilles' closest friend, was killed did Achilles enter the fray. The final scenes of the *Iliad* describe how "swift-footed" Achilles and Hector "of the shining helmet," a son of King Priam, chased each other in their chariots around the walls of Troy until Hector stood his ground and refused to give chase any longer. At that moment, Achilles hurled his spear and missed, but the goddess Athena, unseen, retrieved the spear and gave it

ANCIENT GREEKS

Homer

BORN

Around 700 B.C.
On the coast of Asia Minor, perhaps in Smyrna or on the island of Chios

DIED

Date and place unknown

PROFESSION

Epic poet

ACCOMPLISHMENTS

Credited as the author of the epic poems the *Iliad* and the *Odyssey*

"Bards are honored and revered throughout the world, because the muse has taught them songs and loves the race of bards."

—from the Odyssey

back to Achilles. Hector threw his spear and, when he missed, turned to get a second spear. Only when he found no second spear did he realize that Athena had deceived him. "Yet his courage did not fail him. He drew his sharp sword and prepared to swoop down like an eagle that darts through dark clouds on his way earthward in order to snatch a tender lamb or a cowering hare. Achilles, his heart bursting with anger, rushed at Hector where the collarbones part the neck and shoulders, and there drove his spear...." The *Iliad* ends with Priam in Achilles' tent, seeking to ransom the body of his son.

The *Odyssey* continues the tale but focuses on the return home of the Greek hero Odysseus. The opening lines clearly set the stage for the rest of the poem: "Tell me, O Muse, of that man, so in need of help, who wandered far and wide, after he had sacked the sacred city of Troy...." The poem retells how the Greeks built an enormous wooden horse, filled it with armed men, and wheeled it to the gates of Troy. There a Greek, pretending to be a traitor, pleaded with the Trojans to quickly drag the horse within the walls, for only then could Troy defeat the Greeks. The Trojans took his advice, but later that evening were defeated in a surprise attack after armed Greek soldiers climbed out of their secret hiding place in the horse.

For Odysseus, however, the joy of victory quickly fades when the gods force him to spend another 10 years struggling to return home. Yet Odysseus is not the only Greek hero to encounter great hardships after the war. Several others died without ever seeing Greece again. Many scholars see this as Homer's way of stating that war is futile and military victory does not ensure happiness or freedom from troubles.

When Odysseus finally arrives home to Ithaca, on the west coast of Greece, he must battle the many suitors who have overtaken his home and have insisted that his wife, Penelope, choose one of them as her husband. The poem ends as Odysseus is reunited with his wife after he, with the aid of his son, Telemachus, has slain the suitors.

Through the centuries, poets and writers from many countries and civilizations, each writing in his or her own language, have imitated, adapted, and even borrowed Homer's verses. Examples of later novels whose authors used Homer as a model are *Tom Jones* (1749), by the English novelist Henry Fielding, and *Ulysses* (1922), by the Irish novelist James Joyce.

FURTHER READING

Baker, Charles F., III. "Odysseus's Homecoming." *Calliope*, January/February 1991, 14–20.

Baker, Rosalie F. "At the Walls of Troy." *Calliope*, January/February 1994, 4–9.

———. "What Is an Epic?" *Calliope*, January/February 1991, 4–6.

Connolly, Peter. *The Legend of Odysseus*. New York: Oxford University Press, 1986.

Homer. *Iliad*. Translated by A. T. Murray. Loeb Classical Library. 2 vols. Cambridge: Harvard University Press, 1976–1978.

———. *The Iliad*. Retold by Barbara Leonie Picard. New York: Oxford University Press, 1991.

———. *Odyssey*. Translated by A. T. Murray. Loeb Classical Library. 2 vols. Cambridge: Harvard University Press, 1966.

———. *The Odyssey*. Retold by Barbara Leonie Picard. New York: Oxford University Press, 1992.

———. *The Odyssey*. Translated by Walter Shewring. New York: Oxford University Press, 1992.

McCaughrean, Geraldine. *The Odyssey*. Illustrated by Victor G. Ambrus. New York: Oxford University Press, 1993.

Podlecki, Anthony J. *The Early Greek Poets and Their Times*. Vancouver, Canada: University of British Columbia Press, 1984.

Wood, Michael. *In Search of the Trojan War*. New York: Penguin, 1996.

Solon

LEADING THE WORLD TOWARD DEMOCRACY

The 6th century B.C. found Athenians struggling with government reform. Both aristocrats (members of the upper class) and ordinary citizens believed that a more democratic form of government would create a better Athens for everyone. What was needed to carry out the necessary changes was strong leadership.

In 594 B.C., a man named Solon became the chief archon, or public official, in Athens. Over the years, Solon had become a leading citizen in Athens and had earned the respect of all Athenians because of his fair handling of difficult state matters. An aristocrat by birth, Solon is said to have traced his ancestry back to Codrus (11th century B.C.), the last king of Athens. Solon was not very rich, however, because his father had used much of the family's money helping others.

Accounts also suggest that Solon was a merchant who had traveled widely and understood finances and money matters. Solon was considered to be very honest, and it was this characteristic that made the poor admire and follow

Solon, who tried to make Athenian government fairer and open to more people, once said, "Justice, even when slow, is sure."

Found in a building at the northeast corner of the Agora in Athens, these bronze wheels are public ballots. To vote for an acquittal, jurors would drop a ballot with a solid axle in a ballot box. A ballot with a hollow axle (center) was a vote for condemnation. To conceal the vote from public view, a juror held the axle between his fingertips.

him. Solon was also honored as one of the Seven Sages, reputedly the wisest men in Greece.

Once in office, Solon immediately began revamping the government. He had learned many lessons from his study of history, including one that involved his ancestor Codrus.

Tradition said that when a group of people known as the Dorians prepared to invade Athens in the 11th century B.C., the oracle at Delphi declared that the victor in the battle would be the side whose king was slain. When Codrus heard the prophecy, he secretly dressed himself as a woodcutter, marched onto the battlefield, and soon met death. So it was that Athens won its freedom but lost its ruler. Because the Athenians believed no one could or should succeed the noble Codrus, the monarchy was abolished.

We do not know if this tale is true, but history does record that the monarchy at Athens was in a state of decline at the time and that public officials known as archons wielded the power. Membership in this group was selective, because only aristocrats could become archons. Originally, archons served for life. Later the term of office was reduced to 10 years, and then to a single year. At the end of his term in office, an archon automatically became a member of the *Areopagos*, or ruling council. Because this method of governing allowed the aristocrats to have all the power and the people to have none, conflicts between the two groups arose.

Sometime around 620 B.C., Solon's predecessor, an archon named Draco, enacted major changes in government policies, such as giving the right to vote to all those men who could buy their own military equipment. Solon's laws were strict, but they signaled a strong move toward fairness and equality among citizens. Still, the poor had few political rights.

Solon understood this gradual shift toward involving all citizens in the governing process, and he approved of it. However, he knew that another problem faced the poor, one that was worse than having no political rights. For many Athenians, the only way they could survive was to borrow money. Too often, though, a poor person found it impossible to pay back the loan. As a result, the debt load kept growing until this individual had only one solution. He, or a member of his family, could become a slave to his creditor. Worse still, creditors sometimes sold these slaves abroad.

Once Solon received the approval of both the aristocrats and the people to do whatever was necessary to end the conflict between the classes, he acted swiftly and with determination. First he canceled all debts that had made poor people slaves and returned "lost" farms to the poor. He then recalled those who had been sold abroad as slaves. Finally, to prevent the same situation from recurring, he banned individuals from selling themselves for money or to pay debts.

To make the government fairer and open to a greater number of Athenians, Solon rewrote the constitution. Athenians had already been divided into four groups for tax purposes. Solon used these groups as the basis of his political reforms. He decreed that membership in a particular group be based on the amount of grain or wine an individual's land produced each year. Those who produced 500 measures (about 700 bushels) were called the *pentakosiomedimnoi* (literally, "500 bushel men") and were eligible to run for all public offices, including the archonship. Those who produced 300 measures were the *hippeis*, or cavalrymen. They were generally wealthy citizens (they could afford to buy their cavalry equipment, including horses) and were eligible for some higher public offices. Those who produced 200 measures were the *zeugitai*, or farmers. They served as foot soldiers and could hold minor offices. Those who produced less than 200 measures were the *thetes*, or day laborers, the lowest class of citizens in Athens. The *thetes* were not eligible to hold public office, but they could serve as jurors and were allowed to participate in the Assembly, the body of adult male citizens that met to consider proposals such as those involving war, peace, and alliances.

The divisions helped, but there was still resentment because only the *pentakosiomedimnoi* were eligible to become archons, the prerequisite for membership in the *Areopagos*, the government body that held the most power. To balance the *Areopagos*, Solon added a new council to be composed of 400 members, 100 from each of the 4 groups. Called the Council of the Four Hundred, its members prepared the laws that were then submitted to the people in the Assembly.

Solon realized that for his laws to work people needed to take part in government matters. He decreed that anyone who refused to participate in public matters or stood by and allowed treasonous acts to be committed would be denied the right to vote and the right to be an Athenian citizen. The same punishment held for anyone who withdrew from political arguments and conflicts and waited to see which side was winning before choosing sides. To ensure justice for all, he made it a law that anyone who witnessed another person being hurt could bring charges against the wrongdoer.

Solon then turned to Draco's laws. He repealed all of them except one requiring the death penalty for a murderer, and he passed a new set of laws with more humane punishments. Solon also addressed everyday problems that could lead to political conflict. He forbade anyone in public to speak ill of a dead person. And if anyone spoke out against another person at a public function, the speaker had to pay a fine both to the public treasury and to the individual he had maligned.

Another of Solon's laws concerned wills, the legal documents that state how a person's possessions are to be distributed after that person's death. Before his time, no one needed a will because all property went automatically to the deceased's family. Solon, however, believed that individuals with no children should be allowed to direct where they wanted their property and money to go. He also enacted laws to punish anyone who tried to be made the heir of a childless person.

Solon's regulations concerning women were quite strict and included a time limit on how long they could mourn a deceased relative or friend. When women traveled away from home, Solon decreed that they could bring only three sets of clothes, a small portion of food, and a small basket. His intent was to keep women fairly close to home. Solon also regulated their clothing and appearance, forbidding women to wear anything that was unsuitable or immodest.

Laziness was not one of Solon's characteristics, and he did not tolerate it in others. He encouraged trading expeditions but allowed the export only of olive oil. He established rules

To ensure a fair measure, two men sit on stools and watch as a third man fills the container on the right until it equals the weight of the sack on the left balance. Solon, who was probably a merchant before assuming government office, had a reputation for honesty in his dealings and was respected for his knowledge of finances.

ANCIENT GREEKS

Solon

BORN

Before 610 B.C.
Athens, Greece

DIED

After 580 B.C.
Athens, Greece

PROFESSION

Statesman and lawgiver

ACCOMPLISHMENTS

Revised the law code of Athens; gave Athenians a greater voice in government matters by dividing them into groups and giving each group specific political rights; abolished the practice of selling oneself into slavery to pay debts

"When giving advice, try to help, not to please, your friend."

—Solon, quoted in *Lives of Eminent Philosophers* (3rd century A.D.) by Diogenes Laertius

stating that olive and fig trees had to be planted at least five feet from the edge of a farmer's property so that the roots could grow naturally and remain healthy.

Because he wanted everyone to know his laws, Solon had them written on wooden tablets and decreed that they were in effect for 100 years. Solon realized that his laws were not perfect, but he also knew they were a beginning. He did admit that he became discouraged and weary when people appeared before him every day asking him to clarify a particular point, to criticize a ruling, or to request an exemption. He felt that he had to respond in order not to discourage or anger the petitioner.

Finally the time came when Solon decided to leave Athens for a period of 10 years. By his own account, he believed that his absence would give Athenians a chance to rule themselves and become familiar with the laws.

Once Solon made the decision to leave Athens, he bought a trading ship. He stopped first in Egypt. According to the Greek biographer Plutarch, Solon later wrote a story of an Atlantic island that he had heard about during his travels in Egypt. In time, this island became known as the lost city of Atlantis. From Egypt, Solon sailed to the island of Cyprus and finally to Lydia, in Asia Minor, where tradition said that he met with the rich king Croesus. (Historically, the dates of the lives of the two men do not overlap.)

Trouble, however, was brewing in Athens, and when messengers brought Solon news that the people were arguing among themselves, he recognized the seriousness of the situation and returned home. Although he was now too old to take control, as he had done some 10 years earlier, he helped by giving advice to the opposing factions.

One man, Pisistratus, seemed determined to rule alone. Solon recognized this and tried to counsel him. Yet even after Pisistratus won control of Athens in a nondemocratic manner, Solon did not fear to voice his opposition publicly. Solon's friends, however, urged him to flee because they were convinced that Pisistratus would hurt or kill the old lawgiver. Solon refused to leave and even placed his weapons outside his door before calmly continuing about his business.

Pisistratus was not about to take the life of someone so noble and honored. Instead, he asked the great lawgiver's advice and then retained many of Solon's reforms and laws. Pisistratus' successors also recognized the value of Solon's laws and used them as a model. So, too, did the Romans and all other nations whose leaders believed in representative government. Thus, it was Solon who took the first major step in leading Athens and the Western world toward democracy.

FURTHER READING

Andrewes, Antony. *The Greek Tyrants*. London: Hutchinson's University Library, 1956.

Freeman, Kathleen. *The Work and Life of Solon*. London: Milford, 1926.

Linforth, Ivan M. *Solon the Athenian*. Berkeley: University of California Press, 1919.

Plutarch. *Parallel Lives: Solon*. Translated by Bernadotte Perrin. Loeb Classical Library. Cambridge: Harvard University Press, 1968.

Podlecki, Anthony J. *The Early Greek Poets and Their Times*. Vancouver, Canada: University of British Columbia Press, 1984.

Lycurgus

SPARTAN REFORMER

"Come home with your shield or on it!" counseled a Spartan mother to her son as he prepared to march out into battle.

Tradition says that her advice was typical, for Spartans believed that a good soldier neither retreated nor allowed himself to be taken prisoner. He either fought and won, bringing his shield home with him, or he died defending Sparta, and his fellow soldiers brought his lifeless body home on the shield.

All of Greece recognized Sparta's soldiers as the most disciplined, the most courageous, and the most successful in the Greek world. For centuries, people have asked how this came to be and who was responsible for creating Sparta's military state. The ancient Spartans traced their unique form of government, unparalleled in the ancient Mediterranean world, to a man named Lycurgus. Through the centuries, however, few have believed that one individual could be responsible for setting up a city-state so concerned with prowess on the battlefield.

The Greek biographer Plutarch chronicled the life of Lycurgus in great detail. Yet even he began his essay

The Spartans honored Lycurgus as the founder of their disciplined way of life, which stressed physical fitness and military prowess.

This bronze Spartan warrior with his crested helmet embodies the traits Lycurgus wished to instill in his people: fearlessness, determination, and confidence.

acknowledging that almost everything written about Lycurgus was questionable. Plutarch and later historians, however, do agree that Lycurgus had to have lived before 600 B.C. and that the Spartan military system had been established by that date.

In ancient times, legend and tradition had made Lycurgus such a hero that many Greeks, especially the Spartans, considered him partly divine. They even traced his ancestry to the most famous of all Greek heroes, Heracles (later known as Hercules to the Romans), whose father was Zeus, the king of the gods.

Lycurgus became one of Sparta's two kings after his older brother died. Since very early times, two kings had always ruled in Sparta. Each came from one of the two royal families, and each acted as a check on the power of the other. Lycurgus' reign, however, was short-lived, for it was soon discovered that his sister-in-law, the former queen, was pregnant. When she gave birth to a son eight months later, Lycurgus stepped down in favor of his nephew Charilaus, the rightful heir. To avoid being connected with any court intrigues, Lycurgus left Sparta and sailed to Crete, where he carefully studied its form of government. He then traveled to Asia, and, according to the Egyptians, to Egypt. What interested him most in all his travels was the manner in which the people were governed.

When Lycurgus heard that the Spartans were eager for him to return because they acknowledged him as the person most able to rule the land, he set sail for home. Once there, he planned a major overhaul of the government, but first he wanted the approval or at least the advice of the gods. He journeyed to Delphi, one of the most sacred areas of Greece, where he consulted the oracle, a priestess who revealed the wishes of the deities. He asked Apollo, the patron god of Delphi, to make known his wishes. Spartan tradition maintained that Apollo, the god of the sun and of prophecy, spoke through his priestess and told Lycurgus that he was well loved by the gods and partly divine. The priestess also said that Lycurgus' laws would be the best, and whoever followed them would produce the world's most famous city-state.

Armed with this prophecy, Lycurgus gradually persuaded several Spartans to help him reform the government. When the young king heard of his uncle's proposals, he decided not to flee or resist but to give Lycurgus the help that he needed. To give more force to the new laws that he wanted to institute, Lycurgus went to Delphi and returned with several *rhetrai*, or directions from the oracle. Lycurgus, however, did not believe in writing down the *rhetrai* because he believed that they should become so much a part of a Spartan citizen that written laws would be unnecessary.

The first change came immediately. Lycurgus saw the wisdom in Sparta's two-king system and allowed it to continue, but to avoid having all the power in the hands of two individuals, he established a 28-member *Gerousia*, or Senate. Every male Spartan citizen older than 60 who, throughout his lifetime, had proven himself loyal to

Lycurgus

BORN

Before 600 B.C.
Sparta, Greece

DIED

Date and place unknown

PROFESSION

Statesman and lawgiver

ACCOMPLISHMENTS

Credited with the establishment of Sparta's rigorous and disciplined military, political, and social systems

the laws of the state was eligible for membership.

Lycurgus then instituted a unique process for electing a senator. A select group met in a room near where the election was to be held. As each candidate appeared before the Spartan people outside, the people shouted their approval. Those in the room listened and rated the volume of the shouting. The candidate who received the loudest voice vote won. Once in office, a senator held the position for life. At first, the senators acted as advisers to the kings, but gradually they came to share equal powers with them.

To involve all Spartans in the governing of the state, every Spartan citizen 30 years of age or older belonged to the *Apella,* or Assembly. This government body met on occasion to listen to and approve by a voice vote proposals made by the senators and kings. But because the people still had little say in the government, decades later the public office of *ephor* was established. Five in number, the *ephors* (government officials) were elected annually by Sparta's citizens and had the power to carry out the will of the Assembly.

With the government offices in place, Lycurgus now began a set of social reforms. Because he felt too few people owned too much land, he persuaded everyone to agree to a new division of lands, one that would apportion the same amount of land to every citizen. Lycurgus felt that merit, not wealth, should distinguish people from one another. Therefore, he divided the land belonging to Sparta (Sparta was the chief and only major city) into 30,000 equal shares and the city of Sparta into 9,000 shares. Tradition says that as Lycurgus traveled about the area checking on the divisions, he said that Sparta seemed like one family to him, with its members sharing the estate peacefully, like brothers.

Still Lycurgus felt he needed more laws to ensure that all Spartans would remain equal as far as material possessions were concerned and that they would not become envious of what others had. He canceled all debts and requested that everyone voluntarily give their gold and silver to the state. Lycurgus also decreed that Spartans could use as money only special pieces of iron weighing at least 20 to 30 pounds each. This law immediately stopped all thoughts of robbery, bribery, and even trading, for who would want to deal with such heavy currency? Still Lycurgus was not satisfied.

To prohibit Spartans from buying or even wanting to buy luxury items, Lycurgus placed a ban on foreign goods. He also ordered that the beams for ceilings in houses could be cut only with an axe, and gates and doors only with a saw. This ensured that all Spartan houses would be simple in design.

Lycurgus imposed a new law stating that all Spartan men were to gather in small groups of 15 or so to share their meals together. (Women ate at home.) Each member was to provide a monthly ration of food and wine from the portion of land assigned to him. It was also customary for young boys to join these groups to learn about politics and other government affairs. Their discussions, however, were kept secret. Anyone wanting to join a "dinner

"A city surrounded by brave men and not by bricks will be well fortified."

—Lycurgus, quoted in Plutarch's *Lives* (around 1st century A.D.)

group" had to be approved by the group's members. The members passed a bowl among themselves, and each threw in a piece of bread rolled into a ball. To vote no, a member squashed and flattened the bread ball before throwing it into the bowl.

Meals were never lavish or costly. In fact, the favored food among Spartans was a so-called black broth, the ingredients of which are now uncertain. Following Lycurgus' belief in strict discipline and simplicity, no Spartan used any candle or light to find his way home after an evening meal. The Spartans instead learned to walk boldly and proudly through the dark.

Not everyone agreed with the policy of communal dining and, on one occasion, some Spartans gathered together and began shouting and throwing stones at Lycurgus. One stone hit the master lawgiver and took out his eye. Shocked at the result of their actions, the Spartans stopped and turned over the individual responsible for the incident to Lycurgus. The lawgiver took the young man, Alcander by name, into his home. After spending a few days with Lycurgus, Alcander realized that the man whom he had recently hated was the most honest and industrious individual he had ever met. Alcander then became a firm believer in Lycurgus' policies and promoted them throughout Sparta.

To end superstitions concerning death, Lycurgus allowed burials within the city walls and even around temples so that everyone would become accustomed to the sight of a dead body and would no longer fear that spirits would affect the living. Lycurgus even forbade mourning for anyone who had died. Because he believed in equality for all Spartans, he decreed that all tombs were to be alike and nameless—with one exception. A Spartan who died fighting bravely on the battlefield won the right to have an inscription on his tomb.

Still Lycurgus was not finished. Because he felt the most important task of a leader was to educate the nation's youth, he turned his energy to the young in Sparta. Military strength was a priority. Yet he did not want his army to fight any enemy too long or too often, for he believed that continued contact would only strengthen the enemy and teach them Spartan tactics. Nor did Lycurgus believe in conquest. He wanted his Spartans to be independent and in control of their land as well as their minds and bodies.

Spartan training began at birth. Only babies considered healthy and strong were allowed to live. All others were abandoned and left to die. Newborns were washed first with wine, not water, because the Spartans felt that wine strengthened an infant's limbs and spirit.

From the ages of 7 to 21, young boys had to leave home and participate in a military-style education program known as the *agoge*. The emphasis was on discipline, self-control, physical exercise, and obedience. Boys had to keep their hair very short, wear little clothing even in cold weather, and go barefoot to build up their endurance to pain and discomfort. After age 12, boys wore no undergarments and were allowed only one coat a year. In addition, bathing was allowed only on a few days during the year.

Groups of boys lived together in barracks-style quarters. The boys made their own sleeping mats out of reeds growing along Sparta's Eurotas River; they broke them with their hands because knives and other cutting tools were not allowed. The best and boldest boy in each group assumed the leadership role, and his commands had to be obeyed. War games and military drills were considered very important, and little emphasis was placed on writing and reading.

Boys were encouraged to find their own food, even if they had to steal it. However, anyone caught stealing was severely punished. The reason for this was that on the battlefield food was often scarce, and in order to survive soldiers were forced to scavenge what they could. The boys took the gathering of food so seriously that Plutarch tells of a boy who stole a fox and hid it under his coat. Rather than be caught, the boy allowed the fox to tear him to death with its teeth and claws.

Spartan girls stayed at home. Yet they, too, were required to dress simply and participate in regular physical training exercises. Unlike females in other Greek city-states, Spartan women of all ages went out in public and even trained outdoors. According to legend, a foreigner once suggested to the queen of Sparta that the women of Sparta were the only women in the world who could rule men. The queen replied, "To be sure, for we are the only ones who give birth to men."

Lycurgus believed simplicity in speech was just as important as simple dress and food. The best answer, rule, or speech was always a short one. In fact, this became a Spartan trait. Once, when a foreigner from another city-state laughed at the short swords used by Spartans, the Spartan king retorted, "Long enough to kill our enemies."

On another occasion, when someone suggested that Lycurgus set up a democracy in Sparta, Lycurgus replied, "After you set up a democracy in your own family." The English language used the word *Laconia*, the name of the area in Greece where Sparta was the chief city, as the base of its word *laconic*, meaning "using few words."

Even after age 21, a Spartan's life was one of discipline and constant physical and military training. On the battlefield, Spartan troops marched in perfect order to the tune of flutes and never showed any sign of fear. Before a battle, Lycurgus encouraged Spartan soldiers to let their hair grow because he believed that long hair made handsome men even more handsome and ugly men more ferocious looking. Also on Lycurgus' orders, Spartan soldiers wore finer garments and had more to eat in time of war.

Because the Spartan lifestyle demanded such military superiority and efficiency, Spartan men had no time to devote to daily chores. A class of people who had no rights and were known as the Helots performed such time-consuming duties as tilling the fields and harvesting the crops. On several occasions, the Helots revolted against their masters, but they were always defeated. In fact, the only fear the Spartans seemed to have was the possibility of a Helot uprising.

After years of reform, Lycurgus was finally pleased with the results in Sparta. According to Plutarch, he called an assembly of all his people and told them that he had one more law to pass. Before doing so, however, he wished to leave Sparta and consult the oracle. He asked the Spartans to continue observing his commands and those of the *rhetrai* until he returned. He also requested that they change nothing until he returned and that they obey whatever the oracle should command. Everyone agreed.

When the oracle at Delphi responded that Lycurgus' laws were good and that the Spartans would continue to be admired for as long as they observed the laws, Lycurgus was well pleased. He sent the oracle's reply to his people and reminded them of their oath to observe his laws and the command of the oracle. He then decided that he had lived long enough and took no more food. Lycurgus believed that even in death he had to set an example of virtue.

According to some accounts, Lycurgus died on the island of Crete. His followers were said to have cremated his body and scattered his ashes over the sea so that the Spartans would not be released from their promise to follow the *rhetrai* until Lycurgus returned home.

For centuries, the Spartans continued to observe Lycurgus' laws. In battle, other Greek city-states and even rulers beyond Greece's borders sent to Sparta for military help. The term *spartan* entered many languages, including English, as a synonym for "strict self-discipline and self-denial." Lycurgus became Sparta's national hero, the founder and writer of its constitution. Over the years, legends grew about his life. Whether he actually existed and what he was like may never be known, but the impact of the laws attributed to Lycurgus and the influence of Sparta on the ancient Mediterranean world have never been doubted.

FURTHER READING

Plutarch. *The Parallel Lives: Lycurgus*. Translated by Bernadotte Perrin. Loeb Classical Library. Cambridge: Harvard University Press, 1968.

Sappho

THE TENTH MUSE

Sappho, a poet for all times, won the admiration not only of her contemporaries but also of all the generations that followed. Today she is considered one of the best, if not *the* best, female poet of classical antiquity.

Home for Sappho was the Greek island of Lesbos in the Aegean Sea. At some time in her life, probably during her youth, Sappho went as an exile to Sicily, an island in the Mediterranean Sea off the coast of Italy where many Greek colonists had settled. Her exile was relatively short, a fact that has led many scholars to believe that political problems or unfriendly rulers must have forced her, and probably her family, to leave Lesbos.

Later writers named Scamandronymus as her father, but they are uncertain about her mother's name. A fragment from one of her poems reads, "I have a beautiful girl named Cleis." Some people believe that Sappho was referring to her mother; others think that she was referring to her own daughter. The latter is possible because, according to ancient accounts, Sappho married a rich man named Cercylas. There are others, however, who think that the name Cleis refers to a girlfriend.

Ancient writings also reveal that Sappho had three brothers, who were probably all younger than she was. Sappho's brother Charaxus earned her wrath by falling in love with an Egyptian slave girl. In one poem, Sappho condemns her brother for spending far too much money buying this girl her freedom and then showering her with expensive presents. In another poem, Sappho prays for her brother's safe return from a trading voyage to Egypt and promises to forgive him. Her favorite brother must have been Larichus because every mention of him is full of praise and love.

Like so many details about her life, Sappho's physical appearance is a mystery. Ancient records document two statues of Sappho, both of which were lost in ancient times and have never been recovered. Several Greek vase designs and a few unidentified busts, which some scholars believe are of Sappho, have survived. All show her with hair pulled back and wrapped in a kerchief or tied up with ribbons.

According to the Greek writer Menander, Sappho committed suicide by throwing herself off a cliff. Centuries later, the Roman poet Ovid wrote that Sappho was so upset when her love for a man named Phaon was not returned that she no longer wished to continue living. Few ever believed this story, and today historians and scholars continue to maintain that the Sappho-Phaon tale is just a fabrication of later times.

Sappho

BORN

Around 600 B.C.
Lesbos

DIED

Date and place unknown

PROFESSION

Lyric poet

ACCOMPLISHMENTS

Wrote lyric poetry; established a school for young girls where she taught poetry, music, singing, and dancing

This is a Roman copy of an original 4th-century bust of Sappho. In a society where few women achieved fame, Sappho produced some of the best-known love poems of ancient Greece.

Scholars do agree that Sappho lived during the latter part of the 7th century B.C., perhaps around 600 B.C. At that time, the Greek language was developed and expanded, people learned to read, and poets began to write down their verses rather than just reciting them. Sappho's vocabulary and writing style prove that she had been educated. According to most scholars, her parents were probably well-to-do aristocrats who believed in teaching their daughter the skills of reading and writing. This certainly was not a common practice of this time among Greeks on the mainland or in the colonies. By custom, the great majority of Greek women were sheltered from the world and expected to work in the home, caring for their children and attending to everyday household duties.

Greek women traditionally had few political or legal rights. However, the situation appears to have been slightly more liberal on the island of Lesbos, where women had many of the same rights as men, including the right to higher education. Still, Sappho was unusual because she formed her own literary group or school where she instructed the members, all of whom were young girls, in poetry, music, singing, and dancing. Because Sappho ran a school for young girls and because her poems involve her feelings for these girls, the name of Sappho's island, Lesbos, became the basis of the English term *lesbian*, which is used to refer to a female homosexual.

Most likely Sappho spent much of her time training her pupils to take part in the processional dances and songs that were performed during the island's religious festivals. Sappho and her students paid tribute to the nine Muses, the goddesses who presided over the arts and sciences, and to Aphrodite, the goddess of love and beauty. Perhaps this was a reflection of the special emphasis that the people of Lesbos placed on beauty and song. According to a passage in Homer's epic poem the *Iliad*, the women of Lesbos were the most beautiful in the world. Beauty contests were held on the island, and many Greeks regarded Lesbos as the home of dance and lyric song.

Sappho's works belong to that class of poetry known as lyric poetry. However, her poems were not meant to be sung by a chorus with a choir and a leader, as most lyric poetry was at the time. Nor were they written to be sung at a specific festival, religious occasion, or drama, as so much ancient poetry was. They could, however, be accompanied by a lyre or other musical instrument or by dancing, as was also the custom. Sappho's poetry was personal and was written to be sung by a single person—herself—before an

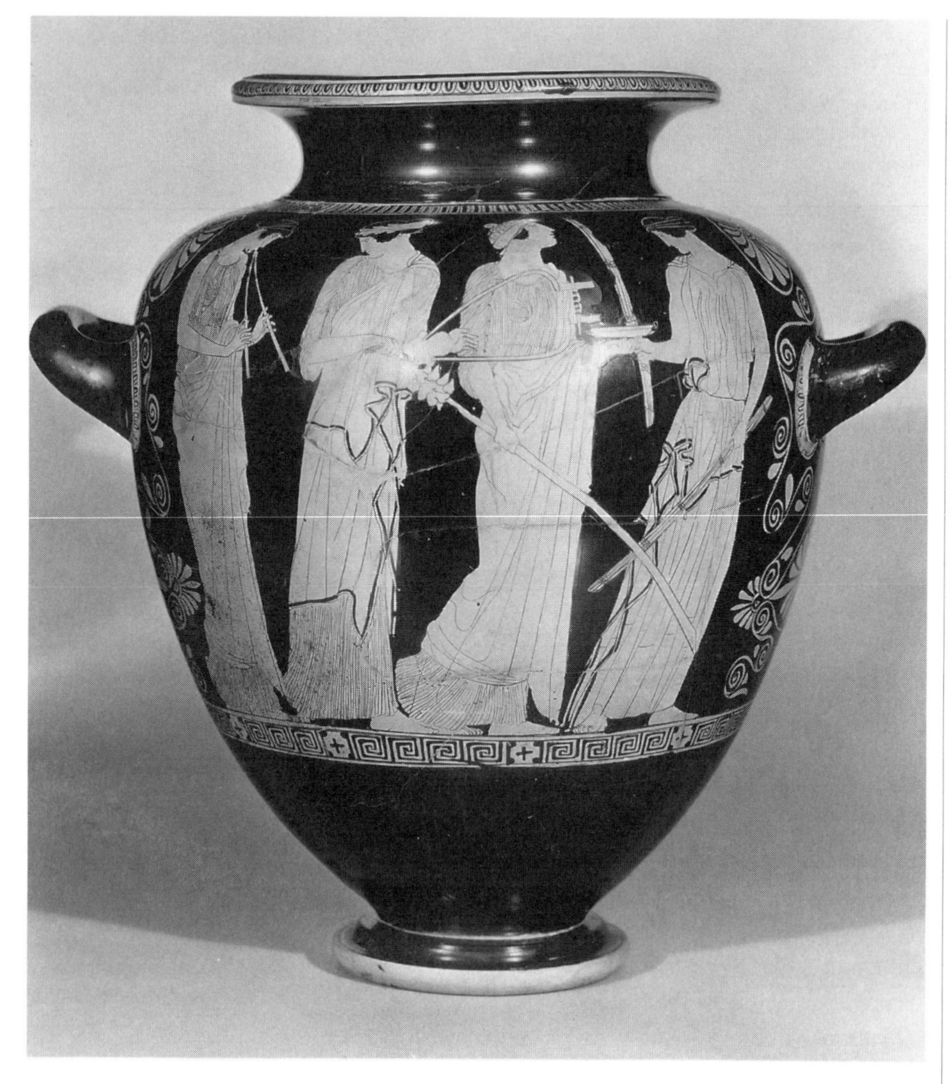

Although Greek women spent most of their time at home caring for their families, they did play an active role in religious festivals, as in this vase scene, in which the two women at left play a double pipe called an aulos and a lyre. At her school for girls, Sappho concentrated on training her students to take part in such festivals.

audience. As such, her poems are addressed to her young pupils and express her feelings on subjects that affected her personally. She wrote, "My fair comrades mine, to you/My thought is ever true."

Many poems are wedding songs, celebrating her pupils' marriages and relating the sadness she feels when a girl leaves. When one particular member leaves for Lydia, on the mainland of Asia Minor, Sappho sings of her disappointment and compares the girl to the moon outshining the stars: "The stars around the lovely moon hide their shining forms when the full moon lights up the earth." Through the centuries, poets have borrowed this phrase to describe Sappho and her place in the literary world.

Because Sappho wrote for herself, her poems come from the heart. The words are honest and direct as they express simple but deeply felt emotions. In one poem, Sappho expresses her anger at the forgetfulness of others and, in another, her hurt when a girl whom she has known for years decides to move and leave the group. On occasion Sappho is philosophical, as when she laughs at a rich woman who thinks money can buy manners and culture. In another passage, she advises that silence is the most dignified behavior when one is angry.

All succeeding generations of poets, including today's, have studied and imitated Sappho, but none has equaled the simplicity of her style and the candidness of her emotion. Perhaps the Greek philosopher Plato, who followed her by a couple of centuries, put it best when he wrote, "Many say there are only nine Muses. How careless! Do they not see the tenth Muse, Sappho of Lesbos?"

FURTHER READING

Barnstone, Willis, trans. *Sappho and the Greek Lyric Poets*. New York: Schocken, 1988.

Podlecki, Anthony J. *The Early Greek Poets and Their Times*. Vancouver, Canada: University of British Columbia Press, 1984.

Sappho. *Sappho, A Garland: The Poems and Fragments of Sappho*. Translated by Jim Powell. New York : Farrar, Straus & Giroux, 1993.

Snyder, Jane McIntosh. *Sappho*. New York: Chelsea House, 1995.

Thurman, Judith. *I Became Alone: Five Women Poets*. New York: Atheneum, 1975.

Aesop

STORYTELLER

Please let me go!" pleaded the tiny mouse. "If you do, I promise that some day I will return the favor and come to your aid."

"Come to my aid!" roared the lion. "You puny little creature, how could you possibly help me, the king of beasts?"

"Just wait and see!" begged the mouse.

"Oh well, you're such a tiny morsel that my stomach wouldn't even notice you," said the lion, and he opened his paw. Without a moment's hesitation, the mouse scampered away from the long, sharp talons, but he did turn once to take a last look at the mighty beast he had promised to help.

Accepting the traditional belief that Aesop was a hunchback, a 15th-century German woodcut artist depicted the Greek storyteller surrounded by images from his fables.

Around 1500, an Italian artist illustrated a Greek-language version of Aesop's tale about men who were turned into ants by the gods because they were always taking their neighbor's crops to add to their own. Despite the change in their appearance, their character was the same and the ants scurried through the fields, still stealing food. Aesop's moral: You may punish thieves, but they do not change.

Soon after, it happened that the mouse was roaming the forest when he heard a mighty roar. He stopped. He heard a second roar. "Someone's in trouble," he thought. "But wait, that roar sounds familiar. Let me have a look!"

There, near some trees, he saw a huge lion trapped in a hunter's net. "You look familiar," squeaked the mouse, "but I must make sure." After asking a series of questions, the mouse realized that this was the very same lion who had set him free only days before.

Quickly, the mouse began gnawing at the ropes of the net, and he made an opening large enough for the lion to escape.

This time, the lion stretched out his paw to say thank you to the mouse. "My friend, for truly we are friends, I

Aesop

BORN
Around 600 B.C.
Samos

DIED
Date and place unknown

PROFESSION
Storyteller

ACCOMPLISHMENTS
Credited with the authorship of fables that teach moral lessons and use animals as characters

thank you sincerely and apologize for laughing so recently at your offer of help. Your kindness has proven that whether big or small, mighty or weak, we can all help each other."

This tale of the lion and the mouse can be found in nearly every bookstore in the world. A variety of animated cartoons and even comic books have also told the tale. One of the best-known fables (fictitious stories meant to teach a lesson) in the world of literature, it traces its roots to at least as far back as the early 6th century B.C. to a Greek storyteller named Aesop.

Most scholars believe that Aesop was originally a slave from one of the Greek colonies in Thrace, a land bordering the northern coast of the Aegean Sea. His master was a man named Iadmon, whose home was the Greek island of Samos in the Aegean Sea. Iadmon later set Aesop free, perhaps because he recognized Aesop's great talent for storytelling. It is impossible to determine, however, whether Aesop was a hunchback and unable to speak, as so many accounts relate.

From all ancient reports, it appears that Aesop's stories won him immediate fame and were told and retold throughout the Greek world. Although Aesop might have borrowed some details and incidents from tales that he had heard, most scholars believe that he was responsible for creating and developing many of the stories now credited to him. Though some were written as poems and others as prose, they are all short and end with a moral. Another characteristic of Aesop's fables is his use of animals to represent human traits and different types of people. In the story above, the lion represents might, pride, force, and superiority, whereas the mouse represents weakness, inferiority, and cleverness. The moral is that size and force do not necessarily bring victory.

Another of Aesop's tales that has been used by philosophers and politicians over the centuries to support their arguments is Aesop's story of the country mouse and the city mouse:

It happened once that a happy little country mouse heard a knock on the door of his humble forest home. "Come in!" he called, and in strutted a fat, proud-looking mouse. The two looked at each other, each remembering days long ago when both had scampered about the fields playing and hunting for food. The visitor had left a while ago for the city, determined to enjoy the so-called high life that he felt awaited him there. The two had not seen each other since then.

"City life sure seems to agree with you, my friend. You look wonderful!" said the country mouse as he greeted his old friend. "Come, won't you stay a while and join me for supper?" and he took out some farmer's cheese, a slab of bacon, and pure spring water.

The two talked of the old days long into the night. The next morning, as the city mouse was about to leave, he said, "My friend, why don't you return with me to the city? My home is a mansion. Our meals are always banquets with the best of everything. It's a lively life, not quiet and boring like the country."

His arguments worked, and the country mouse was soon packing his belongings. It was nighttime when the two approached the city and entered the mansion through a convenient little mouse hole.

"I'm starving!" said the city mouse. "Let's go to the dining room and see what the masters have left us."

The country mouse could hardly believe his eyes. What should he eat

"No act of kindness, no matter how small, is ever wasted. We should look at a person's mind, not his appearance."

—from Aesop's Fables

first? There were cheeses, a variety of meats, breads, desserts, cookies, and champagne. Up the chair leg and then onto the table the two climbed. They began at one end of the table and were working their way across the plates when they heard a dog bark. Both stopped, their short hair standing on end. There was more barking, but this time it was not just one dog barking. There seemed to be many dogs, and they seemed to be coming closer. Suddenly a cat meowed. The two mice froze at the edge of a plate as they watched the cat enter the dining room. More noises! This time it was the servants coming to clear the plates and straighten out the room.

"Good-bye, my friend," called the country mouse, as he hastily but warily crept across the table and back down to the floor. "If this is what you call 'living in style,' you are welcome to enjoy it and all the fears and interruptions it brings. As for me, I much prefer my quiet life in the country. There I can enjoy and appreciate life. It may be simple and perhaps a little boring, but it is peaceful and free from unnecessary worries and cares."

Thus did Aesop advise his audience to appreciate and enjoy what they had, for usually it suited their needs far better than what they thought they wanted. Envy usually hurts rather than helps.

The timelessness of Aesop's stories and characters is what has made his tales so popular. Because they are not set in any particular place or country, they can be understood by people everywhere. There are no lines that must be memorized, for each tale can be retold many times, with each storyteller using his own words. As a result, there are countless versions, especially of the best-known tales—such as the one about the fox who decides that some grapes he had failed to snatch must have been sour anyway, or the story about the slow but steady tortoise who defeats the conceited hare in a race. The theme, the characters, and the moral, however, remain the same.

Ancient accounts mention that Demetrius of Phalerum, a 4th-century B.C. Greek philosopher and politician, assembled a collection of Aesop's fables. In the 1st century A.D., the Roman storyteller Phaedrus used Aesop's tales as the model for his collection of fables. Through the centuries, the tales have been constantly told and retold—the first printed edition in English was published in 1484. In the 17th century, the celebrated French poet Jean de La Fontaine (1621–95) used Aesop's tales as the basis for his *Fables*, which scholars consider a masterpiece of French literature.

Today, as the versions of Aesop's tales continue to multiply, the fame and reputation of this ancient Greek remain almost unequaled in the world of literature.

FURTHER READING

Aesop. *Aesop's Fables*. Retold by Anne Galti and illustrated by Safaya Salter. San Diego: Harcourt Brace Jovanovich, 1992.

———. *Aesop's Fables*. Translated by V. S. Vernon Jones and illustrated by Arthur Rackham. Introduction by G. K. Chesterton. Facsimile of the 1912 edition. Garden City, N.Y.: Garden City Publishing, 1939.

———. *Aesop's Fables*. Translated by John Warrington and illustrated by Joan Kiddell-Monroe. New York: Dutton, 1961.

———. *Aesop's Fables*. Selected and adapted by Jack Zipes. New York: Signet Classic, 1992.

———. *Aesop: Five Centuries of Illustrated Fables*. Compiled by John J. McKendry. New York: Metropolitan Museum of Art, 1964.

Bader, Barbara. *Aesop & Company: With Scenes from His Legendary Life*. Illustrated by Arthur Geisert. Boston: Houghton Mifflin, 1991.

Pythagoras

"REASON IS IMMORTAL"

For a Greek named Pythagoras, numbers were the key to understanding the world and the universe. His years of traveling, in Egypt and in other ancient Middle Eastern lands such as Babylonia, had introduced him to a wide variety of ideas about mathematics, religion, and astronomy. Pythagoras is also thought to have been influenced by Thales, reputedly one of the wisest men in Greece and considered to be the founder of physical science (the natural sciences, such as mineralogy and astronomy, that deal with nonliving matter) and of geometry. As Pythagoras developed his own theories and explained his views, he attracted many followers. However, because Pythagoras wrote no books, it is difficult to establish which thoughts were actually his and which were added or modified by his followers and admirers.

Pythagoras was born sometime around 580 B.C. on the Greek island of Samos in the Aegean Sea. His father was most likely an engraver of gems, a metalworker, or a merchant, any of which would have exposed young Pythagoras to styles and products from other lands. During his young adulthood, Pythagoras traveled extensively in the East, including Egypt and Asia Minor. Ancient accounts indicate that everywhere he went he sought to acquire as much

Proud of their native son, the people of Samos depicted the figure of Pythagoras touching a globe on one of their coins. Since coinage was a mark of independence, citizens carefully chose the figures to represent their city.

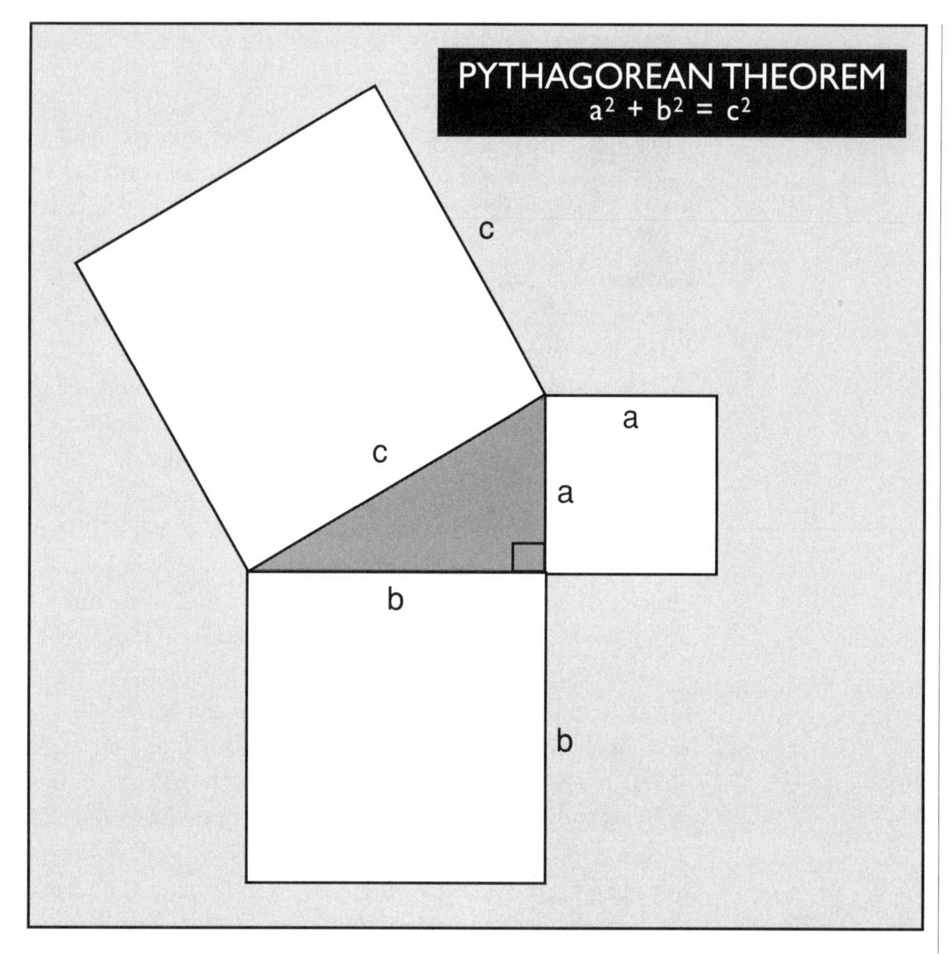

Today, mathematicians throughout the world use Pythagoras' method of calculating the area of the square formed by the hypotenuse, or long edge, of a right-angled triangle. The area of square **a** plus the area of square **b** equals the area of square **c**, or $a^2+b^2=c^2$.

knowledge as possible. Both abroad and at home in Samos, people came to hear his views on life. Exactly what philosophy he taught at this time, however, is uncertain. Then, sometime around 532 B.C., he chose to leave Samos and go into voluntary exile, because he was unable to tolerate life under Polycrates, the tyrant who ruled the island. Some historians suggest that Polycrates was so concerned with money and pleasure that his life-style was unacceptable to Pythagoras. Others believe that his departure was the result of political differences with Polycrates.

From Samos, Pythagoras sailed west to southern Italy, where so many Greeks had established colonies that the Romans later called the area *Magna Graecia*, or "Great Greece." Pythagoras settled in the colony of Crotona at the foot of Italy and was welcomed by its citizens upon his arrival. Many of his Samian pupils and followers also chose to accompany him there. Some historians believe that Pythagoras met his future wife in Crotona and raised a family in this area. Others say that he arrived at Crotona with a wife and family.

At Crotona, Pythagoras' school flourished and the number of pupils steadily increased, along with the number of people who believed in his views on living a simple life and using mathematics as a key to understanding the universe. Most of his 300 or so followers belonged to the aristocratic class and, for them, the philosophy taught at the school became a way of thinking as well as a way of living. Indeed, for many, it was a religion.

Both men and women were welcomed to join the religious society headed by Pythagoras. All members had to undergo an initiation ceremony. Each new member had to vow to keep and observe Pythagoras' ideas and principles and to respect and be loyal to the other members of the group. There was one rule, however, that superseded all others. Every member had to promise never to reveal any of Pythagoras' teachings or anything that was discussed at the meetings. This oath of secrecy was rigidly observed. In fact, a Pythagorean proverb was "Not every thing is for every body." As a result, little is known about the meetings, workings of the society, or the rituals the group performed.

What is certain is that members had rankings and were required to pass a variety of tests to gain full membership. One of the most important tests required a candidate to prove his or her ability to keep a secret. Other tests evaluated a prospective candidate's temper, personality, and mental ability. Only full members are believed to have shared in all the secrets and rituals of the society.

Naturally, Pythagoras' thinking affected the way he and his followers lived. Physical exercise and a careful

"Every person's soul is divided into three parts: intelligence, reason, and passion. Animals possess intelligence and passion, but only humans possess reason."

—Pythagoras, quoted in *Lives of Eminent Philosophers* (3rd century A.D.) by Diogenes Laertius

diet were thought important to keep the body and mind active and healthy. Pythagoras forbade the eating of meat and fish. Some say this was because of his belief in the transmigration of souls. That is, Pythagoras believed that a person's soul or spirit did not die with the body but became the soul or spirit of a newly born creature. Consequently, a person who ate meat or fish might actually be eating an ancestor. According to Xenophanes, a Greek philosopher and contemporary of Pythagoras, Pythagoras once saw a person beating a dog and advised him to stop, saying, "Stop! Stop now! The spirit of that dog was once my friend. I recognized his voice when the dog yelped."

Ancient tales that refer to the followers of Pythagoras always speak of them as honest, conscientious, disciplined, devoted, and loyal friends.

Pythagoras believed in common meals, a custom that was also practiced by all male citizens in the Greek city of Sparta. Pythagoras limited each group to 10 people, because 10 was a special number to Pythagoras. Ten is the number of fingers on a person's two hands. Ten is also the sum of the first unit (1), the first even number (2), the first odd number (3), and the first even square number (4): 1+2+3+4=10. Ten is also the sum of the first unit (1) and the first odd square number (9): 1+9=10.

To write the above equations and to show how special the number 10 was, Pythagoras used a series of dots. The number one was a simple dot (•), the most basic of all symbols. Two was a line composed of two dots (••). Three was three dots arranged to form a triangle (∴). Four was four dots arranged to form a square (∷). In this way, the four numbers, which added together equaled 10, also provided the four basic geometric shapes. But that was not all. Pythagoras took the dots used to represent one, two, three, and four and placed each in a line, one above the other. The result was a triangle that had four dots on each side and that from any one of the three angles looked and was the same.

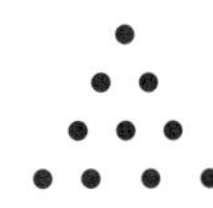

Furthermore, the word *ten* written in Greek letters is ΔΕΚΑ (transliterated *deka*), and the first letter of the Greek word for 10 is the letter *delta* (*d*), written in Greek as a triangle, Δ.

Pythagoras loved numbers and saw them as a logical means of explaining life around him. Numbers were reality. They expressed truth. Two plus two equals four. Three times three equals nine. There are no other answers, not even possible answers. Carrying his theory about numbers further, Pythagoras believed that everything could be explained numerically, and he undertook the task of reducing the world and the universe to numbers. He assigned numbers to concepts, such as justice, opportunity, masculinity, and

ANCIENT GREEKS

Pythagoras

BORN

Around 580 B.C.
Samos

DIED

Around 500 B.C.
Possibly Metapontum, Italy

PROFESSIONS

Mathematician, philosopher, and teacher

ACCOMPLISHMENTS

Established a school of thought that attracted many followers; reduced everything in the universe to a numerical value because he believed that numbers could express concepts and relationships; developed a theory called "The Music of the Spheres" based on harmony in the universe. The Pythagorean theorem is named after him, although his role in proving it is uncertain.

"When humans require laws, they are no longer worthy of freedom."

—attributed to Pythagoras

femininity. The sum of these numbers, he believed, would be a working, complete whole.

Pythagoras is credited as the first person to call the universe *kosmos*, a Greek word that originally meant "harmony." English adopted the Latinized form of *kosmos*—that is, *cosmos*—to mean the universe as an orderly and harmonious system. English also used *cosmos* to form other words, such as *cosmetics*, *cosmopolitan*, and *cosmic rays*. The Russian language used *cosmos* to form the term *cosmonaut*, one who travels in space.

Pythagoras believed in an ordered *kosmos*, and he set about investigating and proving his theories. Because musical notes and sounds seemed so ordered and absolute, he used musical sounds in his experiments. Pythagoras was well acquainted with two commonly used musical instruments—reed pipes of varying lengths and lyres with strings set at different tensions. The ancients knew that the size of the reed and the tightness of the string were responsible for the variety of sounds each instrument produced.

After many experiments with the lyre, Pythagoras discovered several indisputable facts. The pitch of every musical sound depended on the number of vibrations in a set time period—the more vibrations, the higher the sound. Pythagoras also discovered that to produce the sounds of a full octave (do-re-mi-fa-sol-la-ti-do), the A string needed to be only half as long as the G string. But, because the strings on the lyre were traditionally of equal length, a musician could produce twice as many tones on the A string as on the G string. Written mathematically, there was a ratio of 2:1.

Pythagoras continued listening. He found a similar relationship between the three middle strings of the lyre. Then he noticed that the relationships between all five strings could be expressed in ratios using only the numbers 1, 2, 3, and 4. Once again, the sum of these numbers was 10. Therefore, it was only natural that Pythagoras began to see and express musical notes as numbers. The harmony between notes he expressed as numerical ratios. Using the same reasoning, Pythagoras then described the universe and the planets numerically.

For Pythagoras, the earth was one great body that revolved around a great fire. The reason no one saw the fire was because the earth was flat and humans lived on the side that did not face the fire. The sun, moon, five planets (Mercury, Venus, Mars, Jupiter, and Saturn; the other planets were not known at that time), the earth, and a canopy of stars also revolved around the great fire. According to Pythagoras, these nine spheres (the sun, moon, planets, and great fire) resembled the nine notes in the musical octave. Just as there was a harmonious relationship between the musical notes, there was a harmonious relationship between the spheres of the universe.

And like the notes of a musical octave, the nine spheres made sounds. These sounds depended on the speed of each sphere. The speed and time of each revolution depended on how close a particular sphere was to the great fire; the closer it was, the faster the revolution. Pythagoras claimed that he heard these sounds. So did a few of his followers. Yet the vast majority of people do not. Why? According to Pythagoras, that is because we are so accustomed to them that we take them for granted. Because we know only what we have heard, we do not know what the world would sound like without them. Pythagoras' theory of the universe came to be known as "The Music of the Spheres."

The ancient writers who refer to Pythagoras and his teachings say that his chief aim was to help people live a life that would reflect the order and harmony of the universe.

Pythagoras' fascination with numbers led him to develop other theories. One is the so-called Pythagorean theorem: In a right triangle (a triangle with a right, or 90-degree, angle), the square of the hypotenuse (the side opposite the right angle) equals the sum of the squares of the other two sides. This fact was known to mathematicians in Egypt and the Middle East before the 6th century B.C. However, it is possible that Pythagoras was the first to use mathematical calculations and reasoning to prove the theory.

Pythagoras encountered one problem that he could not solve. He firmly believed that everything could be reduced to a number, but this belief led him to the discovery that numbers are infinite—that is, there is no last number. His proof of this fact meant for Pythagoreans that all was not perfect harmony, that there was not always a beginning and an end that could be measured. But this mathematical discovery was one of the great secrets of the Pythagoreans. According to tradition, a member who died at sea had received a just punishment for having broken the Pythagorean code of secrecy; he had, without permission, divulged the fact that numbers were not finite.

As Pythagoras' fame grew, so did his society, and soon admirers in other cities across southern Italy formed groups dedicated to following his teachings. Because Pythagoras' philosophy was not one that meant followers had to devote themselves entirely to learning or mastering specific rituals, some of his followers became involved in politics. Gradually, their policies began to reflect Pythagoras' views of life. In time, this led to conflict between Pythagoreans and non-Pythagoreans, as citizens who believed in democratic principles became dissatisfied with followers of Pythagoras, who were attempting to increase their control over government policies.

Finally the matter erupted in violence. The people of Crotona banded together, marched to a place where many Pythagoreans had gathered, and set fire to the building. Many of them perished, but Pythagoras reportedly survived, fleeing first to the southern Italian town of Tarentum and then to the neighboring city of Metapontum, where he lived until his death, probably around 500 B.C.

Soon, violence against Pythagoras and his followers exploded in other areas of southern Italy. As a result, the number of members decreased, and so did their influence. Yet the movement was not totally destroyed, as active members continued practicing the ordered and disciplined life that Pythagoras advocated and researching their scientific and mathematical theories.

A few decades after Pythagoras' death, another wave of attacks beset the Pythagoreans. Refugees fleeing this persecution took their beliefs to other areas of the Greek world, where they won more followers. In this way, Pythagoras' ideas about life and the universe continued to influence later Greeks, including Plato and Aristotle, two of ancient Greece's most respected philosophers. The scientists and astronomers of the Middle Ages also incorporated the theories of Pythagoras into their work. But it remained his influence on Plato and Aristotle that proved so important to the Western world, because so much of Western philosophy traces its roots to Plato and Aristotle.

FURTHER READING

Diogenes Laertius. *Life of Pythagoras*. Translated by R. D. Hicks. Loeb Classical Library. Cambridge: Harvard University Press, 1925.

Gorman, Peter. *Pythagoras: A Life*. Boston: Routledge & Kegan Paul, 1979.

O'Meara, Dominic J. *Pythagoras Revived: Mathematics and Philosophy in Late Antiquity*. New York: Oxford University Press, 1991.

Terry, Leon. *The Mathmen*. New York: McGraw-Hill, 1964.

Anacreon

A LOVER OF LIFE AND SONG

Although home for the lyric poet Anacreon was the Ionian city of Teos in Asia Minor, he actually spent little time there. As a boy, Anacreon surely heard how the rulers of the powerful Persian Empire to the east were making plans to conquer Asia Minor and the many Greek colonies flourishing there. By the time the Persians did advance into Asia Minor, around 545 B.C., Anacreon was a young man, most likely in his 20s. What his role in Teos was is unclear, but most likely he was writing poetry and winning recognition as a lyric poet.

As the Persian army neared Teos, the inhabitants of the city met to debate their options. Realizing that resistance to such a powerful army would result in slavery or death, the people of Teos, Anacreon included, abandoned their town and set sail as a group for Thrace. There, on the northern coast of the Aegean Sea, they founded the colony of Abdera. In a surviving fragment of one of his poems, Anacreon mentions a dead warrior and fighting against the Thracians.

A decade or so later, the opportunity to serve the court of Polycrates, ruler of the prosperous Greek island of Samos in the Aegean Sea, prompted Anacreon to move again. Polycrates had asked Anacreon to tutor his son in music. Later Greek authors tell of verses Anacreon wrote in honor of Polycrates and about his life on the island. Unfortunately, none of these works has survived.

Sometime around 522 B.C., a Persian satrap (a provincial governor) on the mainland of Asia Minor invited Polycrates to visit him. Several historical accounts mention that Anacreon was at court when the invitation arrived. Unaware of the Persian's secret motives, Polycrates accepted and was promptly executed once he crossed into Persian territory.

Anacreon now had to seek another patron. He found one in Hipparchus, an Athenian who was well known for his strong support of literature and the arts. A few years later, in 514 B.C., Anacreon lost his second patron when Hipparchus was assassinated.

Anacreon left Athens and traveled north to the Greek district of Thessaly, where he composed several works, including a few addressed to members of Thessaly's ruling royal family. Most likely, Anacreon later returned to Athens.

Anacreon also wrote several books of poetry, perhaps as many as five. Many lines and fragments have survived, but only a few complete poems exist. Most are simple, short, and to the point, with a wittiness that reveals Anacreon's quick humor. A man who apparently enjoyed life, Anacreon wrote

Anacreon wrote poems about love, wine, and the pleasures of merry company. Guests at symposia—traditional after-dinner drinking parties—often sang and imitated his verses.

Anacreon

BORN

Around 570 B.C.
Teos, Asia Minor

DIED

Around 485 B.C.
Place unknown

PROFESSION

Lyric poet

ACCOMPLISHMENTS

Wrote several books of poetry

poems that tell mostly of wine, love, and song. One fragment clearly reveals his opinion about himself and his writings: "I sing beautiful songs and I know how to speak beautiful words."

Most of Anacreon's works were written to be accompanied by a lyre and sung at *symposia*. *Symposia* were ancient Greek drinking parties at which guests told riddles and stories and sang drinking songs and selections from Greek drama. A *symposium* (the singular of *symposia*) after the evening meal was a tradition among Greek aristocrats and an important part of their social life.

According to an ancient Greek legend, Anacreon died around 485 B.C., at the age of 85, when he choked on a grape seed that stuck in his throat.

Anacreon's renown as a poet did not die with him. The Athenians continued to honor his memory and even placed a statue of him on the Acropolis, the steep hill in the center of Athens that housed the city's most sacred temples. In later centuries, several poets composed works that were modeled, although not very accurately, on Anacreon's works and themes. This collection became known as the *Anacreontea*.

As the years passed, the close association between this collection and Anacreon led many to believe that Anacreon was its author. During the 18th and 19th centuries, the song "To Anacreon in Heaven" was popular throughout England. It was probably written sometime around 1775 by Dr. Samuel Arnold, a composer at the Royal Chapel in London. Because of the many ties between England and its colonies across the Atlantic Ocean, the song soon became popular with the people in the newly formed United States.

An Italian artist designed this frontispiece for a new edition of Anacreon's works in 1781. The image of the poet as a lover of wine and song inspired the artist to depict climbing grape vines and musical instruments around his portrait.

Only a few decades after the Revolutionary War, England and the United States battled each other again in the War of 1812. An American lawyer, Francis Scott Key, wrote a poem commemorating the American resistance to the British entitled "The Defence of Fort McHenry." Key suggested that the poem be sung to the tune of the then-popular song "To Anacreon in Heaven." The song quickly spread across the nation and soon became known as "The Star-Spangled Banner." In 1931 Congress officially adopted it as the national anthem of the United States of America.

FURTHER READING

Podlecki, Anthony J. *The Early Greek Poets and Their Times*. Vancouver: University of British Columbia Press, 1984.

More Ancient Greeks to Remember

Hesiod (flourished around 700 B.C.) was the poet of peace, according to the ancients. Tradition said that while he was tending sheep on Mount Helicon's slopes near his family's farm in Ascra, in Boeotia, Hesiod believed he heard the Muses calling him to sing the praises of the Greek gods and goddesses. In Greek mythology, the Muses are the daughters of Zeus, the king of the gods, and it is their duty to protect and promote the arts and sciences. Hesiod often mentioned the nine Muses in his poems. In one passage, he credited the inspiration of the Muses for his winning the prize of the tripod in a poetry contest. (A tripod, a three-legged stand made of bronze or of marble, was a common prize.)

When his father died, Hesiod and his brother Perses inherited the family farm. Perses claimed a larger part of the estate than was his due, took his case to court, and won by using persuasion and bribery. Hesiod never forgot the unfairness of this decision and recalled the incident years later in one of his major works, entitled *Works and Days*.

After calling upon the Muses in the opening verses, Hesiod addressed his brother and sought a reconciliation. In other sections of the book, Hesiod stressed the need for justice, honesty, and hard work at a time when he believed tyranny, dishonesty, and idleness were the rule. Hesiod, however, was also quite cynical and believed that the will of the gods affected human actions. There are no expressions of contentment or spontaneous joyous feelings in his works.

Works and Days continues to be a valuable resource for information about everyday life in ancient Greece, early Greek customs, and the social conditions of the time. Included are passages advising farmers how to care for their fields, describing the difficulties winter weather creates, and listing the favorable and unfavorable days for planting and other activities.

The *Theogony* (Birth of the Gods) is Hesiod's other major work. While scholars believe it was composed before the *Works and Days*, both were in the oral tradition—that is, spoken, not written. This was the custom, by necessity, because few people at the time knew how to read or write. Gradually, such poems were written down—not always in the original form because, over the years, changes had been made. Approximately 1,000 lines long, the *Theogony* opens with a description of how the world began. It then proceeds, in a very organized and chronological manner, to describe the lives, loves, and duties of the Greek gods and goddesses. According to Hesiod's count, there were 300 deities.

Ancient artists often used the tripod (a three-legged stool) to represent the god Apollo. At Delphi, one of Apollo's centers of worship, the priestess sat on a tripod as she listened for Apollo to speak through her.

Today, *Theogony* and *Works and Days* give us a glimpse of ancient events and ideas that did not concern wars and fighting but focused on the everyday world in which Hesiod lived.

The Seven Sages (late 7th–6th centuries B.C.) was the honorary title given by the ancients to those individuals whom they considered to be the wisest in Greece. Although the names of the seven varied on occasion, those most frequently mentioned by ancient writers were the philosophers Thales, Bias, and Pittacus and the statesmen Cleobulus, Solon, Chilon, and Periander.

According to the original tale of the Seven Sages, a group of Greek fishermen cast their nets into the Aegean Sea and brought up a golden tripod. Supposedly, this was the same tripod that had been thrown into the sea by Helen (the same Helen whom Prince Paris of Troy had stolen from the Greek city-state of Sparta and whose abduction was the cause of the great Trojan War) on her return home after the Greeks defeated the Trojans. At first, the fishermen quarreled among themselves about who should have the tripod. Then the people in the towns nearby began to quarrel. Finally, they decided to consult the priestess at Apollo's most honored oracle, at Delphi, in central Greece.

The tale continued, with Apollo, through his priestess, advising that the tripod be given "to the wisest." The fishermen agreed that Thales of Miletus, a Greek city-state on the coast of Asia Minor, was the wisest. One of the acknowledged founders of the study of philosophy and mathematics, Thales developed the first principles of geometry. He believed that the earth was a flat piece of land floating on water, and he taught that water is the origin of everything. Thales, did not, however, consider himself the wisest human and advised the fishermen to go to Bias. Bias also felt he was unworthy and said to give it to one of the other sages. And so the tripod made the rounds until it came back again to Thales at Miletus.

The fishermen then agreed to dedicate the tripod to Apollo at his temple in Delphi. Inscribed on this temple were seven proverbs, each giving advice on how to live life. The Seven Sages were considered the authors of these sayings. They are: "Know thyself," "Do nothing in excess," "The greatest blessing is the power to do good," "Pardon is better than punishment," "People find it most difficult to keep a secret, to forgive injuries, and to improve the quality of life," "Too many workers spoil the work," and "Forethought in all things."

Anaximander (around 610–540 B.C.) was one of Greece's earliest philosophers. Like Thales, his mentor, Anaximander was a native of Miletus and he, too, sought to understand and explain the universe. Anaximander believed that everything came from what he termed the "Infinite," something that was divine and could not be described with specific measurements or characteristics. Anaximander placed the earth at the center of the universe. Surrounding the earth like the bark of a tree was first a layer of water, then one of air or mist, and lastly one of fire. When there was a break or hole in the mist, the people on earth could see the stars, the sun, and the other heavenly bodies, all of which were part of the fire mass. When the holes closed, an eclipse occurred. Anaximander's close observation of nature, the water element in the universe, and the way in which humans grow led him to develop a theory of evolution which stated that humans most likely evolved from fish. Anaximander was also the first person to develop a theory of the origin and structure of the universe. For centuries, geographers used his map of the known world.

Draco (lived around 620 B.C.) is recognized as one of Athens' great lawgivers. He was elected to the powerful position of archon and is said to have been the first archon to decree that Athens' laws be written down. This allowed everyone to know exactly what each law stated and what the punishments were for particular offenses.

Draco's laws were supposedly very strict and his punishments quite severe. Under his code, murder and stealing an apple both warranted the death penalty. Draco's explanation was that stealing was the most dishonorable crime and thieves deserved death. As for more serious offenses, Draco explained that there was no greater punishment than death. Later Greek writers would say that Draco had written his laws in blood, not ink. Another reform credited to Draco was the granting of citizenship to any Athenian man who could provide his own military equipment. This opened up the archonship and other lesser government positions to Athenians who were not aristocrats.

Alcaeus (born around 620 B.C.) was a friend of the poet Sappho. He too lived on the island of Lesbos and wrote lyric poetry. Like Sappho's, his poems were direct, simple, and often emotional. His themes, however, were quite different, for Alcaeus often wrote about politics.

Perhaps because he was active in the power struggles in his home town of Mytilene, many of his poems involve conflict. His comparison of a ship to a city-state (the "ship-of-state" metaphor) has been used throughout the centuries by writers and politicians. In this metaphor, Alcaeus compared the growing power of one of Mytilene's rulers to a violent storm that threatens to sink a ship. For Alcaeus, the ship was Mytilene.

Alcaeus was also well known for the songs that he wrote for his countrymen to sing at *symposia* (traditional drinking parties). Decades later, the Greek poet Anacreon would use the same easygoing, direct style.

Corinna (6th–5th centuries B.C.) was a lyric poet from the town of Tanagra, in the district of Boeotia. Mythology was her favorite subject, but her themes were usually related in some way to the life and history of Boeotia.

Corinna used the local dialect. As a result, her poems appealed more to the people of Boeotia than to a wider audience. Her style was said to be simple and unaffected. Only a few fragments have survived.

Telesilla (6th–5th centuries B.C.) was a lyric poet from the town of Argos in southern Greece. Surviving accounts infer that her poems were mostly hymns. Although only a few words have survived, it seems that she wrote mainly for women.

According to legend, Telesilla became personally involved in a war between Argos and Sparta. With her lyre and verses, she encouraged the people of Argos to fight the Spartans and even led a band of her countrywomen into the battle. In honor of her heroism, the people of Argos erected a statue to her in the temple of Aphrodite, the goddess of love and beauty.

Pisistratus (around 560–527 B.C.) had watched his cousin Solon make changes in Athens' government and aimed to do the same, but first he needed to obtain control of the city. To do so, he inflicted his body with wounds and pretended assassins had attacked him. Believing him and fearing for his life, the Athenians allowed him to keep an armed bodyguard. Pisistratus then used the guard as soldiers, took control of Athens' Acropolis, and set himself up as tyrant. His rule, however, was short-lived, and he was driven into exile.

Undeterred, Pisistratus planned another strategy. Accompanied by a beautiful girl whom he announced was

Alcaeus (left), a lyric poet like his friend Sappho (right), once addressed her in a poem as "Violet-haired, holy, sweetly-smiling Sappho."

Athena, the goddess of wisdom, he entered Athens in a chariot proclaiming that the goddess herself had brought him. Again he won control of the government but, like his first attempt, his rule was brief.

Pisistratus returned to Athens yet again, this time with an army, and took the city by force. Once in power, Pisistratus retained many of the reforms begun by Solon. He always made sure that his supporters held positions of power, while extending the rights and government benefits for the poor. His laws led the way to future democratic reforms in Athens.

In addition, Pisistratus supported a public building program and opened a library for the people. A patron of the arts, Pisistratus was reportedly responsible for putting together the first written collection of Homer's works.

Cleisthenes (around 565–500 B.C.) is customarily regarded as the creator of Athenian democracy. He followed and built upon the reforms of Solon and Pisistratus. Cleisthenes reorganized the tribal system by replacing the traditional 4 tribes, whose members traced their roots to the old Ionian families, with 10 tribes, whose members included all male Athenian citizens 18 years old or older. With this new political division, all citizens of the *demes* (small districts or townships) could become members of the *Ecclesia* (Assembly). In addition, he expanded the Senate from 400 members to 500. Senators were to be chosen by lot, 50 from each of the 10 tribes. The result of these changes was that birth and wealth no longer determined rights and privileges.

Several ancient accounts also credit Cleisthenes with another important reform. If, at a special meeting of the Assembly, 6,000 votes were cast against any person, that person had to leave Athens for a period of 10 years. Voters wrote the name of the person they wanted banished on pieces of clay called *ostraca*. This practice was to prevent a tyrant from ever again ruling Athens. Centuries later, the English language adapted the term *ostraca* to make the verb *to ostracize*, meaning "to banish or exclude an individual."

Croesus (560–546 B.C.), king of Lydia in Asia Minor, conquered many Greek cities along the Asia Minor coast and became fabulously wealthy. Accounts show that he remained on very friendly terms with the Greeks, honored their gods, and welcomed their philosophers to his court. According to tradition, Solon of Athens once visited Croesus.

Croesus did, however, have one major problem—the growing Persian menace to the east. Unable to decide whether to attack Persia or not, Croesus sent a messenger to consult Apollo's oracle at Delphi. Tradition reports that the oracle replied, "If Croesus attacks Persia, he will destroy a mighty empire."

Overjoyed at the prophecy, Croesus marched out his army, only to meet defeat and imprisonment. As he sat on the pyre, about to be set on fire by the Persians, Croesus sighed, "Oh, Solon!" The Persian king heard his cry and asked why he had called upon Solon. Legend says that Croesus told him how he had once asked Solon whom he considered to be the happiest person alive. The Greek had replied that the only person who is truly happy is a person who is happy at the moment he dies. The Persian king so liked this response that he ordered Croesus freed and requested that Croesus join his council of advisers.

Croesus acquiesced, but first he needed to solve the "mystery" of Apollo's prophecy. He sent a second messenger to Delphi. This time the oracle stated simply: "The oracle told the truth. Croesus did attack Persia and did destroy a mighty empire—his own!"

Polycrates (died around 523 B.C.) ruled the Greek island of Samos in the Aegean Sea. Under him, Samos became a great naval power, controlling the waters of the eastern Aegean and many of the surrounding islands. Polycrates undertook a massive public works program, including the building of a harbor at Samos. Other projects often credited to him are a temple to Hera (queen of the gods and goddesses) and a tunnel that brought water to the capital. Polycrates became well known as a patron of the arts and literature, inviting artists and poets to his court. Anacreon was one of his favorites.

Aware that his good fortune might cause jealousy, Polycrates asked an Egyptian ruler for advice. The Egyptian told him to throw away his most valuable possession, because doing so would cause Polycrates great grief and thereby make others feel sorry for him rather than envy him. Legend says that Polycrates immediately threw his beautiful seal ring into the sea. Days later, a fisherman appeared at the palace. In his hand was the ring, which he had found in the belly of a fish that he had caught. Unfortunately for Polycrates, his wealth did cause the envy of the Persian ruler across the waters on the coast of Asia Minor. Under false pretenses, the Persian invited Polycrates to his court and then killed him.

Milon (active 532–512 B.C.) was the star wrestler of the ancient Greek world. A native of Crotona, a Greek colony on the bay in southern Italy, Milon competed in several Olympic Games. The original games were held every four years at Olympia in western Greece, in honor of Zeus, the king of the gods. Milon won the Olympic wrestling competition six times. He also entered the Pythian Games, which were considered second in importance to the Olympic Games. At the Pythian Games, held in the third year of each Olympiad to honor the god Apollo at Delphi, Milon won seven wrestling victories. His strength was so great that the ancients reported he once carried a four-year-old cow on his shoulders around the stadium at Olympia and then devoured the entire animal in one day.

Death struck him in his old age. Supposedly, he was walking in the woods when he saw a tree trunk that woodcutters had tried unsuccessfully to split. With his bare hands, he set about completing the task. Something happened and the two halves snapped together, trapping his hands. Unfortunately, a pack of hungry wolves attacked and devoured the "imprisoned" athlete.

The champion wrestler Milon knew well the dangerous sport known as *pancration,* a combination of boxing and wrestling. The athletes wore nothing on their hands and could kick, strangle, or twist their opponents. Umpires enforced the rules of no biting and no gouging.

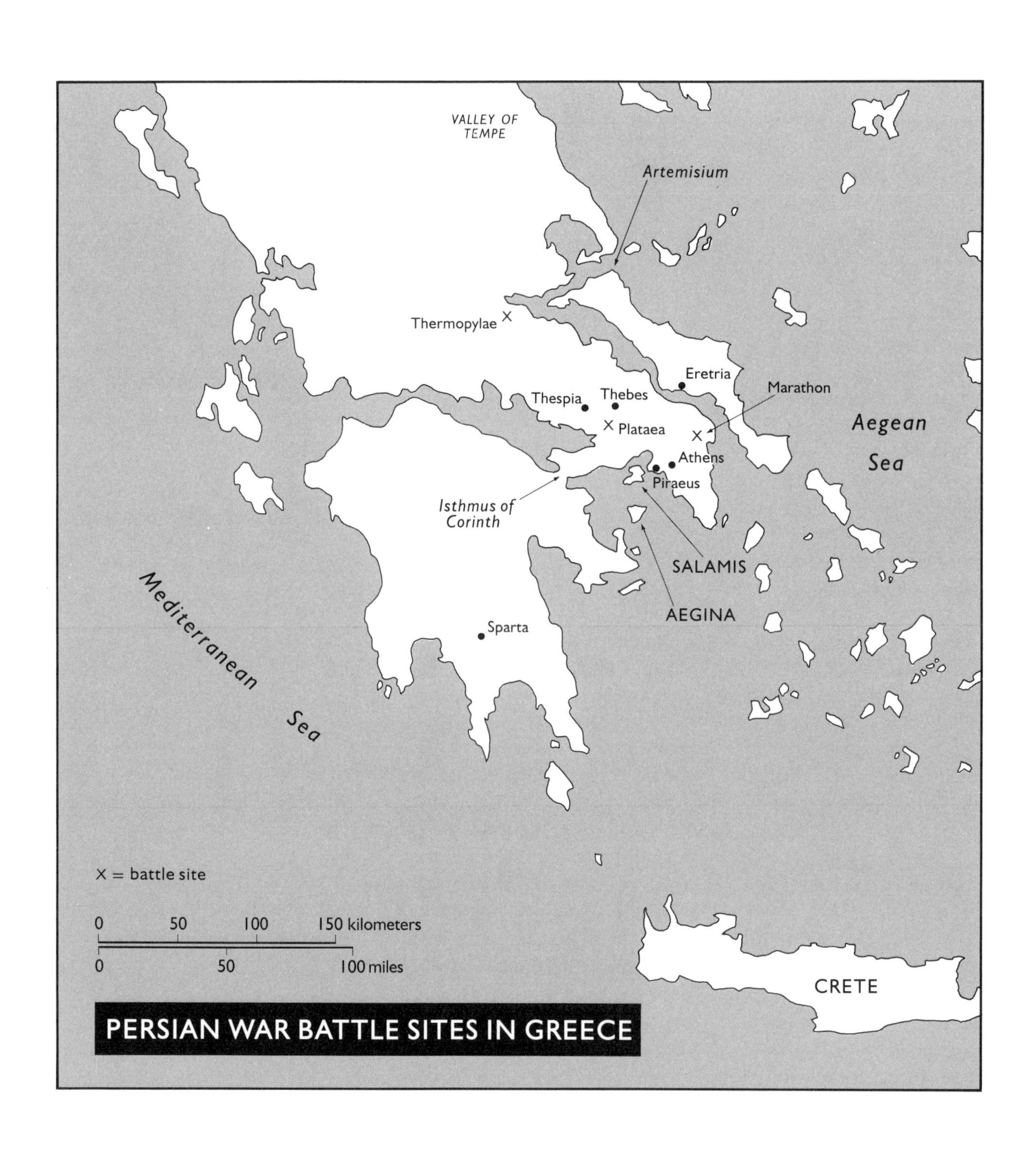

PERSIAN WAR BATTLE SITES IN GREECE

2 The Ascent of Athens (500–410 B.C.)

IN THIS PART

AESCHYLUS

PINDAR

PHIDIPPIDES

LEONIDAS

SOPHOCLES

HERODOTUS

EURIPIDES

THEMISTOCLES

By 500 B.C., the era of invading tribes and great migratory movements across the Aegean had become history. Personal independence was still, however, an important part of Greek life, along with an appreciation of culture, the power of the mind, and simple beauty and harmony. Yet life was changing, especially in Athens, where new laws created a more democratic way of life and established a system of government controlled by its citizens. The Greek city-states on the mainland, the Greek colonies across the Aegean, and the many recently founded colonies on shores bordering the Mediterranean Sea all thrived, economically and culturally. The bonds between them remained strong, and whenever trouble arose the colonies always looked to the mainland Greeks for help.

By the end of the 6th century B.C., trouble seemed to be approaching the colonies along Asia Minor's coast as Persia, a growing military power to the east, sought to extend its empire as far as the Aegean Sea. The Persian king Darius I had already ruled that the Greek colonies should pay a tribute (tax) to Persia. But when the decree came that Greeks were required to serve in the Persian army, the colonists revolted. The year was 500 B.C., and historians have since referred to the uprising as the Ionian Revolt because it began in the area that had originally been colonized by Ionians.

Athens helped the Ionians revolt. The Ionians had first appealed to Sparta because it was the chief military power in Greece, but the Spartans denied them aid. Their next stop was Athens, the city-state that had always considered itself the "mother" of all Ionian colonies. Athenian aid was crucial to the initial success of the revolt, but losses soon disheartened the Athenians and they returned home. Without their assistance, the colonists did not have the military power or the strength to withstand the Persian assaults. By 493 B.C., the Persians controlled all of Asia Minor and were planning a massive invasion of mainland Greece. Athens became their special target because the Athenians had dared to help the Ionians revolt.

This critical state of affairs forced the mainland Greeks to rethink their policy of independence. The result was unprecedented cooperation and unity among the Greeks that led to the overwhelming defeat of the Persian forces in 490 B.C. and again in 480 B.C. Because Athenian commanders and soldiers were responsible for many important victories and strategies, the city of Athens was acknowledged as the most powerful of the Greek city-states.

The Athenians welcomed this honor, but they did not view their role as solely military. The Athenians loved to question life and the role of the individual. Philosophers and writers thrived in such an atmosphere, and soon Athens became an international cultural and intellectual center. The Great Dionysia festival with its dramatic competition featured tragedies by Athens' master playwrights—Aeschylus, Euripides, and Sophocles.

Part 2 of *Ancient Greeks* profiles the individuals who shaped Athens' reputation as the home of the world's great thinkers and writers and those who shaped Greece's rise to power by masterminding the defeat of the Persians.

Aeschylus

"THE WORDS OF TRUTH ARE SIMPLE"

"My tragedies are slices taken from Homer's mighty dinners." So read Aeschylus' humble description of his own plays that was quoted in a commentary written centuries after his death by a Greek named Athenaeus.

Aeschylus may have considered his plays unequal to Homer's epics, but the Greeks felt a special kinship with the tragedian. It is true that his plots included many of the tales and episodes found in Homer, but his treatment was completely different, with actors instead of a bard saying the lines.

Aeschylus wanted his audience to become emotionally involved as they listened and watched. For Aeschylus, the audience, like the actors, should experience the emotions of anger, fear, courage, and tension. These feelings came naturally to Aeschylus because he had experienced them first-hand on the Plain of Marathon.

Certainly no Greek, and particularly no Athenian, would ever forget the Battle of Marathon. In 490 B.C., the

Orestes (left) prepares to avenge his father's death by killing the murderer, his mother Clytemnestra. Unlike Greek playwrights, who did not include such gory scenes in their plays, Greek painters and other artists did.

With a scroll in one hand and the mask of tragedy in the other, Aeschylus lived by a line he once wrote: "He is determined not to seem, but to be, the best."

soldiers of Athens had almost single-handedly defeated the massive Persian force on the plain beyond the town. Aeschylus was a "Marathon warrior," the honorary title given every Athenian and Plataean who had taken part in the battle. (The city of Plataea had sent 1,000 soldiers to join the 9,000 Athenians on the battlefield.)

Aeschylus was in his 30s at the time of the battle; he had been born sometime around 525 B.C. His father, Euphorion, traced his lineage to one of Athens' oldest and most aristocratic families. Their home was in Eleusis, a town just northwest of Athens. This town was well known throughout the Greek world as the center of the Eleusinia, the great festival celebrated every fourth year in honor of Demeter, the goddess of the harvest, and Persephone, the queen of the underworld.

Eleusis was also the center of the Eleusinian Mysteries, one of Greece's most important mystery religions. Because followers of this religion were under oath not to reveal any of their rites or beliefs, not much is known about their customs or practices. A few surviving accounts record that Aeschylus was tried in court for revealing the Mysteries. In his defense, he said he did not realize that what he said was not supposed to be revealed. Other accounts say he was pardoned because he proved he had not been formally initiated into the religion.

Guilty or not, Aeschylus remained a loyal Athenian and marched north to Marathon, determined to keep his city free from foreign control. Ancient records noted that he fought with distinction and that his brother was killed in the battle.

The battle at Marathon did not stop the Persian advance, however. Ten years later, in 480 B.C., Aeschylus once again rallied to his city's defense and fought the Persians at Artemisium and at Salamis. In 479 B.C., he met them near the walls outside the city of Plataea, where the Greeks won the last great land battle of the Persian Wars. With the Persian threat gone, the Greeks could relax, but they would never forget how close they had come to losing their freedom. Writers often incorporated the history of the wars into their works to make certain future generations would not forget.

For Aeschylus, drama was the most effective way of expressing his feelings. Although one of the earliest of the Greek playwrights, he was not the first. That honor goes to Thespis, a lyric poet from Attica, the district of which Athens was the chief city. Around 535 B.C. Thespis introduced the first actor, an individual who played several parts. Thespis' setting was the market square in Athens, an ideal place because many people congregated there, and his background was a simple cart.

Accompanying the actor was the chorus, a group of individuals who traditionally sang their lines while performing some type of dance step. The actor and the chorus interacted when the actor carried on a dialogue with the leader of the chorus. Because there was only one actor, Thespis is believed to have introduced the custom of wearing masks so that the audience would easily recognize which character the actor was representing each time he spoke. (The English language borrowed Thespis' name to form the adjective *thespian*, which means "dramatic." The term *thespian* has been incorporated into the name of many drama clubs.)

Phrynichus followed Thespis, but his plays focused on the Persian Wars and were too realistic for the Athenians. In fact, after the audience broke down in tears while watching his interpretation of the Persian capture of the Greek colony of Miletus, the Athenian court forbade the play from being produced and fined Phrynichus for reminding his fellow citizens of past failures. Phrynichus then wrote *The*

Phoenicians, using the Greek victory at Salamis as his plot but writing from the perspective of how the Persian court received the news.

Aeschylus was well acquainted with these efforts at dramatic writing. In fact, *The Phoenicians* appears to have been the model for Aeschylus' play *The Persians*, produced in 472 B.C. in Athens. According to accounts of the time, Aeschylus began his writing career prior to the Battle of Marathon and often took the part of the actor. Unfortunately, only six, or according to some seven, of the 80 or so plays he wrote have survived, and these date to the last 16 years of his life.

During his career as a playwright, Aeschylus gradually became more aware of what was needed to produce a dramatic effect, and he began to make changes in the production itself. He gave the chorus fewer lines and added a second actor, which increased the amount of dialogue and the importance of the actors.

Like his contemporaries, Aeschylus directed his own plays. He loved to use spectacular costumes, especially on actors who were representing characters from Persia and other Eastern countries where the dress was much more colorful and ornate than in Greece. Stage effects became more important, and Aeschylus dressed his soldiers in real armor, introduced chariots onstage, and even used trumpets when needed. The simple backgrounds and backdrops that had accompanied his early plays gradually became more elaborate, and he even devised stage machinery to show indoor scenes.

In his tragedy *Agamemnon*, Clytemnestra, Agamemnon's wife, literally rolls out a red carpet when her husband returns home after 10 years at war. However, this red carpet, which he walks on to enter the house, is symbolic of the red blood that will soon flow when Clytemnestra stabs him in the bathtub. The audience never sees the killing; it only hears the shrieks and cries of the shocked chorus. This reaction heightens the drama and the suspense, especially as it allows viewers to picture for themselves the terrible scene within. Rarely did the violence in Aeschylus' plays take place onstage. Instead Aeschylus used vivid dialogue and interaction between actor and chorus to make the audience aware of everything happening offstage.

In time, the marketplace at Athens could not hold the number of people both on the stage and in the audience. Tradition says that while one of Aeschylus' plays was being performed in the marketplace, the scaffolding that had been raised to accommodate the viewers collapsed. Supposedly, as a result of this disaster, the stage was moved to an area just a short distance away. The new site was perfect for a theater because it lay at the foot of the Acropolis, an outcrop of rock that rose 170 feet above the city. Spectators could now sit on the hill and watch the play on the flat ground at the foot of the hill with the fields and landscape beyond Athens providing the backdrop.

What made the site even more appropriate was the fact that it was sacred to Dionysus, the god of merriment and wine. Traditionally, tragedies were a major part of the Great Dionysia, the spring festival at Athens in honor of Dionysus. Over the years, it became the custom for three playwrights to present four plays each, three of which were tragedies and one a satyr play. (A satyr play was lighter in tone. The Greeks pictured satyrs as wild woodland spirits with bodies that were half-man and half-goat. Satyrs were also followers of Dionysus.) The plays were short, all four lasting only several hours. For this reason, playwrights normally had the action of their play take place in one day. Drama judges were chosen by lot from Athens' 10 tribes, and the victorious playwright

ANCIENT GREEKS

Aeschylus

BORN

Around 525 B.C.
Athens, Greece

DIED

456 B.C.
Gela, Sicily

PROFESSION

Writer of tragedies

ACCOMPLISHMENTS

Wrote approximately 80 plays, 6 (7 according to some) of which have survived: *The Persians*, *Seven Against Thebes*, *Suppliants*, *Agamemnon*, *Libation Bearers* or *Choephoroi*, and *Eumenides* (the one in question is *Prometheus Bound)*; influenced the development of Greek drama by adding a second actor, placing more stress on dialogue between the actors and less emphasis on the chorus, and using language that reflected the strength and heroic nature of his characters

"God loves to help those who work to help themselves."

—from a fragment of a play

was awarded a wreath of ivy and an automatic entry into the following year's competition.

Records show that Aeschylus won his first victory at the Great Dionysia in 484 B.C. In the years that followed, Aeschylus won at least 12 more victories. In fact, the Athenians enjoyed his plays so much that they bestowed upon him a unique honor after his death—any playwright who wished to reproduce one of Aeschylus' plays could do so and enter the competition. As a result, Aeschylus was winning prizes at the Great Dionysia even after he died.

What endeared the Greek audience to Aeschylus was his style, and for this reason he became recognized as the father of tragedy. His fascination with the East definitely inspired many of the rich costumes his actors wore, while his seriousness of purpose was reflected in the solemn chorus dances. But, more important, Aeschylus brought a depth of character to each major role and gave each a willpower and determination to face situations that seemed unconquerable.

Aeschylus understood such courage, for he had personally experienced the terrible reality of suffering and death on the battlefield and survived. Now it was his stage characters who had to face great odds and win. Before the Persian Wars, the great heroes had all belonged to the age of Homer. Now in early 5th-century B.C. Greece, the heroes were those who had fought at Marathon, Salamis, and Plataea. Because of his personal experiences Aeschylus was able to use words and phrases that reflected heroic actions and thought. A few lines spoken by Clytemnestra in the play *Agamemnon* reveal that the writer knew well the tragedies of war:

"The women have thrown themselves on the lifeless bodies of husbands, brothers. . . . Small children are clinging to the dead that gave them life, crying from throats no longer free. As for the victors . . . a night of roaming after the battle has made them sit down for breakfast hungry to eat what the town might have."

Aeschylus' plays also reflect the Athenian concern with democracy, for he emphasized justice and fairness rather than violence as a means of settling differences. Other common themes are morality and religion. Even though Aeschylus portrayed his characters as having control of their destiny, the gods in his plays still influenced the lives of these characters.

Although Aeschylus spent most of his life in Athens, he did visit Sicily and even spent enough time on his first visit to write a play. In 456 B.C., during this second visit to Sicily, Aeschylus died. Tradition said that an eagle with a turtle clutched in its talons was flying above Aeschylus while he was walking. Thinking he had found a stone when he saw Aeschylus' bald head, the eagle dropped the turtle, hoping it would break open and give him some delicious turtle meat. Instead, the shell cracked Aeschylus' skull and killed him.

Aeschylus was ready for death and had even prepared the epitaph for his tombstone. From it we learn that one of the world's greatest playwrights wished to be remembered, not for his merit or fame as a dramatist, but rather for his courage on the field at Marathon. Aeschylus' epitaph read:

"Here lies the Athenian Aeschylus, Euphorion's son. This tomb in Gela's cornlands covers him. The Plain of Marathon can tell of his proven courage, and of the long-haired Persian who discovered it there."

History, however, did not associate Aeschylus with the Battle of Marathon, but with his plays. While some generations have not favored him as much as others, he has never been forgotten. The development of European tragedy owes much to Aeschylus, and playwrights through the centuries have borrowed from and adapted his works. Today, in theaters throughout the Western world, Aeschylus' plays are periodically staged and drama students continue to study his style and his characters. Thus it is only appropriate that history has awarded him the title "father of tragedy."

FURTHER READING

Aeschylus. *Aeschylus*. Translated by H. Weir Smyth. Loeb Classical Library. Cambridge: Harvard University Press, 1922.

Beck, Robert Holmes. *Aeschylus: Playwright, Educator*. The Hague: Nijhoff, 1975.

Goldhill, Simon. *Aeschylus: "The Oresteia."* New York: Cambridge University Press, 1992.

Murray, Gilbert. *Aeschylus, the Creator of Tragedy*. Oxford, England: Clarendon Press, 1940.

Spatz, Lois. *Aeschylus*. Boston: Twayne, 1982

Pindar

"UNSUNG, THE NOBLEST DEED WILL DIE"

A native of Cynoscephalae, a village on the outskirts of the powerful city of Thebes, Pindar began his writing career early. He learned the art first from his uncle and then at school in Athens. While in Thebes, Pindar also learned to play the flute, either from his uncle or perhaps from his father. This skill was almost a prerequisite for anyone wishing to compose lyric poems. Traditionally, the ancients delivered their poems publicly and often accompanied them with music. Sometimes, poets sang their verses; at other times a choral group and/or dancers performed with the poet. Accounts also mention the poet Corinna as one of Pindar's teachers, and there were reports that he and Corinna competed against each other at Thebes in lyric poetry contests. Corinna is said to have defeated Pindar as many as five times.

A musician plays an aulos (a double reed instrument) for practicing wrestlers, with their hands bound in heavy thongs and their bodies unclothed for ease of movement. Music accompanied a variety of activities in ancient Greece, especially poetry recitals, and Pindar, like many poets, learned how to play the flute.

A prolific and professional poet, Pindar covered a wide range of topics in his verse. Often, he wrote about the victors at chariot races and horse races, but he preferred to praise the horses and those who bred them, not the riders themselves.

By 498 B.C., Pindar was a professional poet who received paying commissions to write poems. As the years passed, Pindar's fame gradually spread beyond the borders of his native region of Boeotia, then beyond Athens, and finally across the entire Greek world. As a descendant of an old aristocratic Theban family, Pindar's connections brought him into contact with the influential leaders of many other Greek cities. Such connections often led to requests for poems. In fact, rulers in Greek colonies as far away as Sicily and northern Africa commissioned Pindar to compose lyric poetry for them. Pindar focused each poem on praising the person who had given the commission or on commemorating an event that that person had sponsored.

Accounts say that when Alexander the Great of Macedonia captured Thebes more than 100 years after Pindar's death, the famed conqueror ordered his soldiers to destroy every structure in Thebes except Pindar's house. This was Alexander's way of showing respect for the poet who had once praised Macedonia so beautifully in a poem.

Surviving poems clearly reveal that Pindar traveled widely throughout Greece and Sicily. Nevertheless, he considered Thebes his home and returned there often. In the early 5th century B.C., when Thebes sided with the Persians against other Greek city-states, Greece did not look too kindly on this "treasonous" city-state. As a result, Pindar suffered the same treatment. Many of his friends continued to support him, and gradually he was welcomed again by the Greek cities that had fought against Persia.

Yet Pindar's poetry never focused on the military, because he did not see courage and victory on the battlefield as the only honorable traits. Instead, he admired those virtues that stayed with an individual throughout his lifetime, not just in war. Pindar knew full well that the threat of a Persian invasion had brought unity to the fiercely independent Greek cities, but he believed that unity and a feeling of national pride were needed in peacetime as well.

Reflecting this way of thinking, most of Pindar's surviving works center on festivities celebrated throughout the

Greek world. These were religious festivals, great athletic contests, and the rites performed at temples honoring the Greek gods and goddesses.

In ancient times, scholars collected Pindar's poems into 17 books and then subdivided these according to type and subject. Only four books, the *Epinicia* (victory songs), have survived intact. Most of these poems were written in honor of victors at the four major athletic festivals held in ancient Greece: the Olympic Games, the Pythian Games, the Nemean Games, and the Isthmian Games. All were national festivals in honor of a particular god.

The Olympic and Nemean Games honored Zeus, the all-powerful king of the gods; the Pythian Games honored Apollo, the god of prophecy; and the Isthmian Games honored Poseidon, the god of the sea. Athletes from cities and towns throughout Greece participated in all four events. A victory won in one contest was a great honor, for it brought lifelong fame, not only to the athlete and his family, but also to his hometown.

Traditionally, a victor's hometown hosted a great celebration in his honor. The festivities began with a procession to a temple, a religious sacrifice of thanksgiving, and finally a grand banquet. On the way to the temple and during the banquet, it was the custom to sing victory songs. The *Epinicia* is the collection of Pindar's victory songs, for he received many commissions to write these choral poems.

Although Pindar was able to incorporate his own ideas and thoughts into the songs, custom dictated that he include praise for the god honored at the festival, a sincere thanksgiving for the victory, a myth aimed at linking the city's present glories to those of the past, and wise proverblike phrases warning athletes about the danger of becoming too proud or boastful.

Because his audiences knew the facts, Pindar rarely used many lines to mention the event or the victory itself. Instead, he focused on praising the athlete and informing his listeners that the games gave athletes an opportunity to display their abilities before an audience representing all of Greece. Pindar felt it was also important to mention how victory was the result of an athlete's skill (or wealth, if the victor had entered the chariot races, because only those who could afford to supply their own horses and chariot could compete).

Pindar often included verses that compared a recent victor with a legendary hero from the same area. This tied his verses to the history of the Greek world, and Greeks everywhere could understand and appreciate Pindar's poems. In this way, he could be considered a national poet because he did not favor any particular region in his verses.

Pindar was very serious about his writing and wanted his poems to instill a sense of honor, create a feeling for the heroic past, and provide a sense of morality. He also believed that the gods would punish those who thought too highly of themselves. Yet his serious nature did not stop him from writing phrases that expressed both joy and pride in being Greek.

Pindar's language matched his thoughts, for neither his style nor his vocabulary is simple. He loved metaphors, proverbs, and lengthy descriptions. As a result, he is considered one of the most difficult of all the Greek writers to read. Sometimes his

ANCIENT GREEKS

Pindar

BORN

About 518 B.C.
Cynoscephalae, Greece

DIED

Probably after 446 B.C.
Place unknown

PROFESSION

Lyric poet

ACCOMPLISHMENTS

Wrote lyric poems that were collected by ancient scholars into 17 books, and these, in turn, were divided into hymns, paeans (songs of tribute or thanksgiving), dithyrambs (choral songs, often in honor of the god Dionysus), processional songs, maidens' songs, dance songs, *encomia* (formal expressions of praise), dirges (funeral songs), and victory songs; the four books of victory songs, called the *Epinicia*, are the only books to have survived intact

"For those who are honorable, time is the best of champions."

—from a poem fragment

verses leave a modern reader exhausted because his images and vocabulary are so involved.

We cannot fully appreciate Pindar's poetry today because we do not know what type of music accompanied his poems. Nor do we know the range of voices, or if the singers danced or stood solemnly. We do not even know how many singers there were.

Surviving verses prove that Pindar's poems were quite moving and descriptive, even if the descriptions were often lengthy. In the last lines of his first Olympic ode, written in 476 B.C. in honor of a chariot race won by Hieron, the ruler of Syracuse, Pindar specifically praises kings while expressing the value of the profession he practices: "Some individuals are great in one area, others in another area; but the summit belongs to kings. . . . May the gods grant that you be honored all your days, and that I may accompany victors all my days and be the best lyric poet among Greeks in every land."

Like all Greeks, Pindar had studied the master poet Homer and his epics, the *Iliad* and the *Odyssey*. Pindar's writings and manner of presentation reflected his admiration for Homer. In fact, many ancients considered Pindar to be the greatest Greek poet after Homer. However, the aristocratic world of Homer, with kings and nobles always in command, was being replaced in Athens by a more democratic form of government. At the same time, Athens was becoming the dominant Greek city-state. This did not mean that Homer would be forgotten; rather, it signaled a period of change.

Yet Pindar does not seem to have changed with the times: he considered himself an aristocrat and believed that aristocrats should rule society. Nevertheless, even as change swirled about him, his outdated beliefs did not detract from his fame. The commissions continued, and his poetry was read and appreciated throughout the Greek world.

For the Greeks, Pindar was the master of lyric poetry. However, in the centuries since his death, his works have been studied less than those of other Greek literary masters, partly because of his difficult style and partly because of passages that almost defy translation. Another reason is his refusal to consider the future and how the Greek world would react to change. Because Pindar preferred to look to the past, many have called him "the last aristocrat."

FURTHER READING

Bowra, Cecil Maurice. *Pindar.* Oxford, England: Clarendon Press, 1964.

Lefkowitz, Mary R. *The Lives of the Greek Poets.* London: Duckworth, 1981.

———. *The Victory Ode.* Park Ridge, N.J.: Noyes, 1976.

Pindar. *The Odes of Pindar.* Translated by Richard Lattimore. 2nd. ed. Chicago: University of Chicago Press, 1976.

———. *Pindar.* Translated by Sir J. E. Sandys. Loeb Classical Library. Cambridge: Harvard University Press, 1915.

Podlecki, Anthony J. *The Early Greek Poets and Their Times.* Vancouver, Canada: University of British Columbia Press, 1984.

Phidippides

THE FIRST MARATHON RUNNER

Phidippides shouted, "I'll do my best, sir!" and off he ran on the road south to Sparta. This was not the first time Phidippides had been given an important message to deliver, because he was, by profession, a courier.

In ancient Greece, this meant he was a long-distance runner. There was no official postal system, and the discovery of electricity was approximately 2,500 years into the future. Any Greek who wanted to communicate with someone in another area could either convey the message in person or entrust it to someone else to deliver. Because most people could not take the time needed to hand deliver a message, it soon became the custom for Greek cities to maintain ships and runners for this purpose.

Vases like this one, filled with oil from the olive trees sacred to the goddess Athena, were awarded to winners in the athletic contests at the Panathenaea. At this major Athenian festival, the footrace was the prized event. Professional runners were important in Greek society, and leaders depended on men like Phidippides to deliver urgent messages quickly.

The Greek writing on this tablet uncovered in Athens is part of an epigram written to commemorate the Battle of Marathon. After fighting the Persians, Phidippides ran the 25 miles to Athens to report the Greek victory.

In fact, runners proved to be one of the most efficient means of safely delivering official messages. Horses were available, as were carts and chariots, but the land of Greece is mountainous and the roads often steep, narrow, and winding. In wartime, generals and military strategists counted on professional runners and their speed.

Phidippides most likely had made many runs for Athens, and he knew well the roads leading in and out of the city. Yet the run to Sparta was a long one—approximately 150 miles round trip. As he ran, he must have thought about the dangers facing Athens at the time.

Just a few years before, in the early 5th century B.C., Athens, the chief city in the district of Attica, and the small city of Eretria, in the district of Euboea, had helped Greek colonists in Asia Minor fight the powerful Persian army. At first the Greeks had won, but after a bitter struggle they met defeat. Angered because the Greeks had caused them so much trouble, the Persians resolved to take revenge, and their main objective became the destruction of Athens and Eretria.

When the massive Persian army marched on Eretria, the outnumbered citizens bravely defended their city. Only after two traitorous Eretrians secretly aided the Persians did the city fall. The Persians burned the city, and all its citizens were enslaved.

After regrouping, the Persians prepared to attack and destroy Athens. Helping them plan their strategy was Hippias, a former tyrant of Athens who had been banished 10 years earlier. Hippias advised the Persians to proceed first to the Plain of Marathon, a short distance northeast of Athens. Following Hippias' advice, the Persians sailed across the waterway separating Euboea and Attica. There they set up camp near the Plain of Marathon.

Now the Athenians were forced to make a decision: whether to fight the Persians at Marathon or wait until they advanced on Athens. The Athenian general Miltiades favored the first choice and persuaded the other military leaders to agree. Athens' fighting force of 9,000 soldiers then marched north to Marathon, where they were joined by 1,000 soldiers from the neighboring city of Plataea. So it was that a force of 10,000 Greeks prepared to face the invading Persians, who numbered more than 20,000.

As Phidippides ran along the road to Sparta, he thought about his 9,000 countrymen and their 1,000 allies. Defeat would mean enslavement for the citizens of both cities. Moreover, if Persia won, what city could stop them from capturing other Greek cities? If only the Spartans would agree to send help.

Spartan soldiers were certainly the best in Greece, perhaps even the best in the world. Phidippides wondered if the Spartans would listen to his message: Send help to the Athenians at Marathon. You can not allow the city that is the oldest in Greece to be enslaved, he said; Eretria has already fallen and all Greece is weakened as a result.

Sparta did listen and promised to send its troops, but not immediately. It was only the ninth day of the month, and the moon was not yet full. Spartan law clearly stated that Sparta's armies could not march out of the city until the full moon, and it was not Phidippides' place to argue. He was only the messenger, and it was his duty to carry Sparta's answer to Athens as quickly as possible.

Approximately 48 hours after Phidippides had left Athens, he returned. It was a remarkable feat, even for a professional distance runner. The Athenians were disappointed with Sparta's answer, because the Persians certainly would not wait until the full moon to fight. And so it was that, in 490 B.C., the mighty Persian force faced a small but determined Greek army on the Plain of Marathon and lost. The Athenian strategy of charging the

"We won!"

—Phidippides' message to the Athenians after the Battle of Marathon, according to legend

enemy at a run and breaking apart its line of defense had worked.

When Sparta's troops arrived after the full moon, the action was over and the Athenians, with the help of the Plataeans, had triumphed. Greece would never forget this day, nor would Athens. Those who fought at Marathon were called "the Marathon warriors," a title of great respect. Contrary to custom, the Greeks buried those who had died in battle right on the field and erected an enormous mound above their grave. Today this "tombstone" still stands, a perpetual reminder of that day in history when so many Athenians and Plataeans died to keep their country free.

As the years passed, many more details were added to the story of the battle, and legends developed that might or might not have been based on fact. Consequently, it is now difficult to separate fact from fiction, but one legend did have a lasting impact on the world, and it involved Phidippides.

According to tradition, Phidippides made it back from Sparta in time to join his regiment at Marathon. But after the battle, he became a courier once again. This time his run was shorter—from Marathon to Athens—and the message was simpler: "We won!" The legend also says that Phidippides was so exhausted that he barely delivered his message before collapsing and dying in the marketplace at Athens. Whether or not this is true, history has never forgotten Phidippides. Today's marathon races are based on his run from the Plain of Marathon to Athens, a distance of about 25 miles.

The first marathon race took place in 1896 in Athens, Greece, at the first Olympic Games held in modern times. Because footraces had always been key events in the ancient Olympics, the 1896 Olympic committee thought it fitting to include a footrace as a major competition. Phidippides' legendary run determined the length of the race, and the name of the battlefield became the name of the event.

In 1897, Boston, Massachusetts, decided to host its own marathon race. When setting the date for the event, Boston thought it only appropriate to hold it on a day that represented an American victory for freedom. Boston officials selected the date April 19, a state holiday known as Patriots' Day, because on this date in 1775 the first battles of the American Revolution were fought at Lexington and Concord. Today's Boston Marathon is considered one of the world's most prestigious long-distance footraces.

Other cities also organized marathon races. For years the running distance varied from event to event and city to city. Then in 1924 the International Olympic Committee set the standard marathon distance still used today—26 miles, 385 yards.

FURTHER READING

Lloyd, Alan. *Marathon: The Story of Civilizations on Collision Course.* New York: Random House, 1973.

Nardo, Don. *The Battle of Marathon.* San Diego: Lucent, 1996.

ANCIENT GREEKS

Phidippides

BORN

Before 505 B.C.
Place unknown

DIED

About 490 B.C.
Place unknown

PROFESSION

Long-distance runner and courier

ACCOMPLISHMENTS

Within 48 hours, he ran approximately 150 miles from Athens to Sparta and back to seek Sparta's aid against advancing Persian forces; according to legend, he fought at the Battle of Marathon

Leonidas

THE HERO OF THERMOPYLAE

It was the summer of 480 B.C., and all of Greece was waiting for news of the advancing Persian army. Earlier reports had told how the Persian king Xerxes stood ready to invade northern Greece with his massive army and a fleet of warships. In Sparta, the city whose highly disciplined army was considered to be the best in Greece, King Leonidas carefully listened to each report. He knew Greece had to act, but the timing was not good. The Olympic Games were about to begin in Olympia in western Greece, and the Carnean Festival in honor of

Leonidas, in the helmet of a Spartan warrior, is remembered for his bravery in leading his troops against the Persians at Thermopylae. Leonidas and all his men were killed at that battle.

This was the first of 18 victories that Sophocles would win at the Great Dionysia. He also entered and won prizes at dramatic contests held at other Greek festivals. Sophocles is believed to have written 123 plays, and he won prizes for the majority of them, 72—more than half of them—at the Great Dionysia. (At each competition, a playwright presented four plays and a single prize was given for the four. So the 18 victories at the Great Dionysia represented 72 plays.)

In his early tragedies, Sophocles often played one of the roles, but he had to give up acting because his voice was not strong enough for the stage. He continued writing, however, and began to take an increasingly active role in government affairs.

In the years following the Persian Wars, Athens became the leader of the Greek city-states that had joined together to resist the Persians. Known as the Delian League, this alliance gradually became the basis of the Athenian empire as Athens' role changed from leader to ruler. In 454 B.C., the treasury of the league was moved from the island of Delos to Athens, and in 443 Sophocles was elected one of the 10 imperial treasurers. Three years later, Athens elected Sophocles one of its 10 *strategoi*, or generals, along with Pericles, one of the city's most distinguished statesmen. When the inhabitants of the Aegean island of Samos objected to Athens' new role as ruler of the Delian League, Sophocles and Pericles participated in the expedition sent against the Samians.

Sophocles, however, was not a general, and he readily agreed with Pericles' assessment of his leadership qualities—Sophocles "knows how to write a tragedy, but not how to command an army." Nevertheless, Sophocles' experiences at Samos did not lead him to withdraw from public duty. In 415 B.C., the 80-year-old Sophocles was one of the special commissioners appointed to govern Athens after the Athenian forces met a disastrous defeat in Sicily. He died a few years later, in 406 B.C., just two years before Athens itself fell.

Throughout his career as statesman, military officer, and playwright, Sophocles was never involved in a scandal. Yet he was not overconfident or proud, for he had seen too many powerful men exiled or assassinated. The fact that his home was chosen as a temporary place of worship for Asclepius, the god of healing, shows the honor Athenians conferred upon Sophocles.

Just months after Sophocles' death, the Athenian comic poet Phrynichus honored the tragedian in his play *Muses*, which was being performed at the Great Dionysia. His words are a fitting epitaph for one of the world's greatest writers: "Blessed is Sophocles, for he was a happy and fortunate individual who lived a very long life. The author of many good tragedies, he ended his life well and did not suffer any misfortunes."

And so it is that Sophocles' life stands in stark contrast to the suffering of so many of the characters in his tragedies. All of his characters have a nobility about them, a sense of duty, and a determination to do what they believe is right. These traits illustrated Sophocles' belief that individuals should use their free will to govern their lives. At the same time, however, Sophocles believed that fate played an important part in each person's life. He reasoned that because only the gods knew the future, they alone understood what an individual should or should not do.

Sophocles' main characters are tragic heroes and heroines who forget themselves and what may happen to them in order to accomplish what they

A politician and a playwright, Sophocles wrote, "I have nothing but contempt for any ruler who is afraid to do what he knows is best for his people; I have no use also for those who value private friendship more than the welfare of their country."

Confident that no one will solve her riddle, the sphinx stares haughtily at Oedipus in this 5th-century depiction of a scene from Sophocles' *Oedipus Tyrannus*. Death is the punishment if Oedipus gives the wrong answer.

see as right. Their determination is the key characteristic in Sophocles' works. In this way, he portrayed his characters as he felt people should be and should act.

Each of Sophocles' seven surviving plays shows how the playwright carefully planned the sequence of events. The scenes flow smoothly, and the action is clearly directed by humans. However, because the stories were taken from Greek mythology and legend, the audience of that time knew that the gods always had the final say and that the wisdom of the oracle would prove to be correct.

Sophocles, as a religious person and a firm believer in oracles, recognized the authority of the gods and did not attempt to change the story. It was how Sophocles treated each tale that made the drama so powerful and gripping. His characters were not the godlike heroes and heroines portrayed by Aeschylus. Nor were they the starkly realistic characters portrayed by the playwright Euripides. Sophocles' characters were ordinary humans whose fierce determination to stand by their beliefs made them heroic.

Unlike Euripides, Sophocles did not use the tragic suffering of his characters just for the emotional effect it would have on his audience. Sophocles portrayed his characters as humans who rose above the ordinary to accomplish their purpose. In this sense, he reminds today's readers of the Greek poet Homer, who wrote the master epics the *Iliad* and the *Odyssey*.

Sophocles also wanted his audience to realize that intense determination could also be a fault because absolute resistance to changing one's goal causes tragic results. For Sophocles, a character's downfall or suffering was to a great extent the result of that character's own actions.

In the play *Antigone*, written in 442 or 441 B.C., Sophocles masterfully portrayed Antigone's determination to disobey King Creon and bury her brother. Her argument is that divine law requires a person to be buried before being allowed to enter the underworld. No human law, she asserts, can ever override divine law. Even when Creon orders her buried alive for refusing to change her mind, Antigone does not yield. King Creon, on the other hand, steadfastly refuses to allow the body to be buried, even when his son Haemon threatens to die with Antigone, who is his fiancée. As a result of their righteousness, both Antigone and Creon suffer terribly. Antigone dies before learning that Creon has suddenly changed his mind. Creon learns first of her death, then of his son's, and finally of his wife's suicide.

For many, *Antigone* is Sophocles at his best. Indeed, many acclaim Sophocles as the greatest of the Greek tragedians. His masterful use of words to reveal the inner thoughts of a character draws the audience closer to the character. This involvement gives a heightened sense of drama because the audience is no longer just observing the action of the play—it is now participating mentally. This ability of Sophocles to involve the spectators also sets them thinking about the rightness or wrongness of each character's actions. Should Creon have been so stubborn? How about Antigone?

There were no set answers, and Sophocles did not offer any. What he did was to portray strong, willful characters whose beliefs governed their actions. The result was almost always suffering, even on the part of the innocent. Yet this too had its purpose because as the plot of each play unraveled, the actions and dialogue showed how pain and grief made the characters wiser. Each main character finally recognizes that the gods are indeed all-knowing and that humans do not know everything. This revelation alone produced a feeling of humility.

In *Oedipus Tyrannus*, certainly Sophocles' best-known work and the one considered by many to be his masterpiece, wisdom and an acceptance of fate come only after much suffering. Like Aeschylus and Euripides, who wrote plays based on the legend of Oedipus, Sophocles used the well-known tale as the subject of two plays that have survived.

According to the Greeks, when Oedipus was born, an oracle predicted that he would one day kill his father and marry his mother. To avoid such tragic events, Oedipus' parents, the king and queen of Thebes, decided to abandon their newborn on a hill outside the city. This was an accepted practice in ancient Greece when parents decided not to rear a sickly or unwanted child.

The servant who had been given the task of leaving Oedipus to die was unable to do so and gave the royal infant to the king and queen of Corinth, who wanted a child. Oedipus' foster parents, however, never told him the true story of his birth. As a young man, Oedipus followed the Greek custom of consulting an oracle. After hearing that he would kill his father and marry his mother, Oepidus immediately left Corinth, determined never to commit such horrible crimes.

One day while traveling along a road, he fell to arguing with some travelers. Words soon changed to weapons and Oedipus, as the strongest, killed all except one member of the group. Believing that he had acted in self-defense, Oedipus continued along the road, unaware that he had just killed the king of Thebes, his real father.

By chance, Oedipus next found himself near Thebes, where a sphinx—a winged monster with a lion's body and the head and breasts of a woman—had been plaguing the entrance and exit to the city. No one could leave or enter the city without first answering the monster's riddle. The punishment for a wrong answer was death.

The situation was serious, and the Thebans were beginning to panic because every Greek who had dared offer an answer had been killed. Oedipus listened carefully to the question, "What walks on all fours in the morning, two feet at noon, and three in the evening?" "A human being!" Oedipus replied. He understood that all fours meant a crawling infant, two feet meant a healthy adult, and three feet meant an old person with a cane.

Hearing the correct answer, the sphinx flung itself from the cliff to its death. Oedipus was made king of Thebes and given the recently widowed queen as his wife. With her, he fathered a daughter, Antigone, and a son, Polynices. Years later, when Oedipus learned the truth, his shame and grief overwhelmed him and he tore out his eyes.

ANCIENT GREEKS

Sophocles

BORN
496 or 495 B.C.
Outside Athens, Greece

DIED
406 or 405 B.C.
Probably in Athens, Greece

PROFESSION
Writer of tragedies

ACCOMPLISHMENTS
Master writer of tragedies and honored by many as the best Greek tragedian; wrote approximately 123 plays and won prizes at dramatic festivals for more than 70 plays (the surviving plays are *Ajax*, *Women of Trachis*, *Antigone*, *Oedipus Tyrannus* [also known as *Oedipus Rex* and *Oedipus the King*], *Electra*, *Philoctetes*, and *Oedipus at Colonus*, produced posthumously); treasurer of the Delian League; elected *strategos* (general); appointed governor of Athens after the city's disastrous military defeat in Sicily

In the 19th century, the French artist Gustave Moreau painted his own interpretation of the meeting of Oedipus and the sphinx. In contrast to the Greek depiction on page 68, this sphinx is a more seductive figure, trying to distract Oedipus from thinking about the right answer.

All Greek audiences were acquainted with this part of the story, but they were eager to see Sophocles' treatment of the tale. He opened his play with the Thebans demanding immediate action to rid the city of a terrible plague. Oedipus informs them that he has already sent a messenger to the oracle for advice. When the oracle replies that the Thebans must rid their land of the man who murdered the previous king, Oedipus vows to find the murderer.

The drama is set and so too the suspense, for although Oedipus believes this oracle, he refuses to believe what the other oracle had said about him. His wife, the queen, also refuses to think about the oracle that said she would marry her son.

Again and again Oedipus and Jocasta, his wife/mother, seem on the verge of learning the horrible truth, but circumstances delay the revelation each time. Oedipus and Jocasta do not intentionally avoid the truth. Rather, Sophocles composed his lines to show that both desperately sought the truth yet failed to recognize what was so obvious. In this way, the action of the play leads to the final scene, in which Oedipus, aware of how blind he has been to the truth, gouges out his eyes to make himself truly blind.

To heighten the conflict of blindness and sight, Sophocles introduced the character Tiresias, a blind prophet. In *Oedipus Tyrannus*, Tiresias tells Oedipus that he has killed his father unknowingly and hints that even worse revelations will be made—that Jocasta is really his mother.

Sophocles was able to maintain a sense of suspense throughout the play, while keeping the action flowing smoothly and the characters believable. To do this, he introduced scenes that required three actors. Whether Sophocles or Aeschylus was the first to do this is not certain, but the addition of another character increased the sense of drama and allowed the playwright to play one person against two others. This interaction also helped define each character's personality more clearly.

The chorus, as an essential part of tragedy, commented on the action being portrayed on the stage. Even though Sophocles did not give his choruses the prominent role they had had in earlier times, he still used them. Cleverly and masterfully, Sophocles matched the chorus dialogue to the gradual unraveling of the truth. As the final scene approaches, the chorus has become, little by little, sympathetic to the main characters and so, too, has the audience.

Here, as in *Antigone*, Sophocles' rendering of the tale posed questions. Because the oracle predicted the horrible events, was Oedipus a doomed man from the time he was born? Or was Oedipus' fall his own fault because he constantly had refused to listen to the oracle's warning? Sophocles' religious faith made it impossible for him to blame the all-knowing gods for Oedipus' downfall. The downfall comes, according to Sophocles, because humans do not know everything.

Unlike today's dramas that use onstage violence to create an emotional scene, Sophocles conformed to the Greek custom of avoiding violence onstage. Cries of mourners and faithful servants acknowledged some terrible act, but only the aftermath was shown. It was not essential to portray blood and gore, because it was how a human felt and and how deeply others were affected that mattered to the playwright and the audience.

One stage effect that Sophocles is said to have introduced, or at least improved, is stage scenery. Like the other Greek playwrights, Sophocles used mechanical devices when necessary. In *Antigone*, the *ekkulema*, or "platform on wheels," revealed the

"When fighting for something that is right, even weakness triumphs."

—from *Oedipus at Colonus* (401 B.C.)

"I have nothing but contempt for any ruler who, for whatever reason, is afraid to do what he knows is best for his people; as for those who value private friendship more than the welfare of their country, I have no use for them either."

—from *Antigone* (around 441 B.C.)

body of Eurydice, who had been killed by a snakebite. The stage setting for *Oedipus Tyrannus* was simply a palace front with entrances for the characters.

Sophocles also followed the custom of introducing at the end of the play the *mechane*, a mechanical device that allowed a god to "fly" above the stage and settle the action. In the final scene of the play *Philoctetes*, the legendary hero Heracles appears above the action in such a device.

Sophocles' last play, *Oedipus at Colonus*, centered on Oedipus' life after his blinding and banishment from Thebes. After much suffering, Oedipus finally finds peace at *Oedipus at Colonus*. Sophocles' craftmanship as a playwright is evident in his choice of words, the smoothly flowing lines, the buildup of Oedipus' character, and the masterful expression of emotions.

As the final scene approaches, Sophocles seems to be saying that despite untold misery and suffering, peace is always possible and that there is a reason for suffering that the gods know and understand. Therefore, humans must trust in the gods and their divine justice. Such a message provided hope, particularly because the play was written toward the end of the Peloponnesian War, when Athens was rapidly losing its place as Greece's chief city-state. Sophocles might have been saying that Athens and the Athenians should trust their future to the gods, who fully understood the city's greatness and destiny. Surely the gods would see that Athens, too, merited divine justice.

Before Sophocles could produce *Oedipus at Colonus*, he died at age 90. Five years later, in 401 B.C., the tragedy won first prize when his grandson, also named Sophocles, presented it at the dramatic festival. The message of hope must have lifted the spirits of the Athenians, who in 404 B.C. had lost the Peloponnesian War.

Sophocles probably would consider his belief in divine justice and destiny justified because Athens, its culture, literature, and philosophy have remained preeminent for more than 2,000 years. Today Sophocles' plays continue to be read, studied, imitated, and performed. For most 16th-century European humanists—who considered humans capable of controlling their own destiny—*Antigone* was their favorite tragedy, and *Oedipus Tyrannus* has been considered a masterpiece of tragic drama since ancient times. Many adaptations and versions have been written of the Oedipus story, such as the one in 1718 by the French writer and philosopher Voltaire. Though later playwrights have added their scenery, costumes, and stage effects, it is still Sophocles' version that remains the focus of the audience's attention.

FURTHER READING

Fitts, Dudley, ed. *Greek Plays in Modern Translation*. New York: Dial, 1947.

Melchinger, Siegfried. *Sophocles*. Translated by David A. Scarse. New York: Ungar, 1974.

Murray, Gilbert, Benjamin R. Rogers, et al., trans. *Fifteen Greek Plays*. New York: Oxford University Press, 1943.

Nardo, Don. *Sophocles*. San Diego: Greenhaven, 1996.

Scodel, Ruth. *Sophocles*. New York: Macmillan, 1984.

Sophocles. *Antigone, Oedipus the King, Electra*. Translated by H. D. F. Kitto and edited by Edith Hall. New York: Oxford University Press, 1994.

———. *Sophocles*. Translated by F. Storr. Loeb Classical Library. Cambridge: Harvard University Press, 1919.

Webster, Thomas B. L. *An Introduction to Sophocles*. 2nd ed. London: Methuen, 1969.

Herodotus

THE FATHER OF HISTORY

From the time that he was a little boy, Herodotus had listened to stories of Greece's courageous fight against the mighty Persian Empire. He heard many tales of Persia's aggressive tactics and Greece's determination to win complete independence against overwhelming odds. Naturally, as a Greek himself, he supported his compatriots and believed that freedom was a right worth defending and that tyranny suppressed creativity.

Tradition places Herodotus' birth in the year 484 B.C., just six years after the Persian king Darius first invaded mainland Greece and four years before the Persian king Xerxes led the second invasion. However, Herodotus' hometown, the Greek colony of Halicarnassus on the southwest coast of Asia Minor (present-day Turkey), had experienced life under Persian control much earlier. The prosperous Greek colonies along the coast had been among the first areas to fall to Persian might. In fact, the Persian assault on the Greek mainland was intended to punish the Greeks for sending aid to the Greek colonies that fought the Persians in Asia Minor.

During his youth, Herodotus heard far more about Greece's victories on the battlefield than about its early defeats. Yet at the same time that he heard of Greece's great deeds, he lived under the tyrannical rule of a Persian-appointed ruler named Lygdamis. Years earlier, when Lygdamis' grandmother ruled Halicarnassus, she and her fleet of five ships had joined Xerxes as he advanced against Greece. It was because of her bravery and forethought that Halicarnassus' fleet escaped defeat and destruction at Salamis. Her grandson Lygdamis did not share the same concern about the welfare of the people of Halicarnassus, and his rule became increasingly more oppressive.

Strong opposition to Lygdamis' policies finally brought civil unrest to the city. Herodotus' family, as aristocrats and leading citizens, became actively involved in resisting Lygdamis. When an epic poet named Panyasis, most likely a relative of Herodotus, was killed by Lygdamis, Herodotus felt he could no longer tolerate such tyranny, and he left Halicarnassus.

His first stop was the Greek island of Samos in the Aegean Sea. Samos was quite different from Halicarnassus, which had been colonized by Greeks known to history as the Dorians. As a group, the Dorians stressed simplicity and preferred physical and military activities to academic studies. The Dorians also looked to the cities of southern Greece, especially Sparta, as their mother country. Samos, on the other hand, traced its roots to those Greeks known to

This statue of Herodotus, representing History, stands in the Library of Congress in Washington, D.C. The U.S. sculptor Daniel Chester French (1850-1931) portrays Herodotus as a traveler searching the world for information for his own *History*.

history as Ionians. Traditionally, the Ionians appreciated beauty, the fine arts, intellectual pursuits, and, above all, independence. They looked to Athens as their mother country.

While at Samos, Herodotus most likely involved himself in reading and the arts. He probably had heard of the Samian poets Aesop and Anacreon and of the philosopher and mathematician Pythagoras. But Herodotus was a very inquisitive man, and after a time he decided to leave the island and travel through the Middle East, Egypt, and parts of southern Europe.

Everywhere he traveled he was intrigued by the different customs, governments, and religious beliefs that he encountered. But Herodotus was never satisfied with a single explanation for an incident or historical event; he spoke to many people and consulted a variety of reference materials. Everywhere he took notes and considered the many ways in which he could convey his experiences and thoughts to others. Soon Herodotus began lecturing in various cities, including Athens, about his travels and observations. Meanwhile, the situation at Halicarnassus had become worse as objections to Lygdamis' tyrannical rule increased. The people launched a revolt, and Lygdamis was forced into exile. Whether Herodotus took part in Lygdamis' expulsion is not known. It is possible that Herodotus was there during the turmoil and stayed for a while, but he no longer considered Halicarnassus home.

He now preferred Athens, and, as a resident, he heard much about the city's role in the Persian Wars. He also

"These books contain the researches of Herodotus of Halicarnassus. The author publishes this work because he hopes to keep from oblivion the memory of what men have accomplished, and to make sure the wonderful and brave deeds of the Greeks and the barbarians receive their rightful glory. He also wishes to record what caused the conflict between the two peoples."

—from the introduction to *Clio*, Book One of *History* (around 444–420 B.C.)

experienced the city's unique form of government, which stressed democratic principles and intellectual freedom. Herodotus enjoyed the Athenians and made many friends, including the playwright Sophocles. It was also during this time that he began arranging and preparing for publication the numerous notes that he had made.

Yet despite his love for Athens, Herodotus chose to leave sometime around 444 or 443 B.C., when he was approximately 40 years old. He moved to Thurii, a new colony established by Athenians in southern Italy. This move, however, did not stop his travels, for Herodotus was too much of an observer, explorer, and listener to stay in one place for very long, and his curiosity and intense desire to know as much as he could pushed him to ask questions and seek answers from all sources.

It was at Thurii that Herodotus wrote his masterpiece, entitled *History*. The Greek writer Lucian of the 2nd century A.D. claimed that the Greeks so loved the nine books of *History* that they renamed each volume in honor of one of the nine Muses. (The Muses were the daughters of Zeus, the king of the gods, and their duty was to support and promote the arts and sciences.) Whether Lucian's tale is fact or fiction, or whether some person at a later date renamed the books of Herodotus' *History*, the names of the Muses—Clio, Euterpe, Thalia, Melpomene, Terpsichore, Erato, Polyhymnia, Urania, and Calliope—are still used to refer to each of his books.

When deciding how to present his material, Herodotus debated whether or not to use poetry, the customary manner of writing at the time. However, after concluding that poetry would not express his message properly, he wrote in prose—and thus became the first of the ancient Greeks to cover so extensive a topic using sentences and paragraphs.

As his central theme, Herodotus chose the Persian Wars, perhaps because of the similarities that he saw between the Persian Wars and the Trojan War. He knew that both had been fought in Asia Minor between Greeks and a foreign power, and he was well acquainted with the *Iliad* and the *Odyssey*, the two epic poems by Homer about the Trojan War. Herodotus believed the Persian Wars would have a lasting effect on Greece and would become an important part of its history, just as the Trojan War had.

Herodotus' preference for and loyalty to Greece and Greek culture are evident throughout his work, for he, like the majority of Greeks, considered

ANCIENT GREEKS

Herodotus

BORN

Around 484 B.C.
Halicarnassus, Asia Minor

DIED

Around 420 B.C.
Thurii, Italy

PROFESSION

Historian

ACCOMPLISHMENTS

Wrote a work entitled *History*, which was later divided into nine books or chapters, each bearing the name of one of the nine Muses

"I must tell of a certain leader named Artemisia, whose participation in the battle against the Greeks, although she was a woman, merits special consideration. Artemisia had taken control after the death of her husband.... Her bravery, spirit, and boldness forced her to enter into the [Persian] war... the five triremes [Greek warships] which she brought to aid the Persian fleet were the second best in the fleet."

—Herodotus' description of Artemisia—queen of Halicarnassus and grandmother of Lygdamis, who ruled the city-state when Herodotus lived there—in *Polyhymnia*, Book Seven of *History* (around 444–420 B.C.)

all non-Greeks foreigners. In his *History*, Herodotus even compared the speech of non-Greeks to the twittering of birds. The Greeks themselves called the speech of non-Greeks *bar-bar*, a phrase the Romans adapted to *barbarus*, meaning "foreigner." Centuries later, the English language used *barbarus* as the basis of its word *barbarian*, originally used to mean "a foreigner."

This word history would have delighted Herodotus because he enjoyed learning about people, their customs, and their beliefs. He wanted his work to tell a story, to be more than just a dull list of facts, dates, and events. For this reason, he incorporated in his *History* many of the tales that he had heard and learned on his travels. Ancient as well as modern readers have found Herodotus' digressions among the most interesting sections in his work.

In the 19th century, many historians and scientists criticized Herodotus for diverging too much from his theme of the Persian Wars and for including information that was most likely legend or myth. They also accused him of not checking his statistics carefully and of using greatly exaggerated figures such as "more than 5 million" to record the number of people the Persian king Xerxes led against Greece.

Today, historians look at Herodotus differently. They see a man who appears to have accurately recorded what he saw and heard, and who chose to include several accounts when he could not decide which was most reliable. In his *History*, Herodotus himself mentioned that some facts might not be true but that he was reporting what he knew and had learned. And it is Herodotus' digressions as much as his accounts of the battles that have helped later generations understand the peoples and times in which he lived.

Although Herodotus was too young to have taken part in the Persian Wars, he knew well the battlefields of Marathon, Thermopylae, Salamis, and Plataea and had spoken with many eyewitnesses, both in Greece and throughout the East. This was important to Herodotus, for he had a keen sense of geography and wanted his readers, present and future, to understand the relationship between places and peoples.

Herodotus knew that many in his audience were not well versed in early Greek history and felt that before he could focus on the Persian Wars it was necessary to explain the events leading up to them. Therefore, he spent the first four books of *History* explaining the incidents that led to the Persian conquest of Asia Minor.

Egypt was another area with which he felt his readers should become

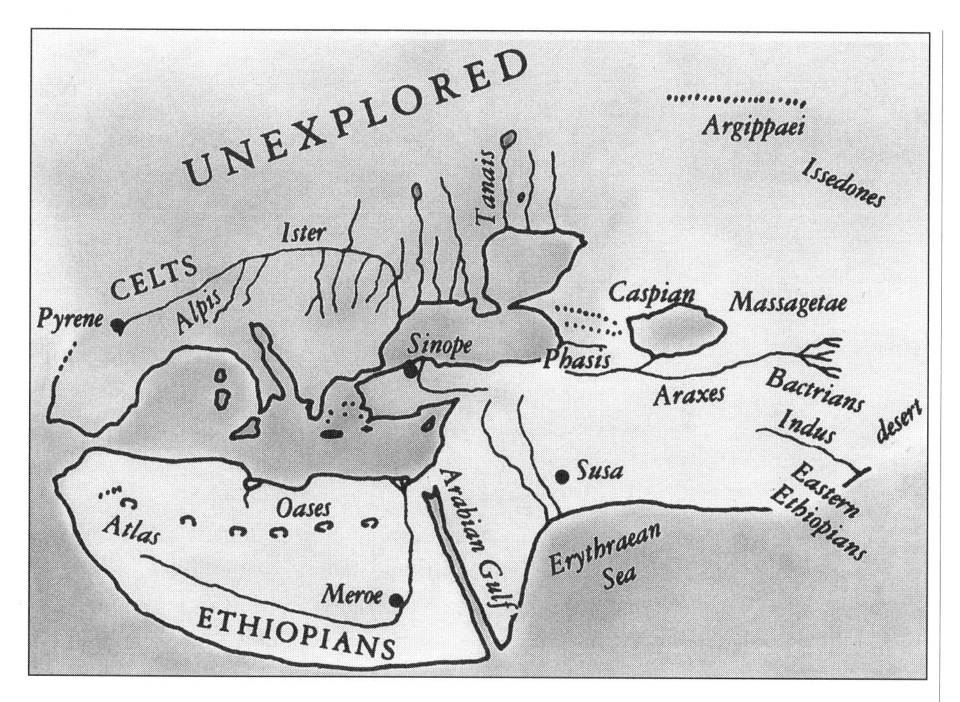

From his limited travels around the Mediterranean and from his questioning of travelers, Herodotus had a surprisingly accurate view of the then-known world. This map is a reconstruction of Herodotus' view of the ancient world. Note the boot shape of Italy and, to the right of the boot, the peninsula of Greece.

acquainted. To work Egypt into his book, Herodotus focused on an early Persian king named Cambyses who had led his army into Egypt and had conquered the country. With such an introduction, Herodotus felt justified in turning his attention from the Persian Wars to describing the Egyptian people and their customs.

Only in Book Five did he begin focusing on the Persian Wars themselves by recounting the revolt by the Ionian Greeks against the Persians. It was this revolt and the aid sent by mainland Greeks that provoked Persia into attacking Greece itself. Yet, even in Book Five and again in Book Six, Herodotus digressed from the wars to explain the divisions within the Greek cities. Herodotus strongly believed that such an explanation was necessary for readers to fully understand why each Greek city reacted as it did to the Persian threat. Books Seven, Eight, and Nine focus on the major battles of the wars.

As a chronicler of the past and an individual keenly interested in presenting events as accurately and objectively as possible, Herodotus has become known as the "father of history."

FURTHER READING

Evans, James Allan Stewart. *Herodotus*. Boston: Twayne, 1982.

Gaines, Ann. *Herodotus and the Explorers of the Classical Age*. New York: Chelsea House, 1993.

Gould, John. *Herodotus*. New York: St. Martin's, 1989.

Hart, John. *Herodotus and Greek History*. New York: St. Martin's, 1982.

Herodotus. *Herodotus*. Translated by A. D. Godley. Loeb Classical Library. Cambridge: Harvard University Press, 1922.

———. *The Histories*. Translated by George Rawlinson. Reprint. Boston: Tuttle, 1994.

———. *The Persian Wars*. Translated by George Rawlinson. New York: McGraw-Hill, 1964.

Thomas, Albertine. *Tales from Herodotus*. New York: Pageant, 1966.

Waters, Kenneth H. *Herodotos, the Historian: His Problems, Methods, and Originality*. Norman: University of Oklahoma Press, 1985.

Euripides

A LITERARY "PAINTER OF PASSIONS"

The ancient Athenians loved the theater, and one of the most eagerly awaited events was the dramatic contest held every spring during the Great Dionysia. This was a festival in honor of Dionysus, the god of wine and merriment. A panel of judges asked each of Athens' top three playwrights to present four plays at the festival. At the scheduled time, throngs of Athenians entered the theater on the side of the Acropolis near Dionysus' temple, anxious to see which playwright would win the coveted prize.

The contests of the 5th century B.C. were the most exciting because Greece's three master tragedians—Aeschylus, Sophocles, and Euripides—were all competing. So honored were these playwrights that, in the decades following their deaths, their fame continued to grow along with the legends about their lives.

One tale was especially popular among the Athenians because it focused on 480 B.C. and the Greek defeat of the

Euripides understood well the importance of education. He wrote, "Whoever neglects learning when he is young, loses the past and is dead for the future."

Persians at Salamis. Over time, it seemed fitting that Athens' three master tragedians should in some way be associated with one of Athens' greatest historical moments. As a result, it came to be accepted as fact that Aeschylus, the oldest of the three, served as an officer at Salamis; that Sophocles, who at 16 had been too young to fight, watched the evacuation of Athens and the city's destruction from Salamis; and that Euripides, the youngest, was born at Salamis on the very day of the battle in 480 B.C.

Exact dates, however, are really not important. What is significant is that Euripides' early years coincided with Athens' rise to power in the Greek world. From the time that he was a child, he had listened to stories about Athens' role in Persia's defeat, of the heroic deeds of his countrymen, and of his city's position as Greece's new leader.

Euripides' parents were both Athenians, making him eligible for full citizenship, with the right to vote and hold office. Several years after Euripides' death, Aristophanes, the renowned Greek comic poet, wrote that Euripides' mother was a greengrocer, or vegetable seller. That most likely meant that his family sent the vegetables grown on their lands in Salamis to the markets in Athens.

According to tradition, Euripides entered athletic competitions at the national festivals, winning at least one prize. At age 17, he presented himself as a candidate for the Olympic Games, but he was refused because the officials believed that he was younger and had falsified his age to qualify. Euripides' athletic career is possibly a fabrication from later centuries, just like the oracle's prophecy to Euripides' father that his son would win sacred garlands. Euripides' father thought the oracle was referring to the wreaths given to victorious Greek athletes, but Euripides would win his garlands in the field of literature, not sports.

Euripides loved solitude and often returned to the quiet of his hometown of Salamis to think and write. There, according to tradition, he spent much time alone, writing in a cave. Unlike so many Athenians who began taking an active part in the government at the legal age of 16, Euripides did not. The philosopher Aristotle later wrote that Euripides did go on a diplomatic mission to Sicily, an island where many Greek colonists had settled. A few centuries later, the Greek biographer Plutarch noted that Euripides wrote a poem in honor of the Athenians who died while attacking the Sicilian city of Syracuse. Yet this type of activity was the exception for Euripides, who preferred to spend his free time reading and discussing ideas with the thinkers and teachers of Athens.

After the Battle of Salamis, the Athenians had immediately begun rebuilding their city. The seeds of democracy that had been sown before the war were beginning to sprout, and bloodlines and family gradually ceased to be the key to political power. The Athenian attitude toward freedom of speech and thought encouraged the people to express their feelings and opinions. As a result, more and more individuals were beginning to enter public life. Some even began to question traditional beliefs and long-established practices. The changing times especially affected artists because they now had more freedom to create.

This bustling environment influenced the young playwright Euripides. Like many of his contemporaries, he wondered about the meaning of life, the role of the traditional gods and myths, and the depth of human emotions. Often Euripides' thoughts broke with tradition. For example, his lack of complete confidence in the righteousness of the gods caused some fellow Athenians to bring a charge of

"Only a quiet conscience is able to endure the joys and sorrows of a person's life."

—from *Hippolytus* (428 B.C.)

At the Theater of Dionysus in Epidaurus, set against the backdrop of Greek hills, directors and actors continue to present Euripides' plays for today's audiences.

disrespect against him. Although no sources give the outcome or verdict, themes and lines in his later works prove that Euripides did not stop questioning or expressing his beliefs.

Because there were no printed programs for performances given in Euripides' day, he opened his plays with a prologue in which he had a character detail the facts the audience needed to know before the action began. Another characteristic of his plays was the vivid and very dramatic messenger scene. An example is found in *The Trojan Women*, when the Greek messenger Talthybius explains to the Trojan Andromache that he must take her young son and kill him because the Greeks want no heirs to the Trojan throne. This is a scene that sears itself into the audience's memory forever, because the grief of a woman who in war loses first her husband and country, and then her only child, strikes at the heart of everyone.

The Trojan Women is, perhaps, Euripides' best-known play and certainly one of his most powerful dramas. First performed in 415 B.C. and awarded second prize in the spring drama contest, its theme was directly pertinent to the times. The Greek unity and victories achieved during the period of the Persian Wars were history. Now the two leading Greek cities, Athens and Sparta, were involved in a deadly civil war. Thousands had died, family life had been torn apart, and the number of widows kept increasing. The disastrous fates of the defeated Trojan men, women, and children began to take on new meaning for Greek audiences. In this way, Euripides' play was a political commentary on the brutality and horrors of war, as well as on the futility of war, which destroys both the victor and the defeated.

Euripides' audiences could identify with his characters, because he made them act and feel like real people. He portrayed them as they were, not as they should be, which meant that their actions were not always glorious, patriotic, or right. To bring tragedy to the level of everyday life, Euripides used action and suspense. Throughout his plays, the audience is involved in intrigue, narrow escapes, sudden changes in a character's life or feelings, acts of terrible revenge, and deeds involving supreme heroism. However, because Euripides was so interested in why people acted the way they did, his characters often gave soliloquies and philosophized about life. As a result, the action did not always flow continuously.

Euripides also liked to introduce scenes to shock his audience. In *Heracles,* which focuses on the life of the legendary Greek hero, even the chorus (the group of people on stage who comment on the action) expresses shock when one of the principal characters prepares to burn Heracles' children alive.

Euripides sometimes used mechanical devices to heighten the shock effect. For example, every Greek knew the story of Medea, a foreign princess who helped the Greek hero Jason and then married him. Her wickedness was also well known, for she killed their children when she discovered that Jason was planning to leave her for another woman. In Euripides' play *Medea,* the audience was not surprised when the boys' deaths were announced (brutal actions always took place offstage) and did not expect to see the bodies. Euripides, however, did not conform to tradition—he had the bodies raised on a wheeled mechanical device and displayed above the stage.

The *deus ex machina,* "god from a machine," was another of Euripides' favorite devices. He often incorporated it into the final scene, in which some god standing in a crane tells the audience the future destinies of the play's main characters. Again Euripides did not conform to custom, because other playwrights of the time usually introduced the *deus ex machina* so that they could have some god resolve the problems presented in the play in a satisfactory way. Euripides, on the other hand, emphasized the role each individual played in his own destiny. The personality of each of his characters was key to the play's plot, and the chorus played a minimal role.

This tendency to be different, especially concerning the role of the gods and the use of myths, often brought criticism from his contemporaries. Euripides' works illustrate that he believed a human being's misfortunes were not caused by the gods and goddesses but were the result of a person's weaknesses and inability to deal with emotions. For example, in the *Medea,* it was Medea's inability to control her anger and jealousy that led her to commit murder.

Medea also incorporated another theme common in Euripides—the position of women in society. In this play, Euripides seems to be questioning whether Medea must accept Jason's abandonment of her as just, while Jason goes unpunished for his callous treatment of the person who saved his life. *The Trojan Women* also addresses the subordinate role of women in a community and the justice of their treatment in defeat.

The manner in which Euripides expressed human emotions and related them to everyday experiences won him the admiration of his Athenian audiences. Soon, his fame spread beyond the boundaries of the city. Archelaus, the king of Macedonia, a country just to the north of Greece, was a devoted patron of the arts and particularly admired Euripides' works. He offered the playwright great rewards if he

ANCIENT GREEKS

Euripides

BORN

Around 484 or 480 B.C.
Salamis, Greece

DIED

Before 405 B.C., most likely 406 B.C.
Macedonia

PROFESSION

Writer of tragedies

ACCOMPLISHMENTS

Wrote 92 plays, of which 17 tragedies and one satyr play survive (the surviving tragedies are *Alcestis, Medea, Hippolytus, Children of Heracles, Andromache, Hecuba, Heracles, Suppliants, Ion, Trojan Women, Electra, Iphigeneia in Tauris, Helen, Phoenician Women, Orestes, Iphigeneia in Aulis,* produced posthumously, and *Bacchae,* produced posthumously; the surviving satyr play is *Cyclops*); won the dramatic prize at the Great Dionysia for the first time in 441 B.C.; one prize was awarded posthumously for the *Bacchae,* a play most likely completed by his son or grandson; given credit by some for the tragedy *Rhesus*; acknowledged as one of Greece's leading tragedians

Judith Anderson plays Medea in Robinson Jeffers' popular 1947 adaptation of Euripides' *Medea*. The ancient story of one woman's wrath at being left for another woman is still a powerful theme.

would come to Macedonia and produce plays for his court. Even though home had always been Athens and Salamis, Euripides chose to spend his final years away from both.

Sometime around 408 B.C., Euripides accepted Archelaus' offer. His stay, however, was brief, for he died probably in 406 B.C. at the age of 75. When news of his death reached Athens just prior to the start of the Great Dionysia, Sophocles immediately asked the members of his chorus to dress in mourning for the parade held before the competition.

During his lifetime, Euripides won few prizes for his plays, and scholars have often debated why this was so, offering as an explanation the fact that some of the ideas included in Euripides' plays were too offensive and irritating and that Athenian judges felt it best not to reward such thoughts. However, the fact that Euripides was selected to present his works at the Great Dionysia is a tribute to the Athenian belief in the freedom of expression.

Today, 17 tragedies and one satyr play survive. (A satyr play is a type of comedy introduced for comic relief; a satyr in Greek mythology is a fun-loving woodland deity with pointed ears, short horns, the head and body of a man, and the legs of a goat.) However, records show that Euripides wrote 92 plays and entered 22 competitions. Because competition at the Great Dionysia allowed a playwright to produce three tragedies and a satyr play, this meant that Euripides won the right to compete, most likely at the Great Dionysia, 22 times with a total of 88 plays.

In 405 B.C., shortly after Euripides' death, the comic playwright Aristophanes included in his comedy *Frogs* a lengthy scene involving Euripides. The scene begins with the god Dionysus journeying to the underworld to pay his last respects to the tragedian. There he finds Euripides in the middle of a lawsuit, claiming that he, not Aeschylus, is entitled to the throne awarded the world's best tragedian. Sophocles does not enter the debate because he had already acknowledged Aeschylus as the better writer when he first entered the underworld. Euripides then explains that he deserves the throne because he contributed so much to tragedy in the way of language and ideas. Aeschylus comments that Euripides' emphasis on emotions and suffering and his unconventional religious views have had a harmful effect on his listeners. Finally a scale is brought out and each playwright must quote a verse from one of his plays onto the scale and symbolically weigh it. Three times they do this and three times Aeschylus wins.

Aeschylus may have won Aristophanes' contest, but in the centuries that followed, Euripides' popularity far surpassed that of Aeschylus and Sophocles. In the 2nd century A.D., when a collection of plays written by great classical authors was compiled for school use, 10 of Euripides' plays were included, making him the playwright with the greatest number of works in the text. In fact, more of Euripides' plays have survived than of any other Greek playwright.

Performances of Euripides' tragedies continue today in the restored theaters of ancient Greece as well as in modern theaters throughout the world. Euripides' themes of war, love, religion, and suffering are just as relevant today as they were in his day. His characters, such as Medea, Orestes, and Andromache, have been borrowed by later writers, playwrights, and composers throughout the Western world.

The French poet and dramatist Jean Racine adopted the plot and many of the characters in Euripides' tragedy *Hippolytus* when writing his masterpiece *Phèdre* (1677). The German composer Johann Wolfgang von Goethe based his opera *Iphigenie auf Tauris* (1779) on Euripides' *Iphigenia in Tauris*. The English poet William Morris knew well Euripides' *Medea* when he wrote *The Life and Death of Jason* (1867). American writers have also used Euripides' works as a basis for their own. The American poet Robinson Jeffers, for example, made verse adaptations of both *Medea* (1947) and *Hippolytus* (1954).

"In a conflict, never judge until you have heard both sides."

—from *Heraclidae* (around 428 B.C.), quoted by Aristophanes in *The Wasps* (422 B.C.)

FURTHER READING

Euripides. *Euripides*. Translated by A. S. Way. Loeb Classical Library. Cambridge: Harvard University Press, 1912.

Melchinger, Siegfried. *Euripides*. Translated by Samuel R. Rosenbaum. New York: Ungar, 1973.

Murray, Gilbert. *Euripides and His Age*. Reprint. Westport, Conn.: Greenwood, 1979.

Murray, Gilbert, Benjamin R. Rogers, et al., trans. *Fifteen Greek Plays*. New York: Oxford University Press, 1943.

Themistocles

DEFENDER OF ATHENS

The year was 490 B.C. and Greeks everywhere were talking about the Athenian victory on the Plain of Marathon. The mighty Persian army so recently encamped within Greece's borders had retreated. No longer did Greeks have to fear that foreigners from the East would sweep across their lands and take away their freedom. Greece was safe. Or was it?

Though most Greeks believed that the answer was yes, an Athenian named Themistocles felt that Marathon

The helmet crowning Themistocles is of the so-called Corinthian style, identifiable by its pot shape. It was the most popular with Athenian commanders and soldiers.

was just the first of many conflicts with the Persians, and he resolved to prepare himself and his city for the future.

By 490 B.C., Themistocles was a well-known political figure in Athens, with admirers and followers among the rich and the poor. This popularity was due mostly to his parentage. Although Themistocles did not trace his roots to the oldest and most aristocratic of Athenian families, he was related on his father's side to the noble Lycomidae family. As a result, Themistocles knew and associated with many of Athens' most prominent citizens. However, because his mother was not Athenian, his rights and privileges were sometimes limited. For example, if he wished to exercise, he had to go to the Cynosarges, a gymnasium located just outside the city gates that was open to those who were not of pure Athenian blood. The biographer Plutarch wrote that Themistocles often persuaded several friends who were full citizens to exercise with him at Cynosarges. This ability to influence others and argue his point of view were two characteristics that later worked to his advantage in politics.

Throughout the 490s B.C., Greece had watched and listened to reports of advancing Persian troops. What at first seemed a distant threat became increasingly more menacing. Themistocles believed that Greece should not wait until Persia stood at its gates but should prepare itself in advance. He saw Athens as the leader, not only in war but also in peace. Themistocles also saw Athens as a commercial power because of its close proximity to the Aegean Sea. Therefore, he argued, preparing for war was not wasteful. If Persia did not attack, Athens would be ready to take on the leadership of Greece and the Greek colonies in the Aegean Sea and along the coast of Asia Minor (present-day Turkey).

In 493 B.C., the Athenians elected Themistocles the chief archon of Athens. Nine in number, the archons had both judicial and executive duties. Because the leading archon, as the city's highest-ranking civil officer, gave his name to the year, 493 B.C. was recorded as the year of Themistocles. Only members of Athens' two highest-ranking classes of citizens were eligible to be archons, and when an archon's term ended, the records involving public funds were checked. If no discrepancies or misuse of funds was found, an ex-archon became a life member of the council known as the *Areopagos*. Members of the *Areopagos* were considered the keepers of the laws, for it was their duty to see that the laws were respected and properly implemented.

When Themistocles' records cleared at the end of his term, he joined the *Areopagos*. He still had the characteristics that he had had as a youth, an impetuous nature and a love of action. Plutarch later wrote that Themistocles learned quickly, enjoyed being involved in serious and important matters, and was eager to climb the political ladder.

As a *strategos* at the Battle of Marathon, one of the 10 annually elected generals, Themistocles welcomed the fame and glory that he and his troops received as victors, and he was willing to work to achieve more. Plutarch wrote that Themistocles thought constantly of Marathon's greatest hero, Miltiades, and when asked why he looked so tired, Themistocles answered, "The trophy of Miltiades will not let me sleep."

His ambitions and long-range plans for Athens, however, brought him into conflict with other powerful Athenians. One rival was the conservative statesman Aristides, who had also been a *strategos* at Marathon. Aristides and his followers no longer saw Persia as a threat to Greece and believed that, should the Persians ever plan a

"Tuning and playing the lyre cannot be counted among my accomplishments, but making a city that was small and inglorious glorious and great can."

—Themistocles, quoted in Plutarch's *Lives* (around 1st century A.D.)

second invasion, the Athenians would defend themselves as they had at the Battle of Marathon.

Themistocles disagreed with Aristides. Persia, he argued, had a powerful army as well as navy. If Greece planned to defeat Persia, Greece must also have trained soldiers and sailors. Athens, Themistocles continued, had already proved itself on the battlefield. Now it was time to prepare for a naval encounter. Themistocles ended his argument by appealing to the patriotism of his fellow Athenians. After acknowledging that Greece recognized Sparta's soldiers as the best on land, he asked why Athenians could not build the best Greek navy. Athens was perfectly situated, he continued, just a few miles inland from the Aegean Sea, which in turn flows south to the Mediterranean Sea and east toward the Black Sea. Naturally, he concluded, if Athens ruled the seas, it would control the trade on those waters.

To prove his argument Themistocles needed money to build ships. Miners had discovered a new silver vein at the Laurium mines just south of Athens. Although it was the custom for any extra revenue from the mines to be divided among the citizens, Themistocles asked that the money be used to start a navy. When some people disagreed with his reasoning, Themistocles mentioned that Athens' rival and enemy, the neighboring island of Aegina, already had a strong navy. This argument was forceful enough to win Themistocles a vote of confidence, and the money from the mines went to building a fleet of 200 triremes (warships with three banks of oars).

But the conservatives and their leader Aristides continued to oppose Themistocles. A special meeting of the *Ecclesia*, or assembly, the political body composed of all adult male citizens, was called, and its members decided to implement a new political practice called ostracism. This process gave the members of the assembly the right to decide whether Aristides and his political viewpoint threatened the safety of the state. Each member of the assembly who believed Athens was threatened wrote Aristides' name or the name of any politician they felt threatened Athens on a piece of clay known as an *ostrakon*. If at least 6,000 such votes were cast, then the person who received the most votes was ordered to leave Athens for a period of 10 years.

Although ostracism was supposed to prevent people from abusing power, not every person who was ostracized was actually a threat to Athens. On occasion, ostracism was used to get rid of a political rival. In fact, of the surviving *ostraka* (plural of *ostrakon*) that date to the 480s B.C., Themistocles' name has been found written on one-third of them. Fortunately for him, he never received the most votes. Yet many of his rivals did. Therefore it seems likely that his popularity was strong enough to end the political ambitions of those opposed to his views. As a result, Themistocles became the strongest and most powerful politician in Athens.

Another political reform of the 480s also helped Themistocles. Archons were now chosen by lot for a single one-year term instead of being elected. This change increased the power of the *strategoi* because the 10 generals could be re-elected. No records survive that prove Themistocles was re-elected *strategos*, but it is probable that his popularity kept him in that office during much of the 480s.

Themistocles

BORN
Around 524 B.C.
Athens, Greece

DIED
Around 460 B.C.
Magnesia, Asia Minor

PROFESSION
General and statesman

ACCOMPLISHMENTS
Persuaded Athenians to build a navy and led them against the Persians at Artemisium and Salamis; his strategy won Salamis, which directly led to the end of the Persian threat to the Greek mainland

As work on the fleet progressed, Themistocles argued for a good harbor for the ships. He thought that the waters near the old port of Phalerum were too exposed to storms and enemies, whereas the harbor of Piraeus was large enough to be a naval station and had its own natural defenses—a piece of land jutting out into the water on either side of a narrow entrance. Themistocles won, and today Piraeus continues to be Athens' chief port.

In the year 481 B.C. almost 10 years had passed since Marathon. However, news reports were reaching Greece that the Persian king Xerxes, son of Darius, had gathered the largest army the world had ever seen and was heading west. Fearing for their city, the Athenians decided to consult the oracle of the god Apollo at Delphi, in central Greece. The priestess listened to their plea and answered, "Wooden walls alone will remain and benefit the Athenians and their children." Baffled by such a reply, the Athenians began to ask: What did she mean? What was Apollo telling them? Finally, Themistocles gave his interpretation: "Wooden walls must mean a battle line of wooden ships." Soon all Athens was convinced that Themistocles was correct, and the Athenians set to building more ships.

Themistocles was not satisfied, however, for he knew victory depended on strength and unity, and he encouraged the Greek cities to work together. Although this would be difficult, because for decades they had fought each other continuously, Themistocles argued that without unity Greece would lose its freedom. He even encouraged the Athenians to ally themselves with their archrival, Sparta, and advised recalling exiles, including Aristides, because he thought their services could only aid the Greek cause.

Still he feared for Athens. In 480 B.C., the Athenians passed what was known as the Decree of Themistocles. A piece of marble inscribed with the decree was found in 1959 in Troezen, a city to the south of Athens. It confirmed what historians had always believed: Themistocles knew that the Persian king wanted to destroy Athens and enslave its people. As a result, he decreed that, if a Persian attack seemed imminent, the Athenians were to take their wives and children to Troezen and their possessions and old people to the island of Salamis just across the bay. The priestesses and guardians of the Acropolis were to remain and protect the temples of the gods, and all males of fighting age were to prepare for the Persian attack.

After he made this decree, Themistocles turned his attention to the battlefield and argued vehemently for an approach by land and sea. His arguments finally won approval, but he was not named commander in chief. Instead, the Athenians voted to let a Spartan hold that title, and Themistocles agreed to the wishes of the people.

In the spring of 480 B.C., a force of 10,000 Greeks marched north to Tempe, the northernmost point in Greece that could be properly defended. Themistocles led the Athenian troops, but when the Greeks realized that Tempe was just one of many passes in the area, they immediately abandoned their positions and retreated south.

Themistocles now resolved to persuade everyone to fight the Persians on land and on sea. This time, the Greeks listened and a land force led by the Spartan king Leonidas marched to defend the pass at Thermopylae, while

Excavators in Athens have uncovered many *ostraka* inscribed with names of leading Greek citizens, including that of Themistocles (top right). Although about one-third of the *ostraka* discovered have his name on them, Themistocles never received enough votes to be exiled.

Themistocles, as head of the Athenian navy, sailed to Artemisium, just east of Thermopylae. Tactically, the spot was perfect and the strategy should have worked, except a Greek traitor secretly led the Persians behind the Greek line of battle at Thermopylae.

Meanwhile, the Greek navy under Themistocles' guidance and encouragement had prevented the Persian ships from stopping along the coast for rest or from bringing aid to their soldiers at Thermopylae. In addition, because of the position of the Greek fleet, the Persians had had to head a little further out to sea, exposing themselves to late-summer squalls that destroyed many of their ships. Nevertheless, when the Greeks learned the fate of Leonidas and his troops, they abandoned Artemisium and headed south.

The Greeks now debated where to make their third stand. Many wanted to withdraw as far south as the Isthmus of Corinth, which meant abandoning all of northern Greece, including Athens, to the Persians. Themistocles refused to accept this alternative and argued that the fleet now resting at Salamis after its retreat from Artemisium should immediately prepare for battle.

Determined to face the Persians, yet knowing defeat was a possibility, Themistocles invoked his decree and the Athenians abandoned their city. Themistocles made the decision at the right time, for the Persians advanced and destroyed his beloved city.

Again Themistocles tried to convince the other Greek cities to use their "wooden wall" and meet the enemy at Salamis, but no one wanted to listen to him. Plutarch recorded that when the Spartan commander in chief said, "Remember that at the Olympic Games the athletes who make an early start are whipped," Themistocles replied, "True, but remember that those who are left behind are never crowned." Then another Greek challenged Themistocles' authority: "You no longer have any say, Themistocles! Your city is gone!" Themistocles immediately retorted, "If Greece votes to move the line of battle to the Isthmus,

I shall lead the Athenian fleet away and found a new homeland."

It was this ultimatum that ended all debate because the Greeks knew defeat was almost certain without the Athenian navy. Themistocles had won, but he still did not trust the other Greek cities and believed that some might retreat once they saw the massive number of Persian soldiers and ships advancing toward them. To prevent such action, he gave a message for King Xerxes to a trusted slave named Sicinnus who happened by chance to be Persian.

Xerxes eagerly listened as Sicinnus told him how Themistocles wished to warn the great king that the Greek fleet was about to abandon its position at Salamis and head south. "If you want to stop them, you must attack now" was Themistocles' advice.

So excited by the prospect of victory, Xerxes did not even question the message, but sent troops to close off an escape to the east and part of the fleet to block any escape to the west. Everything was working according to his plan, for Xerxes had trapped the Greek fleet and the Greeks would be forced to fight.

Confident of victory, Xerxes had seated himself on a golden throne on a hill above the bay and prepared to dictate the events to his secretaries as they happened. But within hours, Xerxes' confident attitude had turned to one of despair. The Greeks were winning and the Persians were in retreat. Themistocles' strategy had worked. Because the number of Persian ships far outnumbered his own, he had forced them to battle in a narrow, confined strait where skill, not numbers, was key to victory.

At night the fighting ended and the Greeks regrouped and prepared to renew battle the following day. Xerxes, however, had had enough and ordered his forces to retreat. The next morning the Greeks found the bay empty. Themistocles became a national hero and was honored for his strategy, which had led to victory at Salamis and made Athens the acknowledged ruler of the Greek seas. Two more Greek victories in the following year ended Xerxes' dream of conquering Greece.

Now that the Persian threat had been crushed, Themistocles began to focus on making Athens the chief city in Greece. His leadership during the war had won him the respect of all Greece. Even the Spartans publicly praised his wisdom and skill and showed him special honor by presenting him with their best chariot.

At home, Themistocles encouraged all Athenians to return to their city and begin the work of rebuilding the defensive walls and the buildings, because he believed that a strong city needed protective walls. The Spartans, who had no walls of their own and did not believe in them, began to wonder if the victory at Salamis had made Athens too self-confident and too powerful.

To prevent problems between the two cities, Themistocles offered to travel to Sparta and discuss the situation with the Spartans. Once there, Themistocles talked and wasted time with excuses and lies until he felt he had given the Athenians enough time to rebuild the walls. Excavations in the 1990s show how the Athenians, in their haste to finish the construction, even used tombstones and column drums from destroyed buildings.

Themistocles, however, was not content with just fortified city walls. If Athens was to be the leader on land and on sea, its harbor of Piraeus also needed defensive walls. The Athenians agreed with Themistocles and construction began on the port. Such actions made Sparta and even some

"My son wields more power than anyone in Greece because the Athenians rule the Greeks, I rule the Athenians, the boy's mother rules me, and the boy rules his mother."

—Themistocles, quoted in Plutarch's *Lives* (around 1st century A.D.)

conservative Athenians increasingly uneasy about Themistocles and his policies. Leaders of the Athenian opposition included Aristides and Miltiades' son Cimon. Gradually, Themistocles' influence began to decrease, and sometime around 471 B.C., just nine years after the Battle of Salamis, the Athenians voted to ostracize him.

Themistocles went first to the neighboring city of Argos, but when he learned that the Athenians had condemned him to death because they believed that he had joined with the Spartan traitor Pausanias, he left for northern Greece. His next stop was the court of King Admetus in Epirus. There, according to Plutarch, the queen placed one of the royal children in Themistocles' arms and told him to sit on the floor of the palace until Admetus entered. Acknowledging and accepting that Themistocles' actions meant he was asking for refuge, Admetus refused to surrender Themistocles to the envoys from Athens or Sparta.

Still Themistocles found life difficult, and after he arrived in Asia Minor he was forced to disguise himself as a woman and take advantage of the Persian custom that required women to travel in covered carriages in order to escape being discovered himself. Meanwhile, his friends in Athens had helped his wife and children leave the city and then gathered his possessions to send on to him.

When Themistocles learned that Artaxerxes, the son and heir of King Xerxes, was offering a reward for his capture, he decided to seek a meeting with Artaxerxes. Without revealing his identity, he asked for an audience and was told he must be willing to bow before the king. Themistocles agreed and, after bowing to Artaxerxes, clearly announced that he was "Themistocles the Athenian, banished from Athens by his own people. I have brought great harm to Persia, but I have also shown kindness for it was I who persuaded the Greeks not to follow your father's defeated forces home."

The king could scarcely believe his good fortune. After careful thought, he decided to befriend the Athenian and make use of his military and political expertise. Themistocles asked only that he be given time to learn the Persian language before entering into the king's service. Artaxerxes agreed.

A year later, Themistocles returned and spoke directly to the king, using no interpreter. The Persian king was so impressed by Themistocles' courage and directness that he treated him royally. But not all of Artaxerxes' advisers were so impressed by the Athenian, and Themistocles decided it was safer to move away from the court to Magnesia, one of the places Artaxerxes had put under Themistocles' control.

When Themistocles died at the age of 65, the people of Magnesia were so grieved that they buried him in a magnificent tomb in the center of the city and granted special privileges to his family. Years later, the Greeks reported that Themistocles' relatives had secretly taken his bones back to Greece and buried them near Athens.

FURTHER READING

Bradford, Ernle. *Thermopylae: The Battle for the West*. 1980. Reprint. New York: Da Capo, 1993.

Lenardon, Robert J. *The Saga of Themistocles*. London: Thames & Hudson, 1978.

Podlecki, Anthony J. *The Life of Themistocles*. Montreal: McGill–Queen's University Press, 1975.

More Ancient Greeks to Remember

Xenophanes (latter half of the 6th century B.C.) was a native of Colophon, an Ionian city in Asia Minor (present-day Turkey). He left home around the age of 25 and spent the rest of his life, more than 60 years, in exile, probably because Colophon and Asia Minor were conquered by the Persians. As he traveled around the Greek world, Xenophanes asked pointed questions about Greek gods and religious beliefs that had a lasting influence on contemporary and future philosophers. He disagreed completely with the idea of anthropomorphic gods—that is, gods who look and act like humans—and reasoned that if animals such as cows had hands to draw, then they would draw their gods in the shape of cows. Xenophanes believed that there was only one god and that this god did not create any other deities. He further stated that this one god gave life to the entire universe. Only fragments of his poetic works have survived.

Heraclitus (active around 500 B.C.) of Ephesus, on the coast of Asia Minor, saw the world as a constantly changing place where ideas remain the same but life is one continuous flow of restless activity. A surviving fragment from his writings neatly summarizes his thoughts: "No person can step into the same river twice, for different waters are always streaming past."

Nicknamed by his contemporaries as "the Obscure" and "the Riddler," Heraclitus wrote pieces that were confusing and difficult to understand. He does not appear to have been a very happy individual, distrusting most humans for their lack of knowledge and understanding. He wrote, "People do not remember what they do when they are awake, just as they forget what they do when they are asleep."

Heraclitus saw the world as a constant conflict between opposites and gave as an example, "The road going up and the road going down is actually the same road." For Heraclitus, the image of a constantly burning fire represented stability produced through change. The *logos*, or universal principle, that governed everything gave meaning to this change. This recognition of a unifying force was Heraclitus' main contribution to philosophical thought. Heraclitus' ideas influenced the 4th-century B.C. Greek philosopher Plato.

Miltiades (around 550–489 B.C.) is credited with making the decision to fight the Persian army on the Plain of Marathon. Accounts also say he was instrumental in devising the strategy that brought Greece victory. After defeating the Persians, Miltiades persuaded the Athenians to make a forced march to Athens before the defeated Persians could attack the empty and unprotected city. Miltiades' quick

Still visible on the surviving remains of this Athenian helmet is the phrase "Miltiades dedicated me." Most likely, the Greek hero wore it in battle.

thinking saved Athens, and he was given a hero's reception there. The Athenians erected one statue to him in Athens and another at Delphi, the center of worship to the god Apollo and one of the most sacred religious sites in the ancient world.

In 480 B.C., when the Persians advanced for a second time against Greece, Cimon (before 510–around 450 B.C.) immediately joined the Athenian forces and proved himself a capable fighter. After the Persians had been driven away, a fleet was sent to free the Greek colonies in the Aegean Sea from Persian control. A Spartan named Pausanias took command of the operation and Aristides, a close associate of Cimon, led the Athenian forces.

Victory came quickly, and the Greeks wrested control of the colonies from Persia. Pausanias' haughty rule, however, and his close association with the Persians soon brought about his fall from power. Cimon and Aristides, who had proved themselves trustworthy leaders, assumed command of the entire Greek fleet and decided to form a league of Greek cities that would fight to keep Persians off Greek soil. The league chose Delos, the Aegean island sacred to the god Apollo, as its headquarters, and the new organization was called the Delian League. All members were equal, but Athens was recognized as the head.

With each victory against the Persians, Cimon's popularity grew, and so too did the number of cities that joined the Delian League. Reports of his kindness, justice, and wisdom also spread and won him respect, but his popularity invited jealousy and his enemies looked for a way to discredit him.

In 462 B.C., when Sparta asked Athens for help against rebelling Helots (the people who worked Sparta's lands but who had no rights), Cimon argued that Athens should send an army. After much debate, the Athenians voted to send Cimon to Sparta with 4,000 soldiers. Soon after Cimon's arrival, however, the Spartans changed their mind and ordered the Athenians home. Pericles, the leading statesman of the time, and all those who had opposed Athens' intervention in the revolt took this as an insult and argued that neither Sparta nor anyone who had favored cooperation with Sparta was to be trusted. The insult gave Cimon's enemies the opportunity to request a vote for ostracism, and Cimon was banished from Athens.

The tensions between Athens and Sparta grew until 457 B.C., when the two cities met on the battlefield at Tanagra in Boeotia. Always a loyal Athenian citizen, Cimon requested permission to join the fight, but he was rebuffed. Undeterred, Cimon rallied his followers who had not been ostracized and encouraged each one to prove himself a true Athenian patriot by fighting bravely. They followed his orders so ardently that none survived.

The Athenians were stunned when they learned of the deaths and regretted their unfair judgment of Cimon. Pericles proposed a measure to recall him, and once home from exile, Cimon worked at arranging a truce between the two warring cities. Around 451 B.C., Athens and Sparta signed the Five Years' Peace. Cimon's work, however, was not over.

Persia was still a powerful empire, and the Greeks planned a new offensive with Cimon as the leader. Soon after leaving Athens, Cimon died, either from illness or from a wound received in battle.

Aristides (elected archon in 489–88 B.C.) is best remembered for the honorary title awarded him by his fellow Athenians—"Aristides the Just." A supporter of democratic reforms and a true patriot, Aristides believed strongly in defending the freedom of the Greek city-states. One of the 10 *strategoi*, the generals who led the Athenians to victory against the Persians at the Battle of Marathon in 490 B.C., Aristides was elected the following year to the highest office, archon. In all his judgments, Aristides tried to be fair and not show favoritism.

As a staunch conservative, Aristides often found himself opposed to the leading progressive, Themistocles. In 482 B.C., probably as a result of Themistocles' influence, Aristides was ostracized and forced to leave Athens for 10 years. Two years later, however, when the Persians advanced against Greece, Themistocles urged that Aristides be recalled to Athens. Aristides was recalled, and he immediately led the Athenian forces to victory.

Soon after, Themistocles himself was ostracized and Aristides returned to power, along with another conservative named Cimon. When Sparta was forced to recall its general, Pausanias, as commander of the Greek fleet because he was suspected of conspiring with the Persians, Aristides was given the command. This increased Athens' influence and power, and in 477 B.C. Aristides formed the Delian League, whose purpose was to keep the Persians away from Greek lands. Aristides also established the tribute system, which determined how much each member of the league had to contribute. This league came to form the basis of Athens' empire in the following years.

Polygnotus (active 475–447 B.C.) was ancient Greece's first great painter. Born on the northern Aegean island of Thasos, he learned the art of painting from his father. In honor of his skill as an artist, the Athenians granted Polygnotus the rights of citizenship. The Athenian statesman Cimon was his patron. None of Polygnotus' paintings survive, but records show that they adorned many public buildings in Athens, including the "Painted Porch" of the Propylaea, the enormous gateway to the Acropolis.

A painter of mostly mythological and historical subjects, Polygnotus placed his figures up and down the painting to give an idea of perspective, instead of on a single line at ground level as was the custom. Because he wanted to portray his characters as individuals with a moral purpose, he did not have his figures interact, but depicted them deep in thought or concerned with what they were doing.

The positioning of the figures on this 5th-century Athenian vase—not in a line, but up and down the space—reflects the influence of Polygnotus, who used this technique to show perspective.

Pausanias (died around 467–66 B.C.) was the son of a Spartan king and had been trained since birth to live according to the very strict Spartan code. His courage and military skill won him the position of commander in chief of the Greek land and sea forces against the Persians at Plataea. His victory there in 479 B.C. finally drove the Persians from Greek soil and ensured Greek independence. Pausanias then continued his drive against the Persians, expelling them from the Greek city-states along the coast of Asia Minor.

After capturing Byzantium (present-day Istanbul), Pausanias changed his life-style. He no longer followed the rigid Spartan life-style but began to spend the riches that he was accumulating on luxuries. His fellow Greeks resented his arrogance toward them and his acceptance of Eastern customs. In addition, many Greeks began to suspect that Pausanias had entered into negotiations with the Persian king, and envoys were sent to Sparta with this information. The Spartans recalled Pausanias, and the Athenians were given the right to name a new commander in chief of the Greek forces. Pausanias was not convicted for his behavior but returned to Byzantium, where he was exiled by Cimon for actions not befitting a Greek.

After settling in Colonae, another Greek city-state in Asia Minor, Pausanias soon fell under suspicion of conspiring with the Persians. Again he was recalled to Sparta, and again he managed to get himself acquitted. Soon after, he was suspected by the Spartans of plotting with the Helots (the state-owned class of people who

In this illustration from about A.D. 1200, the artist has borrowed Empedocles' idea that the universe is composed of four basic elements. Here, the elements are depicted as people: Aer (air), Ignis (fire), Terra (earth), abbreviated as "Tra," and Aqua (water).

tilled the lands of Sparta) and of inciting a revolt.

Realizing his danger, Pausanias took refuge in a temple in Sparta. Unwilling to kill him on sacred ground, the chief officials decided to wall up all the entrances to the temple, leaving Pausanias to starve.

Parmenides (born 515–510 B.C.) is said to have emigrated to Athens from Elea in southern Italy at the age of 65. As the first Greek philosopher to use rigorous and continual arguments to seek answers to questions about life, Parmenides greatly influenced his successors, including Zeno, Socrates, Plato, and Aristotle. The first philosopher to consider the meaning of "to be," Parmenides argued that only what exists can be understood and that what does not exist is impossible to understand. As a way of explaining his philosophy, Parmenides wrote a poem entitled *On Nature*. Using himself as the main character, he journeyed in a chariot from night into day, where he was welcomed by a goddess who proceeded to tell him the truth about what is. She also informed him that ideas put forth by humans cannot be accepted with complete confidence.

Empedocles (around 492–432 B.C.), an aristocrat from Acragas in Sicily, was not only a philosopher but also a statesman, orator, and doctor. There are many stories about his curing very sick individuals and even about raising people from the dead. A believer in democracy, Empedocles is said to have refused the kingship of Acragas when it was offered to him. Later, when exiled from his hometown, he settled in southern Greece.

In his poem *On Nature*, Empedocles presented his explanation of the universe. Although he was influenced by Parmenides, who believed in the unity of all things, Empedocles held the conviction that the universe was composed of four basic elements—earth, air, fire, and water. Believing that nothing could come from nothing,

Empedocles argued that things change only as the four elements change in relation to one another. What creates change are the forces of love and strife. Love makes the elements mingle together, whereas strife makes them move away from each other.

In another poem, entitled *Purifications*, he discusses the transmigration of souls. Empedocles believed that the soul of anyone who commits a sin must wander the earth in many bodies and be tossed about from one element to the other. Empedocles believed that his need to wander the earth was almost at an end because his spirit had already spent time in various bodies, including those of a bird, a bush, a fish, a boy, and a girl. Therefore he said of himself, "I live among people as an immortal god."

Protagoras (around 490–about 420 B.C.) was a native of the prosperous Greek city of Abdera in Thrace. Like so many other thinkers and artists of the time, he migrated to Athens, the intellectual and cultural center of the Greek world. A respected and righteous individual, Protagoras was chosen by the statesman Pericles to draw up a code of laws for the new Greek colony of Thurii, founded by Athenians in Italy in 444 B.C. By profession Protagoras was a teacher who traveled from town to town and was paid to give lessons. Recognized as one of the first sophists—teachers who used persuasive and clever arguments as their means of instruction—Protagoras was very successful and spent most of his time teaching in Athens. Two of his sayings neatly capture his philosophy on life: "The human being is the measure of all things" and "As for the gods, I do not know whether they exist or do not exist. What prevents me from knowing is the difficulty of the topic and the shortness of human life."

Zeno (born around 490 B.C.) was a friend of Parmenides and admired his rational way of thinking. Like Parmenides, Zeno was a native of the Greek colony of Elea in southern Italy. Around the age of 40, he is thought to have accompanied the much older Parmenides to Athens. At the time, the followers of Pythagoras' philosophy were considered scientific and mathematical experts. Parmenides' philosophical ideas, however, ran opposite to those of the Pythagoreans, and Zeno spent his life proving that Parmenides' theories were correct. To do this, he posed several arguments, all involving motion, and then used logic to prove them.

The most famous debate involved a theoretical race between the Greek hero Achilles and a turtle. Because Achilles gave the turtle a headstart, Zeno said Achilles could never win, for every time Achilles reached a point that the turtle had reached, the turtle was already at a point farther ahead. Another argument involved a flying arrow. Zeno asked, "If at every instant of its flight a flying arrow is at rest, then when does it move?" Zeno's questions encouraged others to use logic as a means of discussing and proving ideas. It also forced his contemporaries to analyze Pythagorean ideas.

Democritus (born around 460 B.C.) loved to learn, and he spent much time traveling and studying the customs and practices of peoples in Persia, Egypt, Babylon, Ethiopia, and India. A native of the Thracian city of Abdera, on the northern coast of the Aegean Sea, Democritus is believed to have visited Athens. His stay, however, was brief. The writer Diogenes Laertius of the 3rd century A.D. quoted Democritus as saying, "I went to Athens, but no one knew me." Yet Democritus was not a cynical person. For him, the goal of a good life was cheerfulness, which meant that a person should live in peace and not be afraid of anything. To accomplish this, Democritus believed people needed to know their own abilities and live accordingly. Because of his belief in cheerfulness, later generations referred to Democritus as the "laughing philosopher."

Only fragments survive of the more than 60 books Democritus wrote on subjects that ranged from music to mathematics to ethics to philosophy. Democritus was interested in how the world was formed and said, "nothing exists but small particles called atoms and empty space."

For Democritus, atoms were solid, uncuttable, and unable to be destroyed. All were identical in composition but differed from each other in shape, size, and perhaps weight. According to Democritus, atoms continually moved through the emptiness or void that existed wherever there were no atoms. Sometimes they collided with each other and combined to form various clusters of atoms. Such collisions were always random, but the manner of collision, as well as the shape, size, and weight of the atoms involved, determined the nature of the combined form. The result of atoms colliding and combining was the world and everything that exists in the world, including humans.

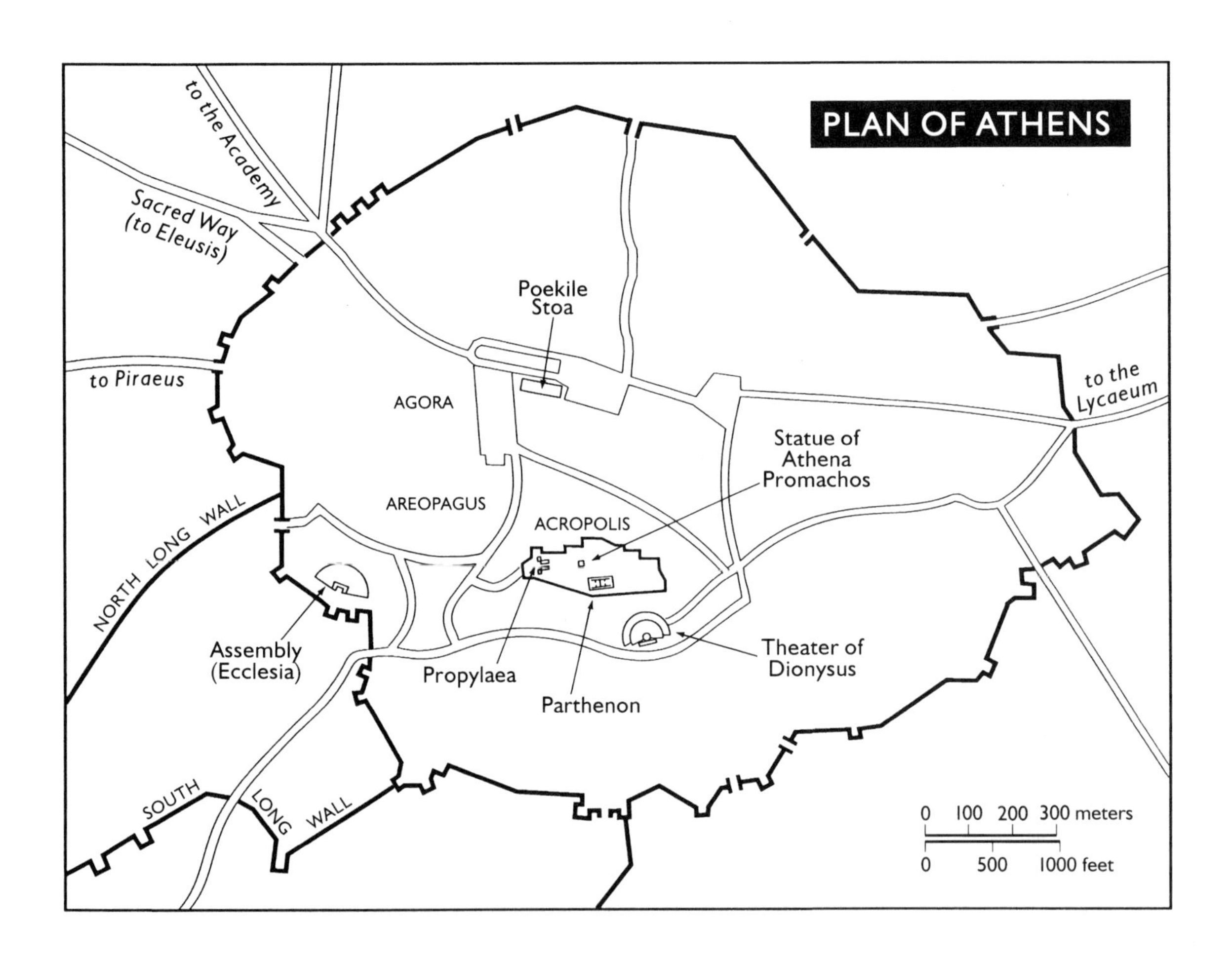
PLAN OF ATHENS
to the Academy
Sacred Way (to Eleusis)
to Piraeus
Poekile Stoa
AGORA
AREOPAGUS
ACROPOLIS
Statue of Athena Promachos
to the Lycaeum
NORTH LONG WALL
Assembly (Ecclesia)
Propylaea
Parthenon
Theater of Dionysus
SOUTH LONG WALL
0 100 200 300 meters
0 500 1000 feet

Pericles

STATESMAN OF ATHENS

As a young boy, Pericles experienced firsthand the intrigue, exile, and assassination that were part of the political scene in Athens in the 5th century B.C. His father, Xanthippus, was a member of one of Athens' oldest

Always ready to fight for freedom and for Athens, Pericles recognized the value of human life: "Trees, even if they are cut and trimmed, quickly grow again, but if men are destroyed, it is not easy to get them again."

3 Defending the Tradition (460–400 B.C.)

By 450 B.C., the Greek city-states, especially Athens, had proved their military power on land and on sea. The Greek world seemed secure and trade across the Aegean and Mediterranean seas prospered once again. As the acknowledged cultural center of the Mediterranean world, Athens was bustling with activity. This was the period of Athens' master statesman, Pericles, who was determined to make his city reflect its global standing. Under his patronage, the arts and sciences flourished and creativity was encouraged. Later periods would call this the Golden Age of Greece, although it should really be called the Golden Age of Athens because Athens was where everything was happening.

But the period was short-lived. The Greeks' fierce independent streak brought their city-states, especially Athens and Sparta, into conflict. Athens saw itself as the leader and strove continually to assert its influence and to amass more power. Several Greek city-states—especially Sparta—disagreed with such actions, and in 431 B.C. the Peloponnesian War broke out between Sparta and Athens. The Peloponnesus, in the southern part of Greece, was an area controlled by Sparta. As in all wars, both sides suffered casualties, the disruption of the daily routine, and irreparable damage to economic and cultural life.

Part 3 of *Ancient Greeks* profiles the individuals who valued Greek tradition and spent their lives defending what they considered to be the essential ingredients of that tradition. Not all Greeks agreed on the essential ingredients, and because the Greek sense of independence was strong, the people who held contrasting views of this tradition often felt that the battlefield was the only way to protect their interpretation of it.

IN THIS PART

aristocratic families and a prominent political figure. During the 480s, Xanthippus was ostracized—forced to leave Athens for 10 years when political rivals accused him of aiding the Persians.

In 480 B.C., Pericles experienced the joy of Xanthippus' return home after Athens' leaders declared a general amnesty for political exiles. The reason for the amnesty was political—the Athenian leaders realized that to defeat the advancing Persian army, every Greek would be needed to fight. In 479 B.C., the Athenians elected Xanthippus one of the 10 *strategoi*, or generals, and as commander of the Athenian fleet at Mycale, he routed the Persian navy.

Pericles' mother, Agariste, also traced her roots to one of Athens' noblest families. Her uncle Cleisthenes is traditionally regarded as the creator of Athenian democracy. As a teenager, Pericles probably heard many discussions about the merits of democracy and the rights of individuals. Helping him shape his own opinion were his teachers, especially Damon, Zeno of Elea, and Anaxagoras. All three made Pericles look more critically at the world about him by encouraging him to ask questions about existing laws, traditions, and customs. From them he also learned to stay calm, to be even-tempered, and to analyze a situation before taking action.

According to the Greek biographer Plutarch, Anaxagoras had the greatest influence on Pericles. Anaxagoras argued that the *nous*, a supreme Intelligence or Mind, rather than chance, controlled creation. Pericles listened closely to Anaxagoras, especially when the latter used reason to explain the workings of the universe and natural phenomena such as earthquakes and eclipses. To Pericles, Anaxagoras' reasons made much more sense than the traditional beliefs, in which gods and goddesses were the cause of everything. Such liberal thinking was contrary to Greek religious rules and would later form the basis for criminal charges against Anaxagoras, but it freed Pericles from clinging blindly to the traditional attitudes that governed much of Greek life. Plutarch later recorded an incident that clearly illustrates Anaxagoras' influence on Pericles.

It was midday and the sun was shining above the blue Aegean Sea, when suddenly the sky darkened and the waters turned gray. Pericles, about to command his Athenian fleet to set sail, saw the terrified faces of the crew and knew exactly what they were thinking—that the gods had caused the weather to change because they did not want the Athenians to sail. Then, just as suddenly, the sun began to reappear and the day brightened. Pericles knew he had to act quickly to convince his crew that the eclipse was a natural occurrence and had nothing to do with the gods. He took his cloak and placed it in front of the eyes of the steersman.

"Does the darkness caused by my cloak frighten or hurt you?" asked Pericles. "No," answered the steersman. "Then how does this darkness differ from the first darkness, when it was only something larger than my cloak that covered the sun?" With this argument, Pericles eased the minds of his sailors and the naval expedition set sail.

The ability to think quickly and, at the same time, to analyze a situation and act accordingly were traits that helped Pericles win power and respect. Reared in a family that had always taken an active part in politics, Pericles aspired to do the same. But the time was not yet right, and his first major public act was in the theater, not in politics.

Every year, the chief magistrate of Athens chose three playwrights to present their plays at the Great Dionysia

Rising on an outcrop of rock above the Agora was the Acropolis, crowned by the Parthenon, the temple dedicated to Athena. During the Golden Age of Athens, Pericles hired architects and artisans to refurbish buildings and temples on the Acropolis and to construct new ones, such as the Parthenon. This scale model represents the area during the 2nd to 1st century B.C.

festival held in honor of Dionysus, the god of wine and merriment. The magistrate also named three Athenians as *choregoi*, each of whom was personally responsible for providing one of the playwrights with a chorus for his plays. In 472 B.C., Pericles was chosen to provide the chorus for the playwright Aeschylus. When Aeschylus' plays won first prize, Pericles also won public recognition because his name was inscribed on the victory lists.

The next few years were relatively quiet ones for Pericles. He watched as the statesmen Themistocles, Aristides, and Cimon struggled to impose their rule on the city. Ousting them was impossible, for each had played a major role in the wars against the Persians and each had many staunch supporters.

Political events, however, worked to Pericles' advantage. By 471 B.C., support for Aristides had waned and Themistocles was banished forever from Athens. Cimon alone remained to oppose Pericles. Cimon led the conservative party, which supported limited political rights for all Athenians. Yet he recognized Athens' dependence on a strong navy, and he honored Athens' sailors and soldiers. Cimon saw Sparta as an ally, not as an enemy, and promoted good relations between the two cities. Pericles, on the other hand, recognized the rising class of Athenians who had fought to make Athens the leader and he promoted more rights for them. Pericles was not pro-Sparta, because he saw the potential for great conflict between the two cities.

Nevertheless, Cimon's following was too strong for Pericles to challenge, and the growth of the Delian League was bringing great prestige, power, and wealth to Athens and to Cimon. Pericles saw the battlefield as the only way for him to prove his ability and courage, and he devoted himself to becoming a strong military leader.

Meanwhile, trouble was brewing in Athens between the aristocrats and the liberals. Ephialtes, Themistocles' successor as leader of the liberals and a man known for his honesty, had begun to push for more political rights for the lower classes. When one of Cimon's military campaigns resulted in heavy financial losses, Ephialtes decided to attack Cimon in Athens and charge him with accepting a bribe. The accusation was weak and difficult to prove, but it was the liberals' attempt to defeat the conservatives.

At the time, the legal profession did not exist and Athenians were responsible for presenting their own cases to the courts or sending an eloquent speaker to do it for them. Ephialtes chose Pericles to prosecute Cimon. Plutarch tells us that Cimon's sister Elpinice disregarded the Athenian custom that kept women at home and personally asked Pericles for mercy for her brother. According to Plutarch, Pericles replied, "Elpinice, you are too old to meddle in such affairs as this."

Whether Elpinice's visit influenced him or whether he realized the evidence was only circumstantial, Pericles presented the case clearly and well but did not use aggressive tactics. Cimon was acquitted. Yet the trial brought Pericles fame and served to make him a leader of the liberals.

Cimon was still the most powerful man in Athens, but he remained so for only one more year. In 462 B.C., Sparta asked Athens for help in quelling a Helot revolt. (Helots were a class of people who worked as slaves for the Spartans and had no political or personal rights.) The Spartans found it difficult to raise an army because two years earlier an earthquake had leveled much of the area and killed many citizens. Despite opposition from the liberals, Cimon convinced the Athenians to send help to Sparta.

Then, for no apparent reason, the Spartans sent Cimon and his 4,000 Athenian soldiers home. Taking this as a personal affront, the Athenians voted to ostracize Cimon in 461 B.C. In retaliation, Ephialtes was assassinated, a murder presumably engineered by the conservatives. Pericles now stood alone as the leading Athenian statesman.

Immediately he began making many reforms aimed at giving more power to the lower classes—those people who had fought in the infantry, rowed the warships, and fed the Athenians with the produce from their farms. Under Pericles' guidance, the people's assembly became the most powerful governing body. Every male Athenian citizen over the age of 18 could become a member, voice his opinion, and propose measures on which the assembly would vote.

Pericles also pushed for legislation that opened up the office of archon (a high-ranking, elected public official) to a larger segment of the population, not just members of the upper classes. Because archons automatically became members of the *Areopagos* (Senate) after their year in office, this government body became increasingly more representative. Pericles strongly believed that it was the duty of every citizen to participate in government affairs and considered those who did not to be worthless.

Yet Pericles' democracy did not include everyone. Slaves had no political rights, nor did resident foreigners. In 451–450 B.C., Pericles introduced a law that restricted citizenship to men born to Athenian parents. Although it was a limited democracy, Athens' form of government became the basis of many modern democracies, including those of Great Britain and the United States.

With the right to govern Athens in the hands of its citizens, Pericles turned his attention to making the courts more democratic. Trial by jury was the accepted rule, with jurors drawn from the whole body of Athenian citizens. To be one of the 6,000 jurors, a male citizen had to be at least 30 years of age and had to volunteer for the position. A minimum of 201 jurors was selected to hear minor offenses; additional jurors were needed for serious offenses. Pericles approved of the system, but he argued that poor citizens could not afford to lose a day's pay to serve on a jury. And so he decreed that jurors would be paid daily for their services. Gradually, he extended payment benefits to members of the council, archons, other public officials who were chosen by lot, and soldiers and sailors on duty. The philosopher Aristotle estimated that more than 20,000 citizens received pay for serving as public officials at any given time during Pericles' rule.

Not everyone, however, agreed with Pericles' belief in payment for services. Some believed such a system would hurt Athens financially. Others, mostly aristocrats, saw payment as a threat to the power of the upper class. Nobody, however, was strong enough to outmaneuver Pericles.

Although he was extremely energetic, Pericles did not spend time at parties or at social gatherings as so many of his contemporaries did. Pericles preferred to work toward his goal of making Athens the capital of the Greek world, the leader in the arts, and the center of philosophical thought.

Under Pericles' leadership, the Delian League gradually changed from a confederacy of Greek cities united as

"Outstanding individuals have the whole world as their memorial."

—Pericles, quoted in *History of Peloponnesian War* (5th century B.C.) by Thucydides

allies against the Persians to a confederacy of cities guided and dominated by Athens. Again, not all agreed that Athens should use military might or persuasion to force Greek people to acknowledge Athens as the leader, but no one dared to oppose Pericles openly.

Aware that Persian loyalists were causing unrest in the cities of the Delian League, Pericles began to worry about the safety of the league's treasury on the island of Delos, so he proposed that the treasury be transferred to Athens. This meant that all league members had to pay their dues directly to Athens. Originally, the dues had been payable in ships and troops, but over time many cities had found it easier to pay in gold. Fearing retaliation, few cities refused to pay their share, and the coffers in Athens soon overflowed.

With league matters settled, Pericles turned his attention to Sparta because he believed Athens and Sparta needed to settle their differences in order to ensure peace throughout the Greek world. Pericles asked Cimon, his former rival, to seek a lasting peace agreement with Sparta. In 451 B.C., Cimon negotiated a five-year truce.

Pericles then focused his energies on ending hostilities with Persia and sent Cimon with a flotilla of Athenian warships to attack the Persian forces on the island of Cyprus. When Cimon fell ill and died during the campaign, Pericles asked Cimon's brother-in-law, Callias, to meet with the Persian king Artaxerxes to negotiate a peace agreement. In 449 B.C., after 40 years of warfare, Persia and Athens signed a peace treaty.

Still Pericles was not satisfied. He wanted an agreement of cooperation ratified by all the Greek cities, so he sent representatives throughout the Greek world asking envoys from the major cities to meet in Athens. Many approved of the meeting, but Sparta, miffed that Athens, not Sparta, would host the all-Greek conference, refused to participate. Cimon had died and there was no other Athenian who could persuade the Spartans to change their minds. Sparta's allies also refused to join, and consequently the conference was never held.

Undeterred, Pericles turned his attention to Athens and made plans to rebuild the city in a manner befitting its position in the Greek world. Because the Athenians had played the major role in defeating the Persians, Pericles thought it proper to use the league's funds to rebuild what the Persians had destroyed. Pericles also argued that a building program would create jobs for the many Athenians left unemployed because of the peace with Persia. One of the first projects undertaken was the construction of defensive walls connecting Athens with Piraeus, the neighboring city that served as Athens' port and harbor. Known as the Long Walls, these fortifications were a series of parallel walls designed to prevent enemies from blocking Athens' access to the sea and to its warships.

Sparta, meanwhile, had been watching Athens and feared that its neighbor was becoming too powerful. To further its own cause, Sparta began to arouse anti-Athenian feelings in cities that had not always agreed with Athens. Sparta's tactics worked, and Athens was forced to send troops to help its allies defend themselves against the Spartans and their allies.

Pericles, however, had no intention of involving himself in a war that would destroy what he had worked so hard to accomplish. He sought peace with Sparta and sent envoys to speak with King Plistoanax. No one knows exactly what happened, but the king suddenly withdrew his forces from Athenian territory and returned home. Soon after, the Spartans exiled Plistoanax on bribery charges. Plutarch later wrote that when Pericles submitted an account of what he had spent in this campaign against Sparta, one entry read: 10 talents (a very large sum of money) for necessities. Because surviving records show that no assembly member asked Pericles to account for this expense, it is possible that the Athenians understood that Pericles had paid the money as part of an agreement that would protect the city.

In the winter of 446–45 B.C., Sparta and Athens signed the Thirty-Years' Peace. Finally peace seemed to have settled on Pericles' world. Yet Athens knew it must maintain its military strength to keep this peace. Consequently, the *strategoi* continued to be the most powerful public officials and were the only ones eligible for re-election. Pericles was re-elected to this post every year from 443 until the year he died, 429 B.C.

The relative calm that followed the signing of the peace treaty between Athens and Sparta gave Pericles the chance to return to his building program. The buildings that rose, as chisels, mallets, and carts hauling marble slabs and drums replaced swords, shields, and warhorses, would over the centuries become the symbol of Athens. This brief 14-year period has become known as the Golden Age. Centered in Athens, its effects reached beyond the city to all of Greece and eventually throughout the Western world.

Pericles placed the sculptor Phidias in charge of the work on the Acropolis and assigned the master architects Ictinus and Callicrates as his assistants. The chief focus of their work was to be a massive temple dedicated to Athena, the patron goddess of Athens. Athena, who never married, was also worshiped under the title Athena Parthenos (Athena the Maiden). Thus the temple came to be known as the Parthenon. Inside was a regal, colossal statue of the goddess, approximately 39 feet tall and sculpted by Phidias. Such a masterpiece needed an appropriate approach, so the architects designed the Sacred Way, a road leading up to the Acropolis and through a magnificent marble entrance known as the Propylaea before winding its way to the Parthenon.

Because Pericles believed the city's past as well as its present deserved to be honored, he commissioned artists and architects to refurbish the old temples and buildings on the Acropolis. New styles emerged as artists and sculptors no longer crafted stiff human forms but attempted to capture the human body in action. They reasoned that the human body that had won the Athenians so many victories deserved to be portrayed more realistically. As news of these works of art reached the cities of the Greek world, many artisans chose to see for themselves the accomplishments of the Athenian artists.

Pericles' dream of a capital city was coming true. Philosophers, mathematicians, and writers traveled to Athens from around the Greek world, and soon the ideas of Athens began to circulate around the lands bordering the Aegean and Mediterranean seas. The great majority of Athenians admired and respected Pericles and saw in him qualities that were almost divine. They even nicknamed him the Olympian because he seemed in some ways godlike.

There were some Athenians, however, who envied Pericles' power and believed that his role as "leading citizen" for almost 30 years had prevented the rise of other potential leaders. Although afraid to attack Pericles personally, these people were determined to undermine his popularity, and in 438 B.C., they began to attack his friends. First they accused Anaxagoras of impiety, saying that he considered natural causes rather than the gods responsible for earthquakes and the like. To escape imprisonment or death, Anaxagoras went into exile.

Next they accused the sculptor Phidias of stealing some of the gold he had been given for the statue of Athena Parthenos. Phidias proved his innocence when he removed all the plates of gold from the statue and their weight equaled what he had been given. In fact, it was Pericles' foresight that saved Phidias, for Pericles had requested that all the gold used on the statue be detachable in case Athens needed money for an emergency.

The third attack was the most vicious and caused Pericles the most pain. As a young man, Pericles had married a relative, but the marriage soon ended in divorce. Years later, Pericles fell in love with Aspasia, a non-Athenian native of Miletus in Asia Minor. Whether they were ever legally married is not known, but when his enemies accused Aspasia of failing to show proper reverence to the gods, Pericles himself entered the court to plead her case. As he begged the jurors not to convict her, he lost his composure for the first time in public and began crying. Overwhelmed by the sorrow such an accusation had caused their leader, the jurors acquitted Aspasia.

Pericles must have been relieved when no more accusations followed. However, there was still one personal matter that caused him much grief. Pericles' son Xanthippus knew that everyone regarded his father as a care-

ANCIENT GREEKS

Pericles

BORN

Around 490 B.C.
Athens, Greece

DIED

429 B.C.
Athens, Greece

PROFESSION

Statesman

ACCOMPLISHMENTS

Created the so-called Golden Age of Athens; promoted culture and learning and made Athens the intellectual and cultural capital of the Greek world; planned the refurbishing of the Acropolis, including the building of the temple known as the Parthenon; introduced pay for government workers; instituted many democratic reforms; transformed the Delian League into the Athenian empire

ful and honest businessman who never squandered money, but he resented what he considered a meager allowance. To get more money, Xanthippus borrowed some from a friend of his father's, saying that his father needed the money. The friend gave Xanthippus the money, but when he came to collect from Pericles, Pericles refused to pay and sued his son. The angered Xanthippus then spread malicious rumors about his father.

In public matters, however, there was never a hint of scandal surrounding Pericles until war broke out between Sparta and Athens. The year was 431 B.C. and the Thirty-Years' Peace negotiated between Athens and Sparta still had 16 years remaining, but Sparta had been watching jealously as Athens remained the acknowledged leader of the Greek world. Sparta also feared that some of its citizens might prefer Athens' democratic government to Sparta's oligarchy, or rule by a privileged few. When the city of Corinth sent to Sparta for help defending itself against the city of Corcyra, Sparta hesitated because it knew Corcyra was an ally of Athens. Instead of breaking the treaty, Sparta asked Athens to make concessions. On Pericles' advice, the Athenians refused and voted for war.

Pericles based his strategy on Athens' strong navy and did not plan for Athenian soldiers to battle Spartan soldiers, who were acknowledged as the best in the Greek world. Pericles believed he was well prepared for war because he had saved enough public funds to support the navy. He advised the Athenians to abandon their farms and homes and live within the Long Walls. He believed that the navy could keep the Athenians supplied with food and Sparta would tire of waiting for a battle that would never come—and would ask for peace.

Although hesitant because they knew the Spartans would destroy their crops and homes, the Athenians did as Pericles requested. Pericles' strategy probably would have worked if the unexpected had not happened. In the summer of 430 B.C., foreign ships laden with supplies docked at Piraeus. Unknown at the time, the ships also brought the plague. The cramped quarters within the Long Walls, where thousands of Athenians now lived, were the perfect breeding grounds for the deadly disease. Within months, one-third of Athens' population had died, including Pericles' two sons.

Pericles was on a naval expedition at the time, but his victories against Sparta's allies were offset by the losses within the Long Walls. On his return home, he learned of the death of his sons. As Pericles approached the coffin of his son Paralus, the Athenians for the second time saw their hero in tears. Pericles now had no legitimate heir, because by his own decree his son by Aspasia was not an Athenian citizen and could not inherit Pericles' property or be elected to any office.

At the end of the first year of fighting, the Athenians held a public funeral for everyone who had died. Pericles gave the Funeral Oration, one of the most celebrated speeches ever delivered and one often compared to Abraham Lincoln's Gettysburg Address. In his oration, Pericles chose to focus not on the defeats of the past year but on the glories of Athens.

"Athens is the educator of all Greece," he proclaimed. "To be happy, we must be free, and to be free, we must be courageous."

Happiness, however, seemed a dream to many Athenians. They listened to Pericles' words, but their eyes rested on the 11 coffins that held the remains of those who had given their lives in defense of Athens and its freedom. Ten of those coffins held the remains of soldiers who had belonged to the 10 tribes into which Athens was divided. The 11th, set a distance apart from the others, was empty and honored the soldiers whose bodies had not been recovered.

Pericles' enemies saw the frustration among the people and decided to attack the Olympian of Athens. They accused him of embezzling public money. Frustrated and weary of the war, the Athenians voted to depose Pericles and to fine him heavily. Within months, however, the Athenians became disillusioned with the new leaders and in 429 B.C. they again elected Pericles one of the 10 *strategoi*. Once again Pericles prepared to lead his city. But he was ill, most likely stricken by the plague that had killed so many Athenians. With both of his legitimate sons dead and no heirs to inherit his property and name, he asked the Athenians if they would permit an exception to the law he had enacted 20 years earlier that allowed only men born of Athenian mothers and fathers the rights of citizenship. That exception would make his only surviving son a citizen. The Athenians agreed, perhaps because they believed Pericles had suffered enough and should be granted his final wish.

As Pericles lay dying in the autumn of 429 B.C., his friends gathered about his bedside and began discussing the great events of his life. Pericles, who had appeared to be sleeping, quietly interrupted his friends to say what he believed was his chief accomplishment: "No Athenian has ever worn mourning clothes because of me."

In death, Pericles became a hero, a man respected by all for his devotion to his city and to its people. Unlike so many politicians who use their office to accumulate wealth and honors, Pericles never sought either. When an accounting of his property was made after his death, it was found that the inheritance left to him by his father was exactly what he left to his own son.

Throughout his lifetime, Pericles saw Athens and its citizens leading the way to form a better world. He accepted the responsibility of guarding Athens and guiding its citizens, and he never abandoned his duties. The Athenian historian Thucydides wrote, "Athens, though in name a democracy, was in fact ruled by its greatest citizen." Pericles firmly believed what he told the Athenians in his Funeral Oration: "The greatness of today continues into the future as an everlasting glory."

"Time is the wisest of all counselors."

—Pericles, quoted in *Life of Pericles* (1st century A.D.) by Plutarch

FURTHER READING

Bowra, Cecil Maurice, Sir. *Periclean Athens*. London: Weidenfeld & Nicolson, 1971.

Davies, J. K. *Democracy and Classical Greece*. 2nd. ed. Cambridge: Harvard University Press, 1993.

Hopper, R. J. *The Acropolis*. Photographs by Werner Forman. New York: Macmillan, 1971.

———. "Athens vs. Sparta." *Calliope*, November/December 1994.

Kagan, Donald. *Pericles of Athens and the Birth of Democracy*. New York: Free Press, 1991.

King, Perry Scott. *Pericles*. New York: Chelsea House, 1988.

Plutarch. *Plutarch: The Lives of the Noble Grecians and Romans*. Translated by John Dryden and edited and revised by Arthur Hugh Clough. 1979. Reprint. New York: Modern Library, 1992.

Podlecki, Anthony J. *Plutarch, Life of Pericles*. Bristol, England: Bristol Classical Press, 1987.

Warner, Rex. *Pericles the Athenian*. Boston: Little, Brown, 1963.

Phidias

PERFECTION IN SCULPTURE

Word of Phidias' newest creation spread quickly throughout Greece. It was larger and more magnificent than any of his other statues, and its setting in the town of Olympia perfectly matched the subject of the work—mighty Zeus, the king of the gods.

For centuries, the Greeks had considered Olympia an area especially sacred to Zeus. Every four years since 776 B.C. the Olympic Games had been held there in his honor. Now, in 479 B.C., after the decisive victory of the Greeks over the Persians at Plataea, it seemed only fitting that the Greeks show special thanks to Zeus. For the people in charge of Olympia and the organization of the games, a temple seemed a fitting thanksgiving gift.

Building began in 470 B.C., and when it was completed sometime around 458 or 457 B.C., the Temple of Zeus at Olympia was enormous—approximately 200 feet long by 85 feet wide. Its foundations reached three feet below ground and just over three feet above ground, with columns on all four sides. All it needed was a statue of Zeus himself. For this task Phidias, the renowned master sculptor of the time, was hired.

Phidias set up his workshop just opposite the west front of Zeus' temple, and slowly the creation took shape. By the late 430s, it was finished. Recognized as Phidias' masterpiece, it depicted Zeus seated on a magnificent cedarwood throne decorated with ebony and gold. Approximately 40 feet high, the statue gave visitors and worshipers the impression that if Zeus stood up, his head would go straight through the temple's roof. Like other statues Phidias had carved, this one was chryselephantine, that is, overlaid with gold and ivory. In his right hand, Zeus held an ivory-and-gold statue of Nike, the goddess of victory; his left supported a beautifully decorated scepter, on top of which perched an eagle, the symbol of all-powerful Zeus.

Seated majestically within the temple, Zeus represented the power of the gods and of the Greeks. Absent from the sculpture, however, were Zeus' lightning bolts, his fiery expression, and his fleet chariot and horses. Phidias had deliberately chosen to portray his Zeus not as a warlike god but as a calm, peaceful deity who reigned supreme over a world completely under his control. The size of the statue, the beaten gold used for Zeus' garments, and the ivory used to represent his flesh were all meant to awe the viewer. And so they did, for in the late 3rd century B.C., a Greek writer named Philon of Byzantium listed Phidias' statue of Zeus as one of the Seven Wonders of the World.

Phidias scuplted a statue of Athena dressed as a warrior that stood inside the Parthenon and dwarfed all its surroundings, as this scale model of the interior attests.

Other writers, such as the 2nd-century traveler Pausanias, wrote about visiting Phidias' workshop, which had become a tourist attraction. Mid-20th-century excavations at Olympia uncovered the workshop in the exact location mentioned by Pausanias. Careful digging revealed molds that Phidias had used to cast the sheets of gold he needed to fashion Zeus' garments. After making the gold sheets, Phidias had attached each one to the wood-and-clay inner mold of the statue. Archaeologists also found tiny slivers of ivory, small particles of gold, and several goldsmith's tools.

The best find of all, however, was the bottom piece of a black glazed jug with the hand-written inscription "I am Phidias'."

Nothing survives of the statue of Zeus. In the 4th century, the Roman emperor Theodosius I ordered it removed from the temple at Olympia

The head of Zeus cradled in the figure's left arm indicates that this is an image of Phidias. The ancients considered Phidias' immense statue of Zeus one of best ever sculpted.

and taken to his headquarters in Constantinople (present-day Istanbul in Turkey), the new capital of the Roman Empire. Approximately 100 years later, fire destroyed both the palace and the statue. Even if the statue had remained in Olympia, it would not have fared much better, because through the centuries earthquakes leveled the temple and every one of its columns.

Phidias had begun his artistic career as a painter, but he gradually found himself spending more time carving statues. One of his early works, completed sometime around 456 B.C., was a bronze statue of the goddess Athena Promachos. It stood approximately 30 feet high just inside the Propylaea, or entrance gate to the Acropolis. Symbolizing Athena's role as the goddess of war, *Athena Promachos* wore a bronze breastplate and helmet and carried a spear. Pausanias wrote that the bronze crest of the helmet and the tip of her spear reflected the sun's light and acted as beacons for sailors rounding Cape Sunium, a promontory more than 20 miles southeast of Athens.

Phidias' work won the praise and admiration of all Athenians, especially the statesman Pericles, because it reminded Athenians of their victory over the Persians and of Athena's aid during the war. One statue, however, was not enough for Pericles, who planned to make Athens reflect its new position as leader of the Greek world. The Persians had leveled both the old temple to Athena and the one that the Athenians were in the process of building at the time of the invasion. Consequently, Pericles envisioned an enormous new temple in honor of Athens' patron goddess.

Pericles recognized Phidias' genius and creativity and asked him to oversee the restoration of the Acropolis and its sacred buildings and the construction of the new temple. Phidias accepted the position and the work began around 447 B.C. The task was too great for one master craftsman to undertake, so Pericles employed the well-known architects Ictinus and Callicrates, as well as many other artists, engineers, and workers, to help Phidias. (Both Pericles and Phidias, however, died before the buildings on the Acropolis were completed toward the end of the 5th century.)

Phidias designed a master plan that viewed the Acropolis as a bridge linking humans and gods. However, the chief deity honored on the Acropolis was always Athena, the maiden goddess who protected her city and helped her people win victories on the battlefield. It was only fitting that the new temple be dedicated as *Athena Parthenos*, "Athena the Maiden." Today, millions of visitors travel to Athens just to see the majestic remains of the Parthenon, the base of which is almost 230 feet long and more than 100 feet wide. Restoration efforts, begun in the 1990s and supported by scientists, archaeologists, and governments around the world, are ensuring that the Parthenon will remain an enduring symbol of the skill and expertise of 5th-century B.C. craftsmen like Phidias.

But it was not the temple that won Phidias fame. Nor was it the friezes and designs along the temple's roof or on the pediments at the front and back. Rather, it was the colossal statue of Athena that he fashioned to stand within the temple's walls that propelled him to such prominence. Crafted only a few years before his statue of Zeus at Olympia, it is similar in size, in the materials used, and in the divine majesty of the subject. But unlike Zeus' statue, which was sculpted seated and ready for peace, Athena was portrayed standing and dressed as a warrior.

It is difficult to imagine the overwhelming sense of awe a visitor to the temple probably felt. Over the statue's wooden frame, Phidias carefully attached sheets of beaten gold to craft Athena's ankle-length tunic, the snakes intertwined at her waist as a belt, and the breastplate with the snake-haired Medusa's head in the middle. For Athena's skin, Phidias used carefully wrought plates of ivory. On the outstretched palm of her right hand stood the winged figure of Nike, the goddess of victory. In her left hand she held a spear; at her side rested her great shield and a serpent. Completed in 438 or 437 B.C., Athena's statue won Phidias great fame. It also won him jealousy and envy.

Phidias' friend and patron, Pericles, was also arousing the anger of people who did not approve of his spending the spoils from Athens' victories on buildings. Others disliked the power he had gained and the popular support he had won. However, because no one felt comfortable attacking Pericles, they chose to attack Pericles' close friends, and Phidias was one of the first victims.

Sometime around 432 B.C., formal charges were registered against Phidias with the Athenian courts. His enemies charged that he had kept some of the gold given him for the statue. Phidias knew he was innocent, but he had to prove it.

With Pericles' permission, Phidias went to the Parthenon and carefully removed each sheet of beaten gold that surrounded the wooden frame. On orders from Pericles, the gold had originally been affixed in such a manner that it could easily be detached. Pericles knew his enemies accused him of spending unwisely, and he wanted public funds available in an emergency.

Phidias waited for the court's decision on the gold he had removed. "Innocent," declared the court, for the weight of the gold plates equaled exactly the amount of gold Phidias had been given originally.

The accusers then tried a different approach. They charged Phidias with the crime of impiety—that is, committing an act that was against Greek religious principles. They argued that two of the figures decorating the shield resting against Athena's left leg resembled Pericles and Phidias. The courts agreed and found Phidias guilty of committing an irreligious act.

What happened after the trial is unclear. Some accounts say that Phidias was thrown into prison, where he died from disease or poison. Other accounts say that he was exiled or escaped to Olympia and that it was at this time that he sculpted the statue of Zeus. Yet even if archaeologists discover exactly how, where, and when Phidias died, such facts will have no effect on his contributions to the world of art. Phidias, whose name has become synonymous with perfection in sculpture and artistic style, will always be remembered for setting the standards for classical Greek art with his idealized forms that looked both human and divine.

FURTHER READING

Leipen, Neda. *Athena Parthenos: A Reconstruction*. Toronto: Royal Ontario Museum, 1971.

Macdonald, Fiona, and Mark Bergin. *A Greek Temple*. New York: Peter Bedrick, 1992.

Walston, Charles, Sir. *Essays on the Art of Pheidias*. 1885. Reprint. Washington: McGrath, 1973.

ANCIENT GREEKS

Phidias

BORN

Around 490 B.C.
Athens, Greece

DIED

Around 432 B.C.
Athens or Olympia, Greece

PROFESSION

Sculptor

ACCOMPLISHMENTS

Sculpted numerous statues, mostly of bronze, but also in marble; none of his works survive, except in copies by later (especially Roman) sculptors; most notable were the three statues of Athena: *Athena Promachos* on the Acropolis, *Lemnian Athena* (a thanksgiving offering by the people of Lemnos), and *Athena Parthenos* in the Parthenon on the Acropolis; his masterpiece was the statue of Zeus in the Temple of Zeus at Olympia, which was one of the Seven Wonders of the Ancient World

Socrates

"THE UNEXAMINED LIFE IS NOT WORTH LIVING"

Mention the name Socrates and anyone listening immediately thinks of philosophy—a natural reaction, because Socrates has influenced the development of Western thought for more than 2,000 years. Yet who was this man, and what exactly were his ideas?

It is difficult to answer either of these questions because Socrates left no writings, no records of his beliefs. He did not have time, nor did he wish to make time, for such activities. What mattered to Socrates were the actual exchanges of ideas, questions, and thoughts between people, not the recording of these exchanges. His pupils, contemporaries, and later admirers, however, did find these worth documenting, and history has had to rely on the writings of others for information about Socrates' life and thoughts.

Historians consider the references to Socrates in works by his pupil Plato, the comic playwright Aristophanes, the historian Xenophon, and the philosopher Aristotle to be the best and most reliable sources of information. Of these four, the dialogues written by Plato, in which Socrates is the main character, are the most widely read. Yet a reader of any one of these accounts must always remember that they might be biased, for each author interpreted Socrates' words as *he* understood them. In addition, each might have added details that did not actually occur. Nevertheless, these sources must have captured at least some of the essence of the real Socrates.

Socrates was born in Athens in 470 or 469 B.C., just as the city was becoming the leading Greek power. During the Persian Wars, Athenian troops had led the Greeks to victory, first at Marathon in 490 B.C. and then at Salamis in 480 B.C. Many cities began to look to Athens for direction and protection, and Athenian statesmen such as Pericles encouraged this dependence of other Greek cities on Athens.

During his youth, Socrates probably heard much talk about the Greek cities that formed the Delian League with the goal of resisting and opposing the Persians. The alliance was a good one, but Athens soon became the most powerful member and began to force nonmember Greek cities to join. When Socrates was a teenager, the Athenians moved the treasury of the Delian League from the Aegean island of Delos to the city of Athens. The independent cities of the league now found themselves increasingly obliged to follow Athens' policies.

At the same time, Athens was becoming the cultural and intellectual center of the Greek world and of the eastern Mediterranean. An increasing number of democratic

The 18th-century French artist Jacques-Louis David focused all the light in his painting *Death of Socrates* on the figure of Socrates, who discusses the meaning of life with his friends before drinking a cup of deadly hemlock.

reforms made Athens' government unique in the region. The city hummed with activity under Pericles' extensive building and rebuilding program. On the Acropolis, artists, sculptors, and architects worked on the Parthenon, the massive temple dedicated to the goddess Athena. In the Agora, or marketplace, one of Socrates' favorite places, thinkers and teachers shared their thoughts as they discussed the meaning of life.

As Socrates approached the age of 40, the Peloponnesian War broke out between Athens and its rival, the Greek city Sparta. Ready to defend his city, Socrates fought in several battles and was commended for saving the life of the Athenian general Alcibiades. Therefore, he knew well the joy of victory and the frustration that followed each loss, especially the final defeat in 404 B.C.

The years that followed were perhaps even more frustrating as various individuals vied for control of Athens. Good statesmanship was needed more than ever, and Socrates loved Athens, but he never entered politics. He knew himself well and realized that his outspoken manner did not suit him for political office. In addition, he believed that politicians often had to compromise their principles to stay in power or to attract followers. Such action would have been impossible for Socrates.

After the Battle of Arginusae in 406 B.C., Socrates stood alone in his refusal to condemn the generals who were being tried for neglecting to rescue their shipwrecked comrades. Although most Athenians favored the condemnation, and the *boule*—the legislative council of Athens, whose members were Athenian citizens elect-

"I learn nothing from fields and trees, but I do from the people in a city."

—Socrates, quoted in *Phaedo* (4th century B.C.) by Plato

ed by lot for one year—sentenced the generals to death, the motion to do so was illegal. Socrates, as a member of the council, would not vote on an issue that had been improperly raised.

This courage to stand by his convictions was a dominant characteristic of Socrates' personality. He was determined to let no one influence his decisions or force him to do anything other than what he intended. He disagreed with the teachings of the Sophists (from the Greek *sophistes*, meaning "wise man"), a relatively new profession in the Greek world. Sophists were itinerant teachers who traveled from one city to another giving lessons in the arts and sciences in exchange for a fee.

What Socrates particularly disliked about the Sophists was their disregard for laws. Most Sophists argued that justice, goodness, and wisdom were merely words and should not determine how people lived their lives. Individuals, they said, should act as each occasion demanded. To Socrates, such thinking was hypocritical because, according to the Sophists, in one situation a person might need to tell the truth to prove a point, while in another situation a lie would prove the point.

For truthful Socrates, the arguments of the Sophists could only harm the people of Athens. To prevent this from happening, Socrates became a teacher, intent on helping himself and others understand what was meant by proper conduct. Unlike the Sophists, however, he accepted no fees and did not travel beyond Athens.

Although he never founded a school of his own or had a set roster of pupils, he won many admirers who often met with him in the Agora, in the city streets, and more often in the gymnasia, the sports facilities used regularly by all male Greeks. Some Greeks—Plato, for example—considered Socrates their teacher and later developed their own schools of thought.

Serious and determined to live according to his beliefs, Socrates was not a cynic who found something wrong with everyone else's way of thinking. Nor did he become bitter when events turned out differently from the way he thought they should. He accepted what was impossible to change and placed a high value on what was truly important in life. He prized cleanliness and taking care of one's body, but his short stature, flat nose, and prominent eyes did not bother him. His keen sense of humor and his even temper made him good company.

Clothes meant nothing to Socrates except to provide warmth and coverage. He went barefoot and wore the same simple outer garment year-round. He was not raised in poverty; his father was most likely a stonemason who was able to provide comfortably for his family. Socrates, however, had very little money and probably found it difficult to provide for his wife, Xanthippe, whom he had married late in life, and for their three sons.

As a teacher, Socrates was a difficult taskmaster, for he did not believe in giving answers. Whenever anyone asked him a question, he would reply by asking first one question, and then a second, and so on until the person had answered his own question.

Logic and careful reasoning played key roles as both teacher and student closely examined possible solutions to the question. According to Plato, Socrates used this procedure to make the person asking the question feel that the answer had come from his own mind. Plato likened Socrates to a doctor or midwife delivering a baby. Although the doctor is present to offer assistance, it is the mother alone who gives birth. For Socrates, the baby was truth or knowledge, the goal every person should strive to attain. Today, this

ANCIENT GREEKS

Socrates

BORN

Around 470 or 469 B.C.
Athens, Greece

DIED

399 B.C.
Athens, Greece

PROFESSION

Philosopher

ACCOMPLISHMENTS

Developed a more scientific method of thinking; one of the first, if not the first, to critically debate morality and how individuals should conduct their lives

technique of asking a series of questions of someone in order to force him to think through a problem is known as the Socratic method and is used by teachers in schools and colleges throughout the world.

Like any well-known personality, Socrates had his enemies. They were mostly people who feared that Socrates would uncover and expose the truth about some of their activities. A few felt that Socrates was just an officious busybody who went about Athens asking questions of everybody he met. This was true, but Socrates had a reason for his questions. Years earlier, before he had turned to teaching, Socrates' friend Chaerephon had visited the oracle of the god Apollo at Delphi, in central Greece. To Chaerephon's question, "Is anyone wiser than Socrates?" the oracle had replied, "No one!"

Unable to accept this as the truth, Socrates began cross-examining everyone whom he considered knowledgeable to see if he could find someone wiser than he. Most people answered his first few questions glibly and with little effort, believing that they knew more about the subject than Socrates. But Socrates was a master at asking questions and would phrase the first few questions in ways that made him seem ignorant of the matter being discussed. As the questions became more pointed and more philosophical, the answers did not flow as freely and those being questioned naturally started to feel uncomfortable. As their uneasiness intensified, they realized that Socrates did indeed know far more than they realized. For some people, this encounter marked the beginning of their dislike for the "seeker of truth."

Socrates, on the other hand, was amazed and began to wonder if the oracle had indeed been correct, for he had found no one who could answer all his questions. Not that he could answer them, but at least he recognized the fact that he could not. Too many of those questioned refused to admit any lack of knowledge. Therefore, because he knew he understood only a little about the world and was unafraid to admit this fact, Socrates decided that he was truly wise.

As a result, "Know thyself," the maxim inscribed on Apollo's temple at Delphi, became the key principle of Socrates' teachings. For Socrates, goodness, justice, and wisdom are all the result of knowledge, for without knowledge, the truly "good life" is impossible to achieve. He counseled all who came to him to examine themselves and their lives closely to discover what really mattered. He wanted them to see that wealth, material comforts, position in life, and even health were not essential to making an individual good or happy.

Socrates considered those people who chose not to find out more about themselves to be ignorant, for he believed they would never acquire true knowledge. Continuing his reasoning, Socrates believed that such ignorance on the part of Athens' leaders had caused the city's steady decline and the prolonged war with Sparta. He wanted so badly to change this state of affairs and bring some knowledge to the leaders that he made his feelings known publicly. He considered himself a gadfly that kept after the Athenians to look at themselves and their city and to try to make it better.

Naturally, this brought him into conflict with those in power. When Critias and his colleagues (members of the oligarchy known as the Thirty Tyrants who ruled Athens in 404 B.C.) advised him to stop talking about matters affecting the state, he ignored their warning. The Thirty Tyrants then ordered Socrates and four other men who were also thought to be upright citizens to arrest Leon of Salamis, a man the Tyrants wanted murdered. Refusing to commit an unjust act,

Found guilty of "corrupting the young" and the "neglect of the gods," Socrates was sentenced to death. The remains of the prison in Athens where he took his life have been excavated and restored.

Socrates did not obey the order. Had the Thirty Tyrants not been deposed in the following year, Socrates' act of disobedience would have cost him his life.

But the new leaders also considered Socrates' teachings and cross-examinations a threat to their power. Socrates was outspoken in his opposition to their democratic reforms—not because he wanted a monarchy or any other form of government, but because he disapproved of the democratic belief that every person's opinion on morality and justice is worthwhile.

But, at the same time, he did not believe that anyone voluntarily would choose to do something that was bad. According to Socrates, bad actions were the result of ignorance. Therefore, good government meant leadership by individuals who tried at all times to help their people improve and know themselves. Yet in order to help others become more knowledgeable, the leaders themselves first had to understand what "good" meant.

By 399 B.C., Athens' leaders had had enough of Socrates' talk about good government. They charged him with "corrupting the young, neglect of the Greek gods, and the introduction of strange gods" and had him arrested.

Socrates defended himself, according to the custom in Athenian courts, where there were no lawyers and citizens were tried by their peers. By a vote of 280 to 220, Socrates' peers convicted him, and the prosecutors asked for the death penalty. According to Athenian custom, the defendant then had the right to make a counteroffer. Socrates' friends persuaded him to offer to pay a fine. The judge, however, rejected his offer and voted for the death sentence. The three dialogues of Plato—*Apology*, *Crito*, and *Phaedo*—recount the events of the trial and the discussions Socrates had with his followers and students after the trial.

Socrates offered an honest defense of himself and his actions. He maintained that his belief in "good government" and in "examining one's own life first" corrupted no one. That he was turning to strange gods was also a false accusation because he believed a divine power or god ruled the world. How people chose to worship this divine power was their own choice, and he had never interfered with Greek religious rites and rituals. There was, however, the *daemon,* an inner voice, like a divine sign, that at various times throughout his life had stopped him from doing something. But, certainly, this was not contrary to Greek beliefs.

As for a counterproposal, Socrates would not ask for a reduced punishment. To do so would have been an admission that he had committed a crime—and he believed that he had not. Socrates argued instead that he deserved to be rewarded, not punished, for the great service his questionings had rendered Athens. He ended by asking that Athens honor him as a public benefactor and grant him free room and board. As the prosecutors and judges listened to Socrates' request, their anger increased. How could he be so arrogant, so self-righteous? They did not see, or they refused to see, that he was a principled man who was not about to lie or contradict everything that he had taught just to save his life.

Socrates' friends begged him to reconsider, and to use their money to pay a fine. Socrates did agree to tell the court that his friends would pay a small fine, but he refused to stop his so-called corrupting practices, because his teachings were far more important to him than life itself.

With little hesitation, the judges voted the death penalty. Under normal circumstances, a convicted person had to be executed within 24 hours after the judges had made their decision. However, the sacred ship had just left Athens on its yearly trip to the island of Delos, and custom forbade any executions while it traveled on its religious mission. The execution was therefore delayed a month.

Socrates' friends took advantage of the delay, bribed the jailers, and planned an escape route, but Socrates refused to cooperate. For 70 years, he had lived in accordance with the laws of Athens and enjoyed the privileges of being an Athenian citizen. He did not intend to start breaking the law now just because it had ruled against him. The decision had been a legal one and he intended to abide by it. Furthermore, he reasoned, the next life might be even better than the present one.

When the sacred ship returned, the time was set for his death. Socrates was given a cup of hemlock, a powerful and deadly poison. With his friends around him, Socrates drank the hemlock and then calmly talked about the nature of the human soul and the possibility of its continued existence after the body's death. As he asked questions of his friends in his customary manner, the poison slowly numbed his limbs. Although Plato was not at the prison that last afternoon, he gave a very moving account of Socrates' final hours in the *Phaedo,* ending with: "Thus did our friend die, a man who was, of all those whom we had ever met, the noblest, the wisest, and the most just."

"Knowledge is the only good and ignorance the only evil."

—Socrates, quoted in *Lives of Eminent Philosophers* (3rd century A.D.) by Diogenes Laertius

FURTHER READING

Brickhouse, Thomas C., and Nicholas D. Smith. *Plato's Socrates.* New York: Oxford University Press, 1994.

Guthrie, William K. C. *Socrates.* London: Cambridge University Press, 1971.

Navia, Luis E. *Socrates, the Man and His Philosophy.* Lanham, Md.: University Press of America, 1985.

Plato. *The Last Days of Socrates: Euthyphro, Apology, Crito, Phaedo.* Translated by Hugh Tredennick and Harold Tarrant. New York: Penguin, 1993.

Hippocrates

MAKING MEDICINE A SCIENCE

"The gods simply cannot be held responsible for every ailment that afflicts human beings," said Hippocrates. In 5th-century B.C. Athens, such thinking was revolutionary. For centuries, the Greeks had believed that pain and disease were caused by angered deities and evil spirits. For example, when a person complained of severe stomach pains, an ailment known today as gastritis, the Greeks said it was the curse of the god Apollo because the symptoms of gastritis resembled the droppings of swallows, the bird associated with Apollo.

Unable to accept such reasoning, Hippocrates began suggesting other explanations. Born around 460 B.C. on the Greek island of Cos, off the southern coast of Asia Minor (present-day Turkey), Hippocrates was well acquainted with the medical practices of the day because his father was a physician. Hippocrates' two sons and a son-in-law would eventually enter the same profession.

Hippocrates left no records, making it difficult to determine what treatments he prescribed and what philosophy guided his life. What is certain is that the Greeks soon recognized Hippocrates as one of the greatest physicians who had ever lived, and they called him the Father of Medicine. The accounts of many ancient writers mention Hippocrates and refer to books written by him. Yet modern scholars believe that it was not Hippocrates who wrote these texts but a series of people who carried on his practices—his sons, pupils, admirers, and fellow physicians.

Known as the Hippocratic Collection, these books included approximately 70 works, most of which have survived to the present. They were written over a period of more than 100 years. All were written in the Ionic dialect, the language spoken by inhabitants of the Greek colonies along the central west coast of Asia Minor and the adjacent islands. As a result, the Ionic dialect became the language of Greek science.

Included in the collection are sections on anatomy, women's diseases, childhood diseases, predicting the course of particular diseases, treatments based on diet and on medication, surgical practices, and medical ethics. Many of the ideas included in the ethics section are quite broad and apply to nonphysicians as well as physicians. Examples are: "Too much sleep and too much wakefulness are both bad." "No individual who is very hungry should undertake strenuous work." "Neither fasting nor overeating, nor anything else that is done to excess is good."

Although the collection may not actually include any writings by Hippocrates, the work as a whole reflects his basic philosophy that the human body is one organism whose parts interact constantly. For Hippocrates, health was a matter of how well the parts interacted. He believed that no doctor could heal one area of the body without knowing how that part depended on the rest of the body. According to a 4th-century B.C. writer named Meno, Hippocrates gave the following explanation of disease: If any food remains undigested in the human body, it begins to excrete or send off particles of moisture or gas. When these particles enter the body's working system, the individual becomes ill.

Yet the Greeks knew little about the inner workings of the body because religious practices dictated that Greeks should respect the human body even in death. Dissecting corpses was not approved of, even though, according to tradition, the medical school at Cos, where Hippocrates taught, owned a skeleton. It was the sports arena, however, that provided physicians like Hippocrates with wonderful opportunities to look inside a working human body. While training and competing, athletes frequently experienced broken and fractured bones. Dislocations were also common, as were cuts and abrasions. Doctors became quite proficient at dealing with such problems, because treatment was essential if an athlete planned to continue to be active.

As a naturally keen observer, Hippocrates kept careful records of every wound that he treated and how it healed. He also noted the effectiveness of different medical procedures. As he traveled throughout Asia Minor and Greece practicing his medical skills and teaching, he constantly sought more information about diseases and potential cures. Everywhere he spoke with other physicians and compared what they had learned with his own observations. In time he learned to recognize the various stages of an infection as well as the positive and negative effects of different medical practices.

A passage on surgery from the Hippocratic Collection tells how Hippocrates operated on a young man who came to him with a swollen area in his lower back. After carefully examining the infected area, Hippocrates recognized the problem as pus in the cavity around the lungs. To determine where to make the cut in his patient's skin (the inner workings of

For Hippocrates, disease was something natural that affected the body, not a punishment sent by the gods. He wrote: "Science produces knowledge, opinion ignorance." A Byzantine artist in the 14th century produced this image of the Father of Medicine.

Dating from a century or so after Hippocrates, these surgical instruments were similar to those he used. Surgeons probably probed areas within the body with the curved-fork device at the far left. Dentists most likely extracted teeth with the pliers-like instrument to the right.

the body were still a mystery and there were no charts or X rays to show the position of veins, arteries, and the body's vital organs), he took some wet clay and laid it on the swollen area. He then marked the spot that dried first, because he knew the infection must be the worst in the area that produced the most heat. After cutting into the spot with a knife, he let the pus ooze out. The treatment continued for the next 10 days, and Hippocrates carefully checked the color of the pus every day. He knew that if the pus was green and smelly, the infection was beyond hope of curing, but if it was white, the chance of curing the infection was quite good.

To ensure complete recovery, Hippocrates made a cut in the arm of patients who had undergone surgery. He reasoned that as the blood flowed from the cut, so too would any "bad blood" that remained in the patient's system from the infection. He also advised surgery patients to follow a rigid diet of thin barley mush because he believed this simple diet would prevent "bad blood" from forming. To remove unwanted particles within the body, he prescribed enemas.

Practice and experience had taught Hippocrates that superstitions, magic, and evil spirits could play no part in his treatments, and he frowned on all who encouraged such beliefs. Yet he knew that the Greeks honored Asclepius, a legendary hero and the god of healing, as the master physician and took their sick to his temples to be cured. Treatment involved spending one or more nights in the Asclepeum, or temple, under the care of special attendants. The Asclepeum in Hippocrates' hometown of Cos was well known for its miraculous cures. Stories were told throughout Greece of how many ill visitors awoke after a sound sleep in the temple to find their ailments gone. As reports of such miraculous cures spread, so too did the belief that Asclepius came during the night to heal his followers.

According to Greek legend, Asclepius could cure any ailment brought to him. It was even said that he had once restored a dead man to life. Asclepius inherited his medical knowledge from his father, Apollo, the god of medicine, but he was not a god because his mother had been a mortal named Coronis. When Asclepius died, Apollo was so grief-stricken that he pleaded with his father, Zeus, the king of the gods, to honor his son's memory. Zeus granted Apollo's plea by turning Asclepius into a star and making him the patron of all physicians.

"Healing is a matter of time, but sometimes it is also a matter of opportunity."

—from *Precepts* (5th century B.C.)

ANCIENT GREEKS

Hippocrates

BORN

Around 460 B.C.
Cos

DIED

Around 360 B.C.
Larissa, Thessaly

PROFESSION

Doctor

ACCOMPLISHMENTS

Practiced medicine using what he had learned from observation and experimentation; freed himself from the widespread belief that cures depended on superstition, myths, and magic

Although Hippocrates could not change Greek society—nor did he have any wish to do so—he intended to show that medical practices could not be governed by myths but should be treated as a science. He believed that doctors needed to use reason and analysis when caring for their patients. According to Hippocrates, a person's diet was central to his health. Therefore, he told doctors to advise their patients about what to eat. Hippocrates also believed that strong medicines hurt rather than helped an illness and that gentle treatment brought the best results.

The times were right for Hippocrates' beliefs. His youth and early manhood coincided with the Golden Age of Athens, a time of great intellectual and artistic activity. Many Greeks, both in Athens and in cities around the Aegean, were beginning to question the order of the world, the power of the gods, and the merits of democracy. Hippocrates questioned them too, not as a philosopher, but as a scientist. His questions and answers revolutionized the practice of medicine and influenced its development in the centuries that followed. Today, as part of the graduation exercises at many medical schools, students solemnly recite the Hippocratic oath, a code of ethics attributed to Hippocrates that is supposed to be the physicians' guide wherever and whenever they practice:

> I swear by Apollo the physician, by Asclepius . . . and all the gods and goddesses, making them my witnesses, that I will carry out, according to my ability and judgment, this oath. . . . I will follow that system of regimen to help the sick according to my ability and judgment, but never with a view to injury and wrongdoing. I will not give a poison to anybody when asked to do so, nor will I suggest such a course. Similarly, I will not give to a woman anything to cause abortion. I will keep pure and holy both my life and my art. . . . In whatever houses I enter, I will enter to help the sick, and I will abstain from all intentional wrongdoing and harm, especially from the pleasures of love with women or men, slave or free. And whatever I shall see or hear in the course of my profession, . . . if it be what should not be published abroad, I will never divulge, keeping them to be secrets. Now if I carry out this oath, may I enjoy life forever and practice my skill, respected always among all men; if I break this oath or violate it, may the reverse be my lot.

FURTHER READING

Heidel, William Arthur. *Hippocratic Medicine, Its Spirit and Method*. New York: Columbia University Press, 1941.

Hippocrates. *Hippocrates*. Translated by W. H. S. Jones and E. T. Withington. Loeb Classical Library. Cambridge: Harvard University Press, 1923.

Levine, Edwin Burton. *Hippocrates*. New York: Twayne, 1971.

Nuland, Sherwin B. *Doctors: The Biography of Medicine*. New York: Knopf, 1988.

Smith, Wesley D. *The Hippocratic Tradition*. Ithaca, N.Y.: Cornell University Press, 1979.

Aristophanes

COMIC POET OF ATHENS

The ancient Athenians loved the theater and eagerly awaited the annual dramatic competitions when prizes were awarded to the best Athenian playwrights. The Great Dionysia held in the spring and the Lenaea held in January or February both honored Dionysus, the god of wine and merriment. At the Great Dionysia, playwrights presented mostly tragedies, whereas at the Lenaea, comedies were the favorite.

As a resident of Athens, Aristophanes knew both festivals well and had been chosen on several occasions to enter his comedies into the competition. His first play, titled *Banqueters*, was performed in 427 B.C., when he was probably in his twenties. Whether he was an Athenian citizen is uncertain, because on one occasion, the statesman Cleon charged Aristophanes with claiming citizenship rights illegally. Cleon's charge was defeated in the courts, as was his accusation that Aristophanes had slandered public officials

A conservative and a traditionalist, Aristophanes used his comedies to express his dislike of intellectuals and of Athenian politicians who favored warfare.

in one of his plays. Such accusations, however, caused ill feelings between the two and, in 424 B.C. at the Lenaea, Aristophanes won first prize for his play *Knights*, in which he bitterly attacked Cleon.

One of the play's main characters is a corrupt and deceitful tanner named Paphlagonian, a fictitious figure whom the audience easily recognized as Cleon. At one point in the play, Aristophanes even mentioned Cleon by name. However, if Aristophanes had hoped to influence the Athenians against Cleon, he failed; just months after the play's production, Cleon was elected to the high-ranking position of *strategos*, or general.

This vote of confidence in so corrupt a politician did not stop Aristophanes from mixing playwriting and politics. In fact, all his comedies had political themes. Perhaps this was only natural because his lifetime coincided with an extremely turbulent and distressing period in Athens' history. The city was at war with archrival Sparta and defeats were beginning to outnumber victories. The Peloponnesian War —supposed to have brought glory to Athens—was instead causing its ruin.

Aristophanes strongly opposed the Athenian "hawks" and wished for peace. He disagreed with those in power and longed to return to the time when the statesmen Miltiades and Pericles ruled Athens. In his comedy titled *Acharnians* (completed in 425 B.C., six years after the start of the Peloponnesian War), an Athenian farmer makes his own private treaty with Sparta and enjoys the benefits of peace. Despite the seriousness of the theme, the play is quite amusing. To help the farmer decide the length of a proper treaty, a peacemaker gives him three draughts of wine to taste. The first represents a 5-year peace, the second a 10-year peace, and the third a 30-year peace. The farmer prefers the taste of the last.

In 421 B.C., at the Great Dionysia, Aristophanes won second prize with his comedy titled *Peace*. The timing was perfect, for Cleon and Brasidas had just been killed on the battlefield and the 50-year Peace of Nicias was about to take effect. The play begins with an Athenian farmer named Trygaeus journeying to heaven on the back of a dung beetle. Once there, he learns that the gods have abandoned their home in frustration over the constant clashes between the Greeks, and that War (in the form of a person) is now in control of Greece. To safeguard his authority, War imprisons Peace (also portrayed as a person) in a cave and then gathers the cities of Greece into a bowl where he plans to grind them down for his supper.

Unable to accept such a fate for his country, Trygaeus convinces a great number of Greeks to help him pull away the stones blocking the entrance to the cave where Peace is being held. With great difficulty they make an opening large enough to let down ropes that they then use to free Peace, along with her two beautiful attendants, Harvest and Festival. As the play ends, Trygaeus and Harvest are attending their wedding feast. Unfortunately, Trygaeus' successful rescue of Peace did not persuade Athens' politicians to attempt a similar exploit, and the casualties and defeats continued to mount.

In 411 B.C., Aristophanes presented *Lysistrata*. The message of the play again was peace, but the scope was much broader. As the play opens, Lysistrata is determined to stop the constant warfare and has called together the women of Athens, as well as representatives from other Greek cities. Her plan is simple: until the Greek men agree to make peace, the Greek women will refuse to make love. Not all of the Greek women agree with her, but Lysistrata soon persuades them to take command

"The wise learn much from their enemies."

—from Birds (414 B.C.)

A piper stands between two dancing men dressed as birds, probably actors in Aristophanes' comedy *Birds*. Crested masks with vicious hooked beaks fit over their heads, and body tights reach to their wrists and ankles.

of the Acropolis and remain there until terms of a peace treaty can be settled.

When an official threatens to force his way onto the Acropolis, Lysistrata and the others voluntarily come to meet him. But the women have no intention of changing plans and make it known that they will remain on the Acropolis, along with all the public funds they have found there, until a peace treaty among the warring Greeks is signed.

With both sides refusing to yield, the time passes and there are defections on each side. After learning that one woman has asked to leave the Acropolis so that she might return home to mothproof her blankets and that another has feigned pregnancy by placing a helmet under her tunic and asked for permission to have her baby at home, Lysistrata calls for a general meeting to rally her followers.

Realizing that the women will never surrender and unable to remain any longer without them, the Spartan and Athenian soldiers send ambassadors from each city to ask Lysistrata's aid in drafting a peace agreement.

Certainly, Aristophanes' message about peace was timely and serious and the leaders of the warring cities would have done well to listen, but the audiences at the Lenaea and Great Dionysia came to laugh, not to be persuaded or lectured. And they did laugh, for Aristophanes' comedies were hilariously funny with their mix of slapstick, fantasy, satire, obscene jokes, and vulgar humor. There was a sense of freedom and license in Aristophanes' Athens that allowed him to criticize everything and everyone, even the gods. Throughout his comedies, one feels a tremendous energy and exuberance. Athenian citizens probably identified with the scenes and situations, faults and weaknesses he presented in his plays, for his characters and their lives reflected the Athens of his day. Aristophanes never tried to hide his meaning, soften his criticisms, or curb his often indecent language. He was the master of directness, frankness, and often obscene expressions. Yet to understand the humor and the literary and political references in Aristophanes' comedies, the audience had to be educated.

Whether Aristophanes was the best comedian in the late 5th century B.C. is not known because only 11 comedies from this period have survived and all were written by him. The first eight belong to what later historians called the Old Comedy period. All were political in nature and involved scenes that bordered on what today might be called science fiction. For example, in *Birds*, two Athenians who wish to live in a city not ruled by money and politics sprout

"You have all the traits of a popular politician: a horrible voice, bad upbringing, and a vulgar manner."

—from *Knights* (424 B.C.)

wings and work with birds to build the "perfect" city.

Typical of Old Comedy was the chorus, a group of 24 individuals who spoke to the audience, commenting on the action taking place. At some central point in the play, the chorus spoke directly to the audience in what was known as the *parabasis*. Often these lines were the playwright's personal opinion on a particular matter. In Aristophanes' play *Wasps*, which attacked the Athenians' love of court action and serving on juries, the jurors form the chorus and are dressed in yellow and black to look like wasps and carry "stingers." In the play *Birds*, in which two Athenians found an ideal city named Cloudcuckooland with their feathered friends, the chorus is costumed and masked to represent birds. In *Clouds*, which ridicules Aristophanes' contemporary, the philosopher Socrates, the teaching practices of the Sophists (itinerant paid teachers who used clever arguments to prove their statements), and the tragic poet Euripides, whose thinking often conflicted with traditional customs, the chorus dresses in costumes fashioned to make each look like a cloud.

In this make-believe world of Old Comedy, even the gods were treated with little respect. The audience immediately sensed that the characters in the play were using humor and fantasy to voice their objection to the real world, in which gods, generals, politicians, and scholars were all superior to the ordinary person. In fact, Aristophanes' characters often represent a type of individual rather than a specific person. For example, two characters in *Clouds* are Right Argument and Wrong Argument, and the name Lysistrata actually means "army breaker." Adding to the comic effect were the grotesque masks and heavy padding used by the actors.

Of the 11 surviving plays of Aristophanes, the two written after the fall of Athens show a marked difference from the earlier plays. Both belong to what scholars call Middle Comedy. In *Ecclesiazusae* (*Women Holding an Assembly*), the Athenian women take control of the city and introduce reforms aimed at allowing everyone to participate in government matters. In *Plutus*, the god of wealth, Plutus, is cured of his blindness and becomes able to distribute his riches on the basis of merit. The themes of both plays focus more on everyday Athenian life than on politics and politicians, and neither play includes a *parabasis*. The chorus, too, has lost its importance.

After Aristophanes died, around 388 B.C., his son Ararus, who was also a playwright, undertook the production of two previously unpublished plays, *Aiolosikon* and *Cocalus*, neither of which have survived. This was not the first time Aristophanes' plays had been produced by someone other than himself. In 427 B.C., Aristophanes entrusted the production of his first play, *Banqueters*, to someone else. He did the same with his next two plays and with several others in later years. Why

ANCIENT GREEKS

Aristophanes

BORN

Between 455 and 445 B.C.
Perhaps Athens, Greece, or the island of Aegina

DIED

Around 388 B.C.
Probably Athens, Greece

PROFESSION

Writer of comedies

ACCOMPLISHMENTS

Wrote more than 40 plays, 11 of which have survived; his first play, *Banqueters*, was produced in 427 B.C.; his earliest surviving play is *Archarnians* (425 B.C.), which won first prize at Lenaea; other surviving plays are *Knights*, *Clouds*, *Wasps*, *Peace*, *Birds*, *Lysistrata*, *Frogs*, *Ecclesiazusae*, and *Plutus*

In 1896, in Richmond, Virginia, a group of young women is dressed to perform as the chorus in a Greek play. There is hardly a region of the Western world that has escaped the influence of the ancient Greek playwrights.

he did this is not clear, but he probably considered himself, at first, too young and inexperienced to undertake such a responsibility, and then later perhaps he preferred to spend his time writing, not training actors.

In the centuries that followed, other comic poets, both Greek and Roman, studied Aristophanes' techniques, colorful language, and fast-flowing lyrics. Yet few have been able to match his quick wit, his bold fantasy, and his strong verbal abuse of characters and situations. However, because jokes lose their impact when they have to be explained, it is difficult for modern audiences to appreciate Aristophanes' artistic skill and humor.

Although today's audiences have little feel for Athenian life in the late 5th century B.C., they can still laugh at Aristophanes' witty remarks about daily life and basic human traits. On restored ancient stages throughout the Greek world and in many of the world's playhouses and university theaters, actors continue to perform the plays Aristophanes wrote almost 2,500 years ago.

FURTHER READING

Aristophanes. *Complete Plays of Aristophanes*. Edited by Moses Hadas. New York: Bantam, 1962.

MacDowell, Douglas M. *Aristophanes and Athens: An Introduction to the Plays*. New York: Oxford University Press, 1995.

Murray, Gilbert, Benjamin R. Rogers, et al., trans. *Fifteen Greek Plays*. New York: Oxford University Press, 1943.

Thucydides

IN RELENTLESS PURSUIT OF THE FACTS

Thucydides was a careful writer who expressed himself in a concise and direct manner. He offered this observation, for example: "Suffering can be somewhat lessened if borne in company with another."

Here is the opening paragraph of one of the greatest historical accounts ever written: "I, Thucydides the Athenian, wrote the history of the war waged by the Peloponnesians [Spartans] and the Athenians against each other. [I] started the work at the very beginning of the war, thinking that this would be the greatest and most noteworthy of all the wars ever fought."

Titled simply *History*, Thucydides' account does not cover the entire Peloponnesian War but stops suddenly in the middle of the winter of 411–410 B.C. Why he chose to end his account here is unknown, but many historians believe Thucydides died before he could complete it. Through the centuries, some scholars have argued that the abruptness of the ending proves that his death was completely unexpected and that perhaps he was killed by paid assassins.

Certainly murder was a possibility because the Peloponnesian War had caused great enmity not only between the Greek cities but also between opposing factions within cities. Thucydides' death at the end of the 5th century B.C. coincided with Athens' defeat. The city was in turmoil and many of its leading citizens were in disagreement with each other. What role Thucydides played at this time is hard to determine, for he had just returned to Athens after an exile of 20 years.

Thucydides was probably in his late fifties at the time of his death. He most likely was born by 454 B.C. because he was elected *strategos*, or general, in 424. By law, a *strategos* had to be at least 30 years old.

Scattered references in his *History* and other contemporary records indicate that Thucydides was born into an aristocratic and well-to-do Athenian family. On his father's side, he was related to the Athenian statesman Cimon, whose father, Miltiades, was the hero of Marathon. Miltiades had married a princess from Thrace, an area bordering the Aegean Sea to the north. Thucydides owned rights to gold mines in the region and wielded considerable influence there.

Thucydides spent his early years, however, in Athens, at a time when the city was the acknowledged center of the Greek world. He most likely knew the playwrights Aeschylus, Sophocles, and Euripides. He probably also listened to the philosophers Anaxagoras and Socrates and watched as the craftsmen Phidias, Ictinus, and Callicrates executed their designs for the buildings on the Acropolis. Thucydides welcomed Pericles' plan to make Athens the capital of the world and approved of, although he did not always agree with, Pericles, whom he considered to be a master statesman.

For almost 30 years, the Peloponnesian War pitted Greek against Greek, often in hand-to hand combat, as this marble fragment reveals. Thucydides made this war and the personalities involved the subject of his multivolume *History*.

As the years passed, Thucydides became keenly aware of the growing rivalry between Athens and Sparta. He was too young to take a leading role when the war began in 431 B.C., and he fell victim to the plague that struck Athens the following year, but he recovered. Athens' leader, Pericles, was also struck by the plague, but he did not regain his health, and Thucydides watched as various political groups attempted to implement their own plans to resolve the war.

When Thucydides was elected *strategos*, he was put in charge of seven Athenian warships and sent north to Thrace because of his influence there. Soon after his arrival, he was called to defend Amphipolis, a Thracian town that had been taken and colonized by Athenians in 437 B.C. Athens considered Amphipolis important because it was a great trade center and gave the Athenians access to nearby gold and silver mines.

The Spartans also recognized Amphipolis' significance and had ordered their troops under General Brasidas to take the town. Thucydides rushed his fleet to the area but arrived just hours after the townspeople, believing defeat was inevitable, had surrendered. Although unable to retake Amphipolis, Thucydides prevented the Spartans from conquering the neighboring port of Eion.

Furious at the loss of Amphipolis and unwilling to look at the reasons, the Athenians blamed Thucydides and voted to exile him. Cleon, an archenemy of Thucydides, probably organized the opposition and pushed through the exile vote. Thucydides consequently had to find a new home, but the war limited his options. Because no area allied with Athens could be considered safe, Thucydides spent much of his time in lands allied with Sparta. He later wrote that his exile had given him the opportunity to quietly watch the course of events and "to become more aware of both sides of the war, especially the Spartan side."

Exactly when he began writing the *History* is not known, but Thucydides most likely took notes, wrote, and edited passages throughout the course of the war. In Book 1, Thucydides wrote:

> As for the speeches made by the different leaders, either at the start of the conflict or during the war itself, it has been difficult for me to recall with absolute accuracy the words which I myself heard and for others to repeat to me exactly what they heard. Therefore, the speeches are presented using language which I feel the speakers would have used for the specific occasion, while at the

> same time I have stayed as close as possible to accounts of what was specifically said at the time.
>
> As far as facts are concerned, I have considered it my responsibility to present them, not having learned them by chance from any individual or situation, but only after investigating each detail with utmost care. This was done in every situation in which I had taken part and also in those situations concerning which I had to get my information from others. This was indeed a difficult and time-consuming task as eye-witnesses at the same event did not always give the same information. Reports varied according to which side they favored and also according to what they remembered.

Although Thucydides did on occasion show some bias—especially toward Cleon, the Athenian statesman responsible for his exile—he was concerned about the truth and made a conscious attempt to present a calm and unbiased account of the war. For this work he earned the honorary title of Father of Scientific History. It is a fitting tribute, for Thucydides is credited as the first historian to write a political and moral analysis of a nation's policies during wartime.

Unlike so many of his predecessors and even his contemporaries, whose works were meant to be spoken before an audience, Thucydides intended his *History* to be read by the people of his day and by the generations that would follow. For this reason, he believed it was important to include events that preceded and caused the war, as well as the early history of Greece, with a special emphasis on how Sparta came to be a land power and Athens a naval power.

Yet Thucydides' style was not dry. Nor was it merely a listing of facts and speeches. Thucydides knew his subject matter well and strongly believed that individuals and their personalities affect the events of any war. For this reason, he incorporated into the *History* descriptions of key personalities in the conflict between Athens and Sparta, such as Themistocles, Pericles, Brasidas, and Alcibiades.

In Book 2, chapter 65, for instance, Thucydides' carefully chosen words paint a vivid picture of Athens' leader: "Because Pericles proved himself an incorruptible statesman, he was able to control the Athenians while at the same time respect their liberties. He led them rather than was led by them; he did not seek power dishonestly and had no need to flatter the people. On the strength of his reputation, Pericles could oppose the people, and even at times anger them. Whenever he felt they were becoming too arrogant or overconfident, with words alone he made them afraid. But, when he saw that they were afraid, he restored their confidence. And so Athens, although in name a democracy, was in fact a government ruled by its greatest citizen."

In Book 5, chapter 9, Thucydides included Brasidas' pre-battle speech to the Spartans and their allies: "Men of the Peloponnesus, let it be enough for me to remind you of the land from which we have come, of our freedom that is due to your courage, and of the fact that you are already accustomed to defeat those whom we are about to fight . . . show yourselves brave men, as Spartans always do . . . and remember the three traits of a good soldier: enthusiasm, a sense of honor, and loyalty. . . . Do not act as cowards . . . as for myself, I will prove that I am not better at giving advice than at following that same advice."

Thucydides did not confine his descriptions to individuals, because he firmly believed that his readers needed to know the characteristics, sufferings, and actions of the cities involved. Thucydides saw individuals as temporary rulers who often fell from power or

ANCIENT GREEKS

Thucydides

BORN

Before 454 B.C.
Athens, Greece

DIED

Between 404 and 400 B.C.
Athens, Greece

PROFESSION

Historian

ACCOMPLISHMENTS

Wrote *History*, an account of the Peloponnesian War and a brief history of early Greece

died during or after a crisis. What continued was the city, its customs, and its philosophy of life. As a result, he included sections that informed his readers about the chief cities involved in the conflict, namely Sparta, Athens, Corinth, and Syracuse. Such passages were intended to help readers understand how the war began and why it continued. Thucydides told how Spartans were not excited by success, nor downcast in time of defeat. The Athenians, he said, were very daring and quick to develop new plans.

These pointed descriptions also show Thucydides' style. He did not waste words, nor did he feel he had to include every detail he had recorded on his extensive travels. He used only what was necessary to tell his story.

Thucydides' *History* was as much a commentary on human nature as it was a history of the war. The terrible events of the times in which he lived did not allow him to incorporate passages of joy into his work. For Thucydides, the quarrels that caused the Peloponnesian War had destroyed the vitality, patriotism, and democratic ideals that followed Greece's victory over the Persians. He saw the power won by the Athenians as the basic cause of their problems. History, according to him, constantly proved that an excess of power corrupts individuals and causes them to disregard justice. In Book 3, section 82, Thucydides wrote, "The cause of today's problems is the desire to rule, a desire caused by greed and ambition."

As an example of how the conflict gradually destroyed the integrity of the Athenians, people who once prided themselves on their democratic way of life and their belief in justice, Thucydides described the Athenian treatment of the Melians. When the inhabitants of the small Aegean island of Melos told Athenian envoys that the Melians wished to remain neutral, the Athenians haughtily replied, "Those who are powerful demand what they can, while those who are weak must yield what is necessary."

When the Melians answered that the Athenians were acting unjustly, the arrogant Athenians retorted, "We plan to conquer you with as little trouble for ourselves as possible and certainly that will be best for you."

Again the Melians spoke. "Are you saying that Athens will refuse to let Melos remain neutral and be a friend?"

"We do not want your friendship," was the curt reply. "Friendship would imply that we Athenians are weak. But, if you hate us, that will prove we are powerful." So the Athenians defeated Melos.

For the first 100 years following Thucydides' death, writers rarely mentioned him. However, ever since the philosopher Theophrastus credited Thucydides and Herodotus as the founders of historical writing at the end of the 4th century B.C., Thucydides' fame as a historian has continued to grow. His evaluation of himself as the chronicler of events for future generations has, indeed, proved true. Through his words, the modern reader can visualize "one of the most noteworthy wars ever fought."

FURTHER READING

Connor, W. Robert. *Thucydides.* Princeton, N.J.: Princeton University Press, 1984.

Hornblower, Simon. *Thucydides.* Baltimore: Johns Hopkins University Press, 1993.

Thucydides. *History of the Peloponnesian War.* Edited by W. Robert Connor and translated by Richard Crawley. Boston: Tuttle, 1993.

———. *Thucydides.* Translated by C. F. Smith. Loeb Classical Library. Cambridge: Harvard University Press, 1935.

Alcibiades

PATRIOT AND TRAITOR

"They love, they hate, they cannot do without him." So spoke an actor performing in the Greek poet Aristophanes' new comedy *Frogs* at Athens' Theater of Dionysus. The year was 405 B.C. and the Athenian audience knew immediately that "they" referred to themselves and "him" to Alcibiades, a patriot-turned-traitor who lived in exile at the time. Any reference to Alcibiades always brought a rush of memories to Athenians, for his traitorous acts of switching his allegiance first to Sparta and then back to Athens won him the enmity of his fellow citizens and prevented any cooperation between the two cities.

Born sometime around 450 B.C., Alcibiades was a member of one of Athens' enduring aristocratic families. His father's influence on him, however, was very brief, for he was

Handsome, intelligent, and rich, Alcibiades pursued personal gain over devotion to country.

killed in 446 B.C. while trying to quell a revolt in the town of Coronea, to the north of Athens.

Alcibiades inherited a considerable fortune, for his father had been one of the richest men in Athens. Because Alcibiades was then far too young to manage his own affairs, by law the responsibility passed to a close male relative. For Alcibiades, this meant his maternal uncle Pericles, the most respected and powerful man in Athens.

According to the Greek biographer Plutarch, Alcibiades was a precocious but spoiled and strong-willed youngster. Although some of the details Plutarch mentioned in his account may not have been strictly historical, they most likely reflect the impression Alcibiades made on the Athenians.

One incident involved an encounter with a teacher who did not have in his possession a copy of Homer's epic poems the *Iliad* and the *Odyssey*. Angered and amazed at such an oversight, Alcibiades punched the teacher. Plutarch also told how Alcibiades became so frustrated when a schoolmate bound him firmly in a wrestling hold that he bit the boy's arm. Tauntingly, the bitten boy sneered, "Alcibiades, you bite like a woman." "No," was the reply, "I bite like a lion."

A third tale recounted the time when Alcibiades cut off the tail of a large and very beautiful dog for which he had paid an exorbitant sum of money. When asked why he had done such a thing, he retorted, "So that Athenians will speak only about this incident when they talk about me, and not concern themselves with knowing too much else about me." Although this response may seem conceited, it was well founded, because the Athenians did talk about him, especially about how he liked to spend money.

According to another story, he once entered seven chariots in the Olympic Games, something no Greek had ever done before. When he won the first, second, and fourth (or as the Greek playwright Euripides recounted, third) prizes, his name and reports of his wealth spread across the Greek world.

Alcibiades was considered one of Athens' most attractive young men, with a carefree, almost reckless attitude that fascinated his friends. The fact that he spoke with a lisp seemed to heighten his charm, for he used the lisp to accentuate what he was saying. Plutarch recounts that Alcibiades, for no reason except that he had told his companions he would do so, publicly punched the ears of a well-known and respected Athenian citizen named Hipponicus. The very next morning, he knocked at the door of the man whom he had so grievously insulted, tore off his clothes, and offered to be whipped as punishment for his crime. Won over by such actions, Hipponicus welcomed Alcibiades into his home and soon gave him his daughter Hipparete in marriage, along with a substantial dowry to seal the agreement.

Alcibiades, however, failed to remain faithful to Hipparete and continued his wild and spendthrift ways. When Hipparete filed for divorce and appeared in court, as Athenian law required, Alcibiades marched into the court, lifted Hipparete up into his arms, and carried her home. According to Plutarch, no one intervened, and the couple continued to live as husband and wife until Hipparete died a short time later. About their son, also named Alcibiades, little is known.

Although his personality won him critics as well as flatterers, Alcibiades had great potential, according to a former teacher, the philosopher Socrates, whose way of living was the exact opposite of Alcibiades'. Socrates' life was marked by simplicity;

Alcibiades' by luxury. Yet the two were often seen together—the older man barefoot and in shabby clothes and the younger man dressed in the latest fashions.

Their friendship was sincere, however, and when Socrates saw Alcibiades wounded at the Battle of Potidaea in 432 B.C., he bravely rushed to position himself in front of his friend, allowing Alcibiades to withdraw and save himself. Several years later, at the Battle of Delium in 424 B.C., the Athenians were in retreat when Alcibiades, who was on horseback at the time, saw Socrates trying to make his way back to camp on foot. Alcibiades placed himself and his horse between Socrates and the advancing enemy, thereby saving his teacher's life.

Nor was this Alcibiades' only notable act, for he repeatedly proved himself a capable warrior and leader during the Peloponnesian War, the bitter struggle between Athens and Sparta that had begun in 431 B.C. When Pericles died soon after the war began, Alcibiades was too young and too inexperienced to lead the Athenians, but he watched and waited as the statesmen Nicias and Cleon vied for control of Athens.

When Cleon died in 422 B.C., Nicias became Athens' leading statesman. A firm believer in peace, he negotiated the treaty with Sparta known as the Peace of Nicias. According to the terms of the agreement, the two cities pledged not to fight for 50 years. But Nicias was not the forceful personality Pericles had been, and he found it difficult to enforce the treaty.

It was about this time that Alcibiades became actively involved in politics. His ability to assess situations accurately and make decisions quickly fitted him to the profession, but his unprincipled nature brought him into direct conflict with Nicias and other prominent Athenians.

In 420 B.C., Alcibiades was elected one of the 10 *strategoi*, or generals. Because this office wielded the most power in Athens, Alcibiades was now in a position to persuade the Athenians to look west for lands to add to their empire, and he urged them to aid their ally, the Sicilian town of Segesta, against its rival, Selinus. Those Athenians who saw great advantages for their own welfare in bringing Sicily under their control quickly gave their support to Alcibiades.

Nicias vehemently opposed such action, but Alcibiades' eloquent arguments convinced the Athenians that they should approve his plan. However, the Athenians voted to send Nicias to Sicily because they were unwilling to entrust Alcibiades with the entire expedition. Despite his opposition to the plan, Nicias, a loyal patriot, did not refuse their wishes.

Soon all Athens was stirring with activity as ships, supplies, and recruits were being readied. Past defeats were forgotten in anticipation of future victories—until one morning the Athenians awoke to find that vandals had attacked their statues of the messenger god Hermes. Known as *hermae*, these statues stood on the city's street corners and were considered sacred by the Athenians. They wondered who could have committed such a sacrilege. Surely it was an omen that the Sicilian expedition would end in disaster. But Alcibiades was determined to set sail, even when the evidence pointed to him and his rowdy companions as the offenders. In 415 B.C., the fleet left for Sicily as planned and the investigations continued in Athens.

With Alcibiades gone, his accusers actively sought evidence against him, and they found more than they had anticipated. In addition to vandalizing the *hermae*, Alcibiades and his friends had also participated in a ceremony imitating the sacred rites in honor of

Alcibiades

BORN
Around 450 B.C.
Athens, Greece

DIED
404 B.C.
Phrygia, Asia Minor

PROFESSION
General

ACCOMPLISHMENTS
Led several Athenian armies to victory over Sparta during the Peloponnesian War; also led several Spartan armies to victory over the Athenians during the same war

This fragment from the Athenian Agora gives notice of the sale of Alcibiades' property after his condemnation for vandalizing the *hermae*. Included is a reference to cloaks "sold individually and with prices and sales tax recorded."

Demeter, the goddess of the harvest. Convinced that Alcibiades was guilty of sacrilege and that his crimes should be considered acts of treason, the Athenians arrested the accomplices who had remained in Athens and sent envoys to Sicily to relieve Alcibiades of his command.

"Stand trial, not I!" sneered Alcibiades when he heard of Athens' decision, and he slipped away from the Athenian camp to offer his services elsewhere. When he reached Italy and the colony of Thurii, which had been established years earlier by Athenians, he learned that the Athenian courts had sentenced him to death, confiscated his property, and ordered all priests and priestesses to curse his name. Believing that he could never return to Athens, Alcibiades turned to Sparta.

The Spartans eagerly welcomed him into their city after hearing that he had offered to turn traitor. The fun-loving and free-spending Alcibiades quickly adapted to the stern Spartan ways. He wore their simple coarse garments, ate their plain "black broth," bathed as they did in cold water, and participated actively in their rigorous daily athletic exercises. In his biography, Plutarch commented that Alcibiades changed his habits more quickly than a chameleon changed colors.

But it was Alcibiades' advice to attack the Athenian forces in Sicily that won the Spartans' gratitude. The Spartans immediately set sail for the island and ended the Sicilian expedition in a crushing defeat that left barely an Athenian alive. That same year, 413 B.C., Alcibiades counseled the Spartans to take Decelea, which they did, and from this garrison northwest of Athens they were able to harass the Athenians and ravage the countryside, destroying the city's grain supply.

Yet all was not going well for Alcibiades. Outwardly he played the part of a true Spartan, but his reckless nature and lack of respect for others brought him into trouble with Sparta's king, Agis II. When the king learned that Alcibiades had seduced his wife and fathered a child with her while he was away, he was outraged. For the moment, however, he controlled his anger because Alcibiades' services were still valuable to Sparta.

However, after Athens rebuilt its forces and succeeded in subduing many of the cities that had revolted against Athenian control, the Spartans began to suspect that Alcibiades was again switching his allegiance, this time to Persia.

Their suspicions were correct. Alcibiades knew that King Agis despised him and that some Spartans disapproved of his leadership. He also knew that the Athenians had not reversed the death sentence issued against him. Consequently, he reasoned that his only option was to ally himself with Persia, the enemy of both Athens and Sparta.

Tissaphernes, the Persian satrap (governor) in southern Asia Minor, welcomed the wily Greek, who now adapted himself to Persian customs and manners of dress. He eagerly listened to Alcibiades' plan: Persia should stand aside and let Sparta and Athens fight each other until both sides were so exhausted that a third party, namely Persia, could easily conquer both of them.

Tissaphernes, who had previously decided to help Sparta in an attempt to weaken Athens, followed Alcibiades' advice and stopped aiding the Spartans. When the Athenians learned of this change in policy, they thought that Alcibiades might once again be on their side, and they began to regret the harsh sentence their courts had passed on him. At the same time, Alcibiades was beginning to question Tissaphernes' loyalty. Believing that Athens now offered him the only possibility of safety, Alcibiades approached the Athenian generals who were stationed with the fleet on the island of Samos, a faithful Athenian ally. He advised them to take control of Athens and make it an oligarchy (a government ruled by a few individuals). Once this was accomplished, he said, the generals could then seek the help of Tissaphernes against Sparta.

Following Alcibiades' advice, the generals agreed to send Pisander (one of the generals) to Athens to bring about a change in government, start the proceedings to recall Alcibiades, and consider an alliance with Tissaphernes. Pisander began implementing all three plans, but when Tissaphernes heard of the proposed alliance, he switched allegiance and renewed ties with his old ally, Sparta. Pisander and his allies also changed course. They decided to forget Persia and Alcibiades, take control of Athens, and align themselves with Sparta.

When this news reached Samos, the generals declared the new government illegal and proclaimed themselves the legal Athenian government. They then recalled Alcibiades and elected him a *strategos*. Alcibiades attacked the Spartan fleet, and in 410 B.C. won a decisive victory at Cyzicus, on the coast of the Sea of Marmara. Alcibiades then attacked Byzantium (present-day Istanbul) and brought it and other cities under Athenian control. His victories won him the support of Athenian merchants because he had opened trade routes to ports along the Black Sea. They also won him the admiration of the people he defeated, for unlike so many conquerors, Alcibiades did not believe in destroying towns or murdering their inhabitants.

In 408 B.C., seven years after he had left on the Sicilian expedition, Alcibiades returned to Athens and was welcomed as a hero. As proof of their trust, the Athenians gave him command of all the Athenian forces, both on land and on sea. Their joy, however, soon changed to anger when in 406

"Any individual under indictment would be foolish to seek an acquittal when he can get away."

—what Alcibiades said, according to Plutarch, when he went into hiding after being summoned from Sicily to stand trial in Athens

B.C. news reached Athens that the Spartans had defeated the Athenians at Notium on the coast of Asia Minor. Believing that with Alcibiades as commander no Athenian force should meet defeat, the Athenians removed Alcibiades from his post as commander in chief.

Hurt and dejected, Alcibiades refused to return to Athens to defend his honor or to accept a lesser rank in the military. Instead, he withdrew to his castle home in rocky Thrace, on the northern shores of the Aegean Sea. The following year, Athens prepared to meet Sparta in the waters just below his home. Watching the proceedings, Alcibiades immediately recognized the vulnerability of the Athenians and his loyalty to Athens once more compelled him to act. Mounting his horse, he rode down to the shore to warn the Athenian commander that he should lead his fleet out of the harbor because it offered no protection. Unfortunately, his advice went unheeded, and a few days later the Spartans attacked and completely destroyed the Athenian fleet. Months later, Spartan troops entered the city of Athens, destroyed the Long Walls that connected the city with the sea, and burned the Athenian ships in the harbor at Piraeus. The Peloponnesian War came to an end.

With Sparta as the new leader of the Greek world, Alcibiades became the unwanted enemy. The Spartans feared his persuasive manner and his preference for the democratic form of government practiced in Athens, and they condemned him to permanent exile. Yet Sparta's leaders could not relax, for they wondered what plans Alcibiades might be making. When they learned that he planned to ask the king of Persia for help against Sparta, they decided to act quickly.

According to Plutarch, Sparta hired assassins to kill Alcibiades before he could meet with the Persian king. In a small village in Phrygia, a country in Asia Minor, the assassins surrounded the house where Alcibiades was living and set it on fire. As the flames devoured the walls, Alcibiades tried to smother the fire with clothes and furniture. He then wrapped his cloak about his left arm and, brandishing a sword in his right hand, walked quickly through the flames and escaped the house unharmed. Fearful of engaging in hand-to-hand combat with such a warrior, the assassins retreated and from a distance used their bows and arrows to kill Alcibiades.

FURTHER READING

Ellis, Walter M. *Alcibiades*. New York: Routledge, 1989.

Green, Peter. *Armada from Athens*. Garden City, N.Y.: Doubdeday, 1970.

Plutarch. *Plutarch: The Lives of the Noble Grecians and Romans*. Translated by John Dryden and edited and revised by Arthur Hugh Clough. 1979. Reprint. New York: Modern Library, 1992.

More Ancient Greeks to Remember

Anaxagoras (around 500–around 428 B.C.) left his hometown of Clazomenae, a Greek city on a small island off the coast of Asia Minor, and went to Athens in 480 B.C. Perhaps he accompanied the Persian king Xerxes' invasion forces, but Anaxagoras was a thinker and not a soldier. Once in Athens, he decided to stay there and began teaching and writing.

Considered Athens' first philosopher in residence, Anaxagoras questioned the formation of the world and the universe. He did not agree with the prevailing belief that everything came from a single basic element such as fire or water. Anaxagoras reasoned that for a tree to be a tree, it had to have the essence of a tree from the beginning. For Anaxagoras, the beginning was a great mass made up of everything that would eventually exist. Gradually, this mass began to rotate and, as it did, the basic elements—water, air, cold, and the like—began to form and separate from the mass. From these came everything that makes up the world. Nothing new ever formed, only substances or elements that had been part of the original shapeless mass.

Anaxagoras also believed that nothing could be destroyed completely. He reasoned that every substance contained particles of every other substance and that what made a tree a tree was that it had more "tree" particles than any other particle. Consequently, when a tree burns, smoke, fire, and ash are able to form because their particles were already present in the tree.

There was one exception, however, which he called the *nous*, or "mind." Separate and distinct, the *nous* did not belong to the original great mass but was the moving force that made the mass rotate and spewed forth elements and substances. It continued as the moving force responsible for the development of everything that makes up the world.

Anaxagoras became friendly with many of Athens' leading citizens, including the tragic playwright Euripides and the statesman Pericles. When Pericles' enemies decided to hurt him by attacking his friends, Anaxagoras was one of the first to be prosecuted for his beliefs. Pericles did manage to save his friend from the death sentence, but Anaxagoras had to leave Athens. From 450 B.C. until his death, he lived in Lampsacus in northern Asia Minor.

Myron (active around 460–440 B.C.) won the admiration and praise of his contemporaries for his magnificently crafted statues. Working mostly in bronze, Myron was able to capture that moment when the body has just completed one action and is about to begin another. An ancient

Myron's *Discus Thrower* is executed in a realistic style that captures the moment of action.

Roman copy of Myron's *Discus Thrower* depicts a trim yet muscular athlete, having maneuvered the discus into position, seconds away from hurling it as far as he possibly can.

Myron was considered to be an Athenian because the residents of his hometown of Eleutherae, in Boeotia, had been granted Athenian citizenship. He helped bring about a revolution in the arts. His works clearly broke from the archaic tradition of crafting stiff, stern figures with stylized hair ringlets and unexpressive faces. Myron's sculptures showed the body in action, with muscles, veins, and limbs reflecting that action. Moreover, his statues were idealized portrayals of the human body. For example, *The Discus Thrower* illustrates perfect form, and the athlete's face is very calm and controlled, making the action seem effortless.

Parrhasius and Zeuxis (active in the 5th century B.C.) were two of Athens' most respected artists, and for years Athenians had debated who was better. Ancient accounts tell us that, one day, the two men decided to settle the controversy themselves and challenged each other to a contest. They asked the citizens of Athens to judge their work.

Parrhasius was a native of the Greek city of Ephesus on the coast of Asia Minor (present-day Turkey), where he had studied with his father, the painter Evenor. However, Parrhasius chose to spend most of his time in Athens, and in later centuries it was reported that the Athenians had so admired Parrhasius that they had granted him the rights of Athenian citizenship.

Zeuxis, on the other hand, hailed from Heraclea, a Greek colony near the Black Sea, and he kept the city as his base but traveled extensively throughout the Greek world.

Unfortunately, only written descriptions of their works survive, but from them we learn that the Greek world acknowledged Parrhasius as the master of the line because his subtle outlining of the contours of each body gave his figures a three-dimensional look. The majority of Parrhasius' paintings centered on a single figure, usually a god, goddess, or mythological hero.

Zeuxis also used realism in his paintings, but instead of using lines as Parrhasius did, Zeuxis became the master of chiaroscuro, the use of light and shade to produce a dramatic effect or a feeling of depth.

Although fame made both Zeuxis and Parrhasius very wealthy, it also made them arrogant. Parrhasius boasted that he was a descendant of the god Apollo. And Zeuxis began to give away his paintings because he said no price could ever match their worth. It is easy to understand why, as a result, all Athens hummed about the contest between two such notable characters. For weeks, Parrhasius and Zeuxis had worked daily in their studios, keeping their work hidden from everyone. When the two stood before the Athenians, a hush gradually spread across the assembly. Beside each artist, covered by a curtain and bound by a gold cord, was his painting.

After Parrhasius graciously motioned to Zeuxis to unveil his painting first, Zeuxis slowly pulled the gold cord from his entry with one hand, and with the other hand opened a small birdcage that he had brought with him. Immediately, several birds flew out, circled the assembly, and then flew straight at Zeuxis' painting.

The Athenians looked and then gasped. Zeuxis had painted a still life of a table set with a bowl of grapes—and the birds headed straight for the grapes. Thunderous applause rang out across the assembly as the Athenians cheered Zeuxis' skill.

Parrhasius then asked Zeuxis to pull the cord binding Parrhasius' entry. Without hesitating, Zeuxis put out his hand to take the cord. But all his

An Athenian bride and groom sit in the wedding cart as friends lead the way to the groom's house. The typical Athenian woman was subject to strict rules that kept her inside her home. Aspasia, a foreigner not subject to such rules, was able to visit and entertain writers, philosophers, and other public figures. Through Pericles, with whom she lived, she may also have had some influence over public affairs.

hand hit was a painting, for Parrhasius had painted just a curtain bound by a gold cord.

Zeuxis then turned to Parrhasius and conceded defeat for he, Zeuxis, had deceived the birds but Parrhasius had deceived him.

Aspasia (active in the 5th century B.C.) was regarded as one of the most intellectual and cultured women in Athens. A native of Miletus, a prosperous Greek city in southern Asia Minor, Aspasia migrated to Athens and won the respect and love of the city's leading citizen, Pericles. While the two lived together until Pericles' death, it is unknown whether they ever actually married. Under Athenian law, Athenian citizens who married foreigners were subject to severe penalties. However, as a non-Athenian, Aspasia was not subject to the rigid rules that kept Athenian women at home. A close friend was the well-known philosopher Socrates, with whom she spoke and debated frequently. And many of Athens' thinkers and writers visited her house regularly to discuss ideas.

Many contemporaries spoke of Aspasia's influence on public affairs through Pericles. Sometime in the 430s, Pericles' enemies tried to harm him by attacking his close friends. Aspasia became a target of their jealousy and was tried for impiety. Only after Pericles appeared in court and broke down in tears did the jurors vote to acquit her.

Hippodamus (active in the 5th century B.C.) achieved fame as a designer of cities. A native of the Greek city of Miletus in southern Asia Minor, Hippodamus emigrated to Athens, where he met and worked for Pericles as a city planner. Although he was not the first to use the gridiron design (straight, parallel roads that intersect each other at right angles), Hippodamus was the first to apply it so effectively to Greek cities. For Hippodamus, it was only natural that a city be divided into sections that accommodate the different activities taking place within that city. Therefore, he assigned residential quarters to one area, public buildings to another, craftsmen's working quarters to another, and so on.

Sometime during the middle of the 5th century B.C., Pericles commissioned Hippodamus to design a new city plan for Piraeus, the city that served as Athens' port and harbor. In 444–43 B.C., when Athens established the colony of Thurii in southern Italy, Hippodamus was one of the new settlers. The orderly rectangular plan of Thurii likely reflects his influence.

Ictinus (active around 450–420 B.C.) was the architect responsible for the design of the Parthenon, the temple on the Acropolis dedicated to Athena. Ictinus wrote a book describing the temple's design and the innovations he used to correct optical illusions.

Realizing that a straight, even column gives the illusion of being thinner in the middle because the light shining behind the column "eats" away at the central portion, Ictinus used entasis. That is, he made his columns swell gently in the middle and then taper slightly at the top. Ictinus also observed that perfectly straight columns give the appearance of slanting outward. The columns he designed leaned slightly inward from bottom to top. Ictinus also made his corner columns a bit wider than the others because he knew that corner columns reflect light on both sides, making them appear thinner than the side columns.

Acknowledged by his contemporaries as a master architect, Ictinus

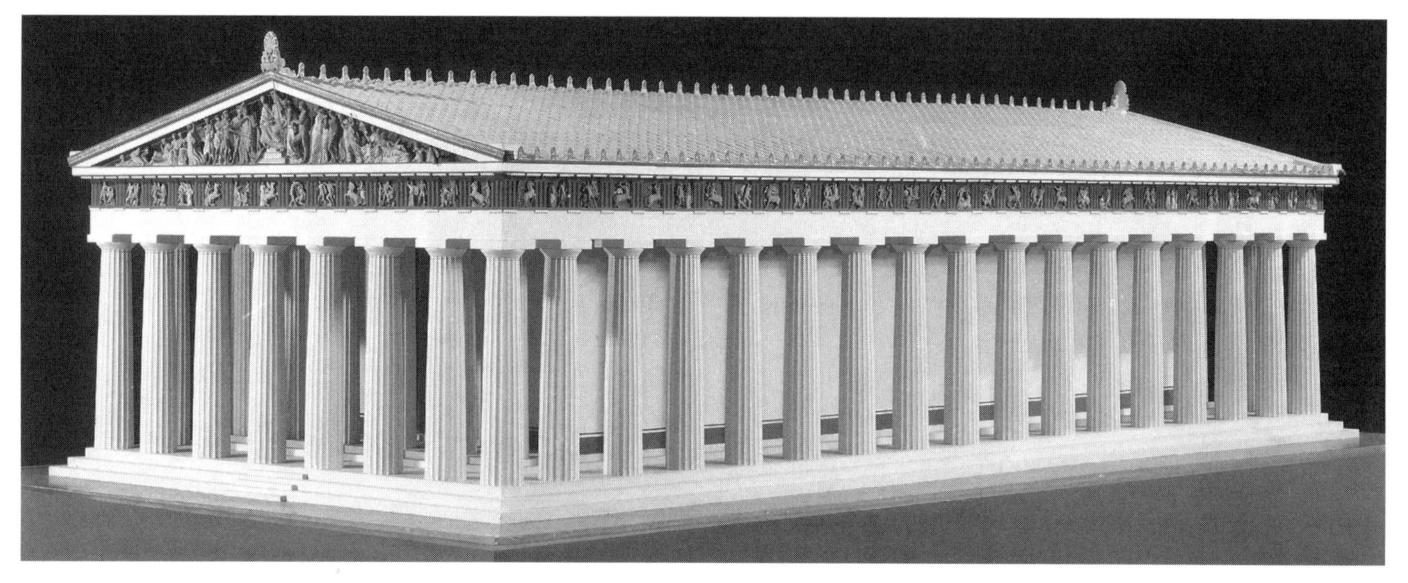

This scale model of the Parthenon shows how Ictinus, the architect responsible for its design, envisioned the finished project. Architects and engineers are now working to rebuild and restore the structures on the Acropolis, including the Parthenon.

received many commissions for other works. His most famous was the majestic temple to Apollo at Bassae in southern Greece, whose columns and base still stand today. Another of his magnificent creations was the Telesterion at Eleusis, just west of Athens. In this great covered hall, the followers of the goddess Demeter conducted their secret religious rituals.

Mnesicles (active after 445 B.C.) designed the Propylaea, the majestic gateway leading to the Acropolis. Like his contemporaries, Phidias and Ictinus, Mnesicles was also commissioned by the Athenian statesman Pericles to rebuild Athens. What made Mnesicles' job difficult was the unevenness of the terrain leading up to the Acropolis. As a result, he had to adjust his design to accommodate a gateway that reached across several levels. Construction began in 437 B.C., but the outbreak of the Peloponnesian War stopped the work and the gateway was never completed. Much of the Propylaea has survived, and today architects and engineers are involved in an effort to restore Mnesicles' structure.

According to legend, Mnesicles once fell from the heights of the Propylaea while inspecting the construction. His injuries were so severe that death seemed inevitable until Pericles brought him a healing herb that the goddess Athena had revealed to him in a dream.

Brasidas (died in 422 B.C.) is considered one of Sparta's greatest generals. In 425 B.C., after the Athenian Cleon captured a Spartan contingent in southern Greece, Brasidas opposed the peace offers suggested by many Spartans. Like Cleon, Brasidas favored an aggressive policy and continued warfare. Gathering a force of mercenaries and Helots (people who ranked just above slaves and who belonged to the state, but had no rights and were forced to work for the Spartans), Brasidas marched north beyond the borders of Greece and into Thrace, where Athenian influence was strong.

In quick succession, Brasidas subdued several areas allied to Athens, including the important city of Amphipolis. His ability to inspire confidence and his military leadership won him many admirers among former Athenian allies.

In 422 B.C., Cleon also marched north, hoping to regain lost territory. On the battlefield before the walls of Amphipolis, Cleon met Brasidas, but the Spartan's maneuvers outflanked the Athenians. Cleon died fighting, as did Brasidas. Grieved by the death of a leader they considered a hero, the townspeople of Amphipolis buried Brasidas within the city walls and honored him with yearly sacrifices and athletic contests. With Brasidas and Cleon dead, the peace factions in Sparta and Athens came into power.

Nicias (died in 413 B.C.) ably led Athens' forces during the Peloponnesian War. Respected for his caution on the battlefield, Nicias was elected *strategos*, or general, several times and led his troops to many victories. Yet he was always urging a peaceful resolution to the conflict and explaining how peace would benefit both Athens and Sparta. After Pericles' death, Nicias' views brought him into direct conflict with Cleon, the new leader of the democratic, or people's, party.

Cleon's death in 422 B.C. allowed Nicias to push his policies more forcefully and in 421 B.C., Athens and Sparta signed a 50-year peace treaty known as the Peace of Nicias. But opponents of the treaty tried to force both sides back to the battlefield. When the Athenian general and statesman Alcibiades proposed sending Athenian troops to conquer areas in Sicily, Nicias vehemently objected. After much debate, Alcibiades won the argument by convincing the Athenians that a victory in Sicily would expand Athens' empire and control in the west.

Against Nicias' wishes, the Athenians named him and Lamachus co-commanders of the expedition with Alcibiades. Soon after the Athenians arrived in Sicily, Alcibiades was recalled to face criminal charges in Athens and Lamachus was killed in a skirmish outside the walls of the city of Syracuse. Nicias now became the sole commander of the expedition, one he had bitterly opposed. He sent a message to Athens, asking to be relieved of the command. Not only was his request refused, but Athens sent reinforcements under the command of a general named Demosthenes. Even though Nicias was now ill, he remained commander until several defeats convinced him that retreat was his only option. He ordered his troops to prepare for a secret nighttime withdrawal. Just as they were leaving, an eclipse of the moon occurred. Nicias immediately consulted a soothsayer, who told him that the eclipse was a sign from the gods that the Athenian troops should remain in Italy until the next full moon. Nicias canceled all orders for retreat. Demosthenes strongly protested the foolishness of such action, but Nicias, a very religious man, refused to listen.

A disastrous naval defeat followed, and the Athenians, unable to escape by sea, tried desperately to escape by land. The Syracusans overwhelmed and destroyed the Athenian forces, killing Demosthenes and Nicias. The historian Thucydides later wrote, "The Athenians suffered no regular defeat in Sicily, but were completely annihilated—army, fleet, and all. Of the many thousands who had sailed to Sicily, only a very few ever saw their homes again."

Lysander (died in 395 B.C.) was an outstanding military commander, perhaps the best Sparta ever produced. His arrogance and his constant desire for praise, however, lost him the respect of both the Spartans and the Athenians.

Although he was not a member of Sparta's royal family, Lysander won the recognition of the city's leaders because of his leadership on the battlefield and in political discussions. He also gained the confidence of the Persian commander Cyrus, who was reported to have given Lysander money to pay his soldiers. Lysander's crushing defeat of the Athenian forces at Notium resulted in the permanent removal of Alcibiades as commander of the Athenians. Soon after, the Spartans named Lysander commander of their navy.

In 405 B.C. Lysander destroyed the Athenian fleet in the Battle of Aegospotami, making it impossible for the Athenians to import grain through the Hellespont, the strait between Europe and Asia that connects the Aegean Sea with the Sea of Marmara. The Athenians now had the choice of starvation or surrender, and they chose the latter. When the Peloponnesian War began in 431 B.C. Athens was the acknowledged capital of the Greek world. Just 27 years later, in 404 B.C., Sparta took control and Lysander became Greece's leading citizen.

With his approval, Athens' Long Walls and the fortifications around the port of Piraeus were destroyed. Lysander then installed as Athens' new leaders a group of pro-Spartan rulers known to history as the Thirty Tyrants. To each of Athens' former allies, Lysander sent a Spartan commander, accompanied by a 10-member board.

In 403 B.C. the prodemocracy Athenians revolted and, despite Lysander's nearly successful attempt to quell the uprising, the Thirty Tyrants were ousted, as were the Spartan commanders in the allied communities. Although Lysander immediately lost his influence at home, he refused to admit defeat and plotted to make the monarchy in Sparta an elected position. When his efforts proved futile, Lysander used his influence to help Agesilaus succeed his brother, Agis, as king of Sparta, bypassing Agis' son as the rightful heir.

Nevertheless, Agesilaus refused to favor either Lysander or his policies. Perhaps he disliked Lysander's haughty attitude. Lysander always commissioned the best poets to celebrate his accomplishments, considered himself worthy of being honored as a god, and even had Greek cities make sacrifices to him and hold festivals in his honor.

When several cities, including Athens and Corinth, revolted against Spartan control in 395 B.C. Lysander was again given command of a Spartan army. He was killed the same year while leading his forces in Boeotia, a district just northeast of Athens.

THE CONQUESTS OF ALEXANDER THE GREAT

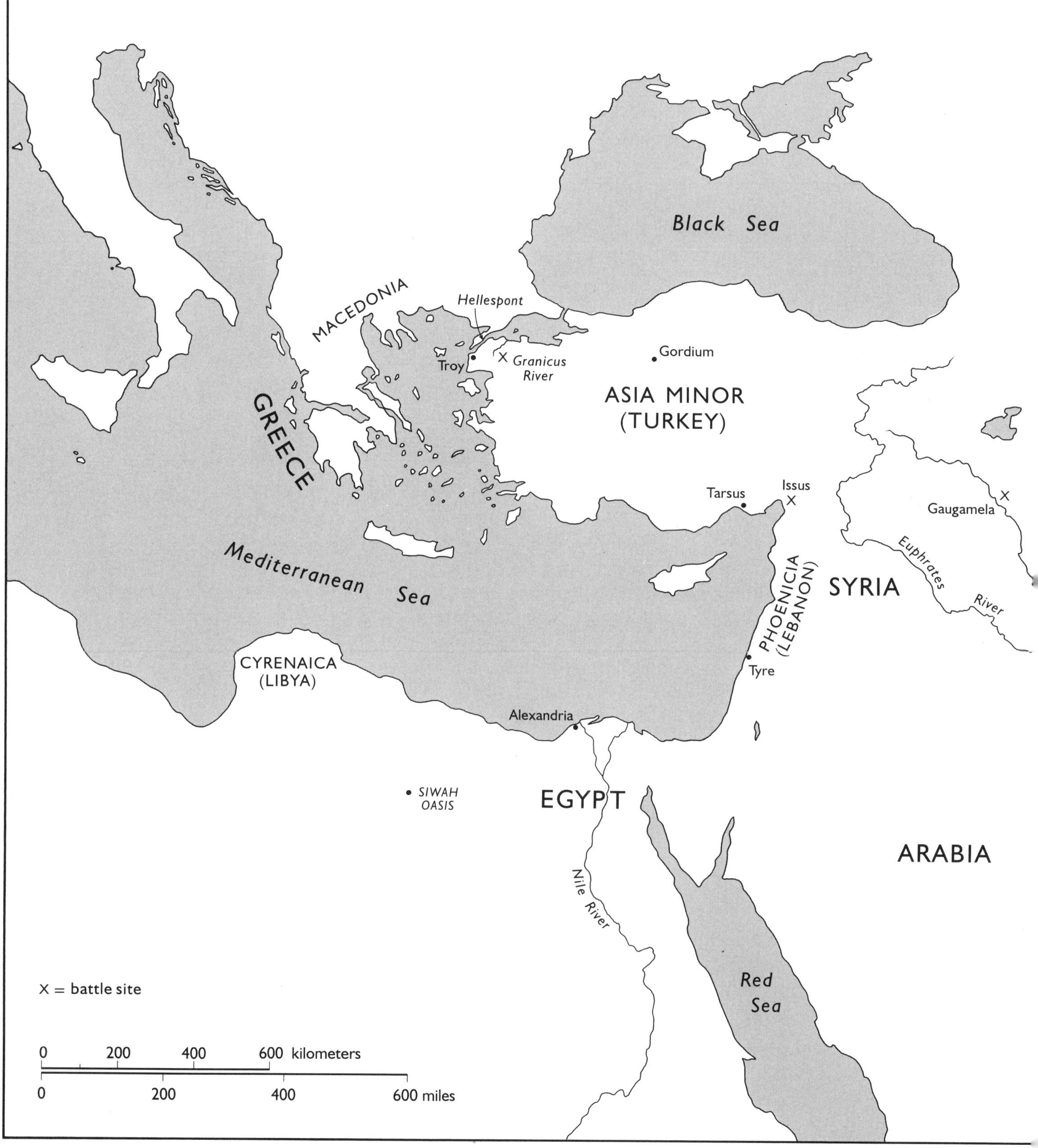

Black Sea
MACEDONIA
Hellespont
Troy
X Granicus River
Gordium
GREECE
ASIA MINOR (TURKEY)
Tarsus
Issus X
Gaugamela X
Mediterranean Sea
PHOENICIA (LEBANON)
SYRIA
Euphrates River
CYRENAICA (LIBYA)
Tyre
Alexandria
SIWAH OASIS
EGYPT
ARABIA
Nile River
Red Sea

X = battle site

0 200 400 600 kilometers
0 200 400 600 miles

Aral Sea
Caspian Sea
ASIA
HINDU KUSH MOUNTAINS
BACTRIA
Taxila
Ecbatana
Indus River
Jhelum River
Tigris River
abylon
Susa
Persepolis
INDIA
PERSIA
Pura
GEDROSIA DESERT
Persian Gulf
Arabian Sea

4 Expanding the Greek World (400–300 B.C.)

The 4th century B.C. ended with Athens a considerably weakened city-state, having lost the Peloponnesian War to its archrival, Sparta. Still Athens continued as Greece's cultural leader, while Sparta sought to prove its military might by extending its power and influence across the Greek world. In such an atmosphere, many Greeks turned to philosophy and found comfort in the ideas fostered by thinkers such as Plato and Aristotle.

Meanwhile, to the north of Greece, a determined ruler named Philip II watched and waited as the Greek city-states fought among themselves. He saw in their disunity an opportunity to extend his power across the entire Greek peninsula. Events proved him right, and the Greeks who had so prided themselves on freedom and independence lost both to a foreigner. But the Greek tradition continued, for Philip and his son Alexander believed strongly in preserving what so many Greeks had spent decades crafting, shaping, and guarding.

Part 4 of *Ancient Greeks* profiles people who cultivated the Greek tradition and whose accomplishments led to the spread of Greek culture far beyond the borders of the Greek world.

IN THIS PART

Plato

KNOWLEDGE IS RECOLLECTION

"Plato is philosophy and philosophy is Plato." So wrote the Greek biographer Plutarch 450 years after Plato's death. Nor did Plato's influence wane after Plutarch's time, for his writings affected the thinking of the entire Western world.

Born of aristocratic Athenian parents, Plato traced his ancestry on his father's side to Codrus, the king who voluntarily sacrificed himself to the enemy so that Athens might remain free. On his mother's side, the line stretched back to Solon, the renowned Athenian lawgiver. Interest in politics was a family trait, and 5th-century B.C. Athens found Plato's family active in the government of Athens' master statesman, Pericles.

Plato's first years, however, were not very happy times for Athens. Ancient sources placed his birth sometime between 429 B.C. and 427 B.C., when the Peloponnesian War was raging and Pericles had just died of the plague. Whether Plato was born in Athens or on the nearby island of Aegina is unclear. In 431 B.C., Athens had seized the island and expelled the inhabitants for their part in instigating the war and siding with Sparta. Plato's family, along with the family of the Greek playwright Aristophanes, was among those sent to Aegina to establish a new settlement.

The war had little effect on Plato's education, however, and he received the best available. Because Athens was still the cultural and intellectual center of the Greek world, he was exposed to many ideas and ways of thinking. Yet it was the teachings of the Athenian philosopher Socrates that intrigued him the most. In 399 B.C., when the city's leaders condemned Socrates to death, Plato was devastated. He abandoned all plans for a political career because Socrates' death proved to him that no one with a conscience had a chance of becoming a politician.

With several companions who had also been followers of Socrates, Plato left Athens and settled in the neighboring city-state of Megara. Thinking that Athens would not be safe for anyone who had been closely associated with Socrates, Plato spent the following years traveling in Greece, Egypt, and Italy. When he was about 40 years old he visited Sicily, where he became friendly with Dion, the brother-in-law of Syracuse's ruler, Dionysius I. This relationship greatly influenced Plato's life and opinions.

Everywhere he traveled, Plato critically observed the successes and failures of the government in power. Using his findings, the teachings of Socrates, and his own beliefs,

Plato began writing dialogues in which two or more characters discussed their ideas about human nature and government.

Around 387 B.C., Plato returned to Athens. A few ancient sources recorded that, while on his way home, Plato was captured, imprisoned, and sold at a slave market before ransom money, paid by a philosopher named Anniceris, bought him his freedom. The tale is impossible to prove, but ancient records note that soon after Plato returned to Athens, he opened his own school in a house and garden near a grove about a mile outside the city's walls. Because the nearby park was dedicated to a legendary Athenian hero named Academus, the school came to be known as the Academy. Through the centuries, many schools have been called academies.

Here Plato welcomed students who wished to pursue philosophical and scientific research. Admission was open to all who applied, including women (the names of two women have been found on surviving rosters). Because Plato had a keen interest in mathematics and law, the Academy became known for its expertise in both areas. Set above the entrance to the school was the inscription "Let no one enter who has not studied geometry."

Plato saw his school as the place where he could teach young people about politics and life to prepare them to become responsible public officials. Unlike Aristotle's Lyceum or Isocrates' school of rhetoric, Plato's Academy was much more organized and not dependent on one instructor. Plato was headmaster of the Academy and oversaw the other teachers. There were provisions for nominating an interim head whenever Plato left Athens and for electing a new head after Plato's death. This organization ensured the Academy's survival, and it remained open, attracting pupils from around the Mediterranean for more than 900 years, until A.D. 529, when the Roman emperor Justinian ordered all philosophical schools closed.

Plato sincerely enjoyed his work at the Academy and remained its principal instructor for 40 years. Among Plato's pupils were many Greeks who later achieved prominence, including the philosopher Aristotle and the general Timotheus. Although no records exist of the exact curriculum or teaching methods, Plato's writings, especially his dialogues, clearly reveal his philosophy. Because of the fame he achieved during his lifetime and the faithfulness of his followers at the Academy, Plato's works were copied word for word on many occasions and have survived intact through the centuries.

A reading of Plato's dialogues illustrates how his thought processes gradually changed over the years. His early writings reflect the influence of Socrates in the use of a series of questions to arrive at true knowledge—the same format that Socrates had used to teach philosophical ideas. In fact, Plato even used Socrates as a principal character in his early works. It was also Plato's intention to compile and defend his master's teachings against further criticism.

In his later works, Plato turned more to understanding the essence of his ideas and what qualities characterized them. The character of Socrates in these works is absent or of little importance.

Two of the most powerful dialogues involving Socrates are the *Apology*, which centers on Socrates' defense against the charge that he corrupted Athens' youth, and the *Phaedo*, which deals with Socrates' final days in prison. In both, Plato moves from the actions of the court and Socrates' grieving followers in his prison cell to questions about the gods, the sanctity of laws, and the immortality of the soul.

This mosaic from a villa near Pompeii, Italy, is believed to represent Plato (third from the left, holding a stick) teaching his pupils in the garden of the Academy.

In both dialogues, Plato followed Socrates' manner of teaching, asking question after question. The first questions were general and the answers obvious. Gradually he introduced questions that required more serious and abstract thought. There were no right or wrong answers, for the participants in the dialogue were encouraged to find the answers within themselves. As a result, Plato's writings offered few definite conclusions to problems or situations, although he ended some dialogues with a myth intended to make a particular point.

Plato's style was very effective because it allowed participants in his dialogues, as well as readers of succeeding generations, to arrive at the answer themselves. His manner of reasoning

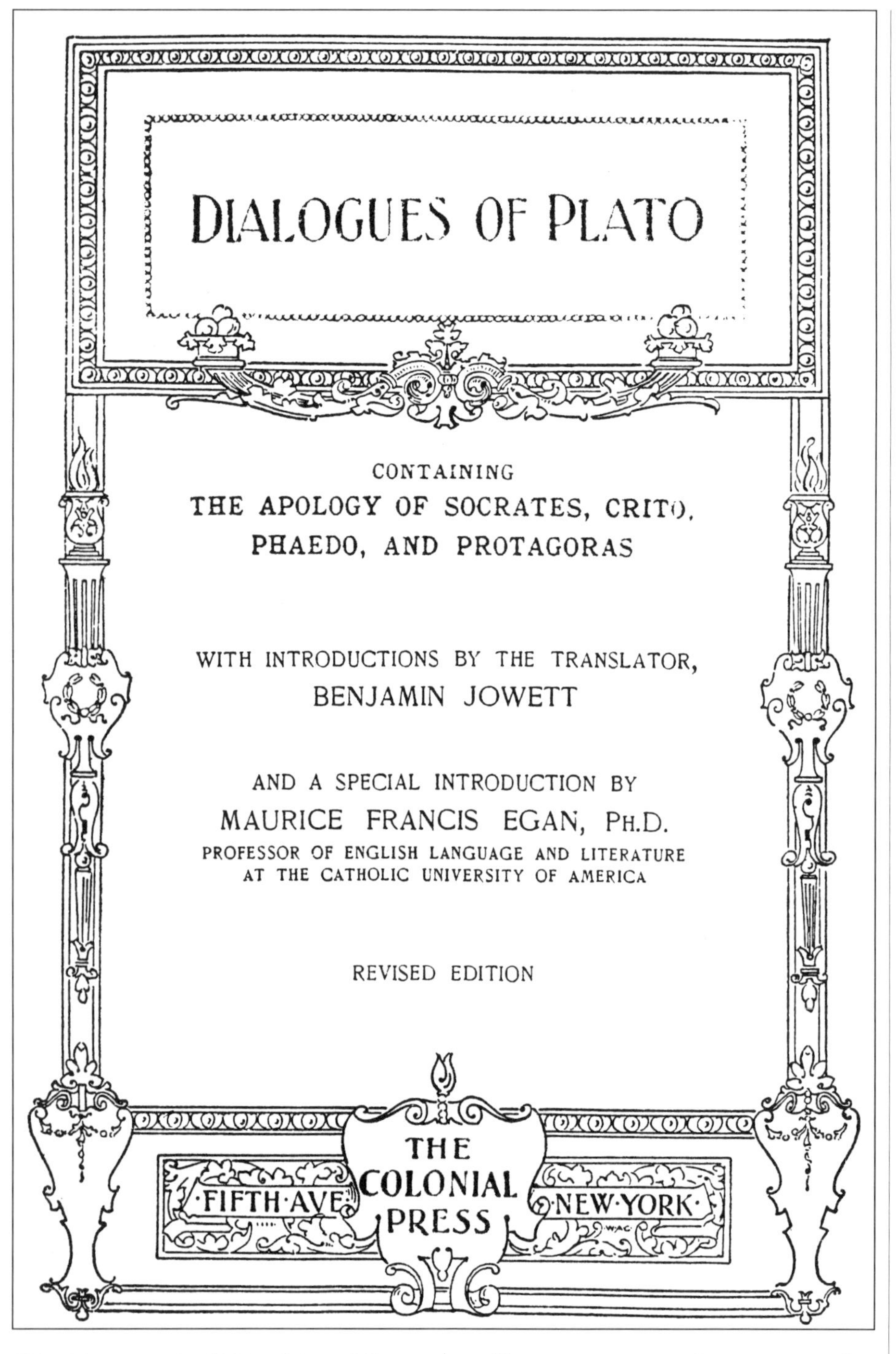

This title page of a 1900 edition of Plato attests to the ancient philosopher's continued popularity. In the *Dialogues* Plato had two or more characters, such as Socrates, discuss their ideas about human nature and government.

and his presentation of questions and arguments were designed to open up new possibilities and expand a person's way of thinking.

Perhaps the reason why Plato's dialogues seem so alive is that he incorporated into them his own quest for answers to the meaning of life, the nature of the soul, and the need for good politicians. His search, however, led him to question the actual meanings of terms like *good, beautiful,* and *just,* because each one could apply to people, animals, and things. For example, it was proper to say a good person, a good horse, a good law. But in each case, the criteria for determining a "good" example were different. A good person was one who was honorable and treated others fairly, but a good horse was one that was suitable for a particular purpose, such as plowing.

Plato reasoned that everyone had a common idea of what *good* was supposed to mean and used the word accordingly. His questioning led him to believe that within each person was something that at one time had perfect knowledge of the meaning of *good* and all other concepts. For Plato, this "something" was the soul that existed within, yet separate from, the body.

In his dialogue called the *Republic*, Plato discussed his theory about various concepts, including the nature of what is good and beautiful, and their relationship to the life of the soul. According to Plato, before a soul entered a human's body it existed in a perfect world where it experienced the "perfect good," the "perfect beautiful," the "perfect just." When a soul prepared to enter a body, it first had to cross a very hot, dry area that made it very thirsty. Then it had to pass the river Lethe (in Greek mythology, the river of forgetfulness). The stronger the soul, the greater its ability to resist the temptation to drink too much. The weaker the soul, the more it drank.

When the soul entered its new body on earth, the extent of its memory of the perfect world it had left behind depended upon how much water it had drunk. Only when a soul had advanced far enough in philosophy and the understanding of the mys-

Plato

BORN

Between 429 and 427 B.C.
Athens or Aegina, Greece

DIED

347 B.C.
Athens, Greece

PROFESSION

Philosopher

ACCOMPLISHMENTS

Established the school in Athens known as the Academy; wrote the *Apology*, in which he had his teacher Socrates reply to the charges made against him by Athens' leaders; 25 philosophical dialogues are credited to him, including the *Republic*, *Crito*, *Phaedo*, *Laws*, *Timaeus*, *Sophist*, and *Symposium*

tery of life was it capable of resisting the temptation to drink the water. Plato reasoned that once the soul had advanced this far, it no longer had to cross the river Lethe but joined the absolute truth and left behind the images of truth.

Plato taught that no soul ever forgot the perfect world, which Plato referred to as the Ideal, because shadows of that world remained within the soul's memory. Therefore, when a person used the term *good,* that person was comparing what he saw on earth to the soul's shadow image of the "perfect good." This was Plato's so-called Doctrine of Ideas. It expressed his belief in the immortality of the soul and his belief that knowledge is recollection. To help his followers and pupils understand his theory of ideas and to make his point clearer, Plato included a myth at the end of the *Republic*.

Imagine, Plato said, a dark cave in which people live as prisoners, held in chains and allowed to face only the innermost wall. Not one of them has ever been allowed to leave the cave. Behind them rises another wall across which various objects pass. Between the second wall and the entrance to the cave is a great fire, which casts a shadow of each object onto the inner wall that the prisoners face. Because those chained within the cave have seen only the shadows, they consider them real.

However, should one of the prisoners be allowed outside the cave into the light, imagine his surprise and amazement to see the "real" objects and not the shadows he had supposed were reality. And what if that prisoner should reenter the cave and attempt to convince the others to come and see what he has seen. Would they believe him and leave the only world they know, or would they consider him a madman and condemn him?

Because Plato believed that a person's main responsibilities were to his soul and his city-state, he considered it the duty of the prisoner who was led to the light—that is, to truth—to become a leader. For Plato, morality and politics needed to be considered together. The ideal ruler was one who knew the truth, because only that individual could lead the city-state toward what is good. To know the truth, a person needs philosophy because it is philosophy that helps recover the knowledge of that perfect world of ideas, where terms and concepts such as *good* and *just* reside in their perfect forms.

Such learning, however, takes time and requires discipline. Therefore, he suggested that the best youths in the city-state be chosen to enter a strict educational program. For Plato, an ideal city-state needed a group of well-trained people whose primary concern was the political and moral welfare of the state. He believed that the ideal government was an aristocracy where the best citizens were the public officials. He rejected the other four forms of government with which he was familiar, ranking them in order of merit: timocracy (rule by people concerned with power and glory), oligarchy (rule by a privileged few), democracy (rule by the people), and tyranny (rule by a dictator). In the *Republic*, Plato wrote, "Until philosophers are kings or kings are philosophers and until political greatness and wisdom are as one with all else standing aside, no city-state will be free of evil."

Plato advised adopting a system in which preliminary education would end at age 17 or 18. Those who had proven themselves to be the best at this age would begin a three-year peri-

"The direction in which education starts an individual determines his future life."

—from the *Republic*

od of physical and military training. The best from this program would then study mathematics for 10 years. At age 30, the top achievers would be selected to study the highest branches of philosophy for five years. Only at age 35 would a candidate for ruler be ready to accept the weighty burden of guiding the city-state. The position of ruler would certainly not be an enviable one because of its overwhelming responsibilities, but it would make the ideal ruler truly happy. At 50, a leader could leave office and return to his studies.

Plato's ideal city-state included three classes of people: leaders whose strongest characteristic was their intellectual power, soldiers whose chief trait was courage, and the rest of the population, who concerned themselves with material things. Plato did not believe a person automatically belonged to his parents' class. Children of leaders who proved themselves unworthy to follow their parents would be demoted, just as the children of the third class who proved themselves superior would be advanced to the leader class. In Plato's ideal society, women received the exact same training as men and there was no "mine" or "yours" because all property, including children, belonged to everyone.

Plato described his ideal city-state in two of his dialogues, *Timaeus* and *Critias*. According to Critias, a character in both dialogues, the story had been told to his grandfather by the Athenian statesman Solon, who had heard it on a visit to Egypt around 600 B.C.

In the *Timaeus*, Critias speaks of an island lying somewhere beyond the Pillars of Hercules (present-day Strait of Gibraltar) that had existed more than 9,000 years before Solon's time. Known as Atlantis, its rulers controlled lands bordering the Mediterranean Sea as far as Egypt and Italy. When the leaders of Atlantis tried to conquer Greece, the Athenians defeated the invaders and freed the lands under Atlantis' control. Soon after, the island was swallowed up by the sea and its site was lost forever.

The tale continued in the *Critias*, with Critias explaining that Poseidon, the god of the sea, settled on the island with Cleito and their five sets of twin boys. Because the oldest boy was named Atlas, the island came to be known as Atlantis, and the waters surrounding the island as the Atlantic. It was the perfect place, with unsurpassed beauty and endless riches. Plato's description ends abruptly just when the gods agree to discuss why the inhabitants of Atlantis are losing their godlike qualities and becoming more concerned with power and ambition.

For centuries, Plato's Atlantis has intrigued scholars and theorists, many of whom have searched tirelessly for clues to its location. Others, however, deny that it ever existed. Why Plato was not more specific about the location of the island is unknown, but perhaps it was because his interest was purely intellectual or because he was not a traveler. After founding the Academy, Plato left Athens only on rare occasions.

Two of these journeys brought him to Syracuse and his friend Dion. In 367 B.C., Dion wrote Plato about the death of Dionysius I and asked him to tutor the young Dionysius II. Dion saw this as an opportunity for Plato to put into practice his ideas concerning the education of future rulers, for Dion envisioned Dionysius II as Plato's "ideal ruler" and Syracuse as the "ideal city-state." But Plato and Dion soon realized that Dionysius II's weak character and Syracuse's bitter political struggles would prevent the success of their plan.

A few years after Plato returned to Athens, Dionysius II asked Plato for help resolving some problems between him and Dion. Again Plato journeyed to Syracuse, and again his efforts proved unsuccessful. His dialogue entitled *Laws* reflects how the events in Sicily changed his views on politics. Though Plato still believed that the ideal city-state was a community in which property was owned and shared by all, he now rejected carrying any idea to extremes. Therefore, he advised that each citizen be allotted two plots of land, neither of which could ever be taken from him or transferred to anyone else. This land would allow citizens to provide the basic necessities for their families.

Plato also began placing more emphasis on law and spent much time addressing issues of crime and punishment. He saw religion playing a greater role in community life, and philosophy a smaller role. Plato even suggested that atheists, those who believe there were no gods, be punished.

Plato died in 347 B.C., having spent most of his life trying to define and create the ideal city-state. He had lived in accordance with his two goals—attaining wisdom and truth. His writings reflect his sincerity, and his use of the dialogue approach to explain his philosophy made his works accessible. His philosophy greatly influenced not only his contemporaries but all succeeding generations, including both religious and secular leaders. The Jewish philosopher Philo of Alexandria of the 1st century A.D. used his knowledge of Plato and Greek philosophy to defend and explain his own religious beliefs. Philo showed how the ancient revelation given to Moses was in agreement with the teachings of the Greek philosophers, especially Plato. Saint Augustine, one of the first great Christian theologians, considered himself a neo-Platonist before converting to Christianity. The 20th-century English mathematician and philosopher Alfred North Whitehead enjoyed reading Plato, and his concept of a God who is somehow involved in the universe was clearly influenced by the ancient Greek. In classrooms around the world, students still read and discuss the merits of Plato's theory of ideas and his belief in a philosopher-king.

FURTHER READING

Hamilton, Edith, and Huntington Cairns, ed. *Plato: The Collected Dialogues*. Princeton, N.J.: Princeton University Press, 1961.

Hare, R. M. *Plato*. New York: Oxford University Press, 1983.

Melling, David J. *Understanding Plato*. New York: Oxford University Press, 1994.

Plato. *Gorgias*. Translated by Terence Irwin. New York: Oxford University Press, 1979.

———. *Phaedo*. Translated and edited by David Gallop. New York: Oxford University Press, 1993.

———. *Republic*. Translated by Robin Waterfield. New York: Oxford University Press, 1994.

———. *Symposium*. Edited by Sir Kenneth Dover. New York: Cambridge University Press, 1980.

———. *Works*. Translated by H. N. Fowler, W. R. M. Lamb, Paul Shorey, and R. G. Bury. 12 vols. Loeb Classical Library. Cambridge: Harvard University Press, 1967–1986.

Rowe, C. J. *Plato*. New York: St. Martin's, 1984.

Skemp, Joseph B. *Plato*. Oxford, England: Clarendon Press, 1976.

Stein, Wendy. *Great Mysteries: Atlantis*. San Diego: Greenhaven, 1989.

Taylor, Alfred E. *Plato: The Man and His Work*. 7th ed. New York: Routledge, Chapman & Hall, 1960.

Xenophon

LEADER OF THE TEN THOUSAND

Suddenly, cries from the front-line troops filled the air. Xenophon, who was marching near the rear, thought immediately of an enemy ambush and quickly mounted his horse and galloped up the mountain toward the front line. As he approached the crest, the cries grew louder. Then he reached the mountaintop and saw that the troops were shouting in joy, not pain. "The sea! The sea!" they kept repeating, as Xenophon later recorded. And surely it was a most welcome sight to Xenophon and his soldiers, who had been lost for four months on the plains and mountains of Asia.

The expedition had begun in 401 B.C., when 10,000 Greeks enlisted as soldiers of fortune with Cyrus the Younger, a Persian governor and prince. Cyrus had welcomed the Greeks, whom he recognized as skilled soldiers, hardened from years of fighting in the Peloponnesian War. Cyrus knew that his own troops, which numbered more than 100,000, lacked discipline and training, and if he was to wrest control of the Persian throne from his brother Arsaces (known officially as Artaxerxes II), he would need the Greeks.

For the Greeks, Cyrus' call for mercenary soldiers was a welcome opportunity to gain steady employment and regular meals. Since the end of the war and the fall of Athens, jobs had been scarce and public funds low. Many people who had prospered before the war now found themselves in difficult circumstances. Others, like Xenophon, were disillusioned with politics, politicians, and the democratic Greek city-state.

Xenophon traced his lineage to one of Athens' aristocratic families and he had served in the elite branch of the Athenian cavalry during the Peloponnesian War. (Cavalrymen had to be rich, because they were responsible for providing their own equipment and horses.) However, when Xenophon returned home from the war, he disliked the political scene in Athens and soon left to join his friend Proxenus, who had already signed up as a mercenary soldier.

Both Xenophon and Proxenus marched with Cyrus when he led his great army toward Cunaxa, a small town on the Euphrates River, in what is today Iraq. In the battle that followed, Cyrus' troops overwhelmingly defeated those of his brother, but Cyrus was killed, leaving the Greeks without a leader and alone in enemy territory. When Tissaphernes, a Persian ruler who had allied himself with Cyrus, summoned the Greek commanders to his camp, they went immediately.

For days, the Greek soldiers watched and waited for their return. When they spied a man, tattered and bruised,

XENOPHON

IN SEVEN VOLUMES

IV

MEMORABILIA AND OECONOMICUS

WITH AN ENGLISH TRANSLATION BY

E. C. MARCHANT

SUB-RECTOR OF LINCOLN COLLEGE, OXFORD

SYMPOSIUM AND APOLOGY

WITH AN ENGLISH TRANSLATION BY

O. J. TODD

UNIVERSITY OF BRITISH COLUMBIA

CAMBRIDGE, MASSACHUSETTS
HARVARD UNIVERSITY PRESS
LONDON
WILLIAM HEINEMANN LTD
MCMLXVIII

ΞΕΝΟΦΩΝΤΟΣ ΟΙΚΟΝΟΜΙΚΟΣ

I. Ἤκουσα δέ ποτε αὐτοῦ καὶ περὶ οἰκονομίας τοιάδε διαλεγομένου. Εἰπέ μοι, ἔφη, ὦ Κριτόβουλε, ἆρά γε ἡ οἰκονομία ἐπιστήμης τινὸς ὄνομά ἐστιν, ὥσπερ ἡ ἰατρικὴ καὶ καλκευτικὴ καὶ τεκτονική;

Ἔμοιγε δοκεῖ, ἔφη ὁ Κριτόβουλος.

2 Ἦ καὶ ὥσπερ τούτων τῶν τεχνῶν ἔχοιμεν ἂν εἰπεῖν ὅ τι ἔργον ἑκάστης, οὕτω καὶ τῆς οἰκονομίας δυνάμεθα εἰπεῖν ὅ τι ἔργον αὐτῆς ἐστι;

Δοκεῖ γοῦν, ἔφη ὁ Κριτόβουλος, οἰκονόμου ἀγαθοῦ εἶναι εὖ οἰκεῖν τὸν ἑαυτοῦ οἶκον.

3 Ἦ καὶ τὸν ἄλλου δὲ οἶκον, ἔφη ὁ Σωκράτης, εἰ ἐπιτρέποι τις αὐτῷ, οὐκ ἂν δύναιτο, εἰ βούλοιτο, εὖ οἰκεῖν, ὥσπερ καὶ τὸν ἑαυτοῦ; ὁ μὲν γὰρ τεκτονικὴν ἐπιστάμενος ὁμοίως ἂν καὶ ἄλλῳ δύναιτο ἐργάζεσθαι ὅτιπερ καὶ ἑαυτῷ, καὶ ὁ οἰκονομικός γ᾽ ἂν ὡσαύτως.

Ἔμοιγε δοκεῖ, ὦ Σώκρατες.

4 Ἔστιν ἄρα, ἔφη ὁ Σωκράτης, τὴν τέχνην ταύτην ἐπισταμένῳ, καὶ εἰ μὴ αὐτὸς τύχοι χρήματα ἔχων, τὸν ἄλλου οἶκον οἰκονομοῦντα ὥσπερ καὶ οἰκοδομοῦντα μισθοφορεῖν;

Νὴ Δία καὶ πολύν γε μισθόν, ἔφη ὁ Κριτόβουλος, φέροιτ᾽ ἄν, εἰ δύναιτο οἶκον παραλαβὼν τελεῖν τε ὅσα δεῖ καὶ περιουσίαν ποιῶν αὔξειν τὸν οἶκον.

362

THE OECONOMICUS

A DISCUSSION ON ESTATE MANAGEMENT

I. I once heard him discuss the subject of estate management in the following manner.

"Tell me, Critobulus, is estate management the name of a branch of knowledge, like medicine, smithing and carpentry?"

"I think so," replied Critobulus.

2 "And can we say what the function of estate management is, just as we can say what is the function of each of these arts?"

"Well, I suppose that the business of a good estate manager is to manage his own estate well."

3 "Yes, and in case he were put in charge of another man's estate, could he not, if he chose, manage it as well as he manages his own? Anyone who understands carpentry can do for another exactly the same work as he does for himself; and so, I presume, can a good estate manager."

"I think so, Socrates."

4 "Is it possible, then, for one who understands this art, even if he has no property of his own, to earn money by managing another man's estate, just as he might do by building him a house?"

"Yes, of course; and he would get a good salary if, after taking over an estate, he continued to pay all outgoings, and to increase the estate by showing a balance."

363

heading toward their camp, they eagerly ran to meet him. With his dying breath, he told how the traitorous Persians had killed the Greek leaders.

Shock and despair quickly spread throughout the Greek camp, as all realized what the Persians were thinking: leaderless troops are powerless and easy to kill. Seeking a place to think and reflect on all that had happened, Xenophon wandered a distance from the camp and soon fell asleep. In his dreams, a thunderbolt suddenly burst through the sky and hit his home in Greece, where it caused a great light to shine forth. The vividness of the dream woke Xenophon, who saw the vision as a sign from Zeus, the king of the gods that he, Xenophon, was to lead the Greeks to safety. (A thunderbolt is the traditional symbol of Zeus' power.)

Xenophon quickly returned to the camp and urged the despairing Greeks to rise above the misfortunes that presently beset them. Years later, in his account of the ordeal, Xenophon wrote that he asked his men, "Shall it be said that we went willingly to slaughter? No! Our common safety is our common need. Let us march to freedom."

Even though Xenophon had never led an army or even held a command post, the troops unanimously elected him their commander in chief. Because he knew the days ahead would be difficult and dangerous and that freedom would come only with complete cooperation, Xenophon gave everyone a chance to lead, and he even had the soldiers think of their escape as the march of the 10,000 generals.

Whenever there was a crisis or someone disagreed with the route or action being taken, Xenophon called a meeting and invited anyone who had an idea to present it. After discussing its advantages and disadvantages, the idea was put to a vote and the majority ruled. According to Xenophon, no unjust decision was ever made.

Although he was a fair leader, Xenophon was not exempt from accusations and, on one occasion, a soldier argued that Xenophon had wrongly struck another soldier. Xenophon

This side-by-side Greek and English publication of Xenophon's work focuses on the defense of his friend, the philosopher Socrates. In this section, Socrates gives his opinion on the problems of estate management.

"I believe it is much more difficult to find someone who bears prosperity well than to find someone who bears adversity well. Prosperity creates pride in most people, but adversity brings moderation to all."

—from *Kyropaideia* (after 365 B.C.)

immediately admitted that he had struck the man, but only after he had told him to carry a badly wounded soldier to camp and then found him burying the man alive. Xenophon later recorded his defense: "The enemy scouts would have caught up to him and killed him if I had not struck him and jolted his mind into action." The jury of 10,000 acquitted him.

Another time, a soldier complained that life was easier for Xenophon than for his troops because he had a horse to ride. Xenophon immediately jumped down from his horse, pushed the man aside, and marched in his place. Such actions naturally won the respect of all his soldiers and made it easier for Xenophon when he asked the troops to leave behind their extra supplies and the treasures they had captured in battle. With less to carry, they would be able to travel more quickly and easily.

Yet the march was never easy, for without maps, compasses, or any of the equipment modern armies take for granted, they could not plan a route that would avoid mountains or wide rivers. Furthermore, because they were unwilling to travel west across the lands they had marched through on the way to Cunaxa for fear of reprisals at the hands of the Persians, they turned north into unfamiliar territory.

When supplies ran low, they used their ingenuity to replenish them. One trick was for experts with slingshots to shoot enemy cavalrymen. When a rider fell, the Greeks ran in and stole his horse. Another trick involved expert archers shooting beyond the enemy troops. The enemy would respond by shooting their arrows, which, if the Greeks planned the distance correctly, would fall just short of the Greek line. Within minutes, the Greeks could collect a supply of arrows for the next skirmish.

No historical records tell of any march as difficult as the 2,000-mile trek of the 10,000 under Xenophon. But the joy of reaching the Greek town of Trapezus (present-day Trabzon) on the Black Sea in January 400 B.C. quickly evaporated when the Greeks saw the few job opportunities available. Many, including Xenophon, chose to join the forces of King Seuthes of Thrace, a country that bordered the northern Aegean Sea. Soon after, Xenophon and a group of soldiers under his command accepted an opportunity to join the Spartan general Thibron stationed in Pergamum, a city in western Asia Minor.

Desperate for money, Xenophon made a slight detour on his way to Pergamum, kidnapping a rich Persian named Asidates and his family and plundering his house and estate. Although the ransom he received for his captives made Xenophon a very rich man, it did not stop him from joining Thibron's forces. It was at this time that Xenophon met King Agesilaus of Sparta, a man whom he grew to admire and respect.

The timing of his meeting with Agesilaus was perfect, because Xenophon had become completely disillusioned with the political leaders in Athens. When Athenian officials passed the death sentence on Xenophon's friend and former teacher Socrates in 399 B.C., Xenophon was furious. Years earlier, before leaving Athens to join Cyrus' troops, Xenophon had asked Socrates for his advice. The philosopher felt that joining Cyrus might indeed be unwise, because Cyrus was aligned with Sparta and opposed to Athens, and he advised Xenophon to consult the oracle of the god Apollo at Delphi. Xenophon did follow Socrates' advice but, because he was determined to join Cyrus, he asked the oracle only to which gods he should sacrifice in order to achieve success on his mission.

Xenophon thought about Socrates' death and about Athens' leaders. He knew Agesilaus had returned to Greece to command Spartan forces in the Corinthian War that was now raging. Xenophon also knew that Agesilaus would appreciate any seasoned recruits and, at the Battle of Coronea in 394 B.C., Xenophon fought for Sparta's Agesilaus against his native city-state of Athens. Soon after, the Athenians voted to exile Xenophon.

Sparta and King Agesilaus warmly welcomed Xenophon, his wife, and their two sons, even giving them a house, first in Sparta and then at Scillus, a town near the Greek city of Olympia. At Scillus, Xenophon spent many pleasant days hunting and riding. To show his respect for Artemis, the goddess of the hunt, Xenophon took the money he had set aside for his family in case he died while fighting for Agesilaus and built a shrine in her honor.

Around 371 B.C. the people of the city of Elis seized the town of Scillus, forcing Xenophon to find another home. This time he settled in Corinth, but a few years later, when Athens and Sparta joined forces against the city of Thebes, the Athenians voted to recall Xenophon. After decades away from Athens, Xenophon returned in 365 B.C., and so did his sons, who joined their father's old cavalry unit.

The years that followed were probably quiet ones, away from the political arena. It was most likely during this period and during the peaceful years on his estate at Scillus that Xenophon composed the many works that gained him an international reputation as a historian.

His best-known work, the *Anabasis Kyrou* (The Expedition of Cyrus), better known as the *Anabasis*, is Xenophon's personal account of the March of the Ten Thousand. His descriptions of the march revealed to his Greek audience previously unknown areas of the Persian empire, and his graphic details and simple style recorded the events as seen through the eyes of an energetic young officer. To be sure, Xenophon was one of the world's first journalists.

An admirer of Thucydides, Xenophon saw himself as a historian. Recognizing Thucydides' *History* as unfinished, Xenophon undertook to complete the work. In his history titled *Hellenika* (Greek Matters), Xenophon began where Thucydides had left off in 411 B.C. and continued to 362 B.C. and the Battle of Mantinea, at which Xenophon's son Gryllus was killed.

The *Hellenika* is a comparatively short historical piece. Xenophon most likely used Thucydides' notes for the first sections and his own experiences for the rest. But Xenophon was not overly concerned with research and objectivity, as Thucydides had been, nor did he have his predecessor's ability to evaluate events and situations critically. As a result, there are gaps in his records. Furthermore, the preferential treatment he gave Sparta reflects his close personal ties with the city and King Agesilaus.

Sparta, in fact, never seemed to be too far from Xenophon's thinking. In a treatise entitled *Lakedaimonion Politeia* (The Constitution of Sparta), Xenophon praised Sparta's government and the city's customs and practices. His *Agesilaus* is a tribute to the Spartan king Agesilaus and treats him as a Greek hero.

Because of his dissatisfaction with Athenian leadership and the results of full democracy, Xenophon saw monarchy under leaders like Agesilaus and Cyrus as the most stable form of government. In his historical novel *Kyropaideia*, which praised Cyrus, Xenophon included passages focusing on the type of education a true leader and statesman needed and on the importance of family life.

As the years passed, Xenophon began to realize that monarchies also

ANCIENT GREEKS

Xenophon

BORN

Around 428 B.C.
Athens, Greece

DIED

Around 355 B.C.
Athens or Corinth, Greece

PROFESSION

Historian

ACCOMPLISHMENTS

Successfully led the ten thousand Greeks who had signed on as mercenaries under the Persian prince Cyrus through central Persia to the Greek city of Trapezus; wrote the *Anabasis*, a personal account of the march, and *Hellenika*, a continuation of Thucydides' history of the Peloponnesian War, and several other essays and books, including *Memorabilia*, *Symposium*, *Apology*, *Kyropaideia*, *Agesilaus*, and *On Hunting*

The illustrator of this scene, which appeared in a 1703 British edition of *Xenophon's Works,* used artistic license to idealize the figures of Xenophon (left) and Socrates, as well as the locale.

had their problems, many of which were more harmful to a city's well-being than were the problems of democracies. He began to rethink his criticism of democracy and to see advantages to the Athenian system.

Yet Xenophon was not a philosopher. He was far too practical an individual to think deeply about any one subject. Still, the one person for whom he had constant praise and admiration was his former teacher, the philosopher Socrates. Bitterly upset and disappointed with the Athenian leaders who passed the death sentence on Socrates, Xenophon undertook to defend and support Socrates in three works: *Apology*, *Symposium*, and *Memorabilia*.

Plato, another of Socrates' pupils, also came to the defense of Socrates. But Plato's writings focused on philosophical ideas, whereas Xenophon preferred to include the moral and practical side of every argument. As a result, Xenophon's works were much more popular. They were also more informative and presented Socrates as a personality rather than as a person who talked only of ideas.

The *Symposium* recounts lively dinner conversations at an imaginary party where Socrates is a guest. In a well-known passage, Socrates asks his dinner companions if anyone wishes to teach his wife, Xanthippe, something. The muffled whispers clearly reveal that all feel she certainly could use some lessons. One guest, in a restrained manner, asks, "Socrates, why do you not teach her to be good-humored?" The philosopher calmly but sincerely replies, "My aim in life is to get along well with people. Therefore, I chose Xanthippe as my wife, for I believed if I could get along with her, I could get along with anybody."

Country life was of great interest to Xenophon, and he wrote several books, including *On Horsemanship* and *On Hunting,* that reflect his expert knowledge of those subjects and his love for his country estate at Scillus.

In his dialogue titled *Oikonomikos*, Xenophon used simple yet clearly stated phrases to explain how an estate should be managed. The passage on the duties of the landowner's wife and her role in managing the household tells much about the role of women in 4th-century B.C. Athens. By custom, Athenian women led very sheltered lives, spending most of their time at home. Marriages were prearranged by their parents; the bride was usually a young teenager and the groom, a mature man who already had his own household. In *Oikonomikos*, a married man proudly states that his wife is a proper Athenian, and that he had dutifully taught her how to manage a household when he married her at age 15.

Following the custom of the time, he held her responsible for making sure expenses did not exceed the budget, regularly checking the food supply, and caring for anyone who might be ill. Yet he was a fair and thoughtful husband who considered the house to be their joint property and planned to consult with his wife about the upbringing of their children.

As the dialogue continues, the husband advises his young wife to exercise by making the beds, spinning yarn, or supervising the servants. Exercise, he says, is essential to good health and good looks. He then asks that she never use artificial cosmetics to color her face or wear high-heeled shoes, for no husband appreciates falseness. He ends by saying that his wife, after years of marriage, still lives in the same manner as he taught her when she first came as a bride.

As a historical writer, Xenophon was far more popular than either Herodotus or Thucydides. His contemporaries enjoyed his choice of topics and the practical manner in which he wrote. Xenophon's style was not complicated, nor were his themes weighty.

In the centuries that followed, the historians of Rome preferred Xenophon to other Greek historians. They appreciated his interest in the practical side of historical events as opposed to the philosophical, and they imitated his emphasis on moral issues both on the battlefield and in everyday life.

"The most pleasing sound is the one that praises you."

—from *Hieron* (after 365 B.C.), a dialogue about kingship

FURTHER READING

Anderson, John K. *Xenophon.* New York: Scribners, 1974.

Dillery, J. *Xenophon and the History of His Times.* New York: Routledge, 1995.

Household, Geoffrey. *The Exploits of Xenophon.* 1955. Reprint. Hamden, Conn.: Linnet Books, 1989.

Schmeling, Gareth L. *Xenophon of Ephesus.* Boston: Twayne, 1980.

Xenophon. *Xenophon.* Translated by Walter Miller, C. L. Brownson, E. C. Marchant, O. J. Todd, and G. W. Bowersock. 7 vols. Loeb Classical Library. Cambridge: Harvard University Press, 1968–84.

———. *Xenophon: The Education of Cyrus.* Translated by H. G. Dakyns. London: J. M. Dent and Sons, Everyman's Library, 1992.

Aristotle

THE FATHER OF LOGIC

For 20 years, two of the world's greatest thinkers, Plato and Aristotle, studied together as teacher and pupil at Plato's Academy in Athens. Aristotle's father was a court physician to Macedonia's king, Amyntas II, and the family home was in Stagira, a town in Chalcidice, a peninsula jutting out into the northern Aegean Sea. Around 367 B.C., when Aristotle was 17 or 18, his father sent him to Athens to study at the Academy. Plato was in Sicily when Aristotle arrived, but when Plato returned, he quickly recognized the uniqueness and superior mental abilities of his new student. Plato even called Aristotle "the intellect of the school."

When Plato died in 347 B.C., his nephew Speusippus became headmaster of the Academy. Aristotle, who was also teaching at the school at the time, disagreed with Speusippus' emphasis on mathematics and numbers. It is uncertain whether this is why Aristotle and other teachers, including Xenocrates, chose to leave the Academy.

Both Aristotle and Xenocrates accepted an invitation from Hermias, the ruler of Atarneus on the west coast of Asia Minor, to join a study group of former Academy students at his court. Years earlier, Hermias had studied under Plato and adopted Plato's belief that a ruler's chief concern should be the welfare of his city-state and his subjects. In his rise from simple beginnings to a position of power, Hermias had followed Plato's philosophy and, in a sense, he was Plato's "philosopher-king."

Hermias was captured and murdered by enemy Persians just three years after Aristotle arrived at his court. Fearing for his life, Aristotle fled to Mytilene, the chief city on the neigboring island of Lesbos. With him was his wife, Pythias, Hermias' niece.

Aristotle most likely chose Lesbos because the island was home to his favorite pupil, Theophrastus. During his years there, from 344 to 342 B.C., Aristotle became very interested in biology and gathered numerous specimens of marine life along the shore. With his notebook and scalpel in hand, Aristotle carefully inspected each organism and recorded his observations. Gradually, these observations led him away from Plato's doctrine of ideas to the development of his own philosophy, which stated that what we perceive with our senses is the "real thing" and not, as Plato believed, an image of the "real thing."

Sometime around 342 B.C., Philip II invited Aristotle to Macedonia to tutor his 13-year-old son Alexander. Aristotle immediately accepted and for several years taught grammar, literature (especially Homer), and politics to the future

One of the most recognizable paintings in the world is *Aristotle with a Bust of Homer,* by the 17th-century Dutch artist Rembrandt. The artist depicts Aristotle in the clothes of a European and uses dark colors and shadows to set the mood of contemplation.

world leader. (Philip's son later became known as Alexander the Great. Records show that Alexander ordered that specimens of all new plants and animals discovered on his campaigns across Asia Minor and central Asia be sent to his former teacher.)

After Philip's assassination in 336 B.C. and Alexander's assumption of power, Aristotle returned to Athens. His friend Xenocrates was now head of the Academy, but Aristotle knew that his own ideas and outlook on life had changed considerably since his days there as pupil and teacher. Consequently, he chose to start his own school and rented several buildings just outside Athens near a grove dedicated to the god Apollo Lyceus. This school (whose course offerings were comparable to those of today's universities) became known as the Lyceum and attracted many distinguished pupils from around the Greek world.

Always concerned with organization, Aristotle divided his day into two teaching periods. The morning hours he spent with a small select group of pupils, leading discussions about difficult concepts in philosophy and other disciplines, such as zoology. He also took time to acquaint these students with his biological research and to listen to and evaluate their ideas.

Every afternoon, Aristotle spent time teaching a much larger group of pupils subjects such as politics and rhetoric. Aristotle preferred to lecture, rather than converse with, these students. As he lectured, he did not sit, as was the custom of the time, but would stroll with his students along the school's shady walkways. Soon Aristotle's pupils became known as *Peripatetics*. The term comes from the

"Education is the best provision for old age."

—Aristotle, quoted in *Lives of Eminent Philosophers* (3rd century A.D.) by Diogenes Laertius

Greek words *peri* ("around") and *patein* ("to walk").

Aristotle's school also functioned as a museum and library. There, he exhibited his enormous collection of animal and plant specimens. With a gift of 800 talents (a considerable sum of money in ancient times) from Alexander the Great, Aristotle was able to gather additional specimens as well as numerous maps and manuscripts, including the constitutions of 158 city-states. Such information, he believed, would benefit his research and that of his students. Aristotle also asked other Lyceum teachers to gather information in areas such as botany, physics, mathematics, and medicine.

Alexander the Great's unexpected death in 323 B.C. changed Aristotle's life. For more than a decade, the Greeks had endured Macedonian rule and had only dreamed of freedom. With Alexander dead, that dream became a possibility. Loyal Greeks, however, saw Aristotle as a Macedonian sympathizer because of his relationship with Alexander. Charges of impiety and disrespect for the gods were brought against Aristotle and he was ordered to defend himself in court. Aristotle remembered how, in 399 B.C., the philosopher Socrates had been unjustly sentenced to death on similar false charges, and Aristotle decided to leave Athens before the trial. Yet he made it very clear that his departure was to prevent Athens from "sinning twice against philosophy."

In 322 B.C., Aristotle left for Chalcis, a town in the district of Euboea to the north of Athens, where he owned property. With him went Herpyllis, a former house servant and the woman with whom he had lived after the death of his wife a few years earlier. Within months, the 63-year-old Aristotle died of a stomach disease that had plagued him for several years. His body was taken to his hometown of Stagira and buried with great honors, and the citizens celebrated his memory at yearly festivals. The Lyceum continued to operate until A.D. 529, when the Roman emperor Justinian closed all schools that taught philosophy.

Always well prepared, Aristotle left a will that specifically outlined his wishes and revealed his affection for those close to him. Herpyllis was to have her choice of his two houses in Stagira; provisions were made for their son; Theophrastus was named guardian of his daughter, Pythias; the ashes of his wife, Pythias, were to be placed next to his, in accordance with her wishes; and his slaves were to be freed or kept as the family's slaves, according to his instructions. Aristotle also named Theophrastus the new head of the Lyceum and bequeathed to him both his writings and the museum collections.

The story of what happened to Aristotle's writings is both fascinating and involved. After Theophrastus' death, the libraries and works of Aristotle and Theophrastus passed to Neleus of Scepsis, a pupil of Theophrastus. Neleus kept the original manuscripts of both philosophers but sold the library to Ptolemy II, the ruler of Egypt, who was amassing his own great library at Alexandria. After Neleus' descendants inherited the manuscripts, they hid them in a dark cellar because they knew that Ptolemy II's rival, the king of Pergamum, would make every attempt to steal such valuable writings for his library.

For many decades, worms and dampness ate away at the manuscripts, until sometime around 100 B.C. an avid

Athenian book collector named Apellicon tracked them down, bought them, and made new copies. Unfortunately, Apellicon made many errors when he filled in missing passages and lines. In 86 B.C., the Romans captured Athens; Apellicon's library was confiscated and taken to Rome. Their new owner was a writer named Tyrannion, who then passed them to Andronicus of Rhodes, a philosopher and follower of Aristotle's teachings. Sometime around 40 B.C., Andronicus carefully organized Aristotle's and Theophrastus' works, and it is his arrangement that forms the basis of today's editions. Soon after Andronicus completed this tremendous task, he assumed the position of headmaster of the Lyceum at Athens.

Aristotle's works were not originally in book form, however. He had never written for publication or for a general audience but had circulated notes and manuscripts that explained his thoughts to students and other interested people. Because Aristotle meant them for school use and reference, he felt it unnecessary to explain difficult terms and concepts that his pupils learned from his lectures. As a result, his works were concise and technical, not smoothly flowing treatises.

Aristotle did write a set of notes aimed at a more general audience, and it seems that these were circulated while the technical ones lay hidden in Asia Minor. For some reason, the general notes ceased to be reprinted or used soon after Andronicus' edition of Aristotle was published around 40 B.C. Because only his works intended for school use have survived, we know little of Aristotle's literary style. Still, these works clearly show his wide range of interests and knowledge. They also reflect his early support of Plato's ideas and mark the gradual development of his own thinking. He came to disagree with Plato's belief in ideal images (which existed outside of human experience) and instead believed that truth could be found by relying on human reason and by examining the "real" world of matter and form.

In everything, Aristotle was organized, deliberate, and orderly. His was a curious mind that believed a person had to ask "why" and not just "how." The attainment of truth was extremely important to Aristotle, and he set himself the task of analyzing and recording information about all the sciences except mathematics. In his neglect of numbers as a key component of the universe, Aristotle differed from his teacher Plato.

Aristotle believed in using reason to find answers to his questions about the universe. When he focused on a subject or problem, he sought to break it into simpler parts, classifying each section. This insistence on classification was most evident in his works on animal and plant life: *The History of Animals*, *On the Parts of Animals*, and *On the Coming-to-Be of Animals*. Aristotle divided the animal kingdom into two major categories ("animals with red blood" and "animals with white blood") and, with his pupils as research assistants, described more than 400 living species. Under the category of "red-blooded" animals, Aristotle included those that give birth to live offspring and those that lay eggs (birds, reptiles, and fish). The "white-blooded" animals were those with soft bodies covered by scales or a shell and the insects and worms.

For each group within a category, Aristotle then described the organs, their functions, and any other observa-

ANCIENT GREEKS

Aristotle

BORN

384 B.C.
Stagira, Greece

DIED

322 B.C.
Chalcis, Greece

PROFESSION

Philosopher

ACCOMPLISHMENTS

Tutored the teenage Alexander the Great; established a school in Athens called the Lyceum; wrote hundreds of works on a great variety of topics, including biology, physics, political theory, ethics, logic, metaphysics, history, literature, and rhetoric

Fifteenth-century Europeans were fascinated by the wide range of topics Aristotle covered in his writings. The frontispiece of a 1483 Venetian edition of Aristotle's works is decorated with initial letters, miniature pictures, and other elaborate designs in the style of the time.

tions that he had made. After almost 2,500 years, Aristotle's list is still the basis of modern biological classification, although some terms and categories are no longer used. His observation that animals differ in appearance but are structurally similar (that is, some have hands, some have hooves, and some have claws) formed the basis for the field of biology known as comparative anatomy.

Aristotle's concern for truth led him to rely on reason and the mind. He could not accept Plato's doctrine of ideas, which said that the true form of everything had its own separate existence, and what humans see or know is only a shadow or reflection of the perfect form. Aristotle saw the world as real. Such thinking led Aristotle to wonder about "being" and what it means "to be" or "to exist." He called his conclusions the "First Philosophy." Today, this discipline is known as metaphysics.

For Aristotle, every real thing in nature has four causes: the material cause (the component substances that make a thing what it is), the efficient cause (whatever produces the thing), the formal cause (what the thing represents), and the final cause (the purpose or meaning of the thing). If we take Aristotle the human being as an example to illustrate the theory of causes, then the material cause consists of the organs, muscles, and bones that make Aristotle a human. The efficient cause would be the parents who gave birth to Aristotle. The formal cause is Aristotle, the person. And the final cause is Aristotle's inner nature that leads him into adulthood and to becoming a thinking, rational human being.

What makes something different from something else depends on the four causes that brought it into being. Therefore, we can understand why something is what it is only if we know the causes. To explain everything's existence as the result of the four causes required not only much time but also patience and a clear mind, both of which were key traits of Aristotle's personality. It also meant that if Aristotle were to arrive at truth and reality, he had to classify and divide everything into categories, just as he had done with his description of animals.

Once the causes were established, Aristotle classified each "thing" in 10 categories: substance, quantity, quality, relation, place, time, position, state, action, and affection. According to Aristotle, these categories determined the thing's being. Substance, however, was the most important because without it, the thing would not exist.

Again, we can use Aristotle as an example of classification by categories. The substance is Aristotle himself; the quantity is his height (perhaps 5 feet, 2 inches, because ancient sources say he was short); his quality is curious and organized; his relation (his connection to the present) is far removed; his place is Athens; his time is 330 B.C.; his position is walking in the Lyceum; his state is always well dressed; his action is talking and lecturing; his affection (attribute) is being admired.

All of these categories were subject to change, however. For example, an individual's substance changed when he died, just as place changed whenever a person traveled. Yet there was one unchangeable, eternal substance that Aristotle called the "unmoved mover." This substance was pure intelligence and had no beginning and no end. This unmoved mover has been called Aristotle's God.

For Aristotle, human beings were the closest species in substance to the unmoved mover because they alone had the capacity to think. Furthermore, this capacity to think allowed them to have as their goal the search for the supreme good, which for Aristotle meant happiness. Yet this happiness was not gained from pleasure but from reason. For the philosopher, happiness meant a lifetime devoted to thinking and study. For all other humans, happiness was the ability to curb one's desires and seek a middle course—the moral mean. However, the mean was not the same for everyone.

"It is only natural that all humans desire knowledge."

—from *Metaphysics* (4th century B.C.)

"*We go to war in order to live in peace.*"

—from *Nicomachean Ethics* (4th century B.C.)

Aristotle believed that people needed to remember that what is too much for one person might not be enough for another.

Aristotle's analysis of happiness and the supreme good led his thoughts to politics and what was best for the city-state. Unlike his teacher Plato, who sought the ideal state, Aristotle dealt with what was real. He believed that no constitution was in itself perfect because human nature and physical nature were involved. He saw moderate democracy as the best type of government, provided that the best people were allowed to govern. For Aristotle, the best were those who would respect the political rights of all and would work for the good of their state and not just for themselves.

Aristotle's tireless search for truth led him to question everything. Gradually, he developed what is known today as logic, the science of correct reasoning. One type of argument that Aristotle used to prove a point was the syllogism. He would offer two statements or thoughts, both of which were true, and then, using logic, draw from them a third statement or conclusion. For example:

All mammals are warm-blooded.
Dogs are mammals.
Therefore, dogs are warm-blooded.

Every Greek is a human.
Every human is mortal.
Therefore, every Greek is a mortal.

Yet Aristotle realized that if a person was not careful, such reasoning could lead to untruths. For example:

All trees are living.
All roses are living.
Therefore, a tree is a rose.

In the centuries since Aristotle's death, his influence has been extremely widespread. One reason is the great variety of topics he covered, for in addition to biology, logic, metaphysics, and politics, he wrote on the workings of the universe, rhetoric, the arts, and literature. Today, Aristotle is considered one of the world's greatest thinkers, and students continue to study his theories in courses on philosophy and Western civilization.

FURTHER READING

Ackrill, J. L. *Aristotle the Philosopher*. New York: Oxford University Press, 1981.

Aristotle. *The Complete Works of Aristotle*. 2 vols. Edited by Jonathan Barnes. Princeton, N.J.: Princeton University Press, 1984.

———. *Aristotle*. Translated by A. L. Peck et al. 23 vols. Loeb Classical Library. Cambridge: Harvard University Press, 1965-1991.

———. *Physics*. Translated by Robin Waterfield. New York: Oxford University Press, 1996.

———. *Politics*. Translated by Ernest Barker. New York: Oxford University Press, 1995.

Barnes, Jonathan. *Aristotle*. New York: Oxford University Press, 1982.

Ferguson, John. *Aristotle*. New York: Twayne, 1972.

Demosthenes

IN DEFENSE OF FREEDOM

"Demosthenes, if your strength had been equal to your intent, Greece would never have been ruled by a Macedonian." So read the inscription on the statue of Demosthenes erected by the Athenians in 280 B.C. almost 50 years after his death.

For much of his life, the orator Demosthenes had urged his fellow Greeks to preserve their independence. The opposition, however, was stronger, and many times Demosthenes' words were forgotten or pushed aside. Yet he never yielded to despair or frustration but continually presented arguments explaining why the Greek cities should unite to defend their freedom. His determination to be heard forced him to hone his skills as a public speaker. His first experience in presenting a case to the people was not, however, in defense of Greece but in his own defense.

Demosthenes was born in 384 B.C. to a wealthy Athenian sword maker. When he was only seven, his father died and the management of Demosthenes' inheritance was left to his uncles and a friend of his father. At age 18, Demosthenes legally claimed the money and property left to him by his father and discovered that nothing was left.

Angered by the mismanagement of his inheritance, Demosthenes resolved to sue the three men responsible for his financial situation. But legal procedures in ancient Greece were far different from today's, and citizens had to present their own case before a citizen-jury. (Records show that juries had between 201 and 1,001 members.) If a citizen felt his speaking ability was poor, he could hire someone to speak for him or he could present his arguments in writing.

Demosthenes decided to represent himself, but first he had to master the rules of rhetoric (the art of using words effectively). The idea of studying on his own was not a new one for Demosthenes. He had done so often to compensate for an education that was not as complete as that of other Athenians of the same social class because his guardians frequently failed to pay his teachers. One of Demosthenes' favorite subjects was rhetoric, a common subject of study in ancient Greece and one that often led to a career in oratory, or public speaking.

According to the Greek biographer Plutarch, Demosthenes' fascination with oratory began after one of his teachers took him to court to watch Callistratus, the best-known orator of the day, present a case. Awed by his powerful presentation, Demosthenes began studying the styles of the master speakers.

Finally, after much preparation, Demosthenes felt ready to formally prosecute his guardians. Although his arguments

Demosthenes spent his life urging the Athenians to preserve their independence. He wrote, "Small opportunities are often the start of great enterprises."

won him restitution of only a small portion of the estate, they served as his introduction to public speaking and proved that he had potential as an orator. Soon Athenians were asking Demosthenes to write their cases for them and even to represent them in court. Although his arguments were good and well thought out, his first presentations brought little success because his style was awkward and included too many long sentences and complicated terms. In addition, his stammer and weak voice made it difficult for listeners to follow him.

After one particularly discouraging day at court, Demosthenes walked home feeling dejected. Hearing someone behind him, he turned and saw his friend Satyrus, a well-known actor. Demosthenes told Satyrus of his troubles and claimed that although he was the best-prepared and most dedicated orator, the people preferred all the others, regardless of how ill-prepared they were.

According to Plutarch, Satyrus said to Demosthenes, "My dear Demosthenes, what you say may be true, but recite now a passage from Euripides or Sophocles and I will rid you of your troubles."

Demosthenes did as his friend requested and then listened as Satyrus recited the same passage. Demosthenes immediately saw the difference between the two recitations and realized that he had prepared his arguments well but had not spent time thinking about his delivery.

Demosthenes now devoted himself to perfecting both his manner of delivery and his enunciation. He built an underground study where every day he practiced speaking out loud and coordinating the movements of his body with the feelings his words expressed. On several occasions, Demosthenes believed he needed a large block of time to work on perfecting these new skills and spent two to three months in his study totally isolated from the world. To make himself resist any temptation to leave, he shaved half his head.

Demosthenes practiced talking with pebbles in his mouth to correct his stammer, and to learn to control his speech, he rehearsed his arguments when he was exhausted and out of breath from running up and down steep inclines. He stood before a large mirror and carefully coordinated his words to his movements. When he realized that he raised his right shoulder higher than his left, Demosthenes practiced speaking with a sword tied just above the right shoulder. To prepare for speaking before the Athenian Assembly, meetings that could draw up to 6,000 people, Demosthenes delivered speeches by the seashore, yelling to be heard above the crashing waves.

His methods worked, and within a short time Demosthenes came to be recognized as one of Athens' best orators. There were, however, those who criticized his speeches as being stilted and too precise. Still, Demosthenes never felt comfortable speaking extemporaneously and preferred to write and rewrite speeches until they met his high standards.

His private practice of writing defenses and pleading court cases grew steadily. Once, when a defendant asked him to argue a case, Demosthenes listened to the man explain how he had been wronged and then, according to Plutarch, quickly replied, "Certainly, such misfortune could not have happened to you!"

The man indignantly turned to Demosthenes and with great emotion and inflection in his voice expressed his hurt that Demosthenes dared to question his honesty. Plutarch wrote that once again Demosthenes was quick to reply: "Now, sir, you speak as someone who has been wronged!"

It was this lesson—that a speaker's tone and actions reveal as much as a

"The easiest thing for a person to do is to deceive himself; for an individual usually believes whatever he wants is all right."

—from *Olynthiaka* (349 B.C.)

speaker's words—that made Demosthenes such an accomplished orator and pleader. It also helped him when he entered the political arena.

In 354 B.C., at age 30, Demosthenes delivered his first public speech to the Athenian Assembly, a voting body composed of all male Athenian citizens. At the time, Greece's archenemy, Persia, seemed ready to launch another offensive against the Greeks, and Demosthenes urged the Athenians to rebuild their navy and prepare to fight. He did not encourage a declaration of war but rather a readiness for battle. He argued that if Athens attacked Persia, no Greek city would join the cause, but if Athens were attacked by Persia, then every Greek city would rally to Athens' defense. Demosthenes believed strongly in Athenian independence, but he argued continually that Athens should maintain alliances with other Greek cities in case of an emergency.

Although he was respected for his arguments, Demosthenes found it difficult to turn the Athenians' thoughts to war. Peace was the mood both in Athens and throughout Greece, even as Philip II of Macedonia gradually extended his control beyond his borders. Demosthenes saw Philip as a dangerous, deceitful neighbor who made alliances with no intention of keeping them. But even after Philip blatantly used an agreement he had made with Athens to his own advantage, the Athenians refused to believe he was a threat to their freedom.

In 351 B.C., Demosthenes delivered what came to be known as the *First Philippic*. Aimed at discrediting Philip's "friendly" moves and calling on Greece to unite and raise arms against such a foe, the speech did little to change the Athenians' preference for peace. Two years later, when Philip advanced against the cities on the Chalcidice peninsula, Demosthenes again spoke out against Philip and in three speeches, known as the *Olynthiaka*, urged Athens to send troops to defend the city of Olynthus.

> Philip is about to take Olynthus, yet you Athenians sit still and do nothing. . . . It does not amaze me that Philip, a leader who is always in control, ready to fight, and aware of every opportunity, prevails over you who only talk, ask questions, and vote, but take no action. . . . What I do wonder at is how you Athenians, who have often aided others, can now sit still after losing so much of what is yours! To save Olynthus and stop Philip, we must start at once and proceed vigorously and with spirit . . . with each one loyally performing his share of patriotic duty.

Again the Athenians chose not to act, and Olynthus fell in 348 B.C. When the Athenian statesman Philocrates was put on trial for attempting to enter into discussions with Philip II, Demosthenes spoke in his defense and won his acquittal. Philocrates had wanted peace with Philip and after his trial continued to pursue the possibility of a peace treaty between Athens and Macedonia.

In an illustrated children's book, the early 20th-century American artist Tony Sarg fancifully portrayed Demosthenes' lecture to the waves by showing the orator projecting his voice over the roar of the ocean.

In 346 B.C., the Peace of Philocrates was signed. Demosthenes was one of the ambassadors sent to arrange the final details of the treaty. He did not approve of the terms, but he did feel that a period of peace might give the Athenians an opportunity to rethink their position and prepare for what he believed would be inevitable conflict.

Another orator involved in the peace negotiations with Philip was Aeschines. Aeschines, however, favored Philip and urged all Athenians to accept the treaty. In 344 B.C., after Philip had continued his policy of setting one Greek city-state against another, Demosthenes delivered his *Second Philippic*. In it he said, "There is one precaution known to the wise that gives everyone an advantage and a sense of security. Democracies are especially alert to this precaution as a protection against tyrants. It is suspicion."

Aeschines disagreed with Demosthenes' beliefs and in 343 B.C., Demosthenes accused Aeschines of acting against Athenian interests and unfairly representing Philip II and his intentions. But Aeschines refuted the charge, and the bitter feeling between the two orators intensified.

In 341 B.C., Demosthenes delivered the *Third Philippic*, and this time the Athenians not only listened but gave Demosthenes control of the navy's budget. He enacted reforms he felt were necessary to enable the Athenians to defeat the powerful Macedonian army. He also made alliances with other cities, even winning the support of Thebes, Athens' longtime rival.

In the fall of 338 B.C., Philip met the Athenian troops on the battlefield at Chaeronea. The well-trained Macedonian units completely overwhelmed the Greeks, who retreated by the thousands. According to Plutarch, Demosthenes took part in the battle but returned so quickly to the city that many people, including Aeschines, accused him of cowardice. The Macedonian victory at Chaeronea ended Greek independence. Yet Demosthenes was not defeated or ousted by the people. Rather, they saw him as an honest and sincere defender of Greek independence and honored him by asking that he deliver the funeral oration for those who had died defending Greek freedom.

The loss at Chaeronea had yielded Greece to Philip, but his possession was short-lived. Just two years later, an assassin's knife ended Philip's career and brought his son Alexander to the throne. For a moment, Demosthenes and the Greeks thought freedom was imminent, but Alexander quickly proved his intention to keep control of his southern neighbor.

Furthermore, Alexander was well aware that many Greeks had opposed his father's rule, and he demanded that Demosthenes and seven other orators be sent to him. What he planned to do is uncertain, for Alexander withdrew his request after meeting with special envoys from Greece. But other troubles were brewing for Demosthenes.

His longtime rival Aeschines brought a second set of charges of improper conduct against Demosthenes' friend, the statesman Ctesiphon. Aeschines had done the same thing six years earlier, but events had intervened that prevented the case from coming to court. This time Aeschines counted on the pro-Macedonian faction in Athens to help him win the case. Because Aeschines accused Ctesiphon of lying when he praised Demosthenes as a public hero, Demosthenes believed he had to answer the charge.

A date was set for Demosthenes and Aeschines to face each other before a jury of at least 501 citizens. All Athens was stirring and many people planned to attend the trial just to listen to the two greatest orators of the day.

Demosthenes delivered a speech that became known as *On the Crown*, which many historians believe to be his masterpiece. Deliberately, honestly, and convincingly, Demosthenes leveled charges against Aeschines. He reviewed the events of the past 20 years, the loss of freedom under Philip, the continued loss of freedom under Alexander, and then asked what action had been taken in each crisis and who had taken it. "Aeschines, your policies have aided only Greece's enemy. My policies have aided Greece."

Each argument was well thought out and carefully, but boldly, presented. Every sentence added weight to the charges and accusations Demosthenes made. When it came time for the jury to vote, Demosthenes won a resounding victory and Aeschines, who had not received even one-fifth of the votes, was forced into exile.

Six years later, Demosthenes again found himself in court, accused of accepting 20 talents (a large sum of money) from Harpalus, the Macedonian whom Alexander had placed in charge of the empire's treasury and who had unwisely mismanaged the funds. After his misdeeds were discovered by Alexander, Harpalus fled to Athens and became involved in financial dealings with Demosthenes.

Why Demosthenes took the money is uncertain, and it may be inferred from several ancient sources that he intended to use the money to help Athens. Nevertheless, the jury found Demosthenes guilty and fined him 50 talents. Demosthenes managed to flee Athens, probably with the help of several sympathetic Athenian officials.

The very next year, 323 B.C., Alexander died in Babylon and the Athenians not only recalled Demosthenes but also paid his fine. His anti-Macedonian views, however, were not welcomed by the orator Demades, a leading statesman at the time and a supporter of Antipater, one of Alexander's officers and the man in charge of Greece after Alexander's death.

Because Demades saw Demosthenes as a threat to his own power and to Antipater, he persuaded the Athenians to sentence Demosthenes to death. Upon hearing the news, Demosthenes fled to the island of Calauria, just off the coast of Greece, where he sought refuge in the temple of Poseidon, the god of the sea. Antipater's soldiers followed Demosthenes into the temple and their leader

ANCIENT GREEKS

Demosthenes

BORN

384 B.C.
Athens, Greece

DIED

322 B.C.
Calauria

PROFESSION

Public speaker

ACCOMPLISHMENTS

Greece's best-known orator; delivered three *Philippics* against Philip II of Macedonia; encouraged the Greeks to unite against Philip; *On the Crown* is considered his masterpiece

"*Action! Action! Action!*"

—Demosthenes' reputed response when asked what three things make the perfect orator

Archias attempted to persuade him to return voluntarily to Athens.

According to Plutarch, Demosthenes remembered the dream he had had the previous night in which he had acted in a tragedy with Archias. Both were trying for the dramatic prize and, although Demosthenes had performed well, he had lost the competition because he lacked the proper stage props. Believing this dream was an omen that he would lose to Archias, Demosthenes calmly agreed to go with him, but only after writing a short note to his family.

Demosthenes then withdrew into the interior of the temple, took his reed pen and scroll, and prepared to write his letter. All the while he bit the reed, as was his habit when thinking deeply about some matter. From time to time, Archias' soldiers checked to see if Demosthenes was still writing. When they saw him with his head covered by his cloak, they laughed and called him a coward.

But a coward he was not, nor was he afraid to die. Calmly and boldly, Demosthenes advanced toward the soldiers and Archias, saying that he was ready. In the reed pen had been a vial of poison, and he could now feel its effects traveling through his body. In his biography of Demosthenes, Plutarch recorded the orator's last words to Archias: "While I still live, let me leave this sacred place and not desecrate it with my dead body, even though Antipater and you, his soldiers, have polluted everything, including this temple, with your presence." But the poison worked faster than Demosthenes had anticipated and he collapsed on the temple floor.

When news of his death reached Athens, the Athenians felt great sorrow for the man whom they now considered a true patriot. A statue was erected to his memory and his speeches were carefully studied as masterpieces of oratory. Time did not diminish his fame. A century later, his orations were considered among the greatest treasures housed in the renowned library in Alexandria, Egypt. There scholars carefully prepared each one for publication, thereby preserving his speeches for posterity.

The ancient Romans especially liked Demosthenes' orations, and Roman teachers often required their students to memorize his speeches. During the 1st century B.C., the master Roman orator Marcus Tullius Cicero borrowed many of Demosthenes' phrases, especially those found in *On the Crown*. One saying that Demosthenes included in his prosecution of an Athenian named Leptines in 355 B.C. can be read today as a description of the ancient orator's rise to fame: "Small opportunities are often the start of great enterprises."

FURTHER READING

Adams, Charles D. *Demosthenes and His Influence*. 1927. Reprint. New York: Cooper Square, 1963.

Demosthenes. *Selections*. 7 vols. Translated by J. H. Vince, C. A. Vince, and A. T. Murray. Vol. 7 translated by N. W. DeWitt and N. J. DeWitt. Loeb Classical Library. 1926–49. Reprint. Cambridge: Harvard University Press, 1964–89.

Sealey, Raphael. *Demosthenes and His Time: A Study in Defeat*. New York: Oxford University Press, 1993.

Philip II

CONQUEROR OF GREECE

News of the death of Philip's brother Alexander on the battlefield and the slaughter of his army at the hands of invading Illyrians from the north spread quickly throughout Macedonia. So did reports that the Illyrians were continuing their advance southward, while the Paeonians, another tribe to the north, were gathering their forces at the border.

For decades, turmoil and conflict had reigned in Macedonia, a country whose southern border met the northern coast of the Aegean Sea. Only in 392 B.C., when Philip's father Amyntas II became king, had Macedonia entered a period of relative peace and stability. When Amyntas died of old age in 370 B.C., Philip's oldest brother, Alexander, had succeeded him.

Conflicts again erupted, this time with the people of Thebes, a city in central Greece. The two sides agreed to a peace treaty, and in accordance with its terms, Philip was sent as a hostage to Thebes. This was a common practice in ancient times because the leaders of cities that had exchanged hostages were more reluctant to engage in hostilities that would threaten the lives of their people.

Although hostages could not leave the city that held them captive, they were very well treated. Philip took full

Philip saw his rise to power in Macedonia as only the beginning. His goal was the conquest of Greece, and then perhaps the world.

Uncovered at Olynthos, this arrowhead with two straight cutting edges was probably used in Philip's siege against the city. The inscribed name of Philip indicates that it was probably made in a workshop under state control.

advantage of his three-year stay in Thebes to learn as much as he could about Greek society and customs. It was at Thebes that Philip met Epaminondas, whom many called the greatest of Greeks. From Epaminondas, a highly respected general whose innovative strategies led Thebes to victory over Sparta, Philip learned many political and military lessons. Upon his return to Macedonia, these lessons proved invaluable.

Alexander and Perdiccas, another brother, quickly recognized Philip's leadership qualities and gave him command of a Macedonian province. But the first real test of Philip's character came after the deaths of his brothers, when he had to assume the position of regent, or acting ruler, for his nephew, the heir to the Macedonian throne. The year was 359 B.C. and Philip was 23 years old.

Within a few months, Philip maneuvered himself into the position of rightful heir to the throne. He negotiated a treaty that gave Athens control over the important commercial city of Amphipolis. This pleased the Athenians, who for years had fought unsuccessfully to win control of Amphipolis. Philip also entered into agreements with several other neighboring cities whose leaders might otherwise have opposed his plans.

With potential internal problems resolved, Philip now turned his attention to the military. After enforcing new and stricter military regulations, he marched against Argaeus, a man who intended to claim the Macedonian throne for himself and had won promises of help from Athens. After defeating Argaeus, Philip began securing Macedonia's borders. First he engaged the Paeonians, who soon yielded to his control. Next to meet his might were the Illyrians, with whom he arranged a peace treaty that added a portion of their land to his own. In 358 B.C., to strengthen his alliances with countries to the west, Philip married Olympias, a princess of Epirus, a land along the west coast of Greece where his troops had already conquered some territory.

With its western and northern frontiers under control, stability returned to Macedonia, and so too did peace. But Philip was not satisfied. He looked to the prospering cities along the coast, many of which had pledged their allegiance to Athens, and began to make plans. Amphipolis was the first city to fall, followed by Pydna.

There were reports that Philip had used treachery and deceit to extend his domain. Athens had not sent help to Amphipolis, allegedly because the Athenians had promised to make Philip master of Pydna, a city under Athenian control, in return for Philip's giving control of Amphipolis to Athens. Philip, however, had not waited for Athenian help and had captured Pydna without a struggle. He then refused to give Amphipolis to the Athenians, claiming that the terms of the treaty were invalid because the Athenians had not helped at Pydna.

Realizing that this action would offend the Athenians, Philip continued his conquest of Athens' allies. A fearless fighter, he took part in many battles and was wounded on several occasions. In 354 B.C., while laying siege to the port city of Methone, Philip was blinded in one eye. Yet nothing stopped the energetic and determined king of Macedonia and he now prepared to secure his southern border with Thessaly. Here, too, Philip met conflict and disunity.

Peace with Thessaly was important to Philip because its lands lay between Greece and Macedonia. The people in all three areas were considered to be Greek and they all spoke Greek, but the Macedonians were looked down on as "backward" Greeks with little culture or education. Other Greeks found their dialect difficult to understand. Physical strength was important to the Macedonians, and according to an old custom, only those who had killed a wild boar without using a net could recline at the dinner table. Any Macedonian who had not yet proved his strength in this manner was required to eat sitting up. (By custom, the ancient Macedonians, as well as many other Greeks, reclined while eating.)

In the early 350s, Philip won control of several Thessalian border towns before being asked by a group of Thessalians for help against their neighbors, the people of Pherae. This was what Philip needed—an excuse to march as an ally into a land he wished to conquer. The Thessalians were very generous to Philip. They made him commander of their military forces and gave him control of their public funds. After two defeats on the battlefield, Philip finally led the Thessalians to victory.

For Philip, this victory was twofold: it gave him control of Thessaly and allied him with Thebes, which was supported by Thessaly. At this time, Thebes was involved in the so-called Sacred War with Phocis, the city that had helped Pherae fight against Philip.

The people of Phocis had been cultivating the sacred lands around Delphi, where Greeks came to consult the oracle of Apollo. The Thebans, who were responsible for the care and maintenance of Delphi, had imposed a fine on Phocis but had received nothing. The Thebans, however, were not blameless. Many Greeks felt that they had used their influence at Delphi to advance Theban rights. When the Phocians wanted to sell the treasures at Delphi to support their armies, the conflict intensified. Soon all Greece was taking sides. Philip chose to side with Thebes, and his victory over the Phocians won him election as president of the Thessalian League.

Philip now decided to continue his campaign south into Greece and advanced as far as Thermopylae, which was guarded by such a strong Athenian contingent that he was forced to retreat. Philip's attack on Thermopylae awakened the anger of an Athenian named Demosthenes, one of Greece's greatest public speakers. Demosthenes saw Philip as a threat to every Greek city because he sincerely believed that Philip's goal was the conquest of Greece.

Philip, meanwhile, recognized that a forced entry into Greece would not bring the results he wanted, so he led his army back to Macedonia. He still wanted to expand his power and saw the route east as offering the best possibilities. Thrace, the country directly to the east of Macedonia, now began to feel the might and force of Philip's troops. His conquests there brought him control of several gold and silver mines, the money from which he used to support his troops, decorate his capital at Pella, and patronize the arts and literature. At Philip's invitation, many Greek poets and artists traveled to his court. Philosophers and teachers also came, including Aristotle, whom Philip asked to tutor his son Alexander.

Before Philip's reign, Macedonian leaders had not concerned themselves with the arts or culture. Under Philip's guidance the so-called Hellenization of Macedonia began, as the country gradually adopted Greek customs, ideas, and artistic designs. Yet no records mention Philip visiting Athens or any

Philip II

BORN

383 B.C.
Macedonia

DIED

336 B.C.
Macedonia

PROFESSION

King and general

ACCOMPLISHMENTS

Brought the warring factions of Macedonia under his control and unified the country; introduced the *sarissa*, a very long spear carried by heavily armed foot soldiers; his phalanx formation, with the cavalry guarding its rear and sides, became an exceptional fighting force; conquered all Greece and unified the country for the first time in history, but allowed each city-state to retain many rights; won control of Thessaly and much of Thrace

> *"A donkey carrying gold is allowed to enter the gates of any city."*
>
> —attributed to Philip II by Plutarch in *Apothegms* (around late 1st century A.D.)

Greek city except on the battlefield or when negotiating treaties.

There was one area, however, in which Philip did not follow the Greek lead but instituted his own reforms. This was the military, and with funds from the gold and silver mines Philip reorganized Macedonia's army. Under Philip, every Macedonian male was required to enroll in the army. Philip divided the country into districts, with each responsible for providing one cavalry unit, one heavy infantry unit, and one light infantry unit. Training was strict and so was discipline, with the result that soldiers knew exactly what was expected of them and were able to quickly carry out any order given on the battlefield.

Philip's most innovative reform involved the heavily armed soldiers who formed the phalanx (literally, "line of battle"). This formation of foot soldiers in close ranks with their shields overlapping and their spears extended had been used by early Greek soldiers and by the Spartans, but Philip introduced the *sarissa,* a spear approximately 16 feet long and made of pieces of cornel wood (a type of dogwood) riveted together. It had a pointed metal tip. Because a soldier needed both hands to hold the *sarissa,* he could not hold his shield in the usual way. Instead, he placed his shield's inside strap around his neck and then slung the shield over his left shoulder. In order not to impede a soldier's arm movements, the shield was light and small.

Each phalanx was composed of hundreds of soldiers divided into companies and stood eight to ten soldiers deep. The soldiers were known as the Foot Companions. Constant training gave each phalanx such mobility and flexibility that it could move swiftly across the field, destroying the order within enemy ranks and mowing down everything in its path. The Companions in the front line swished their *sarissas* up and down, while those in the center held theirs upright in order to deflect oncoming enemy arrows.

The defense of each phalanx rested mainly on the cavalry units guarding its sides and rear. The Macedonian cavalry under Philip became a fearsome fighting unit. He trained his riders to form a wedge that would cut directly into the enemy's troops. All of Philip's maneuvers had the same purpose—to destroy the marching formation and battlefield strategies of opposing armies. His innovations revolutionized warfare.

Philip's plans for conquering the lands beyond Greece rested with this fighting force. But first he had to win control of Greece, for he did not wish to march east with an unconquered Greece just miles from Macedonia's borders.

Diplomacy, he felt, was the best way to win Greece, and he continued to look for opportunities. Athens was his main goal, but many Athenians had adopted a pacifist policy and no longer wished to send troops into the field. Philip decided to attack the Chalcidician cities along the coast of the northern Aegean, all of which regarded themselves as allies of Athens. When the major port of Olynthus fell in 347 B.C., Athens began to fear that Philip would cut off Athenian trade with the Black Sea and eliminate Athens' principal food supply route.

In 346 B.C., Philip suggested that Athens and Macedonia sign a peace treaty to return the cities of Chalcidice to Athenian control. The Athenians, including Demosthenes, agreed to the treaty, but the war of wills continued

Ready and poised for action, the Macedonian phalanx presented an awesome sight to any opposing enemy. Philip introduced the use of 16-foot spears to make the phalanx more formidable.

because Philip was not to be stopped and Demosthenes continued to distrust the wily king. Finally, at the persistent urging of Demosthenes, Athens entered into an alliance with other Greek cities to resist any further incursions by Philip into Greek lands.

Philip, meanwhile, disregarded the terms of the peace treaty and began attacking Greek cities allied to Athens. He then consolidated his grip on Thrace and confiscated an Athenian food convoy near the Black Sea. Infuriated by such insolence, the Athenians, at Demosthenes' urging, declared war on Philip in 340 B.C.

In November 339 B.C., Philip swept into Greece. When the Athenians learned that his troops had reached Elatea, just miles to the west, they heeded Demosthenes' advice to join forces with their former enemies, the Thebans. In 338 B.C., at Chaeronea, a city between Elatea and Thebes, the two armies met to decide the fate of Greece. Philip won—and Greece lost its independence. But Philip did not wish to punish Athens too severely, for he admired the city. Therefore, Athens was allowed to govern itself and keep its fleet and colonies. The Thebans, however, lost all their political rights.

After Chaeronea, Philip swiftly conquered all of Greece except for Sparta, whose lands he confiscated and laid waste. In 337 B.C., he called for representatives from all the Greek cities except Sparta to meet at Corinth. Philip decreed an end to all conflicts and ruled that each city would keep its own lands and rule itself. While he imposed no taxes on the Greeks, Philip did require each city to send him a contingent of soldiers in proportion to its population. All Greeks were to acknowledge Philip as ruler, and Macedonian garrisons were established in the Greek cities of Ambracia, Chalcis, Corinth, and Thebes.

To provide a forum where cities could discuss and vote on issues, Philip organized the League of Corinth, made up of representatives from each city. The league brought unprecedented unity to Greece and allowed Philip to continue to pursue the goal he had set for himself years earlier—the conquest of Persia.

Early in 336 B.C., just after the league approved Philip's proposal of war, an advance Macedonian contingent set out for Asia Minor under Philip's trusted general Parmenion. Philip planned to follow with his armies, but the calculating master of diplomacy had not been watching events within his own household.

As was the custom in Macedonia, Philip had several wives, most of them acquired through political marriages made to strengthen ties with his allies. Olympias, his first wife and the mother of Alexander, had never before felt threatened by any of the other marriages. Only in 338 B.C., when Philip married a Macedonian princess named Cleopatra, did she begin to fear for her position and her son's claim to the throne. Infuriated and bitter, Olympias decided to leave Macedonia. Alexander soon followed. Although Olympias' departure did not affect Philip, Alexander's did. Philip still regarded Alexander as his successor, so he met with his son and the two reconciled.

Olympias was not the only person who hated Philip. A young Macedonian named Pausanias, from a distinguished family, was another. According to the philosopher Aristotle, who was at Philip's court in 336 B.C., Cleopatra's uncle Attalus had mistreated Pausanias, and when Pausanias spoke with Philip and asked him to bring Attalus to justice, Philip refused to interfere.

Angered by such injustice, Pausanias attended the wedding of Philip's daughter in the summer of 336 B.C. As Philip walked past Pausanias in the wedding procession, the young Macedonian unsheathed his knife and fatally stabbed the king. Philip's attendants caught and killed Pausanias as he tried to escape. Suspicion fell immediately on Olympias and even on Alexander as instigators of the deed, but with no proof to implicate either, officials dropped the case. Philip was 46 at the time and had ruled Macedonia for 23 years.

Centuries later, a legendary account of Alexander's life told how he had commissioned a grand tomb for his father. Little attention was paid to this piece of information until the fall of 1977, when archaeologists discovered a royal tomb at Vergina, the ancient capital of Macedonia. The most significant finds were two gold caskets, one with the cremated bones of a man in his forties and the other with those of a woman in her twenties. Accompanying the caskets were silver cups, a gold-plated silver crown, a gold quiver, and a pair of greaves (leg armor). Because one of the greaves was shorter than the other, many believed the tomb could be Philip's, who was lame because of a wound to one leg. Studies continue to prove the hypothesis that the tomb is that of Philip II and one of his queens.

FURTHER READING

Bradford, Alfred S., comp., ed., trans. *Philip II of Macedon: A Life from the Ancient Sources*. Illustrated by Pamela M. Bradford. Westport, Conn.: Praeger, 1992.

Cawkwell, George. *Philip of Macedon*. Boston: Faber & Faber, 1978.

Ellis, J. R. *Philip II and Macedonian Imperialism*. London: Thames & Hudson, 1976.

Hammond, N. G. L. *Philip of Macedon*. Baltimore, Md.: Johns Hopkins University Press, 1994.

Perlman, Samuel. *Philip and Athens*. New York: Barnes & Noble, 1973.

Alexander the Great

WORLD CONQUEROR

"What an excellent horse! If only they knew how to handle him!" murmured 11-year-old Alexander as he watched his father order the unridable creature taken away.

"What's that, my son?" asked Philip. "Do you pretend to know more than my expert horse trainers?"

"I know I can handle him better than they can."

"And, if you don't, then what?"

"I will pay the full price of the horse!"

After a moment's hesitation, Philip agreed. Alexander quickly ran to the horse, took hold of the bridle, and faced the horse directly into the sun. Alexander had noticed that the horse reared whenever it saw its shadow moving. By facing him into the sun, Alexander eliminated the shadow. Taking the reins in his hands, he allowed the horse to take a few steps forward, stroking him gently all the while. Then, in one leap, he mounted the horse and, drawing in the bridle, slowed him almost to a halt.

On this gold ring, Alexander is crowned with the lion skin used to adorn statues of Heracles. Alexander believed that all Macedonian kings were descended from that Greek hero.

"The sun never sets on my conquests."

—a boast that ancient authors attributed to Alexander

Feeling the horse's muscles relax, Alexander spurred him to a gallop and gave him the freedom to run at will. After a few turns about the field, Alexander led the "unridable" horse back to his father. A round of applause filled the air as Alexander dismounted. Philip, his eyes brimming with tears of joy, said, "My son, you must seek a kingdom worthy of your talents, for my kingdom of Macedonia is too small for you."

Alexander named the horse Bucephalas (ox head) and rode him throughout his youth and later on his campaigns into Asia. In his *Life of Alexander,* the Greek biographer Plutarch created this conversation to illustrate how Alexander had demonstrated determination, courage, and fearlessness at a very early age. There were other stories too, as well as many omens of a life full of achievements and honors.

During her pregnancy, Alexander's mother, Olympias, often spoke of divine signs that foretold the birth of an illustrious son. When fire destroyed the goddess Artemis' temple at Ephesus in Asia Minor (present-day Turkey) in July 356 B.C., soothsayers warned that something had happened that day that would bring ruin to Asia. Years later, when Alexander began his conquest of Asia, soothsayers remembered the fire and said Artemis had left the temple unprotected that day to be present at the future hero's birth. Alexander's father, Philip, saw 356 B.C. as a year filled with successes at home, on the battlefield, and at the chariot races at the Olympic Games.

Philip wished the same good fortune for his son, but he knew that a man's success depended on his leadership qualities and military skills. To train his son properly, Philip hired tutors. Leonidas, who was responsible for disciplining Alexander's body, sent the young prince on frequent all-night marches and rationed his food. The philosopher Aristotle was asked to challenge Alexander's mind by introducing him to the natural sciences, rhetoric (the art of using words effectively), and politics. Under Aristotle's guidance, Alexander studied the Greek poet Homer, whose epic tale of the Greek hero Achilles stirred Alexander's imagination and remained a lasting influence.

Philip carefully monitored his son's progress and was so pleased with the results that when he went on a military campaign in 340 B.C., he left the 16-year-old Alexander in charge of Macedonia. Alexander rallied to the challenge and won his first military victory by crushing a rebellion in Thrace. As a reward, Philip allowed Alexander to settle his first town, Alexandropolis (meaning "City of Alexander"; *polis* is Greek for "city").

Two years later, when Philip defeated the combined Greek forces at the decisive battle of Chaeronea, Alexander again proved his military skills by leading a cavalry charge against the Greeks. After the battle, Alexander made his only visit to Athens when he accompanied the two Macedonian envoys sent to discuss peace terms.

These experiences were to prove invaluable two years later, in 336 B.C., when an assassin fatally stabbed Philip at his daughter's wedding feast. As news of Philip's murder spread, Macedonia's military leaders and soldiers turned to young Alexander. Alexander readily accepted their allegiance and made known his determination to follow his father's plan of attacking Persia. But first he planned to quell some unrest at home.

By executing all potential rivals and the men accused of conspiring to murder his father, Alexander eliminated opposition within Macedonia. He then subdued several border uprisings that had followed his father's death. Meanwhile, the League of Corinth, the confederation of Greek cities, voted him commander in chief of the expedition against Persia. But when false reports of Alexander's death reached the northern Greek city of Thebes, the Thebans declared their independence. Angered at such insolence, Alexander immediately marched against them, covering the 240 miles to Thebes in 14 days. He then ordered his troops to destroy every building throughout the city except for the temples and the house of the lyric poet Pindar. Thousands of Thebans died in the struggle, and those who survived were sold into slavery. This harsh treatment of the people who defied his orders became characteristic of Alexander's foreign policy. But anyone who accepted his orders or demonstrated great courage on the battlefield he pardoned and treated honorably.

Before returning to Macedonia, Alexander spent some time in Greece consolidating his power. Many people came to see their new leader. When Alexander learned that the well-known philosopher Diogenes could not bother himself with such a task, Alexander asked to meet Diogenes and found him stretched out in the sun. Instead of immediately rising in respect for the great leader, Diogenes merely looked up to see who was approaching. Alexander then asked if there was anything Diogenes wanted to ask of him. According to Plutarch, Diogenes replied, "Yes, there is. I would ask that you not stand between me and the sun." Admiring such honesty, Alexander turned to his companions and said that if he were not Alexander, he would wish to be Diogenes.

In May 334 B.C., Alexander set out for Asia Minor, accompanied by 35,000 foot soldiers and cavalry. With him also were surveyors, architects, historians, and others who could help him establish an empire and build new cities. Alexander's chief assistant was his father's trusted adviser and general Parmenion.

When they reached the Hellespont (known today as the Dardanelles), Alexander placed Parmenion in charge of leading the troops across the strait while he and a few trusted companions set off in their own boat. As he reached the shores of Asia, Alexander, dressed in full armor, jumped out, flung his spear into the soil, and proclaimed himself lord of Asia. According to ancient sources, Alexander had slept with a dagger and a copy of Homer's epic poem the *Iliad* under his pillow for years and now saw himself as a second Achilles.

Alexander's first stop was Troy, the site of Achilles' greatest victory. There, following the traditional Greek rites used to honor a special hero, Alexander ordered a companion to crown him and anoint his body with oil. He then ran naked to Achilles' tomb and placed a garland on it.

Meanwhile, some 20 miles from where Alexander's troops had encamped, the local Persian rulers were debating their next move. For years they had anticipated a Greek invasion and were confident that they could successfully defend their land. With their granaries filled with enough provisions to feed everyone for months and with three times as many troops as the Greeks, the Persians prepared to meet the invading foe at the Granicus River.

In a surprise move, Alexander attacked at dawn and ordered his troops to cross the river, march up the riverbank, and charge the enemy. Alexander's cavalry broke through the Persian cavalry, disrupting its formation and leaving the Persian foot soldiers unprotected. Easily recognizable because of the plumes of white feathers on his helmet, Alexander took part in the charge and by afternoon had won his first battle on Asian soil. In honor of this victory, Alexander sent home many of the spoils with this message: "Alexander, son of Philip and all the Greeks except the Spartans, won this plunder from the barbarians in Asia."

Alexander quickly took advantage of this victory at the Granicus and set about freeing the Greek cities of western Asia Minor from Persian control. On land he had outmaneuvered the Persians, but he knew such a victory would be impossible against Persia's mighty fleet. For this reason, he decided to disable the Persian fleet indirectly by capturing the port cities and making the fleet homeless.

His plan worked, and by the spring of 333 B.C. Alexander was ready to meet the army of the Persian king, Darius. At the town of Gordium, Alexander stopped and waited for reinforcements from home. In the town's old palace there was a chariot with a knot of cornel (a type of dogwood) bark around its yoke. Legend said that whoever untied the knot would be the ruler of Asia. Over the years, many had tried without success. Determined to conquer Asia, Alexander quickly slashed through the knot

Alexander the Great

BORN
356 B.C.
Macedonia

DIED
323 B.C.
Babylon

PROFESSION
King and conqueror

ACCOMPLISHMENTS
Ruled Macedonia after the assassination of his father, Philip II; consolidated his rule over Greece and the lands bordering the northern Aegean Sea; defeated King Darius of Persia to win the Persian Empire; extended his empire into India; explored areas and regions of Asia previously unknown to the Greeks

Around 1500, Italian artisans painted this fresco of Alexander in a triumphal procession; Victory places the victor's crown on his head. The fresco was later transferred to wood panels used to decorate the ceiling of a palace in Siena.

"Heaven cannot allow two suns, nor earth two masters."

—reputedly said by Alexander to King Darius, about Persia

with his knife. At just that moment, according to tradition, the heavens thundered and flashed with bolts of lightning.

Alexander continued his advance into Persian territory, while Darius confidently gathered his troops and prepared for a great victory. Near Tarsus, on the southern coast of Asia Minor, Alexander fell ill, most likely with malaria. His fever and symptoms worsened despite numerous treatments, until a physician named Philip offered a cure. Just before Alexander was to drink the potion, he received a message from Parmenion advising him to beware of Philip. To prove his trust in the doctor, Alexander disregarded the warning and downed the medicine. Soon after, he recovered and returned to his troops. This unwavering confidence in trusted friends was one of Alexander's greatest strengths and inspired confidence in those who served him.

Alexander's delay, however, had made Darius even more confident, and the Persian king planned a surprise attack. When Alexander learned the position of Darius' troops, he immediately changed course and marched his men toward Issus, a town at the northern Syrian border. Never anticipating that troops could travel at the pace Alexander set, nor that they could endure a terrible rain-and-wind storm, Darius was taken by surprise. He tried to shift tactics, but Alexander's well-disciplined cavalry, porcupinelike *sarissa* (spear) bearers, and long line of defense met the enemy and routed them.

With defeat imminent, Darius fled the battlefield, leaving behind his mother, wife, and children. Contrary to custom, Alexander did not harm or enslave them but allowed them to bury the Persian dead and then welcomed them to live in his camp in the style in which they had been accustomed.

As reports of Alexander's daring tactics and his treatment of Darius' family spread throughout the area, other cities and towns along the eastern shores of the Mediterranean Sea surrendered to the Macedonian. Many had hated the autocratic and often cruel rule of the Persians, and they believed life would be better under Alexander.

The Phoenician city of Tyre (modern-day Sur in Lebanon) was an exception, because the Tyrians believed no land force could capture their island stronghold with its high protective walls. But Alexander had a strategy. He ordered his men to build a causeway connecting the mainland with the island. Using catapults, battering rams, and 180-foot-tall siege towers with platforms from which archers could rain their arrows upon the enemy, Alexander's troops broke Tyre's defenses after a nine-month siege. Alexander then ordered the complete destruction of Tyre because its inhabitants had resisted his rule.

Darius now wondered whether his remaining forces could defeat the mighty Macedonian. He tried to negotiate a peace settlement by offering Alexander all the lands west of the Euphrates and a huge ransom for his family. Parmenion quickly advised Alexander to accept, but according to Plutarch, Alexander replied, "I would accept them, but only if I were Parmenion." Peace was not part of Alexander's plan.

In November 332 B.C., Alexander marched into Egypt, won the immediate support of the people, and accepted the surrender of the Persian governor. Here, as in Troy, Alexander left his troops to go on a personal mission. Southwest of Egypt, in the Libyan desert, was the oracle of the great Ammon, a god comparable in power to Zeus, the king of the Greek gods. The 200-mile trip to Ammon's temple in the beautiful Siwa oasis was dangerous because raging winds easily smothered all life and covered trails with mounds of sand. Alexander, however, was determined to consult the oracle, and he traveled with a small group, mostly at night when the heat was not as intense. According to Alexander's friend Ptolemy, on one occasion two snakes appeared just as the group veered off course and guided them straight to the oasis. What happened in the temple is unknown, for Alexander never revealed what the oracle said to him privately, but others said the oracle had proclaimed Alexander the true son of Ammon.

Although emperor-worship was a long tradition in the East, in Greece and the West it was not. Therefore, when Alexander began to encourage others to honor him as a god, many Greeks became upset. Some Greeks also disliked Alexander's new preference for Eastern dress, such as a purple-and-white striped tunic and a ribbon crown as a sign of royalty.

Unlike his troops who saw conquest as a means to dominate another country, Alexander planned to absorb aspects of the cultures of the conquered into Greek culture and vice versa. Before leaving Egypt, Alexander made plans to found a new city at the delta of the Nile River. Named Alexandria in his honor, this city would become one of the ancient world's greatest cultural and commercial centers. Alexander, however, could not wait for his city to be built. Darius was still a threat and Egypt was only one of the lands he planned to conquer.

On the plain of Gaugamela (in present-day Iraq), just east of the Tigris River, Alexander's troops met the massive army Darius had gathered in defense of Persia. When the Macedonians urged Alexander to make a surprise attack at night, his reply, immortalized by Plutarch, was curt: "I will not steal a victory." Historians reported that he stayed up the night before the battle making final changes in his maneuvers and then fell so soundly asleep that he had to be awakened the following morning.

Alexander knew victory depended on strategy, for the Persians far outnumbered his troops. As at Issus, he depended on his cavalry attacking in wedge-shape formation, driving a hole into the enemy's defense and scattering the troops in the rear. This wedge formation could also veer right or left and cause incredible havoc. Key to his strategy was the phalanx, which proved its might and effectiveness as its spears plunged through enemy defenses.

Darius soon realized that he had been defeated, and he fled the battlefield, just as he had done at Issus. Alexander followed in pursuit but stopped when reports reached him that Parmenion needed help against Persian forces that threatened to overwhelm his troops. Turning his attention to his own forces, he allowed Darius to escape. By day's end, Persia was his and Alexander prepared for the next conquest.

Again he led his troops eastward, first to Babylon, then to Susa and Persepolis (where supposedly, drunk at the time, he ceremonially burned the great palace), and finally to Ecbatana (where he ordered the Persian spoils kept). At Ecbatana, Alexander sent his Thessalian cavalry and other Greek allies home. Now that the Persians had been defeated and the Greeks avenged, Alexander considered all further conquests his alone.

Still, there was one Persian matter that needed attention—Darius. When Alexander finally found the Persian king, he lay mortally wounded. His wretched condition won Alexander's sympathy and made him recall the king's great courage on the battlefield. No longer did Alexander wish revenge on Darius. He arranged for a royal funeral at Persepolis and even covered Darius' dead body with his own cloak.

In the months that followed, Alexander pushed farther and farther east. There seemed to be no end to his vision of conquest, but there were signs of unrest in his camp, in Greece, and in other western provinces. Not everyone agreed with Alexander's plan of world conquest. Several cities wanted to secede and rule themselves, and a few of Alexander's commanders strongly objected to his policy of appointing conquered peoples to positions of power.

In September 330 B.C., Alexander learned that Parmenion's son, Philotas, had been involved in an unsuccessful plot on Alexander's life. He ordered Philotas tried before the army, as was the custom on a military campaign. The Macedonian troops condemned Philotas and ordered him executed. To prevent any unrest among those who favored Philotas and his father, Alexander arranged for the murder of Parmenion and other potential conspirators. Although some of Alexander's followers questioned the fairness of the condemnation as well as the severity of the punishments, the troops did not waver in their allegiance to their 26-year-old leader.

During his great expeditions, Alexander continued his custom of establishing new Alexandrias. Like the first Alexandria in Egypt, these new cities were meant to be cultural and commercial centers. Greek was the official language of these cities (Alexander never did learn Persian), but in all other aspects, the culture of the inhabitants was mingled with the culture of Greece. Alexander was trying to achieve concord, and for him this meant a harmonious blending of East and West, with Greek culture being dominant.

Since Gaugamela, Alexander had fought several skirmishes with local tribes and groups, but no major battles. His reputation preceded him and few were willing to consider opposing his entry into their lands. A Bactrian ruler named Spitamenes, however, did prove a formidable enemy, and Alexander not only lost many men fighting his swiftly moving cavalry but was wounded himself in the head by a stone. One day, as Alexander's men were striking camp, a spring of dark gooey liquid spurted into the air near Alexander's tent. Because of its taste and odor, many thought it was olive oil and considered it a good omen. It was not olive oil, however, but petroleum. This was the first recorded oil strike by Westerners in Iran.

Another incident that occurred around this time turned many Greeks and Macedonians against Alexander. To relieve the tension of battling Spitamenes, Alexander had spent a night drinking with some of his men, including his old and trusted friend Clitus. When Clitus carelessly insulted Alexander, the latter reached for a spear (tradition said that his bodyguard had taken his sword to prevent any mishaps) and killed Clitus.

Macedonians and Greeks were shocked at their leader's callous behavior. The troops still followed Alexander but discontent grew, especially when Alexander began asking his followers to observe Persian customs. When

Riding Bucephalas, Alexander (far left, with head uncovered) breaks through the Persian lines in the Battle of Issus and prepares to attack Darius (standing in chariot). Formed of bits of colored glass, this floor mosaic was uncovered in Pompeii, Italy.

Alexander tried to make the Greeks and Macedonians honor him as a god, they reacted so strongly against the idea that he had to stop the practice.

Yet Alexander continued to consolidate his power and, in an attempt to promote ties between himself and the peoples he conquered, he arranged for marriages between his soldiers and Eastern women. This was possible because Macedonian law did not forbid polygamy, and many soldiers had both a Western wife and an Eastern wife. Alexander married several Eastern women, including King Darius' daughter Barsine and a Bactrian ruler's daughter named Roxane.

In the summer of 326 B.C., Alexander stood at the gates of India. His meeting with the Indian raja Ambhi, ruler of Taxila, had gone well. Alexander had agreed to Ambhi's request for help against Porus, another Indian raja whose land lay east of the Jhelum River. Porus, however, was determined to stop Alexander's eastward march and positioned himself at the river with his massive army, which included 200 elephants. Military experts rank Alexander's battle against Porus as a masterpiece of strategy.

To confuse Porus and wear down his troops, Alexander made sure Porus saw cartloads of food enter his camp on a daily basis. At night, Alexander had cavalrymen ride up and down the banks shouting as if about to attack. After several such performances—but still no attack—Porus' men stopped their vigilant watch. At that moment, Alexander struck.

Aware that he had to keep away from Porus' elephants, Alexander ordered one contingent to prepare a fake crossing. Porus, who had been watching all the maneuvers, sent his elephants to intercept that contingent. Alexander was secretly preparing for a crossing at another point. A terrible storm struck just as the rafts carrying the horses and the soldiers armed with spears and breastplates began crossing. Undeterred, Alexander, on his trusted horse Bucephalas, led his troops to the opposite shore.

The battle raged for hours until finally victory was Alexander's. To Porus, whose courage and military prowess he admired, Alexander gave control of the lands east of the Jhelum River. Those west of the Jhelum he placed under Ambhi's control. In this way, he ended the rivalry between the two enemies and brought relative peace to the region.

Alexander again looked east, thinking to conquer more lands, but this time his troops refused to follow. For two days Alexander remained in his tent, sulking because his men had abandoned him when he knew he could continue. Then, realizing their decision was final, he agreed to turn back, but only after building altars to each of the 12 principal Greek deities.

In 325 B.C., Alexander headed west for the first time in more than 10 years. He took a different route because he wanted to explore new lands, especially those along the coast that might become commercial centers and ports for his vast empire. Taking command of the land forces, Alexander marched across Gedrosia (today the Makran Desert) on the northern coast of the Arabian Sea. In charge of his fleet was Nearchus, whose route paralleled Alexander's. Perhaps the two had planned to meet at various points along the way to resupply the land forces with food and the sailors with fresh water, but treacherous conditions prevented such meetings.

Alexander and his forces suffered horribly; many died from exhaustion and heat exposure while crossing the constantly shifting and burning sands. Poisonous snakes were another threat, both to humans and to the pack animals and horses. Several times the troops lost their way, but finally the survivors straggled into Pura, the capital city of Gedrosia.

After allowing them time to rest, eat, and drink, Alexander again urged his forces to continue on to Babylon, where Nearchus' fleet once again rejoined Alexander. At Susa, to the southeast of Babylon, Alexander hosted a great feast at which he arranged the marriage of 80 officers and 10,000 of his soldiers to Persian women.

There was still considerable unrest among his troops because many Macedonians and Greeks resented the positions of honor and power being awarded to the conquered people. Many felt that, as conquerors, they alone should rule. Such resentment, however, did not deter Alexander. He began planning a major campaign into Arabia to look for possible trade routes.

In 323 B.C., as Alexander gathered his forces for the planned expedition, he became sick. Records of his symptoms have led many to believe that his illness was malaria. After 11 days of intense suffering, Alexander died—just months before his 33rd birthday. During the 12 years and eight months since he had taken control of Macedonia, Alexander had consolidated his position in Greece and the lands bordering the northern Aegean, defeated the great Persian empire, conquered lands bordering the eastern Mediterranean Sea, including Egypt, and won control of lands stretching across into India. Few rulers in the history of the world have governed such a huge expanse of land and such a variety of peoples.

According to tradition, Alexander's generals stood around his bedside as he lay dying and asked who would be his successor. The Greek historian Arrian quoted his reply: "To the strongest!"

Yet who was the strongest? Alexander left no living heirs, so his generals chose as Alexander's successor his half brother, a man with little intelligence. When Alexander's wife Roxane gave birth months later to a son, he too was named king. Then, after assassins claimed the lives of both these successors, Alexander's generals began their fight for the throne.

Alexander had always been concerned with the future, and he kept a historian with him to record the events of his campaigns. The best known of these historians was Callisthenes, Aristotle's nephew. Yet Alexander need not have worried, for as the centuries passed, his reputation grew, along with the stories of his exploits and achievements. Medieval Europe loved the tales of his conquests and romanticized his life, adding many fictitious details, including an expedition to the ocean's floor in a glass barrel to search for pearls. The Middle East was also well acquainted with Alexander, and his exploits were translated into five Asian languages. Today, Alexander remains one of world history's best-known personalities. Scholars and historians continue to study the impact of his conquests, his policy of merging East and West, and the spread of Greek culture under his guidance.

FURTHER READING

Bosworth, A. B. *Conquest and Empire: The Reign of Alexander the Great.* New York: Cambridge University Press, 1988.

Dupuy, Trevor Nevitt. *The Military Life of Alexander the Great of Macedon.* New York: Franklin Watts, 1969.

Fox, Robin Lane. *Alexander the Great.* New York: Penguin, 1973.

———. *The Search for Alexander.* Boston: Little, Brown, 1980.

Green, Peter. *Alexander of Macedon, 356–323 B.C.: A Historical Biography.* Rev. ed. Harmondsworth, England: Penguin, 1974.

Snyder, John W. *Alexander the Great.* New York: Twayne, 1966.

Theule, Frederic. *Alexander and His Times.* New York: Holt, 1996.

Wepman, Dennis. *Alexander the Great.* New York: Chelsea House, 1986.

Pytheas

THE FIRST SCIENTIFIC EXPLORER

The excitement of exploration pushed fear from Pytheas' mind. For years, he had listened to people in his hometown of Massilia, in Gaul (today Marseilles, France), speak of the Tin Islands to the north. Because Greece had no tin, the Greeks had to rely on imported tin to make the bronze for their tools and weapons.

The Greek colony of Massilia was a well-known trading center whose prosperity depended to some extent on the tin it imported from the Tin Islands and then exported to other Greek lands along the Mediterranean Sea. Yet it was foreign traders who brought the tin to Massilia, and no Greek had ever traveled to the islands or even knew where they were located. Pytheas was determined to solve this mystery.

Historians believe that Pytheas made his voyage around 300 B.C., a time when the Greeks began actively questioning the world about them. Were geographers correct in saying an ocean of water circled the land masses they inhabited? Was the world really flat so that a person who traveled too

Decorating the bottom of a vase made around 250 B.C., these two Greek sailing ships have prows shaped like animal heads. Pytheas, determined to sail through the Pillars of Hercules, hoped to explore the oceans surrounding Greece and locate the Tin Islands.

far in any direction would fall off? There was much speculation, but few people dared to seek answers to these questions.

Because Pytheas believed the Tin Islands lay somewhere in the vast unnamed ocean surrounding the lands he knew, he resolved to sail through the Pillars of Hercules (known today as the Strait of Gibraltar) at the western end of the Mediterranean Sea and into that ocean. Barring his way, however, were the Carthaginians, whose fleet controlled the passageway through the Pillars of Hercules. Relations between the Greeks and the Carthaginians had never been friendly, especially because they were trade rivals.

The Carthaginians had controlled the western Mediterranean for many decades. Their capital city, Carthage (near modern-day Tunis in Tunisia), had been founded as a commercial port some time around 800 B.C. by the Phoenicians. Phoenicia was a land that bordered the eastern end of the Mediterranean (today Syria and Lebanon). Like the Greeks, the Phoenicians were traders and had established colonies in the lands around the Mediterranean. Consequently, as the number of Greek colonies in the western Mediterranean increased, so did the rivalry between the two peoples.

In an attempt to discourage others from passing through the Pillars of Hercules, the Carthaginians circulated tales of fierce sea monsters and dangerous whirlpools that awaited anyone venturing into the vast ocean. Such stories, however, did not deter Pytheas.

How he managed to slip past the Carthaginian guard posts is uncertain, but once he did Pytheas turned and sailed north. Most likely he kept in sight of land as best he could, for he had neither compass nor maps or charts to use as references. His first stop was the Phoenician port city of Gades (modern-day Cádiz, Spain). From there, he slowly maneuvered his vessel until he reached the northern tip of what is today Brittany, in France. What his thoughts were at this point is pure conjecture, but Pytheas must have debated whether to continue hugging the coastline or venture across the water that stretched north before him.

An explorer's zeal led him across the open waters and to the islands known today as the Channel Islands. Thinking these were the Tin Islands, Pytheas began to make inquiries of the inhabitants, but he was told that the lands that exported tin lay a day's sail to the north. Undeterred, Pytheas again set sail, and soon he saw a huge expanse of land stretching out on the horizon before him.

Once ashore, at what is today known as Land's End in Cornwall, England, Pytheas quickly made known the reason for his visit and was shown several underground mines. Satisfied that he had found the Tin Islands, Pytheas then decided to explore the countryside. In his journal, he noted that the people on the island lived very simple lives. They used logs and reeds to build their houses and ate wheat, corn, and other grains that they grew in their fields. What particularly caught Pytheas' attention was their threshing techniques. Here in the north, the people threshed inside barns, whereas in Mediterranean areas, where the climate was warmer, threshing could be done outdoors. They ate very simply and drank *curmi*, a type of beer made from barley, and other drinks made from grain and honey.

Pytheas described the land as very wooded, with a cold and rainy climate. He recognized its shape as a triangle and accurately estimated its circumference to be 4,000 miles. He estimated the distance he had sailed from Massilia to England to be 1,050 miles. (The actual distance is 1,120 miles.)

After hearing that a land called Thule was a six-day journey farther north, he decided to investigate. There he met people who ate grain and wild berries and drank an alcoholic beverage made from honey. Even more fascinating was the fact that the winters in this land were perpetually dark, but the sun never set during the summer. When possible, Pytheas used his sundial to keep a record of the hours.

No one knows for sure what land Pytheas reached, but historians believe there are three possibilities: Norway, the Faeroe Islands of Denmark, or Iceland. Whichever land it was, it seems likely that Pytheas crossed the Arctic Circle because he recorded that the water was too thick to sail through but not solid enough to walk on.

Approximately six years and 7,000 miles after he first set out from Massilia, Pytheas returned home. Using his records and notes as a guide, he wrote *On the Ocean*, a travelogue and record of his findings. Many of his contemporaries laughed as they read the book and questioned the accuracy of his observations. They found it difficult to believe Pytheas' assertions that their scientific theories were incorrect, that the pole star was not really at the North Pole, that the moon affected the tides, and that the ocean water he mentioned differed from the Mediterranean Sea and other seas.

Only fragments of Pytheas' book have survived, but the controversy surrounding what he claimed to have seen kept his name alive.

FURTHER READING

Franck, Irene M., and David M. Brownstone. *Trade and Travel Routes: The Northern World.* New York: Facts on File, 1990.

Lomask, Milton. *Great Lives: Exploration.* New York: Scribners, 1988.

ANCIENT GREEKS

Pytheas

BORN

Active around 300 B.C.
Place unknown

DIED

Date and place unknown

PROFESSION

Explorer

ACCOMPLISHMENTS

Sailed through the Pillars of Hercules (Strait of Gibraltar) into the Atlantic, north to England, and then across the Arctic Circle; explored a land then called Thule, which might have been Norway, Iceland, or the Faeroe Islands; recorded his observations in *On the Ocean*

More Ancient Greeks to Remember

Critias (around 460–403 B.C.) was the leader of the Thirty Tyrants, the pro-Spartan oligarchy that ruled Athens immediately following the end of the Peloponnesian War in 404 B.C. Well educated and a member of one of Athens' richest families, Critias was also a relative of the philosopher Plato and a former pupil of the philosopher Socrates. But Critias had few admirers, and he was treated harshly by later historians. The reason was most likely his cruel treatment of the Athenians and their allies, which included the killing of many of Critias' opponents and the confiscation of their property.

When another tyrant named Theramenes opposed him too strongly, Critias called for his execution. Such despicable behavior antagonized many Athenians and, within a year, those who had been exiled because of their prodemocracy views organized a revolt against Critias and the Thirty Tyrants. Critias died fighting the exiles, who shortly thereafter restored democracy to Athens.

Epaminondas (around 410–362 B.C.) believed strongly in the right of his city, Thebes, to be free, not subject to the military might of Sparta. His family, although aristocrats, had little money and Epaminondas never experienced a luxurious or carefree life. But his father believed in the importance of education and gave Epaminondas the best instruction possible. Epaminondas' favorite subject was philosophy, especially the views promoted by the followers of Pythagoras.

A loyal Theban, he marched with his city's army when the need arose, but he took little interest in politics. His views changed, however, after Sparta took control of Thebes in 382 B.C. and forced its political leaders into exile.

Epaminondas remained in Thebes but kept away from the political scene until his friend Pelopidas, one of the exiled leaders, secretly plotted a coup. Epaminondas joined him. After the coup, Epaminondas again withdrew from politics until Sparta invaded Theban territory in 371 B.C.

Determined to preserve Thebes' independence, Epaminondas resolved to develop a defensive strategy that would crush the mighty Spartan army. At the Battle of Leuctra in 371 B.C., Epaminondas scrapped the traditional strategy of even lines and ordered the left wing built up to a depth of 50 soldiers, with the rest of the army forming the center and right wing. Unaware of the new maneuvers, the Spartans followed their traditional plan of advancing with a front line 12 soldiers deep and the best soldiers marching on the right wing. The result was a crushing defeat for the Spartans, and victory and freedom for the Thebans.

Epaminondas now resolved to break Sparta's power in Greece, and he led an army south. This time the Spartans were uneasy, for no enemy had penetrated so deeply into their territory in almost 200 years. The Spartans grew even more anxious when Epaminondas won the support of the neighboring Arcadians and began encouraging the Messenians to establish their own city. (The Messenians were mostly Helots, the class of people who worked for the Spartans and tilled their fields but had no rights.)

In 368 B.C., Epaminondas again led an army into southern Greece and won more allies for Thebes. As Sparta's power and influence declined, Epaminondas sought to weaken Greece's other major power, Athens. In an attempt to challenge Athens' naval supremacy, Epaminondas led his fleet across the Aegean Sea and as far as Byzantium (modern-day Istanbul), but unrest in southern Greece brought him home unexpectedly.

In 362 B.C., at Mantinea, in southern Greece, Epaminondas' troops faced the armies of Sparta, Athens, and their allies. Using the same innovative tactics he had used at Leuctra, Epaminondas won a decisive victory. But just as the Spartan line broke under the crushing weight of the Theban troops, Epaminondas was fatally wounded. Without his leadership, the victory meant nothing and Theban power gradually declined.

Isocrates (died 338 B.C.) was born before 431 B.C., when the Peloponnesian War started, and he knew well the misfortunes of war. Political maneuverings and the constant use of public funds for military purposes had drained both the public treasury and the reserves of many private citizens, including those of Isocrates' father. With his inheritance gone, Isocrates needed a profession in order to earn a living. He was excellent with words and turned to rhetoric, the art of using words effectively, as a career.

Isocrates began by writing speeches for fellow Athenians to use when they presented their cases in court. (There was no legal profession in 5th- and 4th-century B.C. Athens.) Despite his skill with words, Isocrates was not much of a speaker. But his expertise and teaching ability soon won him students from all around the Greek world. Eventually, his students numbered about 100, each of whom paid a substantial tuition fee. For more than 40 years, Isocrates' school flourished, and he became a very wealthy man.

Isocrates' surviving speeches (none of which he delivered himself) do not reflect spontaneous ideas or a mind whose thoughts flow freely from one topic to the next. Instead, they reveal a man who spent days writing and rewriting passages until he felt they were perfect. Ancient sources recorded that Isocrates spent a minimum of 10 years working on a speech known as the *Panegyrikos* before publishing it. (Even though many of his "speeches" were never delivered to an audience, they were still referred to as such because Isocrates used the traditional format and techniques of speech writing.) The *Panegyrikos* promoted the unification of Greece, a theme that was key to Isocrates' political philosophy. He had always despised the ill feeling that brought so much disunity, poverty, and war to the Greek world.

To create a spirit of unity among the Greek cities, Isocrates believed the Greeks needed a common goal: a joint military venture against the Persians. Isocrates knew that the Persian invasions of Greece at the beginning of the 5th century had helped unite the cities as they prepared to defend themselves. He was so convinced that such solidarity could exist again that he sent pleas to leaders in Sicily, Thessaly, Macedonia, and other areas, asking for their help in uniting the Greek cities

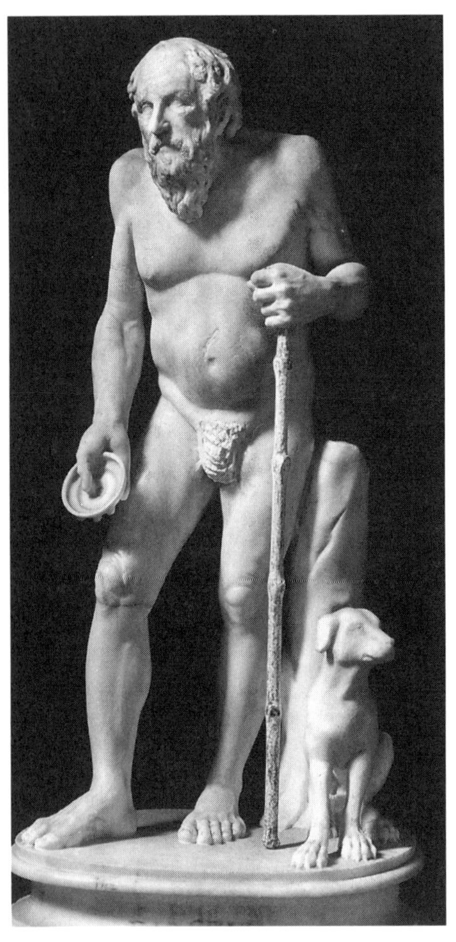

This satirical statue of Diogenes portrays him as a hunched-up man, with a stick and begging bowl. To his left sits a dog, which was Diogenes' nickname.

and attacking Persia. Not one leader answered Isocrates' call.

By 346 B.C., Philip II of Macedonia, a country to the north of Greece, had proved himself a powerful and energetic king. Isocrates saw him as a potential leader of the Greeks against the Persians. He wrote Philip on several occasions, the most important being a speech entitled *To Philip,* in which he outlined his plan. Whether Isocrates' speeches influenced Philip or whether Philip had always planned to unite the Greek cities under his control is not known. But a few years after Isocrates wrote *To Philip,* Philip conquered Greece.

The deciding battle was fought in 338 B.C. at Chaeronea, a town in the district of Boeotia to the north of Athens. When the news reached Isocrates, he was crushed. Although he had encouraged Philip to take on a leadership role in Greece, he had not wanted the Greek cities to lose their independence. In despair, Isocrates starved himself to death. Ancient records claim that he was 98 years old at the time.

Pasion (around 430–370 B.C.) spent his early years as the slave of two well-known Athenian bankers, Antisthenes and Archestratus. Impressed with his accounting ability and his faithfulness, the bankers freed Pasion. He then started his own banking business as well as a manufacturing concern that specialized in making shields. Recognized throughout Greece as a smart and honest businessman, Pasion quickly prospered. Surviving speeches made by two of Athens' greatest orators, Demosthenes and Isocrates, mention Pasion and several of his business transactions.

Because of his substantial donations to Athens, the Athenians granted Pasion and his descendants citizenship and all the accompanying rights and privileges.

Diogenes (died around 320 B.C.) came to Athens as an exile from Sinope in Asia Minor sometime after 362 B.C. It is uncertain whether his father accompanied him, but supposedly the two had been charged with minting their city's money incorrectly. Diogenes quickly became known for his caustic and direct statements and for the extremely simple life he led.

For Diogenes, happiness was to be found within oneself, not through material riches or positions of power. He believed that people should care for their basic needs in natural ways, using the easiest and least costly methods possible. To prove his point, Diogenes ate only if someone gave him food, exposed his body to extremes of cold and heat, wore very coarse clothing, and slept in the porticoes of public buildings. His unconventional lifestyle gave rise to many anecdotes, such as one that said he lived in a tub for lack of other quarters.

It was also said that he was captured by pirates and sold into slavery on the island of Crete. While standing on the auction block, Diogenes was asked by the slave dealer what he could do. Calmly he replied, "I can govern people; therefore sell me to someone who wishes a master." A rich man named Xeniades just happened to be passing by at that moment, heard the remark, and bought Diogenes. Impressed with his ideas and manner, Xeniades brought Diogenes home to Corinth, freed him, and then paid him to tutor his children. While there,

Diogenes supposedly met Alexander the Great.

Because of his insolence and sharp, biting comments, many Greeks referred to Diogenes as a *kuon,* or dog. In time, his followers came to be known as *kunik oi,* or doglike. Using these Greek words as their base, later generations coined the words *cynics* and *cynicism* to refer to Diogenes' followers and his way of thinking. Today's meaning of *cynic* has assumed a stronger connotation and refers to someone who believes selfishness motivates all human actions.

Eudoxus (around 400–350 B.C.) studied mathematics and medicine as a youth in his native town of Cnidus in Asia Minor. During his early twenties Eudoxus traveled to Athens, where he studied at Plato's Academy, and then went to Egypt, where he learned about astronomy from the local priests. After spending some time in Asia Minor and establishing a school of mathematics in Cyzicus, near Byzantium (today Istanbul), Eudoxus returned to Athens.

His contributions to mathematics and astronomy influenced the development of future thought in these two disciplines. In geometry, he invented the theory of proportions, which allowed mathematicians to deal with irrational numbers (real numbers that cannot be expressed as whole numbers—for example, 1 divided by 3 equals .3333 . . . into infinity). Mathematicians today still rely on his theories. In astronomy, he was the first person to use a mathematical formula to explain the movement of the sun, the moon, and the five planets then known. The 3rd-century B.C. mathematicians Euclid and Archimedes built upon the foundations laid by Eudoxus.

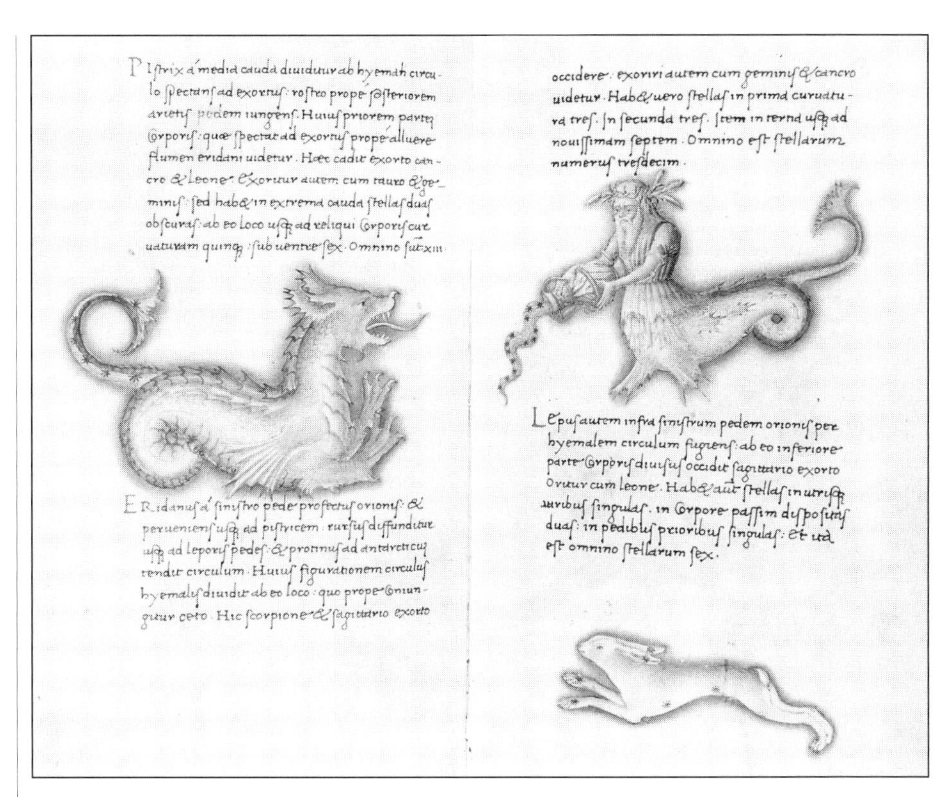
Pistrix a media cauda diuiditur ab hyemali circulo spectans ad exortus: rostro prope posteriorem arietis pedem iungens. Huius priorem partem corporis: quae spectat ad exortus prope alluere flumen eridani uidetur. Haec cadit exorto cancro & Leone. Exoritur autem cum tauro & geminis: sed hab& in extrema cauda stellas duas obscuras: ab eo loco usque ad reliqui corporis curuaturam quinque: sub uentre sex. Omnino sunt xiii

ERidanus a sinistro pede profectus orionis: & perueniens usque ad pistricem: rursus diffunditur usque ad leporis pedes: & protinus ad antarcticum tendit circulum. Huius figurationem circulus hyemalis diuidit ab eo loco: quo prope coniungitur ceto. Hic scorpione & sagittario exorto

occidere. exoriri autem cum geminis & cancro uidetur. Hab& uero stellas in prima curuatura tres. In secunda tres. Item in tertia usque ad nouissimam septem. Omnino est stellarum numerus tresdecim.

LEpus autem infra sinistrum pedem orionis per hyemalem circulum fugiens: ab eo inferiore parte corporis diuisus occidit sagittario exorto. Oritur cum leone. Hab& aut stellas in utrisque auribus singulas. in corpore passim dispositas duas: in pedibus prioribus singulas: Et ita est omnino stellarum sex.

The characters that represent the constellations in this 15th-century Italian manuscript are accompanied by a Latin explanation. The author depended on the calculations and astronomical observations of Eudoxus in writing his text.

Praxiteles (active between 370 and 330 B.C.), an Athenian by birth, was considered one of Greece's best sculptors. *Hermes Carrying the Infant Dionysus,* his only extant sculpture, and surviving Roman copies of some of his other originals clearly reflect his innovative style. Working in both marble and bronze, Praxiteles gave his statues a more humanistic quality than was common. His figures, which included deities and males and females of all ages, have softer curves and more delicate and graceful expressions than previous sculptors' works. Praxiteles intended his viewers to enjoy seeing his statues and to feel a closeness to them. They were not majestic and cold representations of gods and heroes, meant to be honored and revered, but

Strong and willful, Olympias resorted to force to obtain part of Alexander's empire for herself. Her troops were eventually defeated.

figures with emotions and feelings that seemed to come from within the sculpture itself and gave each figure its own personality.

According to the Roman writer Pliny, Praxiteles' representation of Aphrodite, the goddess of love, was the perfect statue. From the numerous Roman copies that have survived, we can see the softness in the contours of her body and feel a closeness to this ancient figure. Later sculptors often imitated Praxiteles' technique of having his figures lean gracefully and lightly against a small post or support.

The white Greek and Roman statues we see in museums today look quite different from the statues that adorned the ancient cities of Athens and Rome. By custom, the Greeks painted their sculpture. And so it happened, according to Pliny, that when someone asked Praxiteles which of his statues he preferred, he answered, "Those which Nicias, the painter, has touched." For Praxiteles, his work was only the base; Nicias' skill gave his creations life.

Olympias (around 375–316 B.C.) was given in marriage by her father, the king of Epirus in western Greece, to Philip II, king of Macedonia. The marriage was a political one, with each side hoping to gain from the alliance. Olympias, however, was a strong-willed woman with a fiery and passionate nature. Years after she gave birth to her only son, Alexander the Great, Olympias began to suggest that Zeus, the king of the gods, and not Philip was his father.

After Philip married a Macedonian named Cleopatra in 337 B.C., Olympias left Philip and returned home to Epirus, where she quickly became a powerful figure in the government. When Philip was assassinated the following year, many Macedonians and Greeks whispered about her alleged involvement, but nothing was ever proven and Olympias returned to Macedonia.

She probably believed her son, Alexander, would include her in his government, but he did not. Alexander always treated her with great respect, and during his 12-year campaign in Asia the two wrote regularly to each other (no letters survive), but they never saw each other again.

Unhappy with her life and opposed to Antipater, the regent Alexander had left in charge of Macedonia in his absence, Olympias returned to Epirus in 331 B.C., where she quickly assumed much power within the country. News of Alexander's unexpected death in 323 B.C. brought her again into Macedonian politics.

Antipater was still regent, but without Alexander his position was weakened, and Olympias constantly attempted to undermine his rule. When Antipater died in 319 B.C., his successor Polyperchon invited Olympias to act as regent for Alexander's young son, Alexander IV. At first Olympias refused his offer, but she changed her mind after hearing that Antipater's son Cassander planned to crown Philip II's son Philip Arrhidaeus as king of Macedonia.

A compromise was reached that named Alexander and Philip Arrhidaeus joint rulers. The agreement was short-lived, however, because Olympias saw the throne as rightfully belonging to her grandson, and to her as regent. Having won the support of Macedonia's soldiers, Olympias knew she would be difficult to defeat and began eliminating her rivals. First she had Philip Arrhidaeus murdered, then his wife and Cassander's brother, and finally 100 political enemies.

Cassander, meanwhile, gathered his troops and hastened to Macedonia, where he attacked Olympias and her troops at Pydna. Forced to surrender, Olympias faced the charges brought against her and was sentenced to death. Because of the belief that Olympias had conceived Alexander with Zeus, Macedonian soldiers regarded Olympias as part divine and refused to carry out the death sentence. Relatives of her most recent victims, however, felt quite differently and executed her themselves.

With no original images available for reference, a late 16th-century Parisian artist used his imagination to portray Euclid at work drawing geometrical figures.

Euclid (active around 300 B.C.) founded a school of mathematics in Alexandria, Egypt, during the rule of Ptolemy I, ruler of Egypt after Alexander the Great. Euclid's reputation as one of the world's greatest mathematicians rests mainly on his *Elements*, a textbook on the principles of geometry. We do not know whether the contents were entirely original or whether the book is Euclid's compilation of all information known at that time with some additions of his own. What is certain is the continued influence *Elements* had on Euclid's contemporaries and on mathematicians right into the 19th century, when some of his arguments began to be questioned. *Elements* continues to be one of the most translated and most read books published in the Western world.

Two anecdotes survive that, if true, give us a glimpse of Euclid, the mathematician. Ptolemy I, an active patron of the arts and sciences, on occasion came to Euclid's school for instruction. Once, after attempting to prove a particular geometric principle and finding the proof extremely complicated, Ptolemy turned to Euclid and asked if there might not be a shorter way. Euclid quickly retorted: "There is no royal road to geometry."

On another occasion, one of Euclid's students asked him how learning geometric theorems would benefit him. Euclid looked at the student and then motioned to a slave to give the young man a coin. He explained, "Since he seems to need a reward for learning, give him this coin."

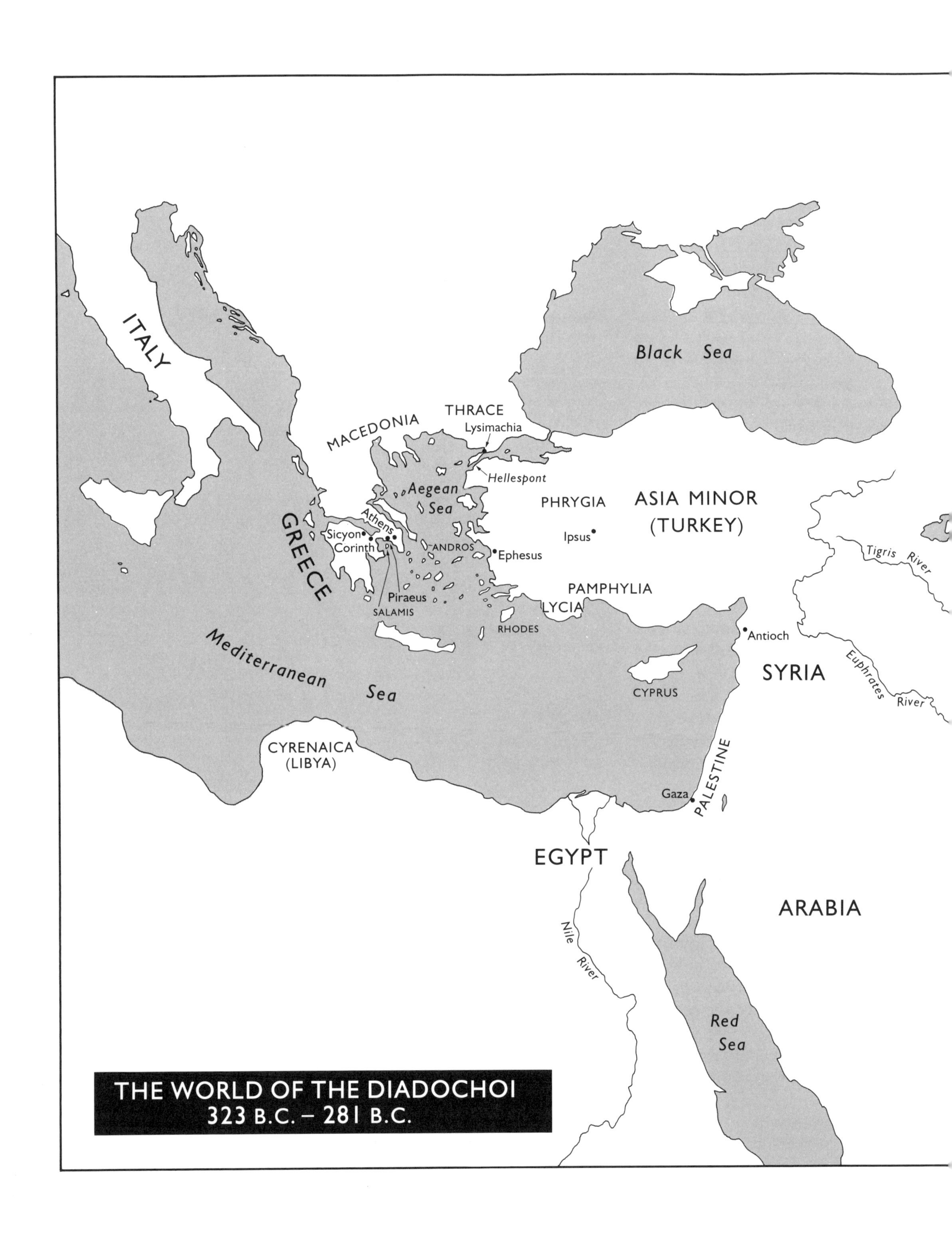

ITALY
Black Sea
THRACE
Lysimachia
MACEDONIA
Hellespont
Aegean Sea
PHRYGIA
ASIA MINOR (TURKEY)
GREECE
Athens
Sicyon
Corinth
ANDROS
Ipsus
Ephesus
Tigris River
Piraeus
SALAMIS
PAMPHYLIA
LYCIA
RHODES
Antioch
Mediterranean Sea
SYRIA
Euphrates River
CYPRUS
CYRENAICA (LIBYA)
PALESTINE
Gaza
EGYPT
ARABIA
Nile River
Red Sea
THE WORLD OF THE DIADOCHOI
323 B.C. – 281 B.C.

0
200
400
600 kilometers
0
200
400
600 miles
Aral Sea
Caspian Sea
ASIA
HINDU KUSH MOUNTAINS
BACTRIA
Indus River
Seleucia
BABYLONIA
PERSIA
Persian Gulf
GEDROSIA DESERT
INDIA
Arabian Sea

5 A Lasting Influence (325–200 B.C.)

Under the Macedonian rulers Philip II and Alexander the Great, Greece finally achieved a unity it had been unable to accomplish on its own. The arts continued to flourish in Athens and Sparta's soldiers were still considered the elite infantry, but the Greek world had grown and changed. The city of Alexandria in northern Egypt was rapidly eclipsing Athens as the international cultural center. Philosophers and mathematicians in Greek colonies around the Mediterranean and Aegean seas were expanding and redirecting the ideas of the early Greek philosophers to shape their own beliefs. Yet the Greek tradition remained strong.

Alexander's untimely death in 323 B.C. shattered the relative peace he had achieved throughout Greece and Asia. Wars and rebellions began erupting everywhere as the *diadochoi* (literally, "successors") sought to gain control of Alexander's empire, or at least a portion of it. The Greek tradition was not forgotten, however. The values were too entrenched, and the *diadochoi* became, although at times only subtly, the promoters of Greek values and ideas.

Part 5 of *Ancient Greeks* profiles individuals who inherited the values of the Greek world and directly or indirectly promoted these values as they came into contact with both Greeks and non-Greeks. All were in part responsible for preserving the Greek tradition and allowing it to become the foundation of what today is considered Western civilization.

IN THIS PART

Antigonus I

HEIR TO AN EMPIRE

"To the strongest!" was, according to the Greek historian Arrian, what Alexander the Great said to his commanders as he lay on his deathbed in 323 B.C. But who was the strongest?

Each of Alexander's generals, all Macedonians, considered himself worthy and felt entitled to a share of the empire. There was Antigonus, who had held a command post under Alexander for more than a decade and was regarded as an outstanding strategist and military leader. Antipater had served first with Alexander's father. Perdiccas was the general to whom Alexander had supposedly given his signet ring on his deathbed and who immediately took over as regent, or acting ruler, in the absence of a sovereign. Craterus was considered Alexander's best soldier, whereas Lysimachus had proved himself a capable leader on the battlefield. Seleucus had first fought under Philip II, and Ptolemy had been one of Alexander's closest friends since their childhood.

Alexander had made no provisions for a successor. If he had, would he have named one of his generals or a blood relative? His generals certainly did not know the answer, but each was determined to retain his position of power, and a bitter struggle followed as the rivals eliminated each other.

In all the turmoil, Heracles, Alexander's son by his mistress Barsine, the daughter of King Darius of Persia, seems to have been ignored and forgotten. Attention focused instead on Alexander's pregnant widow, Roxane, and in due time it

Supported by archers (left) and carrying large shields, 4th-century B.C. Greek soldiers attack a heavily manned fort. For almost 20 years after Alexander's death, Antigonus fought to gain control of the empire and, as a result, Greece experienced almost continuous warfare.

"There was a time when I craved power, but now I crave a reputation and good will among men."

—Antigonus, quoted in *Moralia* (around 1st century A.D.) by Plutarch

was her son whom the generals named Alexander IV and proclaimed heir to his father's empire.

Alexander's soldiers, however, preferred to support as king Alexander's half brother, Philip Arrhidaeus, although it was widely known that he lacked the mental ability to assume any position of responsibility. Finally, an agreement was reached between the generals and the soldiers, and they named the young Alexander IV and the feeble-minded Philip Arrhidaeus joint rulers.

Because neither one was actually capable of ruling the empire, Perdiccas was made the regent and each general was assigned control of a region. Seleucus supported Perdiccas and remained with him, whereas Antigonus took control of Phrygia, Pamphylia, and Lycia, all in Asia Minor. Macedonia and Greece went to Antipater and Craterus, Thrace to Lysimachus, and Egypt to Ptolemy. This arrangement was short-lived, however, because political intrigue quickly disrupted all hope for harmony and unity across the empire.

Antigonus formed an alliance with Antipater, Craterus, Ptolemy, and Lysimachus against Perdiccas. When Perdiccas marched south to conquer Egypt in 321 B.C., his troops mutinied and murdered him. Antipater then assumed the role of regent and Antigonus became commander in chief of all Greek military forces in Asia. Immediately Antigonus began consolidating his power and ousting those opposed to Antipater's rule. When Antipater died in 319 B.C., Asia belonged to Antigonus.

Still peace did not reign over the empire, and the political intrigue continued. Roxane poisoned her rival, Barsine, and in 317 B.C., Olympias (Alexander's mother and a prime contender for power) poisoned Philip Arrhidaeus.

Antigonus, meanwhile, continued to consolidate his power and made plans to bring all the lands Alexander had conquered under his control. Determined to stop Antigonus from accomplishing this feat were Ptolemy, Lysimachus, Craterus, and Seleucus, who formed their own alliance. Between 315 and 311 B.C., the two opposing sides met several times on the battlefield, each winning minor victories.

To gain the support of mainland Greeks, Antigonus promised to remove Macedonia's military garrisons from Greek land and let the cities govern themselves. When the Greeks agreed to back him, Antigonus drove out the Macedonian forces led by Antipater's son, Cassander, and added the country of Greece to his empire, which now stretched from the Hellespont (the present-day Strait of the Dardanelles) to the Euphrates River and Syria. Seleucus, meanwhile, won a decisive victory against Antigonus and gained control of Babylonia and several other eastern regions.

In 311 B.C., a peace treaty between the generals brought a few months of quiet to the empire, but still the political conspiracy continued as Cassander hired assassins to kill Roxane and Alexander IV. In 310 B.C., the peace treaty itself was broken when war burst forth for a second time between Antigonus and the other generals. Antigonus was determined to keep Alexander's empire intact under one ruler—himself—and believed that his able troops and his extremely capable son, Demetrius, would help him achieve this goal.

Subsequent events seemed to prove that Antigonus had every right

Antigonus I

BORN

Around 382 B.C.
Probably in Macedonia

DIED

301 B.C.
At the Battle of Ipsus, in Phrygia

PROFESSION

General and ruler

ACCOMPLISHMENTS

Master general in Alexander's army; never lost a battle until Ipsus, when he was 80 years old; his primary goal was to keep Alexander's empire intact under one leader—himself

to be optimistic. In 306 B.C., after Demetrius had removed Cassander as ruler in Greece, the Athenians saw Antigonus and Demetrius as heroes, and some even began to honor them with sacrifices that had been reserved for the gods. That same year, Demetrius' forces defeated Ptolemy I's fleet and won control of the eastern Mediterranean Sea. The army then proclaimed Antigonus king of the lands and waterways stretching from Greece to the Euphrates River and offered him a crown.

Antigonus took the crown but sent it to Demetrius, whom he appointed his co-ruler. Antigonus' plan was working, and he believed that he would soon be the master of Alexander's empire. But the generals Ptolemy, Seleucus, Lysimachus, and Cassander were not ready to yield their power to Antigonus. When Antigonus demanded that Cassander surrender control of Macedonia to him, the other three generals quickly reacted because they knew that Antigonus would soon make the same demand of each of them.

Ptolemy attacked Syria, Lysimachus crossed with his troops into western Asia Minor, and Seleucus entered eastern Asia Minor. In 301 B.C., at Ipsus in Phrygia, the combined forces of Antigonus and Demetrius met those of Lysimachus and Seleucus. Antigonus, who was 80 years old at the time, bravely led his troops to battle. Demetrius pressed his cavalry attack too far, leaving his father's troops with only limited protection. Overwhelmed by enemy troops, Antigonus was killed—and with him, his hopes for a united empire.

For 20 years after Alexander's death, the lands of Greece and Asia Minor saw almost continuous warfare. Antigonus, who had never lost a battle until that at Ipsus, had been one of the major causes of the conflict. This was because he saw unity as the best means of preserving peace and achieving stability on an international scale, and he had waged war in an effort to unify Alexander's empire. Like his predecessor Alexander, Antigonus strongly believed in the value of Greek civilization and so had allowed the Greeks to govern themselves and had encouraged them to preserve their culture. Future rulers of the Greeks, including the Romans, would grant them the same privileges.

Like Alexander, Antigonus aimed to spread Greek traditions and ideas across the empire and make them the foundation of his empire's culture. He, too, proved himself a very capable statesman and founded cities that eventually became cultural and commercial centers. Of the generals who had assumed power after Alexander's death, only Antigonus had planned to preserve the beliefs of their dead commander. Furthermore, the Greek tradition did not die with Antigonus. For the next 150 years or so, the so-called Antigonid kings (all of them descendants of Antigonus, including Demetrius) ruled Macedonia.

FURTHER READING

Billows, Richard A. *Antigonos the One-Eyed and the Creation of the Hellenistic State*. Berkeley: University of California Press, 1990.

Ptolemy I (Ptolemy Soter)

GREEK RULER IN EGYPT

The sound of bells could be heard across the lands of the Middle East as an elaborate funeral carriage with its vault of gold carried the body of Alexander the Great from the city of Babylon to Macedonia. Believing it only proper that Alexander be buried in his homeland, Alexander's generals had ordered the carriage built. But Alexander was never to return home, for a general named Ptolemy intercepted the funeral cortege and, with little difficulty, seized the coffin.

Ptolemy's reasons were simple. When Alexander's generals divided his empire after his death, Ptolemy was awarded Egypt, and he felt that possession of Alexander's body would help him politically and practically. Egypt had welcomed Alexander years earlier, eagerly accepting him as their ruler in place of their cruel Persian overlords. They also approved of the city of Alexandria, which Alexander had ordered built. Ptolemy felt it only fitting that Alexander be buried in Alexandria and commanded his architects to create a monument worthy of holding the remains of so great a ruler.

Ptolemy and Alexander had known each other since childhood because Ptolemy's father, Lagus, was a Macedonian noble who spent much time at the palace. It was even rumored that Philip II of Macedonia, not Lagus, was

The heads of Ptolemy I and his wife, Berenice I, appear on this gold coin issued in their memory by a successor.

Ptolemy's real father and that Lagus, angered at such a thought, had abandoned the newborn Ptolemy to the elements. (In ancient Greece and Macedonia, a father had the right to decide whether his newborn child was fit to live. If he chose not to accept his child, the newborn would be exposed to the elements and left to die.) But fate had decreed another destiny for Ptolemy, and an eagle swooped down and saved him from certain death. Many historians believe this tale was an attempt to align Ptolemy with the royal family of Macedonia by making him Alexander's half brother.

Whatever the relationship might have been, it is almost certain that Ptolemy was a page at Philip's court, where he acted as both the king's servant and bodyguard. Naturally, Alexander and Ptolemy became well acquainted with each other and with the other pages. In 337 B.C., Philip accused four pages, including Ptolemy, of conspiring against him, and he banished them from Macedonia. The banishment, however, was short-lived because Philip was assassinated the following year and all four were recalled by Alexander.

In the years that followed Philip's murder, Alexander gave increasing responsibilities to these four men. Ptolemy accompanied Alexander as he fought to keep control of the lands left him by his father. By 330 B.C., Ptolemy had become one of Alexander's Royal Bodyguards, which meant he belonged to the king's inner circle of advisers.

One of his first assignments was the arrest of Bessus, a Bactrian official who had killed the Persian king Darius. Ptolemy later wrote that he had pursued Bessus deep into Asia when he received a message saying that Bessus' generals would surrender their leader if Ptolemy would send a few troops to their village. Ptolemy immediately agreed, but the surrender failed to take place until Ptolemy and his men surrounded the village.

Well pleased with Ptolemy's leadership qualities, Alexander continued to consider him an outstanding commander and honored him on several occasions during the campaign in India. However, while in India, Ptolemy almost died.

The conquest of the Indian city of Harmatelia (the location of which is today uncertain) in 326 or 325 B.C. had brought first joy and then great sorrow as, one by one, the wounded were seized with great pains and died. The reason for their sudden illness soon became clear—each had been cut by an Indian sword dipped in snake poison. A frustrated Alexander urgently asked his doctors to find an antidote, but none seemed to be available. When Alexander learned that Ptolemy was one of the wounded, he went immediately to his bedside. There Alexander dreamed that a snake appeared before him holding a plant in its mouth and indicating where he might find the plant. Alexander followed the snake's instructions, brought back the plant, placed a piece on Ptolemy's body, and ordered that medicine be made with the rest. The antidote was given to all the wounded, and within a short time everyone, including Ptolemy, recovered.

The year that followed was a difficult one for Alexander. Faced with mutiny, he was forced to turn back and march west for the first time since he had left Macedonia in 334 B.C. Ptolemy remained one of his faithful bodyguards and again was rewarded with many honors. In 324 B.C., he took part in the great wedding ceremony at Susa, where Alexander married each of his high-ranking generals to a noble Persian woman. Ptolemy's bride was Artacama, the daughter of Artabazus, a well-known and respected ruler in Bactria.

A year later, Alexander lay dead and the generals were fighting among

As ruler of Egypt, Ptolemy I did not try to impose Greek ideas or styles on the Egyptians. Although Ptolemy and his successors were of Macedonian origin, Egyptian artists depicted them as pharaohs, with the Pharaonic crown, as this typical head of a Ptolemy indicates.

themselves to decide the fate of the empire. Several, including Ptolemy, disapproved of Alexander's acceptance of Persian customs, and they divorced the wives Alexander had chosen for them. The matter of a successor to Alexander was far more difficult to solve, and Ptolemy advised the generals to select an heir who was either Macedonian or Greek. Ptolemy proposed that a council of Alexander's top-ranking officials meet and elect a new leader. Most of the generals, however, disagreed with Ptolemy and preferred to name a blood relative as heir.

After months of debate, the generals named two kings, Alexander's newborn son and Alexander's feeble-minded half brother. Because neither one was capable of ruling the empire, they appointed Perdiccas, one of Alexander's generals, to serve as regent to the two kings, and the other generals were each allotted specific areas of the empire to rule.

Ptolemy chose to rule Egypt, Libya, and the neighboring lands of Arabia. Why he chose this area is not known, but many have speculated that Ptolemy appreciated the region's resources, wealth, rich history, and geographic isolation from the rest of the empire. Unlike so many of Alexander's generals who sought to expand their dominions and reunite as much of the empire as possible under their control, Ptolemy seemed content to rule within the boundaries awarded him. Perhaps he recognized the tremendous difficulties any ruler of so vast a territory would experience.

Ptolemy was also aware of the need for allies and for control of areas that would buffer Egypt from surprise attacks by foreign enemies and afford access to prosperous trade routes. To do this, he sent military expeditions to conquer and control Cyrenaica (eastern Libya), the Mediterranean island of Cyprus, and Syria in the Middle East. In the years that followed, Ptolemy won and lost control of these areas on several occasions.

Most important to Ptolemy, however, was winning the allegiance of the Egyptian people. One of his first acts as ruler was to rid the country of Cleomenes, the man Alexander had assigned to oversee the treasury and the building of Alexandria. Cleomenes

"It is more kingly to enrich than to be enriched."

—Ptolemy, quoted in *Moralia* (around 1st century A.D.) by Plutarch

had accomplished both tasks, but he continually raised taxes to enrich himself. As a result, he became the hated enemy of all Egyptians. Ptolemy condemned Cleomenes for his misdeeds and ordered him killed, but instead of distributing Cleomenes' fortune among the Egyptians, Ptolemy used it for his own projects.

The only person truly affected by Cleomenes' death was Perdiccas, who had counted on Cleomenes' allegiance. Ptolemy, on the other hand, was not about to yield any of his power to Perdiccas and informed him of that fact. In 321 B.C., Perdiccas invaded Egypt, accompanied by his war elephants. Ptolemy had already prepared his army and, using a tactic that he would employ successfully on future occasions, he bribed some of Perdiccas' men to desert their commander and join his Egyptian forces.

Meanwhile, Perdiccas planned a surprise attack on one of Ptolemy's forts along the Nile River, but Ptolemy's spies were watching and reported every move. Never one to shirk responsibility, Ptolemy took his position at the front line and hurled his spear at the eyes of Perdiccas' lead elephant. His accurate throw blinded the animal, giving Ptolemy's men time to kill the driver and cast the enemy into disarray.

That night Perdiccas planned a second surprise attack farther south along the Nile, at the capital city of Memphis. Again Ptolemy's scouts were watching, but this time it was the Nile and its current that defeated Perdiccas. As the bodies washed ashore, Ptolemy ordered them cremated and then sent the ashes to their loved ones. Such consideration for his enemies won him their respect and admiration.

As Perdiccas moved to regroup, his soldiers plotted mutiny. Whether Ptolemy aided the conspirators is not certain, but Perdiccas was found fatally stabbed in his tent. Upon learning the news, Ptolemy went to Perdiccas' camp, offered the soldiers food and provisions, and then explained his intentions. Impressed by his leadership and daring, Perdiccas' troops offered Ptolemy Perdiccas' position, but Ptolemy quietly refused. His ambition was not to rule Alexander's world but to make Egypt a stable and prosperous empire.

Past events had proved to Ptolemy that alliances were important, and so in 319 B.C. he married Eurydice, the daughter of Antipater, the new regent of Alexander's empire. Ptolemy, however, did not involve himself in the continuing conflicts that arose between the *diadochoi*, or "successors" of Alexander, but preferred to focus his attention on Egypt and the building of Alexandria.

Years earlier Alexander had ordered the architect Deinocrates of Rhodes to design Alexandria as Egypt's new capital city, but news of Alexander's untimely death had stopped all work. Now Ptolemy was determined to implement Alexander's dream and considered it proper that Alexander's body be laid to rest in a beautiful mausoleum built specially to house the gold coffin.

Like Alexander, Ptolemy saw Alexandria as an international city, a center of learning and the arts where Greek culture would meet and blend with Eastern ideas. To accommodate the many visitors and scholars he hoped would come to Alexandria from around the world, Ptolemy built a museum with lecture rooms and a dining area where they could work and discuss their findings and ideas. He also encouraged scientific research, and soon many of the ancient world's greatest scientists, including the mathematician Archimedes, came to Alexandria to study.

Ptolemy also ordered the construction of a magnificent library, which historians believe might have held as many as 500,000 volumes. It was the most extensive library in the ancient world. Tales were told of how Ptolemy asked Greek cities to send their original literary masterpieces so that librarians at Alexandria could make copies, but then he had the librarians deceitfully keep the originals and return only the copies. For at least 300 years, the library remained a center of learning. Then, sometime between the 1st and 3rd centuries A.D., it was destroyed, although no one knows exactly what happened. Some theories claim that it was burned or damaged by an earthquake. Today, on this very site in Alexandria, a new library with a capacity of 8 million volumes is being built by the Egyptian government, with financial assistance from countries around the world.

The first five years of Ptolemy's rule were relatively peaceful for him, but the other *diadochoi* battled one another in a series of wars. Before Antipater died in 319 B.C., he had chosen Polyperchon as his successor, not his own son Cassander. Offended, Cassander sought to destroy Polyperchon. Ptolemy sided with Cassander, who won the struggle. To further strengthen his ties with Cassander, Ptolemy married his granddaughter Berenice. It is not certain whether he divorced Eurydice, but polygamy was a common practice among Macedonian kings. In time, Berenice became Ptolemy's favorite wife and it was their son, Ptolemy Philadelphus, who succeeded Ptolemy.

The number of *diadochoi* was dwindling, but Antigonus, whose goal was to rule Alexander's empire, was still to be reckoned with. Allied with Antigonus was his son Demetrius, a wily and very effective military leader. Vowing to stop Antigonus, Cassander and Lysimachus sought an alliance with Ptolemy, who agreed to become a third ally of the so-called coalition. Seleucus, the ruler of Babylonia, was also an ally, but for the moment he was without a country. Fearing a takeover by Antigonus, Seleucus had left Babylonia.

From 315 to 311 B.C., the coalition wars raged, with no decisive defeat or victory. Ptolemy did win the battle against Demetrius at Gaza, which gave him control of Syria and Palestine, and Seleucus was able to retake Babylonia with Ptolemy's help. In 311 B.C., a peace treaty was signed, but it did not prevent Antigonus and Seleucus from fighting. Even Ptolemy broke the peace around 308 B.C. when he and his army crossed to Greece and took control of the island of Andros and the cities of Corinth and Sicyon.

Such aggressive behavior was uncharacteristic of Ptolemy and it is unclear why he acted in this way. Perhaps he wanted to be a champion of the Greeks by protecting them from a more aggressive and repressive ruler, or perhaps he, like the other *diadochoi*, was trying to consolidate his power. It was during this period that Ptolemy suffered the most crushing defeat of his career. He lost the island of Cyprus to Demetrius and, even though he would win it back a decade later, his defeat in 306 B.C. gave Demetrius and his father the confidence to invade Egypt. Both men met defeat—the weather stopped Demetrius and the unfamiliar land prevented his father from succeeding.

At about this time, Demetrius and Antigonus each proclaimed himself a king, and the other *diadochoi* soon followed their example. To be sure, the struggle for power was not over, and the island of Rhodes, off the southern coast of Asia Minor was the scene of the next battleground.

Rhodes was a thriving community, with traders passing through its ports from Egypt, the Middle East, and Greece. Because war would destroy their prosperity, the people of Rhodes tried to form alliances and sign peace treaties with other rulers. Antigonus, however, wanted control and sent his son Demetrius to lay siege to the island. The Rhodians requested help from Ptolemy, who agreed to send supplies, as did Lysimachus and Cassander.

Unable to force the citizens to surrender, Demetrius finally agreed to lift his siege after the Rhodians promised to ally themselves with Antigonus. But the Rhodians added one stipulation to the agreement—that they would never go to war against Ptolemy. The Rhodians then followed the advice of the oracle that counseled them to erect a statue in their city honoring Ptolemy. In addition, they gave Ptolemy the surname Soter (savior), and he is known to history as Ptolemy Soter.

Next the Rhodians disassembled Demetrius' gigantic war machines, sold the materials for scrap, and built an enormous statue of the sun god Helios, which stood with one foot on either side of the harbor entrance. No trace of this so-called Colossus of Rhodes survives, but the ancients labeled it one of the Seven Wonders of the World.

In 301 B.C., at Ipsus in Asia Minor, the warring *diadochoi* met on the battlefield. Antigonus was killed and his forces defeated by the combined troops of Seleucus, Lysimachus, and Cassander. Ptolemy had allied himself with the latter, but instead of joining the battle, he stayed behind to regain control of Syria and Palestine. Seleucus, however, questioned Ptolemy's right to these lands and a series of wars between these two generals broke out in the decades that followed.

After Ipsus, Ptolemy devoted himself to affairs in Egypt. He saw political marriages as one way of preserving peace, so he married his daughter Arsinoe II to Lysimachus and his daughter Ptolemais to Demetrius. His stepdaughter Theoxena married

ANCIENT GREEKS

Ptolemy I

BORN

Around 367 B.C.
Macedonia

DIED

Around 283 B.C.
Egypt

PROFESSION

General and ruler

ACCOMPLISHMENTS

Took control of Egypt and the neighboring lands after Alexander the Great's death; forced Demetrius to lift his siege of Rhodes; introduced the worship of Sarapis into Egypt; introduced the first system of coinage into Egypt; continued building Alexander's capital city in Egypt, Alexandria; built the museum at Alexandria and started the library there, which became the most extensive library in the ancient world; founded the city of Ptolemais in Upper Egypt; wrote a history of Alexander's campaigns

Agathocles, ruler of Syracuse in Sicily, and another stepdaughter, Antigone, married Pyrrhus of Epirus, Demetrius' brother-in-law.

Unlike Alexander and other *diadochoi,* Ptolemy founded only one new city, Ptolemais in Upper Egypt. He won the respect of his Egyptian subjects and showed respect to their gods, to the priests who tended the temples, and to the Egyptian nobles.

Ptolemy did not try to assimilate Greeks and Egyptians into one culture, nor did he impose Greek ideas or customs on the Egyptians. However, he did make one attempt at merging Egyptian and Greek religious beliefs when he introduced the worship of Sarapis, a deity especially honored by the people of Sinope on the Black Sea. Under Ptolemy, Sarapis was associated with Isis, the chief Egyptian goddess and the goddess of procreation. In time, it was the cult of Isis, not Sarapis, that spread its influence across the Mediterranean world.

Ptolemy never learned to speak Egyptian, nor did he adopt Egyptian customs for himself. Nevertheless he was sincere in his desire to have the country and his people prosper. He introduced the first system of coinage to make the country's financial system more effective. As a result, almost everyone benefited from the relative peace he brought to Egypt.

Believing that trade was important to Egypt's well-being, Ptolemy sought to protect Egypt's maritime rights and trade routes. To guide ships into the port of Alexandria, he commissioned the building of a gigantic lighthouse on the small island of Pharos at the entrance to the harbor. Begun sometime in the 290s B.C., the lighthouse was made of white limestone or marble and rose to a height of approximately 400 feet. The light itself was probably fire, with huge mirrors reflecting the light and sending beams across the waters to aid incoming ships. Ptolemy died before it was completed, but his son Ptolemy Philadelphus continued the work on it. Recognized as one of the Seven Wonders of the Ancient World, the lighthouse at Pharos dominated the entrance to Alexandria for almost 1,500 years. Through the centuries, earthquakes battered the noble structure, and it finally toppled in the earthquake of 1375. The island's name gradually became synonymous with "lighthouse," and other languages adopted the term: the Romans called a lighthouse *phanus;* the French, *phare;* and the Italian and Spanish, *faro.*

Few documents from this period have survived to provide details of Ptolemy's rule, but records show that he wrote a biography of Alexander that became a standard reference work on the renowned Macedonian king. Our knowledge of it comes from passages quoted by later authors, especially the 2nd-century Greek historian Arrian, who used Ptolemy as the prime source for his own biography of Alexander.

Ptolemy's experiences after Alexander's death had made him think seriously about naming an heir to ensure a smooth transition and the continuation of his policies. In 285 B.C., Ptolemy named his son Ptolemy as his coregent and successor. When Ptolemy I died in 283 B.C., Ptolemy II deified his father and introduced worship of him to the Egyptians. A short time later, he instituted a festival called the Ptolemaieia in his father's honor.

Ptolemy I had done his work well, for his dynasty was not only the longest of all the *diadochoi* but also the most successful. For 250 years, descendants of Ptolemy I ruled Egypt. The last was the famed Cleopatra VII, whose forces lost to the Romans in 30 B.C. The culture of the Ptolemaic world, however, was not forgotten but continued to spread its influence into the lands governed by Rome.

FURTHER READING

Ellis, Walter M. *Ptolemy of Egypt.* New York: Routledge, 1994.

Epicurus

SEEKER OF THE HAPPY LIFE

Happiness is the goal of most people, but how one achieves happiness depends on how one defines it. In the late 4th century B.C., an Athenian named Epicurus began questioning the role of happiness in a person's life. He knew that the fall of Athens in 404 B.C. and the conquest of Greece by Philip II and Alexander the Great a few decades later had robbed many Greeks of happiness. To be a citizen of a Greek city-state had always been prized, but after Greece lost its independence, many people questioned the meaning of this right.

Alexander the Great's sudden death in 323 B.C. caused even more turmoil because his successors began a decades-long battle for the right to control the Greek world. Philosophy seemed to offer the only hope of sanity in a world crazed with the thirst for power.

Although Epicurus was born of Athenian parents and, by law, was an Athenian citizen, he was not born in Athens but on the Aegean island of Samos. In 351 B.C., 10 years before his birth, Epicurus' parents had emigrated to Samos with a large group of Athenian settlers. Studying had been a part of his life since he was a child, especially because his father, Neocles, was a schoolmaster. Epicurus later wrote that he began the study of philosophy at the age of 14. According to tradition, the reason for this early start was Epicurus' dissatisfaction with a teacher who seemed incapable of explaining the early Greek poet Hesiod's description of chaos. The two teachers who did have a strong influence on Epicurus were Pamphilus, a former pupil of the philosopher Plato who lived on Samos, and Nausiphanes, a pupil of the philosopher Democritus.

At age 18, in accordance with Athenian law, Epicurus left Samos to enter military service in Athens for two years. His love of philosophy led him to the Academy, the school founded by Plato and run now by his successor Xenocrates.

When the battles between Alexander's successors intensified in Greece, Epicurus chose to leave Athens and return home. Home, however, was no longer Samos, which had been conquered by the Macedonians, but Colophon, a Greek city in Asia Minor. No records of Epicurus exist for the next few years, but he probably spent his time traveling and studying the various schools of philosophical thought.

Sometime around 311 B.C., Epicurus began teaching, first at Mytilene, the principal city on the Aegean island of Lesbos, and then a year later at Lampsacus, a prosperous city on the Hellespont (the modern-day Strait of the Dardanelles), where he established a school and remained for about four years. Epicurus won the admiration of the citizens

Epicurus, whom this bronze statuette may represent, founded a new school of philosophy in 3rd-century Athens. He said, "Only the just person enjoys peace of mind."

of both cities and his schools flourished, but he was not content. In 306 B.C., he returned to Athens, along with many of his devoted followers.

In Athens, Epicurus bought a house and garden for himself and his followers and established a school of philosophy that became known as the Garden. Epicurus' school found itself in competition with the two older schools, Plato's Academy and Aristotle's Lyceum. Although all three offered courses in philosophy, the sciences, mathematics, and other disciplines, only Epicurus' school was concerned with promoting a way of life, which included advising his students to avoid politics. And only his school admitted both women and slaves.

Soon pupils from all around the Greek world flocked to Epicurus' school. The biographer Diogenes Laertius wrote that there were more pupils in Epicurus' school than there were citizens in a typical major city. Tradition also maintained that many of Epicurus' pupils had left other schools to study at his but that only two ever left his school to study elsewhere.

Epicurus and his followers lived a very simple life at the school. The daily diet consisted mainly of barley bread and water, with a small portion of wine. On one occasion when Athens experienced a severe famine, Epicurus and his students survived on a daily ration of beans.

Although Diogenes Laertius recorded that Epicurus wrote more than 300 volumes, only three letters, several fragments of his works, and two collections of sayings have survived. As a result, scholars have relied on the writings of others to document Epicurus' teachings and beliefs.

Epicurus believed that all humans naturally experience pleasure and pain, and that it is part of human nature to seek the first and avoid the second. According to Epicurus, individuals should try to gain the most pleasure possible, while exposing themselves to the least amount of pain. Furthermore, when Epicurus spoke of pleasure and pain, he referred to the effects of both on the body and on the mind.

Some of Epicurus' contemporaries openly accused him of thinking only of pleasure. They even charged that he and his followers spent their days satisfying their desires. Because later generations continued to make those accusations—even defining his beliefs as an "eat, drink, and be merry" philosophy—Epicurus' name became the basis of the English word *epicure*, which refers to an individual who enjoys fine food and drink and takes great pleasure in indulging in both.

Epicurus, however, would cringe at being associated with such a person, and he would explain that his teachings had been misinterpreted. For Epicurus, seeking pleasure meant staying away from anything that would bring pain. He encouraged his pupils to avoid the restlessness that causes desire because only individuals who are free of desires can fully experience pleasure.

Epicurus believed that pain is caused by desires that have not been satisfied, and he advised individuals to distinguish between desires that are necessary and those that are unnecessary. The next step is to realize that necessary desires are simple desires, such as thirst, which are easily satisfied. However, people who continually seek to satisfy their desires will constantly be in pain. This is because the pain caused by the desire for greater pleasures will not allow them to experience the simple pleasures. Epicurus taught: "If you live according to nature, you will never be poor; but if you live according to the world's opinion, you will never be rich."

For Epicurus, the best pleasures were those that affected the mind rather than those that affected the

"It is impossible to live pleasurably without living wisely, well, and justly, and it is impossible to live wisely, well, and justly without living pleasurably."

—Epicurus, quoted in *Lives of Eminent Philosophers* (3rd century A.D.) by Diogenes Laertius

body, and the greatest pleasure of all was peace of mind. Yet Epicurus maintained that peace of mind is possible only when people make their own decisions about proper conduct. To make such decisions, he said, they need to study philosophy. "Fortune," Epicurus wrote, "seldom interferes with wise individuals because their goals are always directed by reason."

Many of Epicurus' critics charged that his philosophy was too self-centered and that his pupils separated themselves too much from the real world. His followers, they argued, focused far too much on themselves and how to achieve pleasure. In Athens, a city known for politically active citizens, many Athenians were critical of Epicurus for urging his pupils to keep out of public life and in particular not to enter politics. Epicurus, they said, promoted a way of living that focused on the individual and neglected the welfare and well-being of others.

Nevertheless, everyone in Athens was well aware of how loyal and devoted the followers of Epicurus were to each other and to their teacher. This sense of loyalty was a key principle of Epicurus' philosophy, and he believed firmly in creating an atmosphere that allowed individuals to respect one another. According to Epicurus, "The best way to ensure happiness in life and by far the most important is to have friends."

As Epicurus thought about how best to live one's life, his mind turned to the origin and substance of life itself. For Epicurus, the world was made up of matter and the space in which it existed. His matter consisted of small indivisible particles called atoms that came together to form the objects with which we are all familiar. As a result of such thinking, Epicurus came to the conclusion that there was no divine creator, only immortal gods who were made of much finer atoms than humans and lived in an eternal state of happiness, taking no interest in humans.

According to Epicurus, the human soul is also made up of atoms. However, at the moment of death these atoms break up and scatter, with the result that no part of any human being survives this life on earth. Consequently, death never bothered Epicurus and he taught his pupils never to fear death. Wherever death is, he said, no human exists, and where death is not, there a human does exist. For Epicurus, there was no afterlife.

For more than 35 years, Epicurus remained the head of his school in Athens, leaving the city only on a few occasions to visit Asia Minor. At the time of his death, in 270 B.C., he was acknowledged as one of Athens' most influential citizens. His will provided for the continuation of the Garden. Epicurus also made provisions

ANCIENT GREEKS

Epicurus

BORN
341 B.C.
Samos

DIED
270 B.C.
Athens, Greece

PROFESSION
Philosopher

ACCOMPLISHMENTS
Established a school of philosophy, first in Lampsacus on the Hellespont and then in Athens; developed a philosophy of pleasure and pain; wrote approximately 300 volumes

"Simple enjoyment provides as much pleasure as an expensive diet, while bread and water afford the greatest pleasure possible where given to hungry lips."

—Epicurus, quoted in *Lives of Eminent Philosophers* (3rd century A.D.) by Diogenes Laertius

On this reconstructed 5th-century B.C. vase the scene of three women preparing to serve wine is simple and unaffected, qualities that Epicurus admired. He advised his students to avoid the restlessness that comes from always trying to satisfy new desires.

to free his slaves and established a charitable fund to honor both his ancestors and the anniversary of his birth. His trusted follower Hermachus, who had been one of his first pupils years earlier at Mytilene, succeeded him as headmaster.

In the centuries that followed, the Epicurean philosophy and way of life won thousands of followers. Many well-known Romans adopted his teachings, including the 1st-century B.C. poet Lucretius and the 1st-century B.C. orator and statesman Cicero. Epicurus' influence, however, did not end with the Romans. Epicurean communities were founded throughout the Mediterranean, and modern students of philosophy continue to study and discuss his ideas.

FURTHER READING

Hyde, William DeWitt. *Five Great Philosophies of Life*. New York: Macmillan, 1956.

Long, A. A. *Hellenistic Philosophy: Stoics, Epicureans, Sceptics*. New York: Scribners, 1974.

Oates, Whitney Jennings, ed. *The Stoic and Epicurean Philosophers: The Complete Extant Writings of Epicurus, Epictetus, Lucretius [and] Marcus Aurelius*. Translated by C. Bailey, P. E. Matheson, H. A. J. Munro, and G. Long. 1957. Reprint. New York: Random House, 1970.

Panichas, George A. *Epicurus*. New York: Twayne, 1967.

Rist, John M. *Epicurus, An Introduction*. Cambridge: Cambridge University Press, 1972.

Demetrius

THE BESIEGER

War and a thirst for power marked the decades that followed the death of Alexander the Great. For young Demetrius, life was one continuous battle as he watched his father, Antigonus, vie with the other Macedonian generals for control of Alexander's empire. So many alliances had been made, so many treaties signed, but each had been broken, forgotten, or modified to suit the needs of whichever general wielded the most power at the time.

Demetrius was only two years old when his father set out from Macedonia with Alexander in 334 B.C. to conquer Asia. When Alexander died a decade later, Demetrius' father was recognized as one of the *diadochoi* (successors) and given control of the royal army in Asia. By 319 B.C., Antigonus seemed strong enough to defeat the other successors and reunite the empire under his control. In a world filled with political intrigue, Antigonus saw a joint effort between himself and Demetrius, who was 17 and showed great military promise, as the strongest way both to win and to retain power.

The relationship between Antigonus and Demetrius was a good one. Of all those who sought to rule Alexander the Great's empire, only these two never tried to destroy each other. The Greek biographer Plutarch described how Demetrius once ran into the royal chambers while

Demetrius appears on this ancient Greek coin from around 290 B.C. with a headband that is a symbol of his royal powers. The horn, over his ear, represents his connection to the Egyptian god Ammon.

Antigonus was discussing political matters with some ambassadors, kissed his father, and then sat down beside him. Because Demetrius had just come from hunting, he still held several javelins in his hands.

As the ambassadors were leaving, Antigonus asked them to notice how he allowed his son to be in his presence even when carrying dangerous weapons. Unlike the father-and-son relationships of the other successors, Antigonus neither felt threatened by his son nor wished to withhold power from him. Yet Demetrius did have his own opinions.

On one occasion Antigonus urgently summoned Demetrius to his chambers to tell him that he had dreamed that Demetrius' friend Mithridates had harvested and stolen his crops. Antigonus made Demetrius swear never to tell anyone of this dream, especially Mithridates, whom he planned to eliminate. Fearing for his friend's life, but bound by oath not to speak, Demetrius met with Mithridates and, without saying a word, traced the words "Fly, Mithridates!" with the point of his javelin on the ground before them. Forewarned, Mithridates escaped. Within a short time, the dream proved true—because Mithridates took possession of a large tract of fertile land that was under Antigonus' command.

Whether or not Antigonus suspected that Demetrius had helped Mithridates, their bond remained strong. In 312 B.C., Antigonus appointed Demetrius commander of the forces ordered to stop another of Alexander's successors, Ptolemy, in his bid for Syria. With the rashness and optimism of youth, the inexperienced Demetrius bravely led his forces into battle near the town of Gaza, where Ptolemy's troops completely overwhelmed Demetrius' and forced a retreat.

Soon afterward, Ptolemy's envoys returned Demetrius' captured troops and personal belongings with a message that the battle had been for honor and land only. Demetrius graciously accepted everything, but prayed to the gods that he might be able to return this kind of treatment, for he did not wish to feel obligated to anyone, especially an enemy. His opportunity to return the favor came quickly.

Thinking Demetrius was a defeated man, Ptolemy's general Cilles decided to force Demetrius to leave Syria. Cilles, however, did not know Demetrius and was completely taken by surprise when Demetrius attacked him first. This time it was Demetrius who returned the captured treasures. He believed his debt was now paid.

Demetrius welcomed his father, Antigonus, who had come to celebrate his son's conquest of Syria. The joint quest for power and control had begun. They next planned to conquer Athens.

In 307 B.C., Demetrius set sail with 250 ships across the Aegean Sea to Athens, where another successor's son, Cassander, ruled. Because Cassander had earlier allied himself with Ptolemy, when the Athenians saw Demetrius' fleet approaching Piraeus, the port city and harbor for Athens, they thought it was Ptolemy's and did not prevent the ships from entering. Once inside the harbor, Demetrius signaled that he had come in peace and he wished to speak to the Athenians. Given permission to address those who had assembled, Demetrius announced that his father Antigonus had sent him and that it was their joint decision to give the Athenians their freedom and restore the ancient laws of the city.

The Athenians immediately threw down their shields, called Demetrius their savior, and praised him for ridding Athens of Cassander. In the months that followed, the Athenians continued to grant Demetrius and his father great honors. On the spot where Demetrius had first set foot in Athens, they dedicated an altar to him.

But these quiet days lasted only until the next year, when Demetrius received a summons from his father ordering him to take the island of Cyprus from Ptolemy's control. Obedient as always to his father's wishes, Demetrius set sail. He knew well that Cyprus was one of the lands awarded to his father after Alexander's death, and he recognized its importance in the western Mediterranean Sea as both a military base and a trading center. Naturally, Ptolemy saw the same advantages and was determined to keep them for himself.

Demetrius' first encounter was with Ptolemy's brother Menelaus, whom he easily defeated. The battle against Ptolemy was not so easy, for he was well prepared both on land and on sea. Confident of victory, Ptolemy haughtily advised Demetrius to retreat or meet certain defeat. Just as arrogantly, Demetrius replied that he would willingly retreat if Ptolemy promised to withdraw his troops from the Greek cities of Sicyon and Corinth.

With neither man willing to compromise, the battle lines were set at the harbor of Salamis. Ptolemy prepared to outflank and outmaneuver his enemy. In the end, Demetrius won, and Ptolemy managed to escape, but with only eight ships.

As the report of Demetrius' victory spread, the people under Antigonus' control began to hail Antigonus and Demetrius as kings. Not to be outdone, Ptolemy proclaimed himself king of Egypt. Soon after, the other successors also began calling themselves kings.

Antigonus, annoyed at what he believed was insolence on the part of the *diadochoi*, again made it known that he planned to unify Alexander's empire under his control. Believing that they now had the advantage over Ptolemy, Antigonus and Demetrius invaded Egypt by land and sea. But their efforts were unsuccessful and both were forced to retreat.

The next major encounter was at Rhodes, an island off the coast of southern Asia Minor. The Rhodians had tried to stay neutral, but it was difficult because their prosperity depended on trade, especially with Egypt. Antigonus knew this and had sought the Rhodians as allies against Ptolemy. When they used neutrality as their excuse for refusing, Antigonus took it as a sign of their goodwill toward Egypt and ordered one of his generals to seize the cargo of all Rhodian merchant ships caught sailing to Egypt.

But the Rhodians were stubborn and continued to refuse any alliance with Antigonus, who threatened to send Demetrius with his huge war machines, built to attack city walls, to lay siege to their island. Even when Demetrius demanded that the Rhodians surrender 100 nobles as hostages and allow Antigonus' ships to enter their harbor, they refused to be intimidated. They did, however, send messages to Ptolemy asking for his help.

In the spring of 305 B.C., Demetrius advanced on Rhodes with his enormous fleet and war machines. Demetrius had used these machines on earlier campaigns, but his actions at Rhodes were incorporated into all ancient manuals on warfare. The most formidable of his machines was the *helepolis*, or "destroyer of cities," which Demetrius positioned right next to the fortification walls. Reports told how it took 3,400 men to maneuver the 150-foot, eight-wheeled tower into position. With a square base and sides that tapered toward the top, the tower had several shuttered chambers where soldiers stationed themselves and prepared to discharge missiles. It was contraptions such as the *helepolis* that earned Demetrius the surname *Poliorcetes*, the Besieger.

As on previous occasions, Demetrius planned to take an active

ANCIENT GREEKS

Demetrius

BORN

336 B.C.
Macedonia

DIED

283 B.C.
Syria

PROFESSION

General and ruler

ACCOMPLISHMENTS

Took control of Greece and, with his father, almost succeeded in reuniting the lands previously ruled by Alexander the Great; introduced gigantic multistory war machines to batter the walls of besieged cities

Relying on his imagination to compensate for the lack of surviving accounts, a 16th-century engraver offered this reconstruction of the Colossus of Rhodes, which was constructed to celebrate the Rhodian victory over Demetrius. To give viewers an idea of the figure's size, the illustrator placed artisans in the foreground preparing the head for assembly.

part in the campaign. According to Plutarch, Demetrius wore an iron cuirass (armor that fit across the chest and back) that weighed about 40 pounds. To test its effectiveness, he had ordered his men to shoot a catapult missile at the cuirass and was quite satisfied when only a slight scratch showed where the missile had hit.

Rough seas hampered Demetrius' men, as did the daring sorties of the Rhodians, but the *helepolis* caused considerable damage to the walls of the city. Still, the Rhodians refused to surrender and built a second wall, breaking up their houses and temples for the needed construction materials.

In 304 B.C., almost a year after the siege began, Ptolemy's ships arrived with provisions and reinforcements. Instead of risking defeat against the combined forces of the Rhodians and Ptolemy, Demetrius decided to lift the siege and withdraw. At just this time, Athenian messengers arrived from Greece asking Demetrius for help against Cassander, who was threatening to take Athens. Believing that a victory in Greece would be easier to accomplish than one at Rhodes, Antigonus advised his son to set sail for Athens.

The Rhodians were jubilant and commissioned the sculptor Chares of Lindus to create a monument celebrating the Rhodian victory. Tradition claimed that Chares used one of Demetrius' siege towers for scaffolding and pieces of his machines for the statue. Known as the Colossus, it stood as a monument to freedom at the entrance to Rhodes' harbor. Measuring approximately 60 feet around the chest, 11 feet around the thighs, and 5 feet at the ankles, Chares' statue was at the time the largest ever made of bronze. Meant to represent Helios, the sun god, its head was surrounded by a crown of spiked rays, all riveted into place.

The statue's fame spread very quickly throughout the Mediterranean, and it became known as one of the Seven Wonders of the Ancient World. Relatively few people ever saw the Colossus because an earthquake destroyed the statue only 56 years after it was finished. Eight hundred years later, its remains were sold as scrap metal.

In Greece, Demetrius was far more successful than he had been at Rhodes, and he easily drove Cassander from Athens. Yet Demetrius was not content with one victory but continued fighting until all of Greece was under his control. Such easy successes led Antigonus and Demetrius to believe that they could conquer and rule all of Alexander's empire.

The other successors did not want to see this happen and Seleucus, Ptolemy, Lysimachus, and Cassander joined forces against Antigonus and Demetrius. Battle lines were drawn at Ipsus in Asia Minor and, in 301 B.C., both sides met to decide their fate, as well as that of Alexander's empire.

Demetrius led the cavalry charge and quickly routed the troops of Seleucus' son, Antiochus. Overconfidence then led Demetrius to continue his charge, and he soon found his forces cut off from the rest of the army by the enemy's elephants. Having lost the protection of the cavalry, Antigonus' infantry was unable to withstand the assault of the enemy cavalry and troops. Soon Antigonus lay dead, his troops had been defeated, and Demetrius sought refuge in the town of Ephesus on the coast of Asia Minor.

From Ephesus, Demetrius planned his return to Athens, where he believed the citizens would certainly welcome him. But the Athenians did not want him in Athens because they had just voted not to allow any king within their walls. They sent a messenger to advise Demetrius of their decision. Not wanting to antagonize the Athenians, Demetrius changed his plans and sailed to Thrace, where he ravaged the lands ruled by Lysimachus. Meanwhile, Seleucus kept watch over the events and believed that an alliance with Demetrius might aid him against his rival, Lysimachus. He sent messages asking Demetrius for his daughter Stratonice's hand in marriage, and his proposal was accepted.

As had happened so many times since Alexander's death, the successors began making new alliances in their constant bid for power. Like Seleucus, Ptolemy sought Demetrius as an ally and offered him the hand of his daughter Ptolemais in marriage. Demetrius accepted, for polygamy was an accepted practice among Macedonians. But even marriage could not stop the bitter fighting. When Seleucus demanded land from Demetrius, the latter refused, saying he was unwilling to pay such a price for the friendship of a son-in-law.

"I would rather destroy the pictures of my own father than a piece of art that took so much work."

—Demetrius' reputed answer when Rhodians begged him to spare a painting by Protogenes

The battles continued as Demetrius strove to accomplish his father's goal—to control Alexander's empire. In quick succession, Demetrius took Athens, then Thessaly, and finally Thebes. As victory followed victory, Demetrius became more arrogant and less liked by his subjects. In his conflict with Pyrrhus, the king of Epirus in western Greece, Demetrius lost many allies because of his haughty attitude. In fact, many Greeks began to look to Pyrrhus as the king who most resembled Alexander. Such thoughts, however, did not affect Demetrius, who played the royal role with great zest. He wore robes and crowns and hats with double streamers. His shoes were made of felt that was dyed purple and embroidered with gold threads.

Plutarch wrote that once, when Demetrius was approached by a number of his subjects bearing handwritten petitions, he graciously received each one and carefully tucked it into his cloak. The petitioners believed he would read them later and were shocked and furious to see Demetrius cross the nearby bridge and open his coat, letting all the petitions fall into the river below.

Plutarch recorded another incident that showed a different side of Demetrius' personality. Once, after Demetrius had repeatedly refused to listen to an old woman's request, saying that he had no time for her, the woman turned and said, "Then you have no time to be a king." Stung by such a reprimand, Demetrius immediately asked his advisers to arrange a meeting between him and the old woman and with anyone else who might wish to speak with him.

Meanwhile Ptolemy and Lysimachus closely watched Demetrius' troops as they victoriously advanced. Fearing for their own power, the two joined forces to stop Demetrius. After Lysimachus' ally, Pyrrhus, also agreed to march against Demetrius, rumors began spreading through Demetrius' camp about Pyrrhus' bravery and his kind treatment of prisoners. At first, only a few of Demetrius' troops deserted, but the numbers dramatically increased until it seemed as if the entire army was about to change sides.

Unable to stop the exodus, Demetrius fled the field with a few loyal companions and headed toward Asia Minor, where he was stopped by Lysimachus' son, Agathocles. Unable to rouse any support for himself, Demetrius was forced to seek refuge with his son-in-law, Seleucus. Initially, Seleucus agreed to protect him, but after others warned him that Demetrius was a dangerous, power-hungry man, Seleucus reneged on his offer and sent his forces to capture Demetrius.

Desertions again defeated Demetrius, for those troops who had not left him in Greece for Pyrrhus now turned to Seleucus as their master. With the few who did remain loyal, Demetrius fled into the forest, hoping to outwit and evade Seleucus' troops. But the enemy was too watchful, and finally one of Demetrius' friends suggested that he surrender. Infuriated by such a thought, Demetrius drew his sword to kill the friend but was restrained by others.

Finally acknowledging defeat, Demetrius surrendered to Seleucus, who sent him to one of his strongly fortified garrisons in Syria with a guard to watch his every move. However, Seleucus did order that Demetrius be allowed to hunt, exercise, and ride whenever he wished. For three years Demetrius lived as Seleucus' prisoner until he fell ill from overeating and drinking and died in 283 B.C., at the age of 54.

Seleucus had Demetrius' body cremated and the ashes returned to his son, named Antigonus in honor of his grandfather. As the ship bearing Demetrius' remains approached the port of Corinth, the urn with the ashes sat on the bow covered with a cloth dyed royal purple. Xenophrastus, the most prominent musician of the time, played his lyre as the rowers maneuvered the vessel toward land. Antigonus then laid his father's remains to rest at Demetrias, the city Demetrius had founded.

Antigonus succeeded his father as king of Macedonia and for more than a century—until 168 B.C., when the Romans conquered Macedonia—descendants of Demetrius held the Macedonian throne.

FURTHER READING

Plutarch. *The Age of Alexander: Nine Greek Lives*. Translated and annotated by Ian Scott-Kilvert. New York: Viking Penguin, 1973.

Zeno

"LIVING IN AGREEMENT WITH NATURE"

In the 4th century B.C., change and conflict were bringing confusion and uncertainty to the Greek world. The Greeks lost their independence after the Macedonian king Philip II defeated the combined Greek forces at the Battle of Chaeronea in 338 B.C. When Alexander assumed the kingship of Macedonia after his father's assassination, he continued Philip's goal of conquest and gradually absorbed into his empire the Greek colonies that bordered the Aegean and Mediterranean seas.

Nor were Greeks the only people to feel the might of the Macedonians. When Alexander set out in 334 B.C. to conquer Asia, people and rulers throughout the East

Many statues attributed to Roman sculptors, such as this bust of Zeno, are copies of Greek originals. As the founder of Stoicism, he believed in living a simple and disciplined life.

An Athenian teacher unrolls his scroll while a pupil reads from a folding wooden tablet. The tablet would have been waxed so that he could write on it with a stylus. Zeno taught his students in the public area of Athens called the *Poekile Stoa,* or "Painted Porch."

carefully watched his every move. Young people like Zeno, who grew up during these years, must have heard countless tales of Alexander's exploits. When the shocking news of Alexander's untimely death in 323 B.C. echoed across Greece and Asia, Zeno was only 12 years old. The years that followed were marked by great uncertainty as Alexander's successors battled each other constantly in their bid for power and control. For many people, including Zeno, survival depended on developing a philosophy that provided refuge from the turmoil of everyday life.

Born in 335 B.C., just a year before Alexander and his troops crossed into Asia Minor, Zeno became interested in philosophy at an early age. A native of Citium, a town on the Mediterranean island of Cyprus, Zeno was most likely of Phoenician descent. (The early Phoenicians were great sailors who established trading posts in many coastal areas around the Mediterranean.) Zeno's father was a merchant who frequently traveled to Athens and brought his son copies of works by renowned Greek philosophers.

Sometime around 312 B.C., Zeno traveled to Athens, where he attended lectures at the famed Academy, which had been founded years earlier by the philosopher Plato. However, it was not the teachings of Plato that had the greatest influence on Zeno but those of Crates, a well-known Cynic philosopher. (Cynics focused on achieving freedom from worldly desires and

"Each of us has two ears and one mouth so that we may listen more and talk less."

—Zeno, quoted in *Lives of Eminent Philosophers* (3rd century A.D.) by Diogenes Laertius

ANCIENT GREEKS

Zeno

BORN
335 B.C.
Citium, Cyprus

DIED
Around 263 or 237 B.C. (sources vary)
Athens, Greece

PROFESSION
Philosopher

ACCOMPLISHMENTS
Founder of the philosophy known as Stoicism; wrote several works, of which only fragments survive; ran a school at the *Poekile Stoa* ("Painted Porch") in Athens

considered virtue the only good.) In his account of Zeno's life, the 3rd-century A.D. biographer Diogenes Laertius told of Zeno's first encounter with Crates.

Soon after his arrival in Athens, Zeno was browsing in a bookstore and picked up a work by the Greek historian Xenophon. He was so impressed with what he read that he asked the bookseller where he might meet men who wrote so well. At just that moment, Crates happened to be walking by the bookstore. The bookseller pointed to Crates and told Zeno to follow that man.

Zeno did just that, and for a while he regularly attended Crates' lectures. But his eagerness to learn and seek out answers made it difficult for him to accept the Cynic philosophy, which taught indifference to all scientific questioning. As a result, Zeno began attending lectures by other philosophers in Athens, including one named Stilpo. According to Diogenes Laertius, Crates was so incensed that his pupil turned to others that he went directly to Stilpo's school and bodily dragged Zeno out of it. Zeno calmly turned to Crates and said, "You may seize my body, but Stilpo has taken my mind."

Actually, Zeno was not drawn to any one philosophy. Rather, he took from each the ideas he believed best reflected his own thinking and incorporated them into his own philosophy. Not everyone approved of Zeno's methods—especially a teacher named Polemo. According to Diogenes Laertius, Polemo said to Zeno one day: "I know your Phoenician ways, Zeno. I see that your plan is to creep slyly into my garden and steal my fruit."

After much analysis, Zeno began his own career as a teacher on the *Poekile Stoa* ("Painted Porch") in Athens. In this public colonnaded area, the walls of which had been decorated with paintings by Polygnotus and other distinguished artists, students and others who were interested sat and listened to Zeno. They came to be called Stoics, from the Greek word *stoa*, or "porch." Gradually, Zeno's reputation spread beyond Athens. But Zeno liked the city, and when Antigonus Gonatas, the king of Macedonia, invited Zeno to join his court at Pella (the capital of Macedonia), Zeno refused.

Zeno's philosophy was quite simple. He believed in one supreme power that ruled the entire universe and considered all human beings equal. Zeno's supreme power was just and ordered, as were the laws by which this power governed the universe. This power was not separate from the universe but within it.

According to Zeno, the only real good is virtue and the only real evil is moral weakness. He believed that thinking something evil was the same as doing it. Humans, he said, should accept problems such as hunger, death, and suffering but should not worry too much about them. To do this, Zeno advised his pupils to lead themselves away from bodily cravings and desires and to focus more on living morally.

A key principle of Zeno's philosophy was freedom of choice. Yet he maintained that only the truly wise person naturally chooses that which is good. Zeno also believed, however, that because God predetermines what is good, God knows a person's choices beforehand, even though that person has the ability, at every moment, to decide for himself what to do. Zeno therefore taught that people must strive to be wise in order to exercise their free will in such a way that they will choose what is right. Even though God knows what humans will do, this does not deprive them of the choice.

In accordance with his belief in strict moral discipline, Zeno lived very simply. He ate only figs, bread, and honey, and he always wore plain clothes. Most ancient sources noted that he kept no slaves but attended to all his own needs. Furthermore, he spoke freely with everyone and never favored a rich person over a poor one. According to Diogenes Laertius, this stern, demanding lifestyle agreed with Zeno, for he lived to be 98 years old. (Some ancient sources disagreed, however, and said he lived to 72.)

Nor was his death the result of sickness. Diogenes Laertius wrote that one day Zeno fell and broke a toe. Upset that he now had a physical weakness, he pounded the earth beneath his feet and cried, "I am coming! Why do you call me?" He then held his breath and died.

Followers of all ages and nationalities mourned Zeno's death. The Athenians had always respected Zeno; they had even entrusted him with the keys to the city and presented him with a golden crown. After Zeno's death, Antigonus Gonatas suggested that Athens erect a monument in his honor. The Athenians immediately built one.

In the centuries after Zeno's death, his teachings continued to direct the development of philosophical thought throughout the Greek and Roman world. Zeno's philosophy provided a way of thinking that appealed to people of all classes as they tried to survive the many civil wars that ravaged the lands bordering the Mediterranean Sea.

FURTHER READING

Bell, E. T. *Men of Mathematics*. New York: Simon & Schuster, 1937.

Rist, John M. *Essential Works of Stoicism*. Edited by Moses Hadas. New York: Bantam, 1961.

Rist, John M, ed. *The Stoics*. Berkeley: University of California Press, 1978.

Pyrrhus

THE TIRELESS FIGHTER

For Pyrrhus, life was one great battlefield. At age two, he had his first close encounter with death when his father, Aeacides, king of Epirus, an area in northwest Greece that bordered the Adriatic Sea, was deposed by his own subjects. The few Epirots who remained loyal to Aeacides banded together to save the young heir.

In his *Life of Pyrrhus*, the Greek biographer Plutarch described how the two-year-old Pyrrhus was carried in haste to a kingdom in neighboring Illyria. Finding the waters of the river that flowed by the gateway to the city too turbulent to cross on foot, the loyal Epirots tried to shout their message to the sentries, but their cries were of no avail. Then, in a desperate attempt to save Pyrrhus from enemies who were in close pursuit, one Epirot stripped a piece of bark from a nearby tree and used the point of his buckle to write an explanation of the situation.

After attaching the bark to a javelin, the Epirot hurled the javelin onto the opposite shore. When the sentries read

Almost 70 years after Pyrrhus' death, the renowned Carthaginian general Hannibal ranked him as one of the greatest generals that had ever lived.

the message, they immediately lashed together a few hastily hewn trees and set across to rescue Pyrrhus. Within hours, Pyrrhus was presented to Glaucias, the king of the Illyrians. The king, however, was not anxious to act because he knew Pyrrhus' father had been ousted by allies of Cassander, a powerful general and the son of one of Alexander the Great's successors.

It was little Pyrrhus who resolved the situation by crawling either to the king or to a nearby altar and pulling himself up to his feet. Glaucias took this action as a favorable omen and ordered his attendants to take Pyrrhus to his wife with instructions to raise the young boy as one of his own sons. Even when Cassander offered an enormous ransom for Pyrrhus, Glaucias refused it.

When Pyrrhus turned 12, Glaucias judged that it was time to return the boy to his rightful throne. Accompanied by his army, Glaucias entered Epirus, defeated those in command, and placed Pyrrhus on the throne. But Pyrrhus was still too young to rule and Glaucias appointed guardians for him. Plutarch wrote that Pyrrhus was somewhat terrifying to his people, for instead of a set of upper teeth he had one piece of continuous bone marked by lines where the divisions should have been.

Strife again entered Pyrrhus' life when he was 17. While attending the wedding of one of Glaucias' sons in Illyria, Pyrrhus learned that his subjects had seized his throne and named his rival, Neoptolemus, as king. With no army to defend his claim to the kingship, Pyrrhus turned to his sister, Deidamia, for help.

As a child, Deidamia had been engaged to Alexander the Great's son and heir Alexander IV, but when Alexander's untimely assassination prevented such a union, Demetrius had sought her hand in marriage and she had accepted. Because young Pyrrhus knew that Demetrius would prove a powerful ally and might even help him regain control of Epirus, he allied himself with Demetrius and his father Antigonus against the combined forces of Lysimachus, Cassander, and Seleucus. In 301 B.C., at Ipsus in Asia Minor, the two armies fought for control of Alexander's empire. Demetrius and his allies lost the battle. Yet even in defeat, the young soldier Pyrrhus supported his brother-in-law and, as part of the agreement between Pompey (another of Alexander's successors) and Demetrius, served as a hostage in Ptolemy's court in Egypt.

Ptolemy quickly recognized Pyrrhus' leadership skills, gave him his stepdaughter Antigone's hand in marriage, and, in 297 B.C., supplied him an army and a fleet to recapture his throne in Epirus. Pyrrhus, however, did not favor an immediate takeover. He had learned that the Epirots no longer supported Neoptolemus and detested his cruel and autocratic ways. Pyrrhus knew that if Neoptolemus allied himself with the kings of the neighboring countries, such alliances would make regaining his rightful throne even more difficult, and so he offered to rule jointly with Neoptolemus.

All went well for several months, until the loyal followers of Pyrrhus reported that Neoptolemus was plotting against him. Anxious to prevent more conflict, Pyrrhus had Neoptolemus killed. The year was 295 B.C. and Pyrrhus' position finally seemed secure, but a quiet life was not suited to Pyrrhus' personality. He envisioned himself as king of more than Epirus and so did his subjects, who admired his courage and generosity. Many even said that of all the contenders for power at the time, Pyrrhus most closely resembled Alexander the Great in spirit and action.

Pyrrhus first sought to extend his control over Macedonia and welcomed a call for help from one of Cassander's sons. Because Demetrius had also been

The 17th-century French artist Nicolas Poussin dramatically portrayed the harrowing escape of young Pyrrhus when rebellious subjects deposed his father, the king of Epirus. A few subjects who had remained loyal saved the young heir.

asked for help, a bitter conflict developed between the two brothers-in-law. Unfortunately, Deidamia had died just a short time before and was consequently unable to mediate between them.

In 287 B.C., Pyrrhus formed a second coalition against Demetrius in order to strengthen his position. This time his partners were Lysimachus, Seleucus, and Pompey. When Demetrius' soldiers began deserting to join Pyrrhus' army, Demetrius was forced to flee and Pyrrhus and Lysimachus divided Macedonia between them. Lysimachus, however, was not content with joint rule, and he drove Pyrrhus out of Macedonia.

Back in Epirus, Pyrrhus found court life quiet and uneventful and began to look west instead of east for new opportunities. When the inhabitants of the Greek city of Tarentum in southern Italy asked for his help against the advancing Roman army, Pyrrhus eagerly accepted. He had heard of the might and discipline of the Roman soldiers, who, for the past two centuries, had gradually been extending their control across the Italian peninsula. If the Romans conquered the prosperous port city of Tarentum, all of Italy would be theirs. But if Pyrrhus defeated the Romans, all Italy would be open to him.

Pyrrhus had even greater designs. Plutarch recorded that Pyrrhus envisioned first the conquest of Italy, then of Sicily, and then, in northern Africa, of the principal trading town of

"It is impossible for anyone to avoid his fate."

—what Pyrrhus reputedly said at Tarentum as a Roman soldier advanced directly on him

Carthage. Tarentum was just the beginning of an empire that would stretch across the western Mediterranean. Alexander's successors, Pyrrhus reasoned, could fight over the East.

In 280 B.C., Pyrrhus crossed from Epirus to Tarentum with approximately 25,000 soldiers and 20 elephants. Once inside the city, he carefully began to assess the people and their eagerness for war. Believing that the Tarentines were ready to let him fight while they continued to enjoy their luxurious lifestyle, he closed the public gymnasiums and the theaters and forbade all festivities. Pyrrhus also drafted many Tarentines into his army. To express their disapproval of such measures and show they were not to be treated as servants, some Tarentines fled the city.

Pyrrhus was not deterred, for he had his own goals and was determined to accomplish them. He offered to negotiate with the Romans, but they adamantly refused because they felt he had no right to represent the Tarentines, with whom they were at war. With the battle lines drawn at nearby Heraclea, Pyrrhus decided to first scout out the enemy camp. When he saw the discipline, the system of organized lookouts, and the general layout of the encampment, Pyrrhus recognized his enemy as a worthy opponent. Later, in the middle of the battle, Pyrrhus noted the Romans' courage and strength. But when an attendant cautioned Pyrrhus to beware of a Roman cavalryman who seemed absolutely determined to kill him, Pyrrhus merely shrugged off the threat until that Roman lunged toward him, killing his horse.

Barely escaping death made Pyrrhus a little more cautious, and respectful of this new enemy who fought so bravely. He exchanged armor with a friend so that he might move about freely and be less noticeable. Unaware that any changes had been made, the Romans continued pursuing the person dressed in what they knew was Pyrrhus' armor. In a great surge forward, they overwhelmed and killed the man they believed to be Pyrrhus and began yelling that Pyrrhus was dead. Immediately the Greeks fell back, stunned at such a loss, while the Romans regrouped to attack.

When Pyrrhus heard what had happened, he dashed bareheaded to the front line, stretched out his hand to greet every soldier he met, and quickly made it known that he was still alive. Revived by the news, the Greeks again rushed the Romans, who were finding it increasingly difficult to battle Pyrrhus' elephants. By day's end, the victory went to Pyrrhus. However, his losses were so great that he began to wonder how many such victories his troops could withstand, and he decided to advance immediately on Rome.

When Pyrrhus had come to within about 30 miles of Rome, he sent his trusted general Cineas to seek a peace treaty with the Romans and to offer to return all prisoners. Fearing the losses a second encounter with Pyrrhus might bring, many Romans advised considering a peace treaty. But just as the Roman Senate was about to vote on the matter, a blind, elderly statesman named Appius Claudius had his attendants carry him into the Senate.

"What a terrible day today is, if the rumor I heard is true! You Romans seek peace, you who boasted that you would have repulsed even Alexander the Great had he invaded your shores. Now a king who can in no way be compared to Alexander has you terrified after one major battle.

"For some time now, I have grumbled because my old eyes can no longer see. How I wish that I was not only blind but also deaf—then I would not have heard about your cowardice."

Appius Claudius' speech—quoted in Plutarch's *Lives*—quickly changed the minds of the Roman senators, who sent a message to Pyrrhus flatly refusing his offer of peace and suggesting their own terms, which Plutarch also recorded: "Pyrrhus, as long as you remain in Italy armed and with troops, we can not talk of peace or alliances. But once you have returned to Epirus, then, and only then, will we consider an alliance with you."

Cineas faithfully reported to Pyrrhus the details of his meeting with the Romans, commenting that the Romans were a very patriotic people who had already raised another army that was twice as large as the one Pyrrhus had just defeated. Pyrrhus admired such courage on the part of his enemy and decided to withdraw to Tarentum because winter approached.

The Romans, meanwhile, concerned about the many prisoners Pyrrhus had captured, sent the trusted and loyal Caius Fabricius to ransom them. Informed that Fabricius had very little money, Pyrrhus tried to bribe him with gold and other riches. When Fabricius refused, Pyrrhus invited him to return for a meeting the next day. Determined to break Fabricius' calm manner, Pyrrhus led his largest war elephant into his tent and positioned it behind a curtain.

When Fabricius returned the next day, Pyrrhus motioned for him to sit on the stool near the curtain and then signaled his attendant to draw the curtain. Immediately the elephant raised his trunk above Fabricius' head and made a loud trumpeting noise. Unperturbed, Fabricius turned to Pyrrhus and, according to Plutarch, said, "Neither your money nor your elephant impress me!"

Pyrrhus replied, "Certainly, you are an honest and good soldier, Fabricius. I give you permission to take the Roman prisoners back to Rome now, but with one condition: If the Romans do not agree to a peace treaty, you must return all the prisoners to me."

Fabricius accepted Pyrrhus' offer, and when the Romans still refused to negotiate a peace treaty, the prisoners were returned.

Not everyone, however, was as loyal as Fabricius. A messenger delivered a letter from Pyrrhus' doctor to Fabricius, offering to kill Pyrrhus with poison. Furious that anyone would commit such treachery, Fabricius immediately sent the letter to Pyrrhus with his own message, which Plutarch included in his biography of Pyrrhus: "Certainly you have not chosen your close associates well. Be advised that we Romans are loyal and honest men. I would not have it said that we defeated Pyrrhus through treachery because we were not able to do so by force."

In appreciation for Fabricius' upright character, Pyrrhus returned the Roman prisoners without a ransom. The Romans did likewise with their Greek prisoners, so as not to owe Pyrrhus a favor. But with no peace terms concluded, the two armies met soon after, in 279 B.C., near the city of Ausculum. As at Heraclea, both Romans and Greeks fought with such courage and bravery that thousands died and only night was able to put an end to the battle. Even Pyrrhus questioned whether he had won, for he reckoned that the great loss of life had turned his victory into defeat. History has immortalized Pyrrhus' battles against the Romans in the phrase "Pyrrhic victory," meaning a battle won but only after crippling losses.

Frustrated by his inability to win, Pyrrhus welcomed the request for military aid from Greeks on the neighboring island of Sicily. There it was not the Romans who were threatening the area but the army of Carthage, a prosperous trading port in northern Africa (near modern-day Tunis in Tunisia). Pyrrhus and his troops successfully routed the Carthaginians on several fronts, but when he failed to take the city of Lilybaeum, the Sicilians forgot Pyrrhus' victories and condemned him for his failure. In

ANCIENT GREEKS

Pyrrhus

BORN

Around 319 B.C.
Probably Epirus

DIED

272 B.C.
Argos, Greece

PROFESSION

General and ruler

ACCOMPLISHMENTS

Wrote *Memoirs* and books on war that were read and praised by many ancient leaders, including the Roman statesman Cicero and writers such as Plutarch; master military leader and strategist; built a powerful empire in Epirus; aided the Greeks in southern Italy against the Romans, and the Sicilians against the Carthaginians

"One more such victory [over the Romans] and we are lost."

—Pyrrhus, on defeating the Romans at Ausculum in 279 B.C., quoted in Plutarch's *Lives* (around 1st century A.D.)

retaliation, Pyrrhus enacted several cruel laws that so strained his relations with the people that he was forced to withdraw from Sicily and return to Italy in 276 B.C.

Once again the Greeks in southern Italy sought Pyrrhus' aid against the Romans and, willing as always to engage in battle, he agreed to help. In 275 B.C., at Beneventum in southern Italy, Pyrrhus faced the Romans and lost. All hopes of further conquest in Italy were gone and Pyrrhus was forced to return home to Epirus. Only one-third of his troops had survived the campaigns in Italy and Sicily.

But Pyrrhus found court life in Epirus still too quiet and soon began to make plans to conquer Macedonia. In 273 B.C., he attacked Antigonus Gonatas, the son of his old ally and enemy Demetrius, who now ruled Macedonia. It was an easy victory, especially when Antigonus' troops deserted and hailed Pyrrhus as their new leader. Then, for some reason, restlessness again took control of Pyrrhus, for he suddenly decided to leave Macedonia and march his troops into southern Greece. There he laid siege to the city of Sparta but was forced to retreat after a bitter and bloody battle. He then marched to the city of Argos because its leading citizen, Aristeas, had summoned his help against a rival named Antigonus.

According to plan, Aristeas secretly unlocked the gate and Pyrrhus was able to sneak into the city under the cover of darkness. The gate opening was not high enough for the equipment racks on the elephants' backs, so Pyrrhus ordered that the racks be dismantled and everything carried in separately. Once inside, Pyrrhus ordered the racks reassembled and reattached, but his intended element of surprise was gone. Furthermore, the delay had allowed the people of Argos to sound the alarm, grab their weapons, and man their stations.

When Pyrrhus realized his forces were being outmaneuvered, he called a retreat, but the elephants blocked the way, causing confusion and chaos. Pyrrhus, as always, had dashed to the front lines, in the marketplace, where the fighting was hand-to-hand and intense. He was repelling the enemy on all sides when a lance suddenly struck his breastplate. From the roof of a nearby house, a woman had been anxiously watching the battle and saw her son's lance hit Pyrrhus.

Plutarch wrote that she was so overwhelmed with fear and anger when she saw Pyrrhus turn to strike the young man that she grabbed a roof tile and flung it at her son's assailant. The tile hit Pyrrhus in the neck, just below his helmet, and knocked him to the ground. Quickly, the enemy surrounded his body and cut off his head. The year was 272 B.C., and Pyrrhus was just 47 years old.

Antigonus' soldiers immediately summoned their leader to see their dead prize, but the sight of his now-lifeless enemy made Antigonus remember how fickle fortune is and how often defeat follows victory. Antigonus then ordered Pyrrhus' body to be buried honorably and made arrangements for Pyrrhus' son to inherit his father's kingdom in Epirus.

FURTHER READING

Plutarch. *The Age of Alexander: Nine Greek Lives*. Translated and annotated by Ian Scott-Kilvert. New York: Viking Penguin, 1973.

Apollonius Rhodius

RETELLING JASON'S TALE

Egypt's Alexandria gradually replaced Athens as the cultural and intellectual center of the Hellenic world, and by the 3rd century B.C. scholars from around the Mediterranean and beyond were traveling to the city on the delta of the Nile River to study in its massive library. The resources there were phenomenal, with more volumes and artifacts than could be found anywhere else.

Yet what made a visit to this city even more exciting were the people who lived there. The world's best and brightest spent time at Alexandria studying and exchanging ideas. This interchange resulted in the export of philosophies and customs to other lands and people. One of the people who played a role in this interplay was a writer named Apollonius.

Most likely a native of Alexandria, Apollonius involved himself completely in his studies and writing; he had no time for politics or the military. As a result, ancient writers focused less on his life than on those of famous politicians and statesmen. According to one reliable manuscript, Apollonius began writing poetry late in life; another document, also authentic, maintains that Apollonius left as a young man for the Mediterranean island of Rhodes after an audience at a reading in Alexandria rejected one of his poems. The second document says that after Apollonius reworked the poem at Rhodes, it brought him international

The Argonaut hero Jason (left) reaches out to grab the golden fleece that is guarded by a small dragon. In the center is the goddess Athena, and to the right, another deity and the stern of Jason's ship, the *Argo*. The story of Jason is one of the oldest tales in Greek mythology, and perhaps Apollonius' greatest accomplishment is his rendition of it in the *Argonautica* (Tales of the Argonauts).

On this papyrus fragment dating from the 2nd century A.D., Apollonius is listed as one of the early directors of the great library in Alexandria, Egypt.

fame. Whatever the truth may be, Apollonius has become known as Apollonius of Rhodes (Apollonius Rhodius).

Sometime around 260 B.C., Apollonius returned to Alexandria to assume the prestigious position of director of the library. It was at this time that he came into conflict with his former teacher Callimachus. Later historians have focused much attention on the details of this feud, using Apollonius' reworking of several passages from Callimachus' poems as evidence of their intense dislike for each other. Yet there are some who say Apollonius' reworking should be taken as a compliment. However, the answer may not be as important as understanding how the two differed in style.

"Life is short to the fortunate, long to the unfortunate."

—Apollonius, quoted in *Florilegium*, a collection of excerpts from earlier Greek writers, compiled around the 5th century A.D. by Stobaeus

Each represented one side of a controversy that was raging at the time between those writers who believed in the merit of long, traditional epics and those who preferred short, carefully worked poems. The traditionalists, including Apollonius, honored the Greek poet Homer as their model, whereas the innovators, including Callimachus, preferred witty and elegant pieces. As the years passed, the traditional epic won increasing support and became the preferred style. Nevertheless it was Apollonius who emigrated to Rhodes around 247 B.C. and Callimachus who chose to stay in Alexandria.

Apollonius' most celebrated poem and the one on which his fame rests is the *Argonautica* (Tales of the Argonauts). This epic, which the author divided into four books, recounts the story of Jason and the Argonauts, one of the oldest tales in Greek mythology. The Argonauts were Greek heroes who sailed in the ship *Argo* to the land of Colchis at the eastern end of the Black Sea. Their mission was to fetch the golden fleece of a ram that a young Greek named Phrixus had once hung in a grove guarded by a sleepless dragon.

The commander of the Argonauts was Jason, whose crafty uncle had cheated him out of his right to the throne of Thessaly. In order to stay in power, Jason's uncle had sent him on the seemingly impossible task of retrieving the fleece, but he underestimated Jason's determination, especially his cleverness at escaping the evils he would encounter on the journey.

When Jason finally arrived in Colchis and explained his mission to the king, the latter ordered him first to catch two fire-breathing bulls, yoke them to a plow, and plow a field. Jason was then to sow dragon's teeth in the furrows made by the plough and wait for armed soldiers to rise from the planted teeth. As Jason listened to his

the god Apollo was in progress at Sparta. Custom forbade Sparta from sending forth great armies during religious festivals.

Xerxes, however, would not wait, and Leonidas decided to lead an army north. He chose 300 soldiers from the royal guard, all men in their thirties and all of them fathers of sons. For Leonidas and Sparta, this was important, because any Spartan who died in action would leave a son to carry on the family line. Leonidas saw his force as the advance men and, before setting out, made an agreement with Sparta's leaders that the full army would follow once the religious festivals ended.

Scholars believe that Leonidas' contingent also included several hundred Helots. In Spartan society, Helots were the people who tilled the fields, cared for the animals, and worked in the homes of Spartan citizens. Helots had few freedoms and no rights, and male Helots were required to accompany their masters onto the battlefield.

As the Spartan contingent marched north, soldiers from other cities volunteered to join them, swelling the numbers to 10,000. The Persian army, however, counted more than 100,000 soldiers in its ranks.

News of Leonidas' march spread quickly through the cities and towns of Greece. Yet not every Greek was ready to fight the Persians. Several northern Greek cities decided to let the Persians pass through their lands rather than risk defeat and enslavement. Other cities argued that Greece should abandon the north and take a stand at the Isthmus of Corinth in central Greece. An army of 10,000 had recently marched north to the valley of Tempe but had withdrawn after they saw how vulnerable their position was. The commanders decided to make one final stand in the north, at Thermopylae.

The Greek name *Thermopylae* actually means "hot gates," and, according to Greek mythology, Zeus, the king of the gods, had long ago created hot springs in this area to refresh his exhausted son, the Greek hero Heracles. According to tradition, Leonidas traced his ancestry to this legendary Heracles.

Geographically, Thermopylae provided the best defense for an army as small as that of Leonidas. It was a narrow pass, 50 feet wide and wedged between steep cliffs and the Aegean Sea. With two rivers winding their way through the neighboring lands, normal fighting tactics were impossible. Should an army resolve to cross the pass, the defenders of the pass could wait to slaughter each enemy group as it passed through.

Leonidas recognized the advantages of Thermopylae and knew a Greek victory was possible, especially with Spartans defending the pass. Whenever Greek spies brought back reports that made the non-Spartans speak of retreat, Leonidas quickly quelled such fears and encouraged the men to think about victory.

Meanwhile, Persian spies kept Xerxes informed about every Greek move. When they reported that the Greek soldiers were spending time on gymnastic exercises and combing their long hair, Xerxes laughed at such foolish behavior. He did not know that this was all part of how the Spartans trained and prepared for battle.

For four days, Xerxes waited near Thermopylae, convinced that the Greeks would retreat once they saw his huge fighting force. When they did not, Xerxes gave the order to attack. As each group of Persian soldiers surged forward toward the pass, the Greeks waited with calm determination until the enemy reached the pass. The Persians, unable to move or regroup after they were in the narrow space, were easy targets for the Greeks, and once they attacked, the Persian casualties quickly began to mount.

"Come and take them."

—Leonidas' reply when Xerxes asked him to surrender his weapons

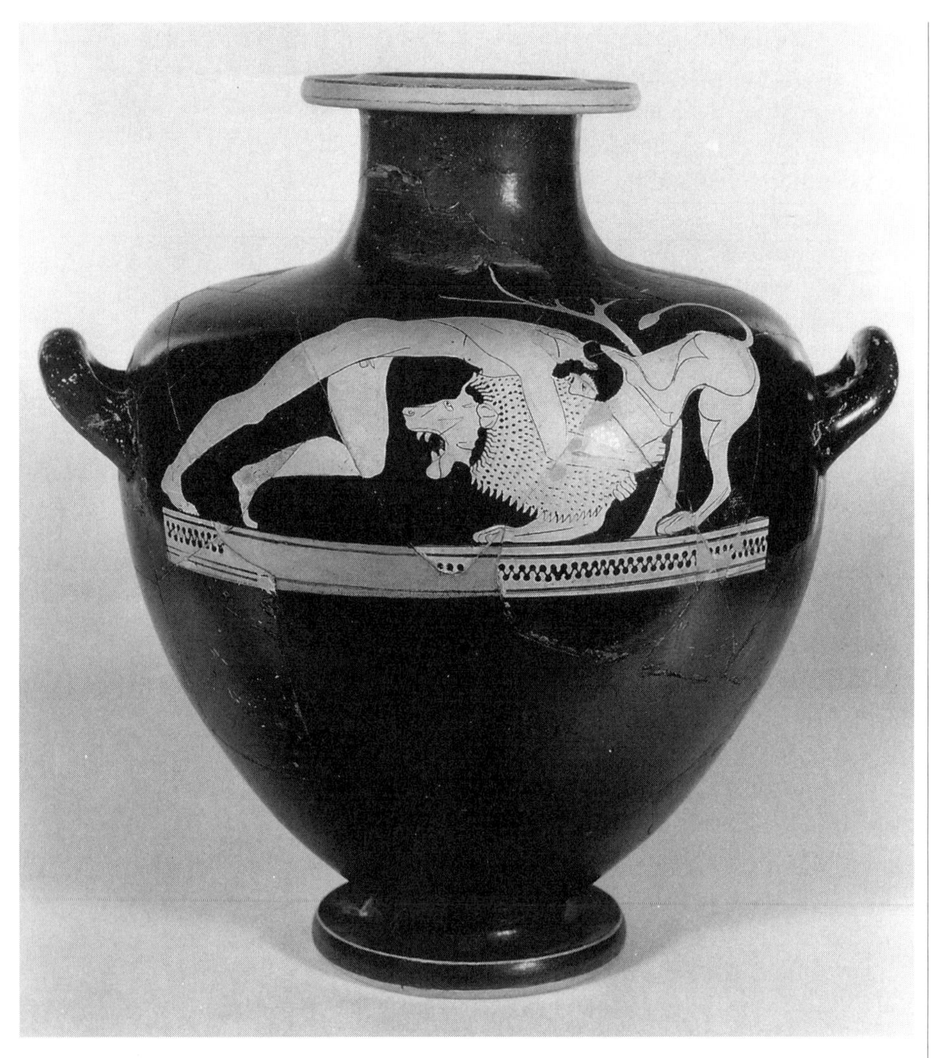

Leonidas claimed he was a descendant of Heracles, son of Zeus, and his fierce spirit certainly matched that of the legendary hero, who barehandedly strangles a fierce lion on this 5th-century vase.

"Send in the Immortals!" commanded Xerxes. The Immortals were the king's personal troops and were so called because anyone who died or left was immediately replaced by another soldier. Yet even this top fighting force could not break the Greek defense.

Leonidas' strategy worked. One Spartan contingent stayed behind the narrow point in the pass while the other marched beyond it toward the Persians. When the second group suddenly turned in retreat, the Persians ran after them. However, as the Persians approached the narrow point of the pass, they had to keep rearranging their battle formation until they finally closed ranks to form a V-shaped battleline. The Spartans, with their superior armor and longer spears, easily overwhelmed and defeated each successive wave of Persians. Xerxes, meanwhile, looked on in disbelief as the two Spartan contingents took turns "baiting" and then slaughtering his troops. Realizing the situation was hopeless, Xerxes ordered his troops to retire to their tents.

For Leonidas and his troops, the impossible had happened. Now they just had to hold out until the religious festivals were over and relief armies arrived. But this was not to happen.

A Greek named Ephialtes decided to tell Xerxes about a little-known path that led through the woods, up the cliffs, and to the Greek camp. The Persian king could barely contain his excitement and immediately ordered Hydarnes, the commander of the Immortals, to take his troops and follow Ephialtes. Xerxes then estimated the time Hydarnes would need to reach the Greek camp and planned his own attack on the Greek forces for the same hour.

As quietly and as quickly as possible, the Persians made their way behind Ephialtes. Only when Greeks standing guard on the cliffs heard the rustling of leaves early the next morning did they realize what was happening. Those on the ridge abandoned their position quickly, without even attempting to fight. A few, however, managed to reach Leonidas and tell him the news. At dawn, Greek scouts rushed in to report that the Persians were again advancing on the pass. Leonidas guessed a traitor had been at work and knew victory would not

orders, his spirits fell, but the gods were watching and Aphrodite, the goddess of love and friend of the Greeks, decided to help the Argonauts.

Aphrodite gave the king's daughter, Medea, a special potion that kindled in her heart a deep love for Jason. Unable to think of anyone or anything but Jason, Medea tried to figure out how she could protect him. An enchantress and crafter of magic brews, Medea secretly handed Jason a jar filled with a special ointment that would protect his body from the fire of the bulls as well as fill it with the strength needed to yoke them. Medea advised Jason to wait until all the soldiers had been born of the teeth and then to throw a stone into their midst. Eager for what they thought was a prize, the soldiers, she said, would scramble and fight to the death for the stone.

Following Medea's instructions, Jason quickly accomplished every assignment and then confidently approached Medea's father to ask for the fleece. Without giving any reason, the king flatly refused, forcing Jason to seek other methods of obtaining the prize. Jason thought of Medea and promised to take her home with him in return for her help. Without a moment's hesitation, Medea took with her some vials and sprinkled the dragon with a sleeping potion. Quickly snatching the golden fleece from the branch, Jason signaled his men to return to the ship and, true to his promise, took Medea with him.

In the *Argonautica*, Apollonius imitated the heroic style and language of Homer but varied the traditional epic phrases and handled the material in such an interesting and innovative manner that he easily won the approval and admiration of contemporary audiences.

Apollonius' epic, however, cannot be considered on the same level as Homer's. Much simpler in scope and style, the *Argonautica* lacks the structural unity and focus of the *Iliad* and the *Odyssey*, and its lines never achieve the spontaneity and beauty of Homer's. Apollonius' version is very uniform in style, with each line carefully prepared for publication.

What was innovative about the *Argonautica* was Apollonius' use of love as a main theme. Previous epics had never focused on this side of the human personality, but Apollonius spent much time carefully and sympathetically describing the principal female figure, Medea, and tracing the development of her love for the principal male figure, Jason. Many later authors followed Apollonius' example and also focused on the tales of characters in love.

In the *Argonautica*, Apollonius successfully merged many of the extant versions of the myth, and his version became the most widely known in ancient times. The Romans especially enjoyed Apollonius, and many Roman poets used his tale as a reference when writing their own editions. Of all the epigrams—short, witty poems—and other poems Apollonius wrote, only the *Argonautica* has survived. Today, students continue to study Jason's tale but few know that many of the passages they read are close translations of Apollonius' *Argonautica*.

FURTHER READING

Apollonius Rhodius. *The Argonautica*. Translated by R. C. Seaton. 1912. Reprint. Loeb Classical Library. Cambridge: Harvard University Press, 1967.

———. *Jason and the Golden Fleece*. Translated by Richard Hunter. New York: Oxford University Press, 1995.

———. *Voyage of Argo*. Translated by E. V. Rieu. New York: Penguin, 1971.

Beye, Charles R. *Ancient Epic Poetry: Homer, Apollonius, Virgil*. Ithaca: Cornell University Press, 1993.

ANCIENT GREEKS

Apollonius Rhodius

BORN
Around 290 B.C.
Probably in Alexandria, Egypt

DIED
After 247 B.C.
Place unknown

PROFESSION
Writer and scholar

ACCOMPLISHMENTS
Wrote *Argonautica* in the traditional epic style, imitating the language and techniques used by Homer; librarian at the world-famous library at Alexandria in Egypt

Archimedes

PROBLEM SOLVER

"Eureka! Eureka!" ("I've found it! I've found it!") cried Archimedes as he jumped from his tub and ran out the door of his house and through the streets of Syracuse. In his joy at solving a difficult problem, Archimedes had completely forgotten where he was and that he was not dressed. The Syracusans who saw him wondered what mathematical problem he had just solved, for they were all well acquainted with his ability to concentrate and disregard the world around him.

Archimedes was Syracuse's most prominent citizen—and its most colorful. Over the years, there were many tales told about his life. Though most were based on fact, a few included more invented details than truths. Such episodes as the "Eureka" incident are probably not accurate and might never have happened at all, but they do give us an idea of how the ancient world pictured this ingenious man.

Born sometime between 290 and 280 B.C. in Syracuse, an important city on the eastern coast of Sicily, Archimedes spent most of his life on the island. As a youth, he probably traveled to Egypt's Alexandria, the renowned cultural center of the Hellenic world. Home, however, was always Syracuse, where Archimedes was a close friend of King Hieron II. Whenever a difficult problem or situation arose, Hieron sought Archimedes' help. In fact, when Archimedes supposedly jumped from his tub, he had just solved a problem for Hieron.

Months earlier, Hieron had commissioned his jeweler to make a crown of gold and silver. But when the jeweler returned with the finished crown, Hieron questioned whether the jeweler had used all the gold he had given him or had kept some for himself and substituted another substance. When the jeweler swore he had done just as the king had asked, Hieron was unable to prove otherwise and was forced to accept the jeweler's statement.

Archimedes loved such problems and returned home, determined to solve the mystery. Despite numerous experiments, the answer had continued to escape him until one day, as he was sitting in his bathtub, he thought about the water his body had displaced when he entered the tub. Suddenly it occurred to him that the difference between his weight in the water and his weight out of the water equaled the weight of the water he had displaced. That was the answer—he had solved his problem.

Archimedes did some further experimenting and proved that the size and weight of an object determined whether the amount of water it displaced would be large or small. He also discovered that when samples of two different materials weighed the same, the denser material (the sample with less volume) displaced less water than the less dense material (the sample with greater volume). Because a unit of gold is denser than a unit of silver that weighs the same amount, the gold displaces less water than the silver.

Archimedes had discovered the principle of hydrostatics (from the Greek words *hydro,* meaning "water," and *statikos,* meaning "causing to stand"), the science that deals with the laws of nature governing how liquids behave when at rest. Not until the experiments of the French mathematician and physicist Blaise Pascal in the 1800s were any new discoveries made in the field of hydrostatics.

After explaining his theory to Hieron, Archimedes asked that the crown and an amount of gold equal to what should be in the crown be brought to him. Archimedes then placed the crown in a container of water and measured the new water level. Next he took out the crown and placed in the container a unit of gold equal to the amount that should have been in the crown. Again Archimedes measured the water level. The jeweler had lied. The new crown displaced more water than the gold unit, proving that the jeweler had substituted another substance for the gold.

This discovery formed the basis of the physical law of buoyancy, known today as Archimedes' principle. A great aid to shipbuilders and sailors, Archimedes' discovery proved that a launched ship sinks in the water until it displaces an amount of water equal to its weight. As more cargo is added to a ship, the ship displaces more water.

Archimedes' ability to solve difficult problems won him the reputation of being the ancient world's greatest mathematician and certainly one of the greatest in history.

Nor did Archimedes wait for problems to be presented to him; he constantly searched for answers to unexplained situations in everyday life. The fact that many of his projects involved ships and water was only natural because Syracuse was a thriving port and merchant ships often moored within its harbor. One day, Archimedes went to the harbor to test a particular theory on which he had been working.

Wanting an eyewitness to this experiment, which involved moving a ship, Archimedes requested that Hieron meet him at the harbor. Archimedes had based his design for this ship-moving device on the principle of the lever and fulcrum, a support on which a lever turns around. As Hieron watched, Archimedes put into place his pulleys and ropes, the only mechanical devices he planned to use. Then calmly

Using as his model Archimedes' portrait on a large bronze medal discovered beneath a Roman town in Sicily, a 16th-century Parisian artist drew his own interpretation of the mathematician, as well as a representation of the siege of Syracuse (on the table) and a model of one of the inventor's war machines (at right).

Some 200 years after Archimedes' death, a sculptor in Alexandria crafted this depiction of a slave using Archimedes' screw to press grapes.

and with little effort, Archimedes single-handedly maneuvered a fully manned and loaded merchant ship toward the shore. He then turned to Hieron and said that his experiment had just proved that a person, standing on firm ground and holding a long lever, could move anything, even the world.

The principle of the lever and fulcrum forms the basis of many modern tools and pieces of equipment, such as oars, crowbars, and scissors.

Archimedes was also acclaimed for his inventions, the best known of which is Archimedes' screw. Whether Archimedes was the first to discover the principle of the screw is uncertain, but tradition and time have granted him the honor. The device consists of a cylinder, inside which is a continuous screw that forms spiral chambers. To bring water from one place to another, one end of the cylinder is placed in water while someone turns the opposite end of the screw. The turning motion then pushes the water into the spiral chambers and forces it to flow upward from one chamber to the next until it finally spills out at the top. In Archimedes' time, this screw allowed sailors to pump bilgewater out of the hold of a ship and helped farmers to lift water from drainage systems and irrigation canals into buckets or pipes.

Archimedes' screw is still used today by some Egyptian farmers to irrigate their fields. In countries such as the Netherlands, where unwanted water needs to be drained from the surface of the land, the screw is used in reverse—that is, the screw forces the water through the spiral chambers from the land back to the canals. Motorboat and airplane propellers are designed on the same principle as the water screw because they drive the boat or plane forward by pushing water or air through the propeller chambers behind them. Modern bilge pumps are also based on the principle of Archimedes' screw.

Archimedes was willing to tackle any mathematical or logistical problem presented to him but chose not to spend time inventing machines that caused destruction. He preferred to spend his time creating designs that would help others. However, around the year 220 B.C., Archimedes was forced to reconsider his thinking.

For several decades, all of Sicily had watched the steady advance of Roman troops down the Italian peninsula and knew well that Rome's next move would be into Sicily. Earlier, invaders from the north African city of Carthage had crossed into Sicily and conquered much of the island. Syracuse was the only city that had managed to retain its freedom, but its people wondered how long it would be before the Carthaginians and Romans would battle each other for control of the island.

To protect his city, Hieron had signed a treaty with the Romans, pledging friendship and cooperation in return for protection against the Carthaginians. Nevertheless, the Syracusans questioned how much help the Romans would actually send in an emergency. Not wanting to find out, Hieron decided to develop his own protection plan for the city and called on his trusted friend Archimedes.

Loyalty and patriotic duty convinced Archimedes that his expertise was needed to create a defense system, and he immediately set to work designing machines that effectively prevented any takeover of the city for years.

Among them were catapults that could fling heavy stones over the city's walls at targets set at varying distances and machines designed to shoot a shower of arrows through specially made holes along the walls. Jutting out from these same walls were long poles with attachments that dropped heavy stones or other objects on approaching enemy ships. One of Archimedes' most feared designs involved iron clawlike devices attached to poles that soldiers could lower onto the prows of approaching enemy ships. By pulling ropes and other mechanisms, the Syracusans could close these iron claws around a ship's prow, lift the ship into the air, and let it swing helplessly. After the sailors had fallen out, the iron claw was released to let the ship fall on the rocks along the shore and be smashed to pieces.

Hieron was pleased with Archimedes' work and gave the order to keep all the machines in working order, ready for any emergency that might arise. When Hieron died around 215 B.C., the machines still had not been used, but they were in perfect condition. In 213 B.C., the Romans under Marcus Claudius Marcellus lay siege to Syracuse. Hippocrates, Syracuse's new ruler, was in part responsible for the attack because he had broken Syracuse's treaty with Rome and allied himself with Carthage.

Archimedes did not like Hippocrates, but when called to his court and asked to prepare the war machines for action, Archimedes patriotically agreed to defend his city. Because the machines had always been kept in perfect working order, no repairs were necessary.

For months, Archimedes' machines protected Syracuse and kept the Romans from capturing the city. Then, one night, Marcellus noticed that a tower and section of wall had been left with little protection. Knowing that the Syracusans were celebrating a religious festival, the Roman general planned a surprise attack. Unable to rally their forces in time, the Syracusans met defeat and the city was sacked, but on Marcellus' orders the citizens were not killed or enslaved as was the custom at the time.

Having heard much about Archimedes and his ingenious defense system, Marcellus ordered that Archimedes be brought directly to him. Tradition has always maintained that the soldier sent to fetch the inventor, who was now in his seventies or eighties, found him so deep in concentration that he was unaware that Syracuse had been captured by the Romans.

When the soldier ordered Archimedes to come with him immediately to Marcellus' camp, Archimedes refused, explaining that he first had to solve a mathematical problem. Furious at such defiance, the soldier killed Archimedes. When Marcellus heard what had happened, he ordered that the soldier be killed and that Archimedes be buried honorably and with much ceremony. Marcellus also commanded that Archimedes' friends and relatives be likewise honored.

In the years before his death, Archimedes had requested that a drawing of a cylinder with the outline of a sphere within it be engraved on his tomb. Next to the drawing, the figures 3:2 were to be written, because they represented the ratio of the volume of a cylinder to that of a sphere. The volume of a cylinder is 1.5 times the volume of the largest sphere that can be contained within it. For example, a cylinder that can hold 7.5 gallons of water is just large enough to contain a sphere filled with 5 gallons of water. Archimedes believed his discovery of

Archimedes

BORN

Around 290–80 B.C.
Syracuse, Sicily

DIED

212 or 211 B.C.
Syracuse, Sicily

PROFESSION

Mathematician and inventor

ACCOMPLISHMENTS

Calculated the approximate value of pi, the ratio of the circumference of a circle to its diameter, as 22/7; calculated the relationship of the volume of a cylinder to that of the largest sphere it could contain as 3:2; credited with the invention and development of Archimedes' screw; discovered the basic principles of hydrostatics and the physical law of buoyancy; mastered the principle of the lever and fulcrum; invented several mechanical devices and war machines for the defense of Syracuse; wrote several treatises on mathematics, including *On the Sphere and Cylinder*, *On Floating Bodies*, *Measurement of the Circle*, and *Method of Mechanical Theorems*

"Give me a lever long enough, and a fulcrum strong enough, and I will single-handedly move the world."

—Archimedes, quoted in *Collectio* (4th century A.D.) by Pappus of Alexandria

this relationship was his greatest achievement.

Archimedes wrote various papers, nine of which have survived. All nine focus on his mathematical theories, not his inventions or mechanical devices, which he believed were insignificant. According to ancient records, Archimedes was also considered to be a master astronomer and his work on the summer and winter solstices was used by later astronomers, including Hipparchus. But Archimedes' works on astronomy have not survived, except for one short section describing a method of finding the sun's diameter.

Archimedes had hoped his work would help successors in his field discover more about mathematical relationships, but in the decades that followed his death his influence was minimal. The ancients did use those theories that were relatively easy to understand and express. One example is Archimedes' discovery of the approximate value of pi, the symbol that represents the ratio of the circumference of a circle to its diameter, as 22/7 or 3.14159265, which became a standard mathematical notation in ancient times.

But the majority of Archimedes' works were forgotten until the 8th and 9th centuries A.D., when they were translated into Arabic and used by Arab mathematicians. Archimedes' greatest influence, however, was on 16th- and 17th-century European mathematicians and physicists. They studied the translated copies of Archimedes' theories that were circulating at the time and expanded upon them. In subsequent centuries, Archimedes' work—including, for example, his mathematical proofs, his methods of finding the area of a parabolic segment, and his discovery that the area of any sphere equals four times that of its greatest circle—lay the foundation for today's mathematics.

FURTHER READING

Bell, E. T. *Men of Mathematics*. New York: Simon & Schuster, 1937.

Bendick, Jeanne. *Archimedes and the Door of Science*. New York: Franklin Watts, 1962.

Heath, Sir Thomas Little. *Archimedes*. New York: Macmillan, 1920.

Ipsen, D. C. *Archimedes, Greatest Scientist of the Ancient World*. Hillside, N.J.: Enslow, 1988.

James, Peter, and Nick Thorpe. *Ancient Inventions*. New York: Ballantine, 1994.

Terry, Leon. *The Mathmen*. New York: McGraw-Hill, 1964.

More Ancient Greeks to Remember

Seleucus (around 358–281 B.C.) proved himself an able general in Alexander's cavalry until the Macedonian king's unexpected death in 323 B.C. left him without a leader. Seleucus watched as Alexander's chief generals parceled out sections of the empire among themselves, and he then chose to pledge his allegiance to Perdiccas, who, as Alexander's second in command, officially became the king's first successor. Two years later, assassins killed Perdiccas and a second division of Alexander's empire began. This time, Seleucus was included in the arrangement and given the rich and strategically important district of Babylonia. But Antigonus, the general who controlled neighboring Asia Minor, threatened Seleucus' authority. Realizing that he could not outmaneuver Antigonus' well-trained troops, Seleucus escaped to Egypt and aligned himself with Ptolemy, yet another of Alexander's generals.

Four years later, Seleucus marched into Babylonia with a small force of Ptolemy's soldiers and won back his land. Historical records date the beginning of the Seleucid dynasty from Seleucus' reentry into Babylonia. (Seleucus' descendants ruled the area until 64 B.C., when the Romans took control.) But Babylonia was not enough for Seleucus

In battle, Seleucus relied heavily on the elephants that he imported from India. This terra-cotta statuette shows an elephant crushing a soldier.

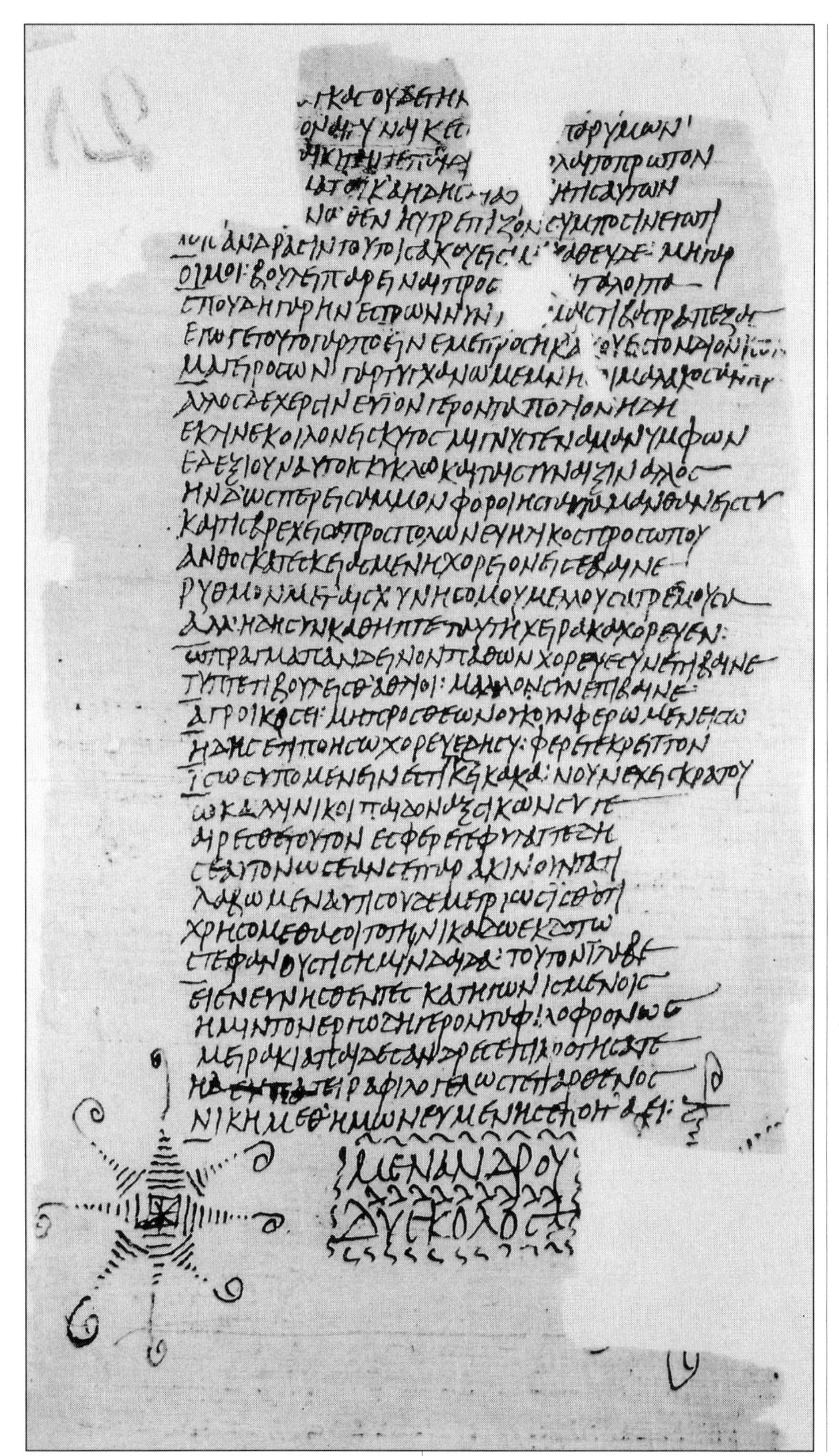

Menander's name and the title of the play, *Dyscolus* (The Disgruntled Man), in the rectangular box at bottom identify this manuscript, discovered in 1956, as the playwright's work.

and he boldly marched into neighboring districts, conquering them all. Only Chandragupta, the Indian leader who founded the Maurya dynasty, stopped his advance in the east.

Then came the opportunity to advance west. In 301 B.C. at the Battle of Ipsus, Seleucus' troops, together with those of the Macedonian generals Lysimachus and Cassander, defeated Antigonus. Seleucus' empire now stretched from the Indus River in India to the Mediterranean Sea. The cities under his control became flourishing commercial and cultural centers that fostered the spread of Greek ideas. In 300 B.C. Seleucus founded Antioch (named in honor of his father) in Syria and made it the capital city. Today Antioch continues to be one of Syria's chief cities.

Seleucus, however, still sought more lands and looked to Macedonia as his next conquest. But one of Ptolemy's sons, Ptolemy Cerannus, wanted Macedonia for himself and murdered the 78-year-old general in 281 B.C.

Lysimachus (around 355–281 B.C.) was Alexander the Great's bodyguard. After Alexander's death in 323 B.C. he was given control of Thrace, the area to the north of the Aegean Sea. For several years, local turmoil kept Lysimachus away from the conflicts involving Alexander's successors, but in 301 B.C. he joined Cassander and Ptolemy against Antigonus. At the Battle of Ipsus, Lysimachus and his coalition were victorious and, when the lands were redistributed, Lysimachus was awarded northern and central Asia Minor. As a result, Lysimachus became one of the most powerful of Alexander's successors, a fact that brought him into direct conflict with Antigonus' son Demetrius.

In 285 B.C. Lysimachus defeated Demetrius and took control of Macedonia and Thessaly, where his arrogant attitude and readiness to raise taxes made him unpopular with his subjects. Family feuds also weakened his authority. His third wife, Arsinoe II, the daughter of Ptolemy I of Egypt, disliked Lysimachus' son and rightful heir, and she persuaded Lysimachus to have him murdered. This violent and unjust act caused much unrest among Lysimachus' subjects and gave Seleucus, another of Alexander's successors, the opportunity to invade Lysimachus' kingdom. In 281 B.C. on the plain of Corupedion in northern Asia Minor, Seleucus' troops killed Lysimachus and defeated his army.

Menander (around 342–292 B.C.) was the last Athenian playwright of great merit and is considered the leading writer of New Comedy, the comedy produced during the last quarter of the 4th century B.C. Concentrating on people's everyday lives, New Comedy did not include political scenes and therefore reflected the fact that the Greek city-states were no longer independent political units. With contemporary Athens as their backdrop, Menander's plays focused on domestic problems, such as abandoned children, strict fathers, crafty slaves, young people in love, and kidnapped daughters. Menander's characters were drawn from all segments of society: rich and poor, young and old, slave and free. In New Comedy, masks were very elaborate and varied, which helped the audience recognize immediately the type of character Menander portrayed.

Menander's plays greatly influenced the Roman playwrights Plautus and Terence, and through them the development of later European comedy. Menander was renowned for his wit, graceful language, mastery of handling, and lifelike characters. Yet for centuries Menander was known mostly through the works and comments of others, because only fragments of his plays survived. Then, in 1958, scholars reproduced an entire play, entitled the *Dyscolus* (The Grouch), which had recently been discovered on sheets of papyrus unearthed in Egypt.

Theocritus (around 300–250 B.C.) is credited as the creator of pastoral poetry, which focused on shepherds and country life. Many scholars believe that Theocritus was a native of Sicily and that he spent time on the Aegean island of Cos, in Alexandria, and perhaps even on the island of Rhodes.

Theocritus preferred the new style of poetry, which stressed innovation and original themes, and enjoyed writing short, carefully worded poems. His dramatic lines and thoughtful but lively descriptions of characters were key elements of his style. Ptolemy Philadelphus of Egypt, son of Ptolemy Soter and a well-known supporter of the arts, recognized Theocritus' talent and became his patron. In the centuries after Theocritus' death, his poems were the model for the *Eclogues* of the famed Roman poet

Virgil and later for the pastoral poems of English poets such as John Milton in the 17th century and Percy Bysshe Shelley in the 19th century.

Hieron II (around 306–216 or 215 B.C.) was one of Syracuse's strongest rulers. A member of one of the city's leading families, Hieron had fought against Carthaginian invaders from northern Africa with his ally Pyrrhus, king of Epirus. After Pyrrhus suddenly withdrew from the island in 276 B.C. the Syracusans found themselves still under siege from both the Carthaginians to the south and Roman forces to the north, and they sought a proven leader to command their troops. All voted to ask Hieron, who accepted the honor and then, to strengthen his position, married the daughter of Syracuse's leading citizen. In the battles that followed, Hieron led Syracuse's troops to victory and was proclaimed king around 270 B.C. The struggle for control of Sicily continued, however, as the Mamertines in northern Sicily tried to outmaneuver the Carthaginians. The Mamertines called on Rome for help and the Carthaginians called on Hieron. In the battles that followed, Rome proved itself the leader and its army led a surprise attack on Hieron and his troops. Hieron withdrew to Syracuse, pursued by the Romans, and eventually asked for peace. The terms of the treaty gave Hieron control of Syracuse and the surrounding area, with the condition that he supply Rome with troops. Despite many battles and skirmishes between the Carthaginians and Romans, Hieron neither broke this treaty nor wavered in his friendship toward the Romans.

During the 54 years that Hieron ruled Syracuse, the city flourished. The poet Theocritus wrote a poem praising Hieron and the prosperity he had brought to Syracuse. Helping Hieron keep the city's defenses strong was the master inventor Archimedes. According to the 3rd-century A.D. writer Athenaeus, Archimedes supervised the construction of one of Hieron's "superships," the *Syrakosia* ("Lady of Syracuse"). Three hundred craftsmen worked on this vessel, which had several entrances, apartments, sleeping quarters, a gymnasium surrounded by garden-lined walkways, a temple, a bathroom with a marble-lined tub, and stalls to accommodate 10 horses. Hieron ordered that this vessel be equipped with weapons to fight off any attacking enemy. When Hieron learned that no harbor was large enough to receive his ship, he gave it to Ptolemy Philopator, the ruler of Egypt and great-grandson of Ptolemy I.

Callimachus (around 305–240 B.C.) was born in the North African town of Cyrene, in Libya, but migrated, probably as a young man, to Alexandria, where he became a teacher. The ruler of Egypt at the time was Ptolemy Philadelphus. Ptolemy recognized Callimachus' abilities and hired him to work at the prestigious library in Alexandria. Callimachus' most significant contribution to the library was cataloging in chronological order the names of the authors and works in the library, making note of the first and last word in each book, the size of the book, and its significance. When completed, this catalog, called the *Pinakes* (Tablets), contained 120 volumes, and ancient scholars based their critical study of Greek literature on it.

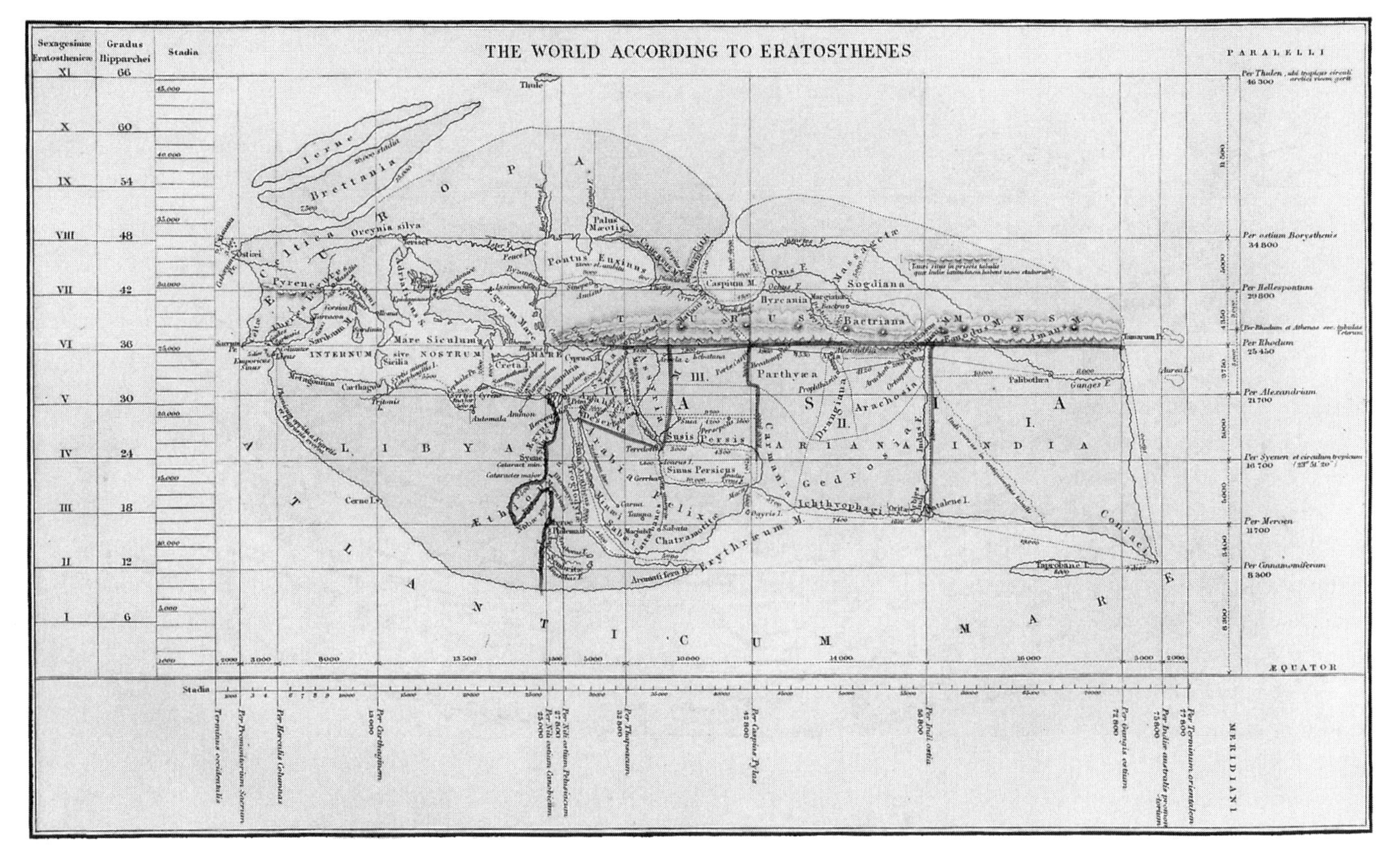

Callimachus wrote hundreds of poems and was respected throughout the ancient world. Later Roman poets, including Catullus and Ovid, imitated his style. Callimachus' most celebrated poem was *Aetia* (Causes), which was published in four books and discussed the foundation of cities and the origins of religious ceremonies, festivals, and legends. Many of Callimachus' poems survive, and of all the ancient Greek poets, with the exception of Homer, Callimachus was quoted most often by ancient writers.

Ctesibius (active around 270 B.C.), a native of Alexandria, Egypt, began studying at Alexandria's great library at an early age. Recognized as one of the ancient world's greatest inventors, Ctesibius is credited with the invention of the water organ and the water clock.

To play Ctesibius' organ, an individual pressed with his foot a pedal that pushed a piston into a cylinder filled with air. The air was then forced through a tube into a globe filled with water. The air coming into the globe forced the water out the bottom of the globe and air out a second tube attached to the globe. The air coming through this second tube entered a small area on which an organ pipe had been positioned. To create a sound, an organ player struck one of the keys on the keyboard. The striking action pulled the stopper from the bottom of the corresponding organ pipe and the air from the box was allowed to enter, producing a specific sound, depending on the length and width of the pipe.

Ctesibius was not the first to invent the water clock, but his

Eratosthenes' world map, as seen in this 1874 atlas, was a marked improvement over the one Herodotus produced earlier. The lands to the east of Greece and the area bordering Arabia are better defined. Also, the British Isles are included.

THE SIEVE OF ERATOSTHENES

~~1~~ 2 3 4 5 6 7 8 9 10 11 12 13 14 15 16 17 18 19 20 21 22 23 24

~~1~~ 2 3 ~~4~~ 5 ~~6~~ 7 ~~8~~ 9 ~~10~~ 11 ~~12~~ 13 ~~14~~ 15 ~~16~~ 17 ~~18~~ 19 ~~20~~ 21 ~~22~~ 23 ~~24~~

~~1~~ 2 3 ~~4~~ 5 ~~6~~ 7 ~~8~~ ~~9~~ ~~10~~ 11 ~~12~~ 13 ~~14~~ ~~15~~ ~~16~~ 17 ~~18~~ 19 ~~20~~ ~~21~~ ~~22~~ 23 ~~24~~

To find those numbers divisible only by one or by themselves (prime numbers), Eratosthenes devised a procedure in which he wrote down a succession of numbers, then crossed out number 1, then every second number after 2, then every third number after 3, and so on to infinity. The numbers that are not crossed out are prime numbers.

improvements on the ancient design earned him credit for the invention. Water clocks were used inside buildings and on cloudy days when sundials could not function. They were especially useful in courtrooms to limit the time defendants and prosecutors could argue their cases.

Although exact details about the workings of ancient water clocks are unavailable, the most accepted theory involves a large vessel with a float at the bottom. Attached to the float was a long rod with a human figure at the top. At the side of this vessel was a small container that allowed water to dribble in slowly. As the water forced the float to rise, the figure pointed to the time on another vessel on which the hours had been marked.

Eratosthenes (around 276–194 B.C.) was a native of the North African town of Cyrene. He spent his early years studying in Athens and Alexandria, the two leading cultural centers of the Greek world. Ptolemy Euergetes, the grandson of Ptolemy I and ruler of Egypt at the time, quickly recognized Eratosthenes' talents and invited him to head the world-famous library at Alexandria. While he served as director, Eratosthenes continued his studies in mathematics, astronomy, and geography.

Acknowledged by his contemporaries as one of the greatest scholars of the period, Eratosthenes was also the most versatile. It was even recorded that the famed Archimedes considered Eratosthenes to be his equal. Like Archimedes, Eratosthenes enjoyed solving difficult mathematical and technical problems. His interest in chronology and history led him to develop a calendar that introduced leap years with 366 days. As his starting date he chose 1183 B.C. the year in which, according to his calculations, the Greeks sacked Troy and the great Trojan War ended.

Eratosthenes' most celebrated achievement was calculating the earth's circumference. Having already noted that at noon on the summer solstice the sun's rays fell vertically in Syrene (modern-day Aswan, Egypt) but at an angle of about seven degrees in Alexandria, Eratosthenes measured the distance between the two cities. Using that distance as the basis of his calculations, he reckoned the circumference of the earth to be 24,662 miles at the equator. (The modern estimate is 24,857 miles.)

Eratosthenes was also the first systematic geographer, and he drew a map of the world with Europe, Asia, and Africa as one solid landmass surrounded by water. Considering the limited amount of information and technical equipment available to him at the time, his map was quite accurate and included Italy's "boot," Greece's "fingered" peninsula, the Arabian peninsula, the Strait of Gibraltar, the Black Sea (known then as the Euxine Sea), the Caspian Sea, and the Persian Gulf.

Eratosthenes also enjoyed solving mathematical and geometrical problems. The principle known today as the sieve of Eratosthenes was his method of determining prime numbers arranged in chronological order. (A prime number is one that is divisible only by itself and 1.) His procedure was as follows: Strike out the number 1; then strike out every second number following the number 2, every third number following the number 3, etc. (See the example at top.)

Tradition maintained that Eratosthenes lived until the age of 80, when either because of blindness or exhaustion he starved himself to death. Little of his work has survived, but the names of his books and the extant fragments illustrate that Eratosthenes was interested in literature as well as the sciences. A short epic poem on the Greek messenger god Hermes was just one of his literary accomplishments.

Appendix 1

Timeline of Events in Ancient Greece

1000 B.C.

Dorian people move south and invade Greece.

AROUND 800

North African city of Carthage is founded by Phoenicians.

776

Olympic Games are held for the first time.

AROUND 750

Writing begins in Greece.

AROUND 700

Homer writes his epics the *Iliad* and the *Odyssey*.

AROUND 621

Athenian lawmaker Draco enacts the first written code of laws.

AROUND 600

Lawmaker Lycurgus imposes a strict military way of life in Sparta.

545

Persian troops advance into Asia Minor and attack the Ionian city of Teos.

Lyric poet Anacreon and others found colony of Abdera in Thrace.

510

Cleisthenes introduces democratic reforms in Athens, including opening membership in the *Ecclesia* to all male Athenian citizens 18 or older.

500

Ionian revolt against the Persians begins in Asia Minor.

490

Persians under Darius invade mainland Greece.

Greeks defeat Persians at the Battle of Marathon.

484

Aeschylus wins his first prize for a play presented at the Great Dionysia festival in Athens.

480

Persians under Xerxes invade Greece.

Under Themistocles' leadership, Greeks defeat Persians at Salamis.

479

Greeks defeat Persians at Plataea and Mycale.

477

Aristides forms Delian League to unite Greek city-states against Persia.

470

Building of the Temple of Zeus at Olympia begins.

468

Sophocles presents his plays for the first time at the Great Dionysia festival.

466

Athenian leader Cimon defeats Persian land and sea forces at Pamphylia.

AROUND 458

Temple of Zeus at Olympia is completed.

456

Phidias sculpts bronze statue *Athena Promachos*, which stood just inside the entrance gate to the Acropolis.

451

Athens and Sparta sign a five-year truce.

449

Persia and Athens sign peace treaty.

447

Pericles orders restoration of Acropolis; architects Ictinus and Callicrates begin work on Parthenon; Pericles commissions city planner Hippodamus to design new plan for Piraeus.

446

Athens and Sparta sign Thirty-Years' Peace Treaty.

441

Euripides wins first prize for a play presented at the Great Dionysia festival.

437

Architect Mnesicles begins work on the Propylaea, the entrance to the Acropolis.

431

Peloponnesian War between Athens and Sparta begins.

424

Aristophanes wins first prize at the Great Dionysia festival with his play *Knights*.

421

Peace of Nicias is signed between Athens and Sparta, but fails to stop the war.

413

Athenian plan to extend control into Sicily meets with a disastrous defeat in Sicily.

404

Peloponnesian War ends with Sparta defeating Athens.

Thirty Tyrants, including Critias, take charge in Athens.

403

Thirty Tyrants are ousted and democracy is restored in Athens.

401

March of the Ten Thousand from Cunaxa on the Euphrates River to Trapezus on the Black Sea begins under Xenophon.

399

Socrates is condemned to death.

387

Plato founds the Academy.

359

Philip II becomes regent of Macedonia.

351

Demosthenes delivers First Philippic against Philip II.

347

Plato dies.

Philip II captures Olynthus on Chalcidice Peninsula.

346

Peace of Philocrates is signed between Greeks and Philip II.

AROUND 342

Aristotle begins tutoring the future Alexander the Great.

Eudoxus calculates circumference of earth.

339

Philip II invades Greece.

338

Greeks lose their independence to Philip II at Battle of Chaeronea.

Philip II marries Macedonian princess Cleopatra.

Philip II is assassinated.

332

Alexander the Great marches into Egypt and takes control.

326

Alexander defeats Indian raja Porus at Jhelum River.

325

Mutinous troops force Alexander to abandon conquests to the east and to head west again.

323

Alexander dies at Babylon.

312

Seleucus defeats Antigonus and his son Demetrius in struggle for control of Alexander's empire. Seleucid dynasty begins and lasts until 64 B.C.

311

Alexander's successors, or *diadochoi*, negotiate peace treaty among themselves.

310

Peace treaty of the *diadochoi* is broken when war erupts between Antigonus and other *diadochoi*.

AROUND 300

Explorer Pytheas makes voyage to the Tin Islands, most likely near Cornwall, England.

300

Seleucus founds city of Antioch in Syria.

283

Ptolemy dies; his descendants continue to rule Egypt until 30 B.C.

270

Hieron II is proclaimed ruler of Syracuse.

213

Romans lay siege to Syracuse but are driven back by Archimedes' machines.

212

Syracuse falls to the Romans.

Appendix 2

People and Places in This Book: A Guide to Spelling and Pronunciation

When the Romans conquered Greece in the 2nd century B.C., they naturally Latinized Greek names. In the centuries that followed, the Latinized spellings became the accepted form and, in many cases, the only form used for Greek names. Only recently has there been a definite movement to transliterate Greek names from Greek into English. For example, when the name of the Greek philosopher Socrates is transliterated from Greek, it is spelled Sokrates. Because that spelling is still not well known, we have chosen to use the Latinized spelling of the ancient Greek names in this book. Listed below are proper names that appear in this volume whose spellings and pronunciations may be unfamiliar. Latinized forms of Greek names that are still widely used today, such as Corinth and Euclid, are not included in this list. Although scholars disagree about exact pronunciations, the following are generally accepted.

ROMAN SPELLING	PRONUNCIATION OF ROMAN SPELLING	GREEK SPELLING
Academus	ak-uh-DAME-uhss	Akademos
Achilles	uh-KILL-eez	Achilleus, Akhilleus
Acragas	AK-rah-gahss	Akragas
Acropolis	uh-KRAWP-ul-ihss	Akropolis
Admetus	ad-MEE-tuhss	Admetos
Aeacides	ee-UH-see-deez	Aiakides
Aegina	ee-JEE-nuh	Aigina
Aeschylus	ES-kih-luhss	Aischylos
Agathocles	uh-GAH-thoh-kleez	Agathokles
Agesilaus	uh-JES-ih-lay-uhss	Agesilaos
Alcaeus	al-SEE-uhss	Alkaios
Alcibiades	al-sih-BYE-uh-dees	Alkibiades
Ambracia	am-BRA-see-uh	Ambrakia
Anacreon	uh-nak-REE-on	Anakreon
Andronicus	an-DRON-ih-kuhss	Andronikos
Antigonus	an-TIG-uh-nuhss	Antigonos
Antiochus	an-tee-AWE-kuhss	Antiochos
Apellicon	uh-PEL-ih-kon	Apellikon
Apollonius	ap-ol-LO-nih-uhss	Apollonios
Ararus	uh-RA-ruhss	Araros
Arcadia	ar-KAY-dih-uh	Arkadia
Archelaus	ar-kih-LAY-uhss	Archelaos
Archestratus	ar-kess-TRAH-tuhss	Archestratos
Argaeus	ar-JEE-uhss	Argaios
Aristides	ar-iss-TYE-deez	Aristeides
Aristodemus	uh-riss-toh-DEE-muhss	Aristodemos
Arrhidaeus	ar-rih-DEE-uhss	Arrhidaios
Artabazus	ar-ta-BAH-zuhss	Artabazos
Artacama	ar-tuh-KAM-uh	Artakama
Artemisium	ar-teh-MEE-zee-um	Artemision
Asclepius	ess-KLAY-pih-uhss	Asklepios
Asclepeum	ess-KLAY-pih-um	Asklepeion
Ascra	ASS-kra	Askra
Athenaeus	ath-uh-NEE-uhss	Athenaios
Attalus	AT-tal-uhss	Attalos
Berenice	ber-eh-NEE-see	Berenike
Boeotia	bee-OH-shih-uh	Boiotia
Calauria	kuh-LOW-ree-uh	Kalaureia
Callias	KAL-lee-ahss	Kallias
Callicrates	kal-lih-KRAH-teez	Kallikrates
Callimachus	kal-lih-MAH-kuhss	Kallimachos
Calliope	kah-LYE-oh-pee	Kalliope
Callisthenes	kal-iss-THEN-eez	Kallisthenes
Callistratus	kal-iss-TRA-tuhss	Kallistratos
Cambyses	KAM-bih-seez	Kambyses

ROMAN SPELLING	PRONUNCIATION OF ROMAN SPELLING	GREEK SPELLING
Cassandreia	kas-san-DRAY-uh	Kassandreia
Ceraunus	seh-RON-uhss	Keraunos
Cerylas	seh-REE-lahss	Kerylas
Chaeronea	kehr-uh-NEE-uh	Chaironeia
Chalcidice	kal-sid-uh-SEE	Chalkidike
Chalcis	KAL-sis	Chalkis
Charaxus	ka-RAH-tsuhss	Charaxos
Cilles	SIL-leez	Killes
Cimon	SEE-mon	Kimon
Cineas	SIN-ee-ahss	Kineas
Citium	SIH-tee-um	Kition
Clazomenae	kla-zoh-MAY-nee	Clazomenai
Cleis	KLICE	Kleis
Cleobulus	kleh-oh-BOO-luhss	Cleobulos
Cleomenes	klee-UM-eh-neez	Kleomenes
Cleon	KLEE-on	Kleon
Cleopatra	klee-oh-PAH-tra	Kleopatra
Clisthenes	KLIZE-thuh-neez	Cleisthenes
Clito	KLEYE-toh	Kleito
Clitus	KLEYE-tuhss	Kleitos
Cnidus	NEE-duhss	Knidos
Cocalus	kok-AH-luhss	Kokalos
Codrus	KOD-ruhss	Kodros
Colchis	KOL-kiss	Kolchis
Colonae	kuh-LOH-nee	Kolonai
Colonus	kuh-LOH-nuhss	Kolonos
Colophon	KOL-uh-fon	Kolophon
Colossus	kuh-LOSS-uhss	Kolossos
Corcyra	kor-SEE-ruh	Korkyra
Coronea	koh-roh-NAY-uh	Koroneia
Coronis	koh-ROH-niss	Koronis
Corinna	koh-RIH-nuh	Korinna
Cos	KUHSS	Kos
Crates	KRAH-teez	Krates
Creon	KREE-un	Kreon
Critias	krih-TEE-ahss	Kritias
Croesus	KREE-suhss	Kroisos
Ctesibius	tes-SIB-ee-uhss	Ktesibios
Ctesiphon	TES-uh-fun	Ktesiphon
Cunaxa	koo-NAX-uh	Kunaxa
Cycnus	SIK-nuhss	Kyknos
Cynoscephalae	sye-noh-SEF-uh-lee	Kynos Kephalai
Cynosarges	sye-noh-SAR-jeez	Kynosarges
Cyrus	SYE-ruhss	Kyros
Cyzicus	SIZ-ih-kuhss	Kyzikos
Darius	dah-REE-uhss	Dareios
Decelea	de-seh-LAY-uh	Dekeleia
Deidamia	dee-ih-da-MEE-uh	Deidameia
Deinocrates	dee-noh-KRAH-teez	Deinokrates
Delium	DEE-lee-um	Delion
Demetrius	dih-MEE-tree-uhss	Demetrios
Democritus	dih-MAWK-ruh-tuhss	Democritos
Demodocus	dih-MAW-duh-kuhss	Demodokos
Diêneces	dye-en-EE-seez	Diênekes
Dionysius	dye-oh-NEE-see-uhss	Dionysios
Dionysus	dye-oh-NEE-suhss	Dionysos
Dyscolus	diss-KOH-luhss	Dyskolos
Ecbatana	ek-ba-TAN-uh	Ekbatana
Elatea	ee-lah-TAY-uh	Elateia
Eleutherae	ee-LOO-ther-ee	Eleutherai
Elpinice	el-pih-NEE-say	Elpinike
Empedocles	em-PED-uh-kleez	Empedokles
Ephesus	EF-ih-suhss	Ephesos
Ephorus	EF-or-uhss	Ephoros
Epicurus	ehp-ih-CURE-uhss	Epikuros
Epirus	eh-PEER-uhss	Epeiros
Euboea	you-BEE-uh	Euboia
Eudoxus	you-DOCKS-uhss	Eudoxos
Eurydice	you-RID-ih-see	Eurydike
Glaucias	GLAW-see-ahss	Glaukias
Gordium	GOR-dee-um	Gordion
Granicus	greh-NEE-kuhss	Granikos
Gryllus	GRILL-uhss	Gryllos
Halicarnassus	ha-lee-kar-NAS-uhss	Halikarnassos
Harpalus	har-PAH-luhss	Harpalos
Hector	HEK-tor	Hektor
Heraclea	heh-RAK-lay-uh	Herakleia
Hercules	HER-kew-leez	Herakles
Heraclitus	her-uh-KLITE-uhss	Herakleitos
Hermachus	her-MAH-kuhss	Hermachos
Herodotus	heh-RAWD-uh-tuhss	Herodotos
Hipparchus	hih-PAR-kuhss	Hipparchos
Hippocrates	hih-PAWK-ruh-teez	Hippokrates
Hippodamus	hih-poh-DAH-muhss	Hippodamos
Hipponicus	hih-PON-ih-kuhss	Hipponikos
Ictinus	ik-TYE-nuhss	Iktinos
Indus	IN-duhss	Indos
Ipsus	IP-suhss	Ipsos
Isocrates	eye-SOCK-ruh-teez	Isokrates
Issus	ISS-uhss	Issos
Ithaca	ITH-uh-kuh	Ithaka

ROMAN SPELLING	PRONUNCIATION OF ROMAN SPELLING	GREEK SPELLING
Lamachus	lah-MAH-kuhss	Lamachos
Lampsacus	LAMP-suh-kuhss	Lampsakos
Larichus	LA-rih-kuhss	Larichos
Leucippus	LOO-sip-uhss	Leukippos
Leuctra	LOOK-tra	Leuktra
Lycaeus	lee-SEE-uhss	Lyceios
Lyceum	lye-SEE-um	Lykeion
Lycia	LISH-ee-uh	Lykia
Lycomedae	lye-koh-MEE-dee	Lykomedai
Lycurgus	lye-KUR-guhss	Lykurgos
Lysimachus	lye-SIM-uh-kuhss	Lysimachos
Lysippus	lye-SIP-uhss	Lysippos
Menelaus	men-eh-LAY-uhss	Menelaos
Miletus	my-LEET-uhss	Miletos
Mnesicles	NES-ih-kleez	Mnesikles
Mount Helicon	HEL-ih-kon	Mount Helikon
Mycale	mih-KAH-lee	Mykale
Nearchus	nee-AR-kuhss	Nearchos
Neocles	NEE-ok-leez	Neokles
Neoptolemus	nee-op-TOL-eh-muhss	Neoptolemos
Nicaea	nye-SEE-uh	Nikaia
Nicias	nih-SEE-ahss	Nikias
Notium	NOH-tee-um	Notion
Olynthus	oh-LIN-thuhss	Olynthos
Orchomenus	or-kuh-MEN-uhss	Orchomenos
Pamphilus	pam-FIL-uhss	Pamphilos
Paralus	puh-RAH-luhss	Paralos
Parrhasius	par-AY-see-uhss	Parrhasios
Patroclus	puh-TROH-kluhss	Patroklos
Peloponnesus	pel-uh-pon-NEE-suhss	Peloponnesos
Perdiccas	PER-dih-kahss	Perdikkas
Pergamum	PER-guh-mum	Pergamon
Pericles	PAIR-ih-kleez	Perikles
Phalerum	fuh-LAIR-um	Phaleron
Phidias	FID-ee-ahss	Pheidias
Phidippides	fye-DIP-ih-deez	Pheidippides
Philocrates	fil-oh-KRAH-teez	Philokrates
Phocis	FOH-siss	Phokis
Phrixus	FRIK-suhss	Phrixos
Phrynichus	FRIN-ih-kuhss	Phrynichos
Piraeus	pye-REE-uhss	Peiraeus
Pisistratus	pye-SIS-tra-tuhss	Peisistratos
Pittacus	pit-TAH-kuhss	Pittakos
Plataea	pluh-TEE-uh	Plataia

ROMAN SPELLING	PRONUNCIATION OF ROMAN SPELLING	GREEK SPELLING
Plistoanax	pliss-TOH-uh-nax	Pleistoanax
Plutus	PLOO-tuhss	Plutos
Polyclitus	pol-ee-KLIE-tuhss	Polykleitos
Polycrates	pol-ee-KRAH-teez	Polykrates
Polygnotus	pol-ig-NOTE-uhss	Polygnotos
Porus	POH-ruhss	Poros
Potidaea	poh-TID-ee-uh	Potidaia
Prodicus	PROD-ih-kuhss	Prodikos
Propylaea	PROP-uh-lee-uh	Propylaia
Proxenus	PROX-een-uhss	Proxenos
Pyrrhus	PIR-uhss	Pyrrhos
Satyrus	SAY-tir-uhss	Satyros
Scamandronymus	scuh-man-DRON-ih-muhss	Skamandronymos
Scepsis	SKEP-siss	Skepsis
Scyros	SIGH-ross	Skyros
Seleucia	suh-LOO-shee-uh	Selukeia
Seleucus	suh-LOO-kuhss	Seleukos
Selinus	suh-LEE-nuhss	Selinous
Sicinnus	sih-SIN-nuhss	Sikinnos
Sicyon	SIK-ih-on	Sikyon
Socrates	SOK-ruh-teez	Sokrates
Sophocles	SOF-uh-kleez	Sophokles
Speusippus	spoo-SIH-puhss	Speusippos
Stagira	STUH-jee-ruh	Stageira
Stratonice	strah-toh-NEE-see	Stratonike
Sunium	SOO-nee-um	Sunion
Talthybius	tal-THIH-bee-uhss	Talthybios
Telemachus	tee-LEM-uh-kuhss	Telemachos
Terpsichore	terp-SIK-uh-ree	Terpsichora
Thasus	THAH-suhss	Thasos
Themistocles	theh-MISS-tuh-kleez	Themistokles
Theocritus	thee-AW-krih-tuhss	Theokritos
Theophrastus	thee-oh-FRAS-tuhss	Theophrastos
Theopompus	thee-oh-POM-puhss	Theopompos
Thermopylae	thur-MOP-uh-lee	Thermopylai
Thespiae	THES-pih-ee	Thespiai
Thucydides	thoo-SID-ih-deez	Thukydides
Timotheus	tih-MOH-thee-uhss	Timotheos
Trapezus	tra-PAY-zuhss	Trapezos
Troezen	TREE-zen	Troizen
Trygaeus	try-JEE-uhss	Trygaios
Xanthippus	zan-TIP-uhss	Xanthippos
Xenocrates	zen-oh-KRAH-teez	Xenokrates
Xenophrastus	zen-oh-FRAS-tuhss	Xenophrastos

Glossary

Academy—the school founded by the Athenian philosopher Plato, whose chief goal was to prepare students to serve the city-state.

archon—one of the highest-ranking public officials in Athens. Originally, there were three archons, each chosen by lot from members of the upper class. Later, the number was increased to nine, the term was limited to one year, and all male citizens were eligible for election. All ex-archons became members of the Areopagos.

Areopagos—Athens' most important governing body, with the authority to supervise and judge all aspects of Athenian life. Originally, only aristocrats were members. But as democratic reforms were introduced into Athens, nine ex-archons were admitted annually and the membership was broadened.

Byzantium—the city founded by Greek colonists around 600 B.C. in southeast Europe at the entrance to the Black Sea on the northern side of the Bosporus Strait. The Romans changed the original Greek name Byzantion to Byzantium; the Roman emperor Constantine changed the name to Constantinople in A.D. 330; and after the Turks conquered the city in 1453, they changed the name to Istanbul.

chorus—the group of people whose dances and songs accompanied and commented on the events in ancient tragedies and comedies.

city-state—an area consisting of an independent, self-governing city and the territory it controlled.

Cynicism—a philosophy that stresses virtue and self-control and urges people to free themselves of material desires.

Delian League—an alliance of Greek city-states founded in 478 B.C.; members pledged to join forces and resources against their common enemy, the Persians.

diadochoi—Alexander the Great's officers who vied for control of his empire after his death.

Dorians—a group of invaders who swept southward into northern Greece during the 11th century B.C. and settled mainly in central and southern Greece.

Ecclesia—the general assembly of the people and the chief governing body, of which, by right, every adult male citizen was a member.

epic—a long narrative poem written in a dignified style detailing the deeds and achievements of a historical or legendary hero. Traditionally, epics are written in dactylic hexameter; that is, the syllables of each line may be divided into six feet (or units), with the fifth foot always a dactyl (one long syllable followed by two short syllables).

Epicureanism—the philosophy practiced by followers of Epicurus, who believed that people should strive to live a calm life, avoid pain, and enjoy moderate sensual pleasures. For Epicurus, the best pleasures were those that affected the mind, not the body.

Great Dionysia—a six-day spring festival held every year in Athens; the highlight of the festival was the three-day presentation of new tragedies and comedies, all in competition for prizes.

Hellenism—the adoption of Greek thought and culture by non-Greeks.

Helots—people who had no political or social rights and spent their lives working for their Spartan masters.

Ionians—those who left northwest Greece in the wake of the invading Dorians and settled on the west coast of Asia Minor (present-day Turkey).

Lyceum—the school founded by the Athenian philosopher Aristotle, who especially encouraged research.

lyric poetry—written verse that expresses a poet's emotions and is suitable for accompaniment by a lyre.

mercenaries—professional soldiers who are hired to serve in a foreign army.

mystery religions—religious sects whose members were sworn to secrecy about the rites and practices involved in worshiping their gods and goddesses.

oligarchy—a government ruled by a few privileged people.

Olympic Games—A Greek festival held every four years in Olympia, Greece, to honor Zeus, king of the gods; it featured athletic, musical, and poetry contests.

omen—an occurrence used to foretell future events.

oracle—advice given to ordinary humans by a person, such as a priestess, through whom the gods or goddesses spoke; also the place where such advice was given.

***ostraca* (singular: *ostracon*)**—pieces of pottery on which Athenian citizens wrote the name of any prominent person they wished to have exiled; if at least 6,000 votes were cast, the person receiving the highest number of votes was forced to leave Athens for at least 10 years.

Peloponnesus—the peninsula forming the southern part of mainland Greece; literally, the "Island of Pelops." In Greek mythology Pelops was the grandson of Zeus, the king of the gods, and ancestor of the Greek king and hero Agamemnon.

phalanx—a type of military formation in which foot soldiers marched with overlapping shields and long, extended spears.

Pyrrhic victory—a hollow victory; the expression refers to the two victories over the Romans won by Pyrrhus, king of Epirus, in which his troop casualties were so great that he considered the victories not much better than defeats.

rhetoric—the art of using words effectively when writing or speaking.

satyr play—a type of satiric or comic play whose themes were based on legends and episodes found in the Greek epics; chorus members were dressed as satyrs, which were ancient woodland deities with the torso and head of a man but the pointed ears, horns, and legs of a goat.

Socratic method—a teaching method based on that used by the philosopher Socrates, in which questions are continually asked of students until their responses gradually help them discover the answers for themselves.

sophist—a member of a class of ancient professional teachers who gave lessons for pay and were known for using clever arguments to prove their points.

Stoicism—the philosophy that teaches that the wise person should seek only virtue and be indifferent to pain and pleasure.

***strategos* (plural: *strategoi*)**—one of 10 generals elected annually to command and organize military expeditions.

***symposium* (plural: *symposia*)**—a "drinking party" at which guests told riddles and stories and sang drinking songs and selections from Greek drama.

trireme—an ancient Greek warship with three banks of oars on either side.

Trojan War—a 10-year war (traditionally, around 1184 B.C.) between the Greeks and Trojans, sparked when the Trojan prince Paris abducted Helen, wife of the king of Sparta; finally, the Greeks destroyed Troy, after sneaking soldiers into the city in a wooden horse, and won the war.

tyrant—in early Greece, someone who won the support of the poor and overthrew an oppressive ruler. Although many tyrants were good rulers, many also abused their power, and eventually the term *tyrant* came to mean a cruel, oppressive ruler.

Further Reading

Each of the major entries in *Ancient Greeks* includes a list of further reading; refer to the index for page references to the individual Greeks profiled in this book.

The following list is intended as a supplement. Although the books do vary in level of difficulty, none is too technical for the interested reader. Titles preceded by an asterisk (*) are especially accessible to younger readers.

Magazines

Archaeology is published bimonthly by the Archaeological Institute of America, 135 William Street, New York, NY 10038.

Calliope: World History for Young People is published nine times during the school year by Cobblestone Publishing, 7 School Street, Peterborough, NH 03458.

General History

*"Athens vs. Sparta." *Calliope*, Nov./Dec. 1994. [Entire issue]

*Baker, Charles F., III, and Rosalie F. Baker. *The Classical Companion*. Peterborough, N.H.: Cobblestone, 1988.

Boardman, John, Jasper Griffin, and Oswyn Murray, eds. *The Oxford History of the Classical World*. New York: Oxford University Press, 1986.

———. *The Oxford History of Greece and the Hellenistic World*. New York: Oxford University Press, 1991.

Bowder, Diana, ed. *Who Was Who in the Greek World*. Ithaca, N.Y.: Cornell University Press, 1982.

Burn, A. R. *The Penguin History of Greece*. New York: Viking Penguin, 1990.

*Burrell, Roy. *The Greeks*. Illustrated by Peter Connolly. New York: Oxford University Press, 1989.

*———. *Oxford First Ancient History*. Illustrated by Peter Connolly. New York: Oxford University Press, 1994.

Cook, J. M. *The Persian Empire*. New York: Schocken, 1983.

*Corbishley, Mike. *The Ancient World*. New York: Peter Bedrick, 1992.

Cotterell, Arthur, ed. *The Penguin Encyclopedia of Classical Civilizations*. New York: Viking Penguin, 1993.

*David, A. Rosalie. *The Egyptian Kingdoms*. New York: Peter Bedrick, 1988.

Fantham, Elaine, Helene Peet Foley, Natalie Boymel Kampen, Sarah B. Pomeroy, and H. A. Shapiro. *Women in the Classical World*. New York: Oxford University Press, 1994.

Finley, M. I., ed. *The Greek Historians: The Essence of Herodotus, Thucydides, Xenophon, and Polybius*. New York: Viking, 1959.

Fitzhardinge, L. F. *The Spartans*. London: Thames & Hudson, 1980.

Grant, Michael. *Atlas of Classical History*. New York: Oxford University Press, 1994.

———. *Greek and Roman Historians: Information and Misinformation*. New York: Routledge, 1995.

Hammond, N. G. L., and H. H. Scullard, eds. *The Oxford Classical Dictionary*. 2nd ed. Oxford: Clarendon Press, 1978.

Hopwood, Keith, comp. *Ancient Greece and Rome: A Bibliographic Guide*. New York: Manchester University Press, 1995.

Kitto, H. D. F. *The Greeks*. Baltimore: Penguin, 1957.

Lévêque, Pierre. *The Birth of Greece*. New York: Abrams, 1990.

Levi, Peter. *Atlas of the Greek World*. 1980. Reprint. New York: Facts on File, 1995.

Livingstone, R. W., ed. *The Legacy of Greece*. Oxford: Clarendon Press, 1962.

Martin, Thomas R. *Ancient Greece: From Prehistoric to Hellenistic Times*. New Haven: Yale University Press, 1996.

McGregor, Malcolm F. *The Athenians and Their Empire*. Vancouver: University of British Columbia Press, 1987.

*"Pharaohs of Egypt." *Calliope*, Sept./Oct. 1994. [Entire issue]

Powell, Anton. *Athens and Sparta*. New York: Routledge, 1988.

*"Queens of Egypt." *Calliope*, Nov./Dec. 1991. [Entire issue]

Robinson, Cyril E. *A History of Greece*. New York: Routledge, 1990.

*Scarre, Chris, ed. *Smithsonian Timelines of the Ancient World*. New York: Dorling Kindersley, 1993.

Starr, Chester G. *The Ancient Greeks*. New York: Oxford University Press, 1971.

———. *A History of the Ancient World*. New York: Oxford University Press, 1991.

Warry, John Gibson. *Warfare in the Classical World: An Illustrated Encyclopedia of Weapons, Warriors, and Warfare in the Ancient Civilizations of Greece and Rome*. New York: St. Martin's, 1980.

Archaeology

Biers, William R. *The Archaeology of Greece: An Introduction*. Ithaca, N.Y.: Cornell University Press, 1980.

Burn, A. R., and Mary Burn. *The Living Past of Greece*. New York: Schocken, 1986.

*Cork, Barbara, and Struan Reid. *The Young Scientist Book of Archaeology*. London: Usborne, 1984.

Etienne, Roland, and Françoise Etienne. *The Search for Ancient Greece*. New York: Abrams, 1992.

Grant, Michael. *The Visible Past: Greek and Roman History from Archaeology, 1960–1990*. New York: Scribners, 1990.

Greece: Temples, Tombs, and Treasures. Alexandria, Va.: Time-Life Books, 1994.

*McIntosh, Jane. *Archaeology*. New York: Knopf, 1994.

———. *The Practical Archaeologist*. New York: Facts on File, 1986.

Pedley, John Griffiths. *Greek Art and Archaeology*. New York: Abrams, 1993.

*Perring, Stefania, and Dominic Perring. *Then and Now*. New York: Macmillan, 1991. [Includes description and illustrations of the Acropolis and Agora]

Arts and Sciences

*Baker, Charles F., III, and Rosalie F. Baker. *Classical Ingenuity*. Peterborough, N.H.: Cobblestone, 1993.

Handley, Eric. *Images of the Greek Theatre*. Austin: University of Texas Press, 1995.

Heuer, Kenneth. *City of the Stargazers*. New York: Scribners, 1972. [About Alexandria, Egypt]

Levi, Peter. *A History of Greek Literature*. New York: Viking, 1985.

Mulroy, David. *Early Greek Lyric Poetry*. Ann Arbor: University of Michigan Press, 1992.

Parker, G. F. *A Short Account of Greek Philosophy from Thales to Epicurus*. London: Edward Arnold, 1967.

Roebuck, Carl, ed. *The Muses at Work*. Cambridge: Massachusetts Institute of Technology Press, 1969. [Description of the arts, crafts, and professions in ancient Greece and Rome]

Sutton, Dana F. *Ancient Comedy*. New York: Twayne, 1993.

Walton, J. Michael. *Living Greek Theatre: A Handbook of Classical Performance and Modern Production*. Westport, Conn.: Greenwood, 1987.

West, M. L., trans. *Greek Lyric Poetry*. New York: Oxford University Press, 1994.

Greek Life

*Archibald, Zofia. *Discovering the World of the Ancient Greeks*. New York: Facts on File, 1991.

*Davis, William Stearns. *A Day in Old Athens: A Picture of Athenian Life*. Boston: Allyn & Bacon, 1914.

*Freeman, Charles. *The Ancient Greeks*. New York: Oxford University Press, 1996.

Hooker, J. T. *The Ancient Spartans*. London: J. M. Dent & Sons, 1980.

Ling, Roger. *The Greek World*. New York: Peter Bedrick, 1988.

Peck, Harry Thurston, ed. *Harper's Dictionary of Classical Literature and Antiquities*. New York: Cooper Square Publishers, 1965.

*Quennell, Marjorie, and C. H. B. Quennell. *Everyday Things in Ancient Greece*. New York: Putnam, 1968.

**The Visual Dictionary of Ancient Civilizations*. New York: Dorling Kindersley, 1994.

Greek Mythology

*Baker, Charles F., III, and Rosalie F. Baker. *Myths and Legends of Mount Olympos*. Peterborough, N.H.: Cobblestone, 1992.

Bowder, Diana. *Bulfinch's Mythology*. New York: HarperCollins, 1991.

*D'Aulaire, Ingri, and Edgar Parin D'Aulaire. *D'Aulaire's Book of Greek Myths*. New York: Doubleday, 1962.

*Flaum, Eric. *The Encylopedia of Mythology: Gods, Heroes, and Legends of the Greeks and Romans*. Philadelphia: Courage Books, 1993.

Hamilton, Edith. *The Greek Way*. 1942. Reprint. New York: Norton, 1993.

*Low, Alice. *The Macmillan Book of Greek Gods and Heroes*. New York: Macmillan, 1994.

Morford, Mark P. O., and Robert J. Lenardon. *Classical Mythology*. New York: Longman, 1991.

Vandenberg, Philipp. *The Mystery of the Oracles*. New York: Macmillan, 1982.

Index of Ancient Greeks by Profession

Explorer
Pytheas

Historians
Herodotus
Thucydides
Xenophon

Long-distance runner
Phidippides

Mathematicians
Archimedes
Pythagoras

Military leaders
Alcibiades
Alexander the Great
Antigonus I
Demetrius
Leonidas
Philip II
Ptolemy I (Ptolemy Soter)
Pyrrhus
Themistocles

Philosophers
Aristotle
Epicurus
Plato
Socrates
Zeno

Physician
Hippocrates

Playwrights
Aeschylus
Aristophanes
Euripides
Sophocles

Poets
Anacreon
Apollonius Rhodius
Homer
Pindar
Sappho

Public speaker
Demosthenes

Sculptor
Phidias

Statesmen
Lycurgus
Pericles
Solon

Storyteller
Aesop

Index

References to main biographical entries are indicated by **bold** page numbers; references to illustrations are indicated by *italics*.

Acknowledgments

Special thanks are owed to the staff of the John D. Rockefeller, Jr., Library at Brown University in Providence, Rhode Island, for its invaluable assistance in helping us search and locate so many of the books used in preparing *Ancient Greeks*.

Picture Credits

Alinari/Art Resource: frontispiece, 41, 67, 84, 114, 125, 129, 136, 146, 164, 181, 188; American Numismatic Society: 198; Archaeological Museum of Thessaloniki: 170, 190; Architect of the Capitol: 19 (neg.# 34081), 23 (neg.# 34073), 99 (neg.# 32199), 108 (neg.# 32198); courtesy The Bancroft Library: 42; Bibliotheca Bodmeriana, Geneva: 234; Bibliothèque Nationale, Paris: 117, 169; British Library: 15; British Museum: 35, 118, 195, 209, 230; copyright © Peter Connolly: 173; George Peabody Library of The Johns Hopkins University: 237; Giraudon/Art Resource, New York: 221; Harvard University Press: 146, 151 (reprinted by permission of the publishers and the Loeb Classical Library from *Xenophon in Seven Volumes*, vol. IV, translated by E. C. Marchant, 1968); collection of the J. Paul Getty Museum, Los Angeles, California: 29, 51, 122; IRPA-KIK, Brussels: 200; Library of Congress: 74, 191; The Metropolitan Museum of Art: 14 (Fletcher Fund, 1930, neg.# 30.11.9), 21 (Joseph Pulitzer Bequest, 1947, neg.# 47.11.5), 30 (Rogers Fund, 1906, neg.# 06.1021.178), 31 (Harris Brisbane Dick Fund, 1937, neg.# 37.39.6), 44 (Gift of Mr. and Mrs. John van Benschoten Griggs, 1946, neg.# 46.129.1), 47 (Rogers Fund, 1916, neg.# 16.71), 55 (Rogers Fund, 1949, neg.# 49.11.1), 59 (Rogers Fund, 1914, neg.# 14.130.12), 64 (Rogers Fund, 1921, neg.# 21.88.1), 70, 107 (Levi Hale Willard bequest, 1890, neg.# 90.35.3), 111 (Lorillard Wolfe Collection, Wolfe Fund, 1931, neg.# 31.45), 126 (Fletcher Fund, 1940, neg.# 40.11.3), 137 (Purchase, Walter C. Baker Gift, 1956, neg.# 56.11.1, rollout photograph by Justin Kerr), 157 (purchased with special funds and gifts of friends of The Metropolitan Museum, 1961, neg.# 61.198), 175 (purchased with funds from various donors, 1910, neg.# 10.132.1), 178 (Rogers Fund, 1910, neg.# 10.231.1), 206 (Rogers Fund, 1910, neg.# 10.231.1), 208 (Rogers Fund, 1921, neg.# 21.88.3), 225 (Harris Brisbane Dick Fund, 1934, neg.# 34.11.7); Musée du Louvre: 93, 120, 183, 216, 233; National Archaeological Museum, Athens: 62; New York Public Library, Astor, Lenox, and Tilden Foundations: 32 (Spencer Collection), 82 (Performing Arts Collection), 189 (Prints Collection, Miriam and Ira D. Wallach Division of Art), 212 (Prints Collection, Miriam and Ira D. Wallach Division of Art), 229; Ny Carlsberg Glyptoteck, Copenhagen: 56, 219; Österreichische Nationalbibliothek, Vienna: 94 (negative from the Bildarchiv); courtesy Holly Pobis: 80; from *Tony Sarg's Book for Children from Six to Sixty*, Greenburg, N.Y., 1924): 166 ; Staatliche Antikensammlungen und Glyptothek München: 45; Thames & Hudson Ltd., London: 77 (from O. A. W. Dilke: *Greek and Roman Maps*, 1985, used by permission of the publisher and Cornell University Press); Ira Toff: cover background photo; The Board of Trinity College, Dublin: 226; The Valentine Museum, Richmond, Virginia: 124; Biblioteca Apostolica Vaticana, Museo Sacro: 52, 68; Wadsworth Athenaeum, Hartford, Connecticut: 13 (Gift of J. Pierpont Morgan).

Rosalie F. and Charles F. Baker III are the editors of the magazine *Calliope: World History for Young People*, which in 1991 was named one of the nation's ten best magazines by *American Library Journal*. They are the authors of *The Classical Companion*, *Myths and Legends of Mount Olympos*, and *Classical Ingenuity: The Legacy of the Ancient Greek and Roman Architects, Artists, and Inventors*. Both are former teachers and Charles Baker is currently an administrator for the New Bedford public schools in Massachusetts. He is also the author of *Struggle for Freedom*, thirteen plays on the American Revolution for classroom perfomance. The Bakers live in New Bedford with their son, Chip.